MW00975806

Tools of the **Trade**

Second Edition

**A Compilation of Programs
and Processes for the Absence,
Disability, and Health and
Productivity Professional**

Disclaimer

The information presented in this publication has been compiled from sources and documents believed to be reliable and represent the best professional judgment of the authors, editors, and Disability Management Employer Coalition, Inc. (DMEC). The accuracy of the information presented is not guaranteed, nor is any responsibility assumed or implied by DMEC for any damage or loss resulting from inaccuracies or omissions.

Laws vary greatly by state. This publication is not intended to provide legal advice or establish standards of reasonable behavior. For specific information regarding any section of this document, you are urged to utilize the advice and guidance of legal counsel.

Foreword

Many loyal and hardworking professionals — also DMEC members — assisted with updating this manual. We used consultants and thought leaders who have the most current information in the areas of absence and disability. We can't thank them enough for their contributions and willingness to volunteer their time on this important project.

Several chapters have been updated in this second edition, providing you with the most current tools and resources. The regulations and laws governing disability and absence are constantly changing, and the publication is current as of the date of revision.

This manual is more than just a compendium of facts. Its intent is to meet the needs of practicing professionals in integrated absence and disability management by offering both background information and the tools/resources needed to complete the job. The 23 chapters hereafter take the reader from basic definitions, through an exploration of programs prime for integration, to program implementation and management. We have heard from many students obtaining their Certified Professional Disability Management (CPDM) and professionals who have already obtained their CPDM about the great information and resources found within this manual. A special thanks to Karen English of Spring Consulting Group, LLC, who assisted DMEC in updating this reference manual.

We hope you will be able use this book each and every day as your desktop guide. We want this tool to be your go-to reference as you build, manage, and monitor your integrated absence and disability management program.

Terri L. Rhodes, MBA, CPDM, CCMP
Chief Executive Officer
DMEC

Introduction

As explained in the first chapter of this book, program integration means different things to different people. It can include a variety of programs ranging from disability to absence to health — as well as a number of processes such as intake, case management, and reporting. Although there are several best practices for employers to consider, building a program that works for a particular population is the single most important point to keep in mind in order to determine success.

It has been my pleasure and honor to be involved with this effort, as I believe there is more than one right way to build an integrated program. Employers, suppliers, and advisors alike need to keep an open mind and a listening ear to each and every member. Using the analogy of building a house, employers who pursue integration truly go down a path of establishing a framework, making improvements over time, and considering additions when they are ready to expand to the next phase. Remodeling is often required and various types of architects and designers are involved from start to finish.

Special thanks go out to all the employers, insurance companies, third-party administrators, consultants, brokers, and friends I have worked with over the years who have given me this perspective, as well as my colleagues at Spring Consulting Group, LLC, who embrace this philosophy for our clients every day. The authors of and contributors to this document share views in this same context, and we collectively hope it proves to be useful to every reader.

Karen Trumbull English, CPCU, ARM
Partner, Spring Consulting Group, LLC
Editor

Contents

Section One

Integrated Disability
Program Definitions

Chapter 1: What Is Integrated Disability Management (IDM), Total Absence Management (TAM), and Health and Productivity Management (HPM)?

Quick Background and Context

As employers battle the rising costs of healthcare, they are also managing a global workforce that is aging and shifting demographically and geographically. They are trying to remain compliant with ever-changing regulations and increased corporate governance while simultaneously boosting their levels of productivity during a time when absence rates are rising and individual health is declining.

Although employers have been interested in benefits integration for over a decade, the culmination of the factors listed above is finally causing notable change. Companies of all types and sizes are turning to program integration as a means to achieve success. Acknowledging that they, as employers, need to do more with less and that proactive solutions may enable healthier and more productive workers is key. In response to these factors, various and distinct approaches have evolved and are becoming more commonplace.

The Disability Management Employer Coalition (DMEC) was established in 1992 as a response to two major forcing factors: 1. The implementation of employer-paid universal healthcare coverage in the state of California; and 2. The need nationally to share best practices in disability and absence management. Sharon Kaleta and Marcia Carruthers formed DMEC to promote the concept of measuring and managing the full cost of disability and absence(s) for a company. Formally incorporated in 1995, DMEC has grown to become a nationally recognized educational organization with 13 chapters throughout the United States. It offers conferences, webinars, publications, and networking opportunities to over 2,800 members. In 1997, a certification program - the Certified Professional in Disability Management (CPDM) - was instituted through a partnership with the Insurance Educational Association (IEA), offering both online and classroom formats. To date, over 3,400 individuals have earned their CPDM designation. Program offerings that explore total health and productivity have expanded the scope of DMEC's original integration agenda.

The concept of combining health and workplace-based productivity first appeared in 1984 at the Stanford Center for Research in Disease Prevention (now Stanford Prevention Research Center). While we would readily accept this approach now, employers and researchers alike did not embrace the idea. In April 1996, the Health Enhancement Research Organization (HERO) was formed with 15 sustaining partners, and health and productivity management made its full-fledged debut. Quickly on the heels of HERO, the Institute for Health and Productivity Management (IHPM) entered corporate consciousness in February 1997 following the publication of the "Two Pens Project: Employer and Physician Dialogue on Health Care and Productivity," which was an effort to address healthcare costs and employer-provided healthcare from physician and employer points of view. The Two Pens Project was a joint effort of the National Business Coalition on Health (NBCH) and National Association of Managed Care Physicians (NAMCP). The term presenteeism entered into the employee benefits vernacular at this time and is often characterized as the opposite of absenteeism, meaning that employees come to work despite illness. Employers experience similar negative repercussions as if the employee were absent.

The Integrated Benefits Institute (IBI), whose focus was on combining the management of occupational and nonoccupational absences into one process, published Linking Medical Care to Productivity: Research on Emerging Health and Productivity Issues in February 2001. This study was the first to propose a linkage between short-term disability and employer-based healthcare costs. This paper proposed that the approximate 10% of employees who are absent every year (and accessing short-term disability) were responsible for slightly more than 50% of employer-based medical costs. Following publication of this study, integration efforts shifted from combined short- and long-term disability processes and/or combined occupational and nonoccupational disability programs to the cost-savings possibilities employers might realize from combining healthcare and disability data and programs.

Finally, the Washington Business Group on Health (now the National Business Group on Health) created the Council on Employee Health and Productivity and EMPAQ® (Employer Measures of Productivity, Absence and Quality) in 2002. The initial purpose of the Council was to establish universal definitions and metrics for measures associated with health and productivity management initiatives, beginning with absence metrics.

What programs are called continues to cause confusion with terms such as integrated disability management (IDM), total absence management (TAM), and health and productivity management (HPM) being quite common, and others such as integrated absence and disability management (IADM), integrated health and disability management (IHDM), and even just health and productivity (H&P) being heavily used.

But these are simply names. The larger question is whether organizations want programs that are truly "integrated" and delivered through one common approach or "coordinated" through separate administration and coupled with constant information sharing.

There is really no right or wrong, and every program has its own differentiation points and interface levels. Therefore, program types can be best described by considering a spectrum of options that we will describe as integrated.

This chapter will provide specific background to help employers determine where their programs fall along the integrated program spectrum and how they can prioritize issues to develop their particular plans. It will outline best practices for implementing an integrated program, recognizing that phased solutions are not only accepted but have become the norm in dealing with so many moving parts.

The Spectrum of Options to Consider

Traditionally, disability management consisted of programs and processes that sought to prevent disability, reduce the cost/impact of absence, and provide mechanisms to promote maximum functional recovery and return to work. As businesses strove to accomplish this, they recognized the importance of integrating disability and leave management with their other like employee benefits.

Integration in this form can be defined as having processes, systems, or related data that is incorporated by two or more programs. Fortunately, a spectrum of program options can be considered (Figure 1.1):

Figure 1.1

Integrated Disability Management (IDM) refers to the concept of integrating various pieces of disability management to achieve cost and administrative efficiencies for the employer and a better "customer experience" for the employee. Programs t programs typically include a combination of short- and long-term disability (STD, LTD), workers' compensation (WC), and/or Family and Medical Leave Act (FMLA) administrations. A single intake source coordinates these programs that can begin the very first day an employee is out of work. The intake coordinator is then responsible for directing the employee to the appropriate claims administrator.

Employers gain several benefits from this approach:

- Reporting a claim uses one simple communications process

- Capability to tracking both occupational and nonoccupational absences to avoid coverage duplication

- Ensuring compliance with city, state, and federal family medical leave laws of notification and certification while still leveraging STD and WC information

- Eliminating reliance on the employee to determine the type of claim they are reporting

Additionally, IDM programs typically encourage early intervention; provide opportunities for common case management across occupational and non-occupational claims; and create an environment in which employers can implement formal return-to-work programs throughout the organization. This integration allows employers to track the data across programs and establish a baseline to measure outcomes against. This also highlights trends across the organization and facilitate the development of prevention and improvement initiatives.

Total Absence Management (TAM) addresses all employee absences, regardless of reason, and provides a process for employers to identify and manage the root cause of the absence. TAM programs track all employee time away from work - sick time (SICK), leaves of absence (LOA), (e.g. military leave, bereavement leave, jury duty, and personal leave), and other paid time off (PTO)(e.g. vacation), plus all the absences covered by IDM. There is a single source of claim intake, as described with IDM programs. This allows for timely communication to the appropriate parties -arming supervisors and managers with information to plan proactively for absences, use budgets more effectively for replacement workers, and make the "present" team as productive as possible.

Health and Productivity Management (HPM) ultimately incorporates the health component into the disability and absence management processes. It goes beyond IDM and TAM to develop a common point of access for all absence and health promotion benefits. HPM incorporates targeted disease management programs, employee assistance programs (EAP), behavioral health (BH) management processes, wellness initiatives, health management programs, and onsite medical facilities. Effective programs even coordinate medical providers for group health and WC. This step often results in appropriate screening of employees for various health risks and ensures referral to suitable intervention programs. Full HPM programs typically utilize a data warehouse for comprehensive reporting and predictive modeling to run hypothetical scenarios for strategic planning across an organization. [i]

Current State of Integration

It is not surprising that the most common approach employers take to benefits integration is to phase in programs over time. The depth and breadth of the options available require organizations to develop a long-term strategy while taking short-term steps to impact their most immediate issues. For some, healthcare costs are at the top of the list and must be addressed before considering anything else. For others, compliance is the main issue and consistent administration is the key. For a third group, reducing absenteeism and impacting attendance may be the focal point. Regardless of where an employer is focused on the integration spectrum, it is important to know that there is a significant competitive advantage to be gained by lowering costs through benefits integration. A 2011 study found that 68.8% of employers of all types and sizes do not have any disability program integration. Further, only 0.6% were projected to integrate by the end of 2012. There is significant interest in integration, though, as 10.1% had plans to integrate, but did not have a target date for implementation. [ii]

Employers often start with parts of IDM, move on to incorporate HPM, and then consider implementation of TAM to round out their strategies (Figure 1.2). Specifically, organizations that integrate benefits generally get started in one of two ways: [iii]

- **Phase I:** Integrate disability (STD and LTD) with SICK and FML administration

- **Phase II:** Focus on population health and incorporate health management initiatives, such as wellness, EAP, and behavioral health and disease management programs

After these initial steps are underway, companies can then expand their integration efforts. Often they use STD as the lever to coordinate with group health, WC and other leave programs (LOA, PTO) to progress toward a total absence management program. Each case, however, will have unique needs and priorities and must implement programs in a matter best suited for its organization.

Figure 1.2

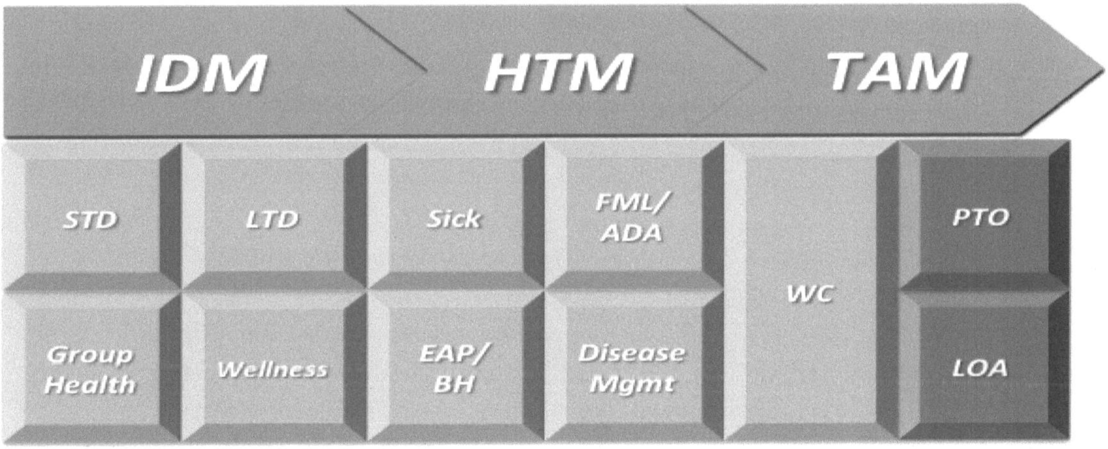

Source: Spring Consulting Group, LLC

Large organizations with more than 10,000 workers are most likely to combine at least a few of their benefit programs. This is due to employer sophistication, internal prioritization of objectives, and product availability. Insurance companies and third-party administrators (providers) have been most successful in targeting large employers in the past because of these factors. However, as the market has matured, employers are more aware of their options and providers have gained experience with their models, causing a down-market shift. Employers with employees numbering between 5,000 and 10,000 are integrating just as much as their larger counterparts. Those with 1,000 to 5,000 workers are integrating more than you might expect. Even companies with fewer than 1,000 employees have begun to realize they need integrated programs and are doing so or have plans to integrate elements of disability and absence management over the next few years.

Disability, WC, and healthcare funding may also inspire an organization's tendency to integrate benefits programs. Organizations that self-insure or use captive insurance to finance their programs are often looking for proactive methods and preventive approaches (e.g., early intervention, common case management, return-to-work) that integrated programs can help resolve. Currently, 73% of employers self-insure their STD,[iv] 32% self-insure their WC, and 60% self-insure their healthcare insurance programs.[v] An even greater number of employers - 84% - insure their LTD programs;[vi] however, that figure is starting to drop due to the use of captive insurance companies for LTD programs.

Data collection and analytics are always important to employers when assessing the impact of integrated benefits programs. Businesses are starting to incorporate overall employee benefits costs into their program analyses, in addition to health and absence information. The use of data warehouses and predictive modeling is becoming a common approach to run benefits scenarios and set strategy for plan design. Provider capabilities, tools, solutions to employee privacy issues, and employer access points determine the successfulness in developing information that is measurable and actionable.

Employer self-service tools have also risen in importance. Companies expect their supervisors and managers to have real-time access to absence information so they can proactively manage employee schedules and plan for replacement workers when needed. Vendors are providing real-time access to absentee information through employer portals, "push" notifications (email, texts) or even mobile apps that help report and record any absence.

Advantages and Barriers

There are several advantages to integrating benefits - some are financial and others are operational. From a financial perspective, employers that combine programs generally experience savings of at least 10% to 15% of direct program costs[vii] or between 0.25% and 1.00% of payroll,[viii] depending on the programs integrated (Table 1.1).

By other measures, employers are able to reduce disability days by between 10% and 35%,[ix] improve return-to-work rates by at least 6%,[x] and experience return on investment (ROI) for the programs they put in place ranging anywhere from 3:1 to 15:1. Once a program has been in place for six months or more, they are able to demonstrate reduced lost time, decreased incidence, and lower absence rates. While the studies that documented these results are somewhat dated, single case and anecdotal evidence suggests that these results continue to be valid.

From an operational perspective, the employer's ability to effectively track claims and employee absences enables that company to move toward viewing the big picture of how the physical and behavioral health of employees impacts workplace productivity. Integrated strategies afford organizations the ability to establish effective return-to-work programs, prevention strategies, and a positive environment. These efforts thus improve the outcomes of employee illness and injuries, and result in fewer absences and improved profitability.

Integrated programs can also lead to simpler processes and increase employee satisfaction. An employee may report claims or absences through one mechanism (e.g., a toll-free number or web portal), receive clear notification of rights and processes, and deal with fewer parties overall.

Table 1.1

Direct and Indirect Costs Summary		2007
Direct Costs	Workers' compensation	1.0%
	Sick leave (not including paid time off bank)	1.0%
	Short-term disability	1.0%
	Long-term disability	0.5%
	Medical coverage	10.9%
Indirect Costs	Overtime	3.3%
	Workstation modification/job accommodation	1.0%
	Replacement workers	2.0%
	Health improvement programs	0.5%
Total		21.2%

Supervisors, managers, human resources, and corporate representatives are usually impressed with the process as well, because they can turn to a common set of instructions for employees to follow, one source of information to interface with, and consistent administration across a number of programs.

Lastly, assured compliance with city, state, and federal laws is yet another advantage of integrated benefits programs. There are specific challenges organizations encounter when employees take FML as a result of a chronic condition, including ongoing injury, ongoing illness, and/or a non-life-threatening condition (Figure 1.3).

Figure 1.3

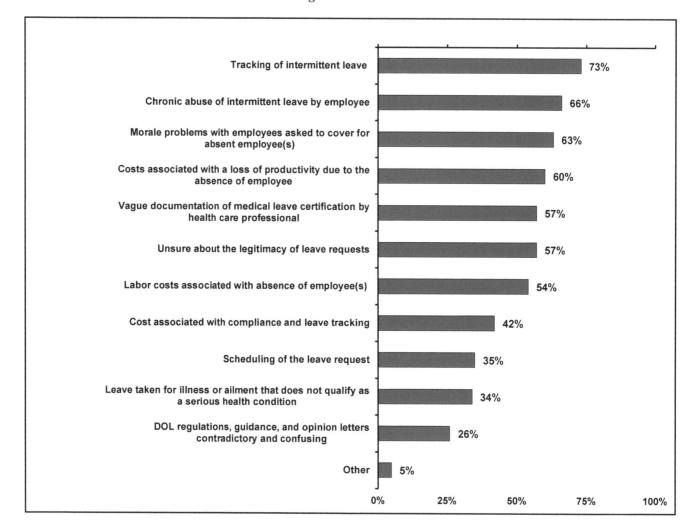

Source: Society for Human Resource Management. Leave administration challenges under FMLA. SHRM. November 2006.

Managing the requirements of the Americans with Disabilities Act, the Americans with Disabilities Act Amendment, the Occupational Safety and Health Act, and other important regulations is often better handled through a combined approach and a data-driven structure that tracks activities and measures outcomes on a continuous basis.

Industry Best Practices

There are several best practices employers can follow to initiate or continue their benefits integration efforts.[xi]

Best Practice 1: Articulate goals and expected outcomes for your company's integrated program.

Benefits integration can embrace many or just a few parts of your overall benefits program. Prior to implementing any changes, decide as an organization what you want to achieve.

- Evaluate your current benefits program and identify areas for improvement. Determine which areas require immediate attention and which can be part of future program enhancements.

- Review your system infrastructure and assess its capabilities. Implementing enhancements such as single claim intake or integrated case management and reporting may require technology upgrades or outsourcing.

- Be specific and don't try to do too much at once. Develop a clear implementation plan that provides enough time to make the necessary internal and external process changes.

Best Practice 2: Clearly communicate benefit policies and procedures to your employees and vendors.

When implementing benefits changes, poor communication can cause confusion and misinterpretation of program policies or processes. Establish a method to clearly communicate with your employees and vendors. If employees do not understand or are not aware of changes, program modifications could result in increased frustration and offset any cost savings.

- Make information about your benefits programs accessible to employees. Provide benefits information through employee training, the Internet, an intranet, direct mail campaigns, or via internal personnel.

- Enforce change consistently across your organization, limiting "one offs" and exceptions.

- Ensure the employees managing your benefits programs have the proper training and resources.

- Educate your vendors on your benefits programs and communication procedures.

Best Practice 3: Designate an internal team to manage your program and monitor vendors.

Different departments may be responsible for collaborating with external vendors and for the day-to-day administration of an organization's integrated program. Having a central resource to manage the overall program and to monitor vendor performance improves consistency and limits costs resulting from administrative errors or duplicate efforts.

- Appoint an internal "advisory" team to communicate and collaborate with external vendors.

- Develop cross-functional teams to assist with program changes (human resources, payroll, legal, etc.).

- Centralize administration to facilitate daily management, tracking, and reporting.

- Provide a central resource to aid managers/supervisors and employees with the return-to-work process.

Best Practice 4: Promote accountability among employees, individual departments, and business units.

An organization may have difficulty integrating its benefit offerings if employees and managers do not understand benefit policies or how their actions affect program success. To achieve favorable outcomes, employers should promote accountability among all internal stakeholders.

- Leverage charge backs as a method to demonstrate absence costs to individual departments or locations.

- Share individual business unit total absence costs or hours corporate-wide to encourage inter-unit collaboration and healthy competition to reduce program costs.

- Include program metrics (such as absence costs or total hours) as part of performance reviews or bonus awards.

- Provide incentives to employees for participation in wellness and other company-sponsored benefit programs.

Best Practice 5: Request regular feedback from key stakeholders.

Employers should request feedback from employees and vendors to ensure that their integrated programs continue to be well administered. This involvement reduces confusion and frustration, and facilitates the acceptance and implementation of any changes.

- Request feedback from employees on your program's service quality, whether it is administered internally or by an outside vendor.

- Encourage your employees to participate in self-training programs that will enhance their understanding of your benefits program.

- Request input from union representatives prior to making any changes.

- Consider program changes as a result of feedback.

Best Practice 6: Challenge your vendor to customize its product and process to best meet your needs.

Vendors may manage several parts of an employer's program. A vendor's willingness to work with you and meet your organization's needs will facilitate overall program administration and increase employee satisfaction.

- Spend time to seek out the best vendors; set up a review process that includes a detailed request for proposal, a site visit, an information technology review, and a reference check.

- Include performance guarantees as a method to measure vendor performance.

- Request a dedicated contact at the vendor to service your program and answers questions.

- Review program details with your vendor prior to implementation.

- Document all policies and procedures, and make sure your benefits department has the appropriate training to assist with any programs administered externally.

Best Practice 7: Leverage technology to gain efficiencies, but understand its limitations.

An organization's ability to successfully develop an integrated benefits program is highly dependent on its internal systems and those of its vendors. While a flexible and secure technology infrastructure can streamline administration, employers should also be aware of any limitations that could delay process enhancements.

- For externally administered programs, determine your vendor's ability to interact with your organization's payroll and human resource systems. In addition, ensure your systems have the flexibility to incorporate changes, such as policy updates or new reporting procedures.

- Confirm that you or your vendor's systems meet all Health Insurance Portability and Accountability Act (HIPAA) privacy regulations and that access is limited to authorized individuals or groups.

- Determine your vendor's ability to work with other outside providers. For example, does your disability carrier partner with one EAP or disease management company, or can they "plug and play" with your preferred providers?

- Utilize a centralized data storage system that makes program information easily accessible to appropriate departments.

- Develop or purchase a strong case management system that will allow for the coordination of leaves and offsetting of benefit payments.

- If your systems are internal, develop a business continuity plan. If your program is outsourced, evaluate your vendor's plans.

Best Practice 8: Capture and make the most of your data.

Capturing and reviewing program data is critical for measuring internal and external performance. Employers should collect information prior to as well as after a change to evaluate its impact. These results may also help an organization to better focus its energy and resources for future planning.

- Ensure your program data is accessible through reporting tools that provides standard and ad hoc queries.

- Utilize program results, such as costs and utilization, to monitor both internal and external performance.

- Be consistent and credible when sharing information, reporting both positive and negative outcomes.

- Clearly communicate what types of information should be captured in addition to the method and frequency of distribution.

Best Practice 9: Integration is a dynamic process — continue to monitor your program and be ready to recommend enhancements.

Proactively adjusting to and taking advantage of both expected and unexpected events will enable an organization to maximize its integrated program results. Employers should routinely evaluate their current programs and vendor relationships to identify changes that may improve overall plan integration and administration.

- Frequently assess your benefit plans to identify which areas are working and which may require additional attention.

- Participate in benefits-related conferences and surveys to view the latest program innovations and capitalize on other organizations' findings and key learnings.

- Benchmark your program versus your peers' on a regular basis to remain competitive and current.

- Leverage the expertise and feedback of internal sources and external vendors when updating or changing policies or processes.

Employer Checklist

An employer can use the following checklist to determine where a particular program falls along the spectrum of options. The key questions below prompt high-level thought as to what is in place today, what could be incorporated tomorrow, and which issues may need to be prioritized to develop your particular future and ongoing plans.

Key Questions	Yes/No	Comments
Which of the following programs are or can be integrated at your organization?		
Short-term disability		
Long-term disability		

Family medical leave		
Sick leave		
Leave of absence		
Paid-time-off programs		
Workers' compensation		
EAP/Behavioral health		
Group healthcare		
Disease management		
Wellness		
ADA		
Other		
Which of the following integration points have been or can be considered at your organization?		
Plan design		
Definitions		
Return-to-work policies		

Case management parameters		
Compliance practices		
Program referrals		
Process		
Intake		
Notification and communication		
Automatic triggers		
Common case management		
Return-to-work programs		
Program interaction		
Outsourcing		
Funding		
Insured		
Self-insured		
Hybrid approach		
Captive insurance		

Technology		
Tracking and management		
Integrated reporting		
Data access by managers and employees		
Electronic data exchange		
Metrics		
Benchmarking		
Software solutions		

Who are the key internal stakeholders at your organization? How can they be aligned?		
Project team leadership		
Senior management		
Subject matter experts		
Stakeholder participants		
Service organizations/vendors		

Can the business case for change be made either through your own available data or by pulling from relevant industry benchmarks?

Financial savings and ROI		
Process improvement		
Employee experience		
Workforce attraction and retention		

Section Two

Programs That Can Be Integrated

Chapter 2: Disability and Workers' Compensation

Background and Context

Disability and workers' compensation programs were the foundation of integrated programs when the industry first started exploring the concept. The theory that an illness is an illness, an accident an accident, and an injury is an injury (regardless of where or how it happened) spawned the concept of "24-hour coverage" and individuals having insurance at all times to cover any situation. A lot of research and development was committed to this effort, and some insurance companies and third-party administrators (TPAs) created new products to respond to the anticipated demand of covering these types of concerns. Unfortunately, employer requests did not materialize to the extent they needed to, and the progress that was made went into a state of dormancy. Over the years, however, it has resurfaced, only in a different form and mostly due to the widened scope of programs that can be integrated.

Disability

Disability coverage provides income replacement when an insured individual is deemed disabled due to a nonoccupational illness, injury, or sickness. Levels of income replacement are based on a percentage of pay and varies by employer and industry. The coverage is typically divided into two parts: short-term disability and long-term disability.

Short-term disability (STD) plans are meant to cover claims ranging anywhere from 13 to 52 weeks, with 26 weeks (or roughly six months) being the norm. Long-term disability (LTD) begins after STD has run its course and typically extends to normal retirement age (65) or slightly beyond. As with most insurance, disability contract provisions vary considerably, but both STD and LTD plans provide income replacement levels that range from 50% to 100% of pre-disability earnings. The most common level is 60%, but many policies are designed to fluctuate based on the length of disability, usually beginning at 100% at the start of a disability (which may even be referred to as sick time) and reducing over time into LTD. Other factors that may impact benefit levels include an employer's desire to tie the benefit to length of service (e.g., 100% for employees with over 10 years of service) or equalization across disability and workers' compensation (e.g., 60% to 70%, depending on state benefit levels).

Premiums for an employer-sponsored plan or program can be paid by the employer in full or by employee contributions, impacting the taxability of the benefits received during disability. Some employer plans include a base plan (paid for by the employer) and a buy-up pay (optional, paid for by the employee and considered a voluntary benefit) in order to provide some level of coverage for all employees.

Within a contract, the definition of disability is the trigger for coverage under both STD and LTD policies. Although it varies among contracts, the root of this definition is linked to the ability to perform certain occupational tasks. For example, some policies define individuals as being disabled if they are unable to perform the essential functions of their own occupation. Other polices may consider an individual disabled if they are unable to seek gainful employment for which they are reasonably suited based on education and qualifications. Still others may consider disability based on a loss of earnings potential (e.g., 15% reduction in earnings or greater) resulting from the injury or illness.

Once a disability has been triggered, the process for managing the disability begins. How aggressive this process is varies by employer, but it is meant to coordinate the activities of labor, management, insurance carriers or TPAs, healthcare providers, and vocational rehabilitation professionals to minimize the impact of the disability to the organization and the individual. This can include ensuring the appropriate level of treatment, as well as facilitating safe and timely return to work in accordance with an employee's ability to do so.

Beyond employer-sponsored disability programs, there are also public-sector disability plans that come into play. State-mandated disability plans required in California, Hawaii, New Jersey, New York, Rhode Island, and Puerto Rico work in conjunction with private STD plans. Social Security (also termed Old Age, Survivors, and Disability Income or Social Security Disability Insurance) works in conjunction with LTD plans. Coverage for veterans and state retirement systems, which may provide disability coverage through policy extension or rider, are also important to consider.

Other than U.S. public-sector disability plans, employers are not required to provide disability coverage; however, many employers do, and individuals who understand the risk, purchase individual disability plans when they are not offered through the workplace.

Workers' Compensation

Contrary to disability, workers' compensation is a federal- and state-mandated coverage that provides income replacement when an insured individual is deemed disabled due to an occupational or work-related illness, injury, or sickness. In addition to income replacement, it also provides medical coverage for the treatment of an injured employee, reimbursement for rehabilitation-related expenses, and death benefits such as a burial allowance and weekly income benefit to help compensate dependents of deceased employees.

Workers' compensation (WC) benefit levels are determined by state statute but can typically be categorized as total or partial disabilities. Total disability benefits, whether they are temporary or permanent, are expressed as a percentage of wages; for example, 66 2/3% of average weekly wages. Partial disability benefits are also based on percent of wage but incorporate a wage loss percentage into the calculation. Scheduled injuries, or those that involve loss or loss of use of specific body parts (e.g., hand, thumb, first finger), are subject to maximum amounts payable.

The United States WC system is intended to be a no-fault program that provides employees who are injured or disabled on the job with monetary awards to eliminate litigation. Prior to the WC statutes, injured employees needed to litigate against their employers (and fellow employees) to prove employer negligence or fault, thus creating a burdensome process for both sides. Therefore, in lieu of legal action, employees are guaranteed certain payment for appropriate WC claims. It is important to note that although the WC system was established to eliminate the need for lawsuits, there remain conditions that may permit lawsuits based on workplace accidents and injuries.

The trigger for a WC claim is that the illness, injury, or sickness is work-related and the incident can be proven to have arisen out of or during the course of employment. Due to the regulatory nature of WC, the management process followed once a WC claim ensues is much more aggressive than that applied to disability claims. Accident prevention and organizational safety plays a major role in WC claims, and return-to-work programs are taken very seriously.

The oversight and regulation of U.S. WC is primarily controlled by each state; however, federal WC statutes do exist specifically for federal employees and others who may be excluded. At the federal level, the following WC regulations apply:

- Jones Act or Merchant Marine Act: Provides seamen with protection against employer negligence

- Federal Employers Liability Act: Provides coverage for railroads engaged in interstate commerce

- Federal Employees Compensation Act: Provides WC benefits to federal employees and their dependents as appropriate

- Longshoremen's and Harbor Workers' Compensation: Provides WC to employees of private maritime employers

- Black Lung Benefit Act: Provides protection for miners suffering from pneumoconiosis (black lung) and requires disability benefits as well as a fund to be established to pay miners when the mine operator is unknown or unable to pay

- Energy Employees Occupational Illness Compensation Program Act: Provides benefits, including monetary compensation and medical coverage, to employees and/or beneficiaries of the Department of Energy at certain facilities and during certain time periods who developed radiation-related cancer or similar diseases related to their occupation

At the state level, 48 of the 50 states consider WC insurance mandatory. New Jersey considers WC insurance as optional, but most employers are required to carry some level of coverage. In Texas, WC insurance remains optional. Employers who do not purchase WC insurance in elective states save on premium costs but expose themselves to lawsuits. Of the 48 states requiring coverage, the majority provides employers with the option of purchasing insurance through a private system, using a state-run insurance fund, or self-insuring. The state-run programs may be competitive, indicating they will compete with insurance companies for business. However, there are a few states (North Dakota, Ohio, Washington, Wyoming) that do not allow private WC policies.

Program Similarities and Differences

Summarizing the above, disability insurance or coverage provides payments to replace income lost when the insured (employee or individual) is unable to work as a result of a nonoccupational sickness or injury. Workers' compensation is a system by which no-fault statutory benefits prescribed by law are provided by an employer to an employee (or the employee's family) due to a job-related injury (including death) resulting from an accident or occupational disease.

Although the goal of both programs is to provide benefits to injured or ill individuals, they do so in varying ways and according to different structures and formats. These similarities and differences are compared and contrasted below under the categories of organization, coverage type, financing and funding, management, and data and reporting.

Organization

Due to the varying nature of the underlying risk ("outside of work" for disability and "inside of work" for WC), disability and WC programs have been handled for years by different constituents within employer organizations. Disability occurrences are considered employee benefits and have historically and commonly been handled by human resources or employee benefits professionals. WC claims occur at work and as a result of the workplace environment and have therefore been handled by risk management, along with other property and casualty risks of organizations.

Coverage Type

Disability and WC require a different approach and treatment. Disability is primarily dependent on employer choice and WC on federal and state mandates. Employers are not required to provide disability benefits to their employees but commonly choose to in order to attract and retain talent. The terms and conditions of disability policies are subjective, and employees may or may not contribute to their cost. When formal policies are in place, they are typically subject to the Employee Retirement Income Security Act (ERISA), which guides the functioning of group policies relating to disability claims.

WC, on the other hand, is mandated for purchase by federal and state law. Employers must provide it and pay for it on their employees' behalf. The coverage form is fairly standardized with variations on benefit levels and policy endorsements by state. Most commonly, a benefit level of 66 2/3% of average weekly wage is paid for income replacement. In addition to income replacement, WC also pays medical benefits for the treatment of the injured employee; rehabilitation benefits to reimburse employees for vocational-related expenses; and death, which includes a burial allowance and a weekly income benefit to help compensate dependents of the deceased. There is typically one policy that covers an employer's risk, unless differing funding types are involved and cause more than one arrangement to be necessary (e.g., fully insured in some states, self-insured in others).

Financing and Funding

Although financing and funding is covered in detail in another chapter of this guide, it is important to note that financing has historically been more advanced under WC programs than it has for disability programs. WC programs routinely consider anything from fully insured to self-insured to captive insurance agreements and build in various levels of risk taking so that employers not only can share in their own experience but can also encourage safe behavior and injury prevention to minimize their exposure. Disability is the most commonly insured; however, STD policies do have a high rate of self-insurance. LTD programs have been the subject of captive arrangements over the last few years, and this trend is expected to continue.

Management

Because WC structures have been in place longer than disability plans, rely on workplace safety conditions, and governing laws and bodies such as OSHA and the National Association of Insurance Commissioners (NAIC) exist, the management of WC programs has been much more proactive from a claims management perspective. They also are more geared toward prevention and minimalizing overall risk. Although times are definitely changing and disability plans have adopted some of the successful aspects of WC management, they are still behind in their level of intervention and treatment parameters and ability to really medically manage a case. WC, at least in several states, has enacted managed care protocols and networks, and has achieved a fairly sophisticated level of case management, bill review, and overall utilization review. Disability programs have case management at their core but are still behind the level and depth of activity common to WC programs.

Data and Reporting

The data fields collected and the ultimate reports produced for disability and WC programs can be similar, especially in the case of integrated programs, but are historically more robust for WC than for disability. WC reporting spans a wide variety of fields. On one side, it captures detail by claim of amounts paid, reserved, and incurred. On the other hand, WC reporting documents the timing of light duty and return to work to the administrator's case notes; OSHA requirements; and other loss control and prevention strategies applied. If plans are in place for disability (versus being paid through general assets as a salary continuation program), reporting can be just as detailed with the caveat that personal health information needs to be protected, and specifically, an employee's nonoccupational diagnosis cannot be identifiable (as it can be under WC). Both program types can be rolled up at an aggregate level, and comparing the two gives an employer a sense of trends occurring across the organization.

Table 2.1 summarizes the key similarities and differences among disability and WC programs.

Table 2.1

Disability and WC Similarities
A waiting period before benefits begin (e.g., seven days) is required.
Income replacement benefit is based on a percentage of wages.
Financing component can include insured, self-insured, or other options.
Claims administration includes case management, return-to-work protocols, and rehabilitation.
Both are usually purchased through brokers and consultants.

Disability and WC Differences	
Disability	WC

Employer choice of benefit: governed by ERISA	State-mandated benefit levels: regulated by National Council on Compensation Insurance, NAIC, OSHA
Purchased by employer, employee, or individual	Purchased by employer
Not work-related/nonoccupational	Work-related/occupational
One or two policies — divided into STD (26 weeks) and LTD (to age 65 or retirement)	One policy — covers life of injury
Variable terms and conditions — carrier, TPA, and insured preference	Statutory terms and conditions
Handled by HR or employee benefits professionals	Handled by risk management professionals
Financing structures are more limited.	Financing structures are more advanced.
Traditionally reactive claim management process: injury did not occur at the workplace, employer may or may not be accountable for the cost	Historically proactive claim management process: injury is work-related, employer is fully responsible for the cost
Non-work-related aspect does not trigger safety concerns.	Involves a strong workplace safety component
Data and reporting is many times nonexistent, especially prior to implementing an integrated program	Data and reporting are more sophisticated and regulated; employer must produce records

Traditional Rationale and Innovative Theory

The rationale for administering disability and WC programs separately within organizations is deeply rooted and easily correlated back to the importance of safety in the workplace and WC claims resulting from situations that could have at least been minimized, if not prevented altogether. It is driven by the different categorization of risk within organizations and the fact that risk management and HR/employee benefits have limited interaction on a day-to-day basis. Although some organizations might understand the advantages and potential savings for managing the two more cohesively, the topic becomes somewhat of a turf issue with neither risk management nor HR/employee benefits wanting to give up a big portion of their responsibilities.

Regardless of what the situation is at any given company, there are several ways to view the risk posed to an organization by disability and WC coverages. When considering the spectrum of integrated program options shared in a previous chapter of this guide, one can start to break down the types of payments offered by both of these coverages and see the value of viewing them differently. For example, WC provides both income replacement (i.e. indemnity benefits) and medical expense benefits within the one policy. If an employee suffers a back injury at work and has to undergo surgery and a six-week recovery time, WC will pay for the costs of the surgery and reimburse the employee for a percentage of their lost work time. Conversely, disability only provides income replacement for the lost work time an employee experiences due to a nonoccupational injury or illness. If an employee had the same back injury as mentioned above, but it occurred at home instead of at work, the disability policy would reimburse the employee for their six-week recovery time, but the cost of the surgery would actually be paid by the employee's health plan. Considering Figure 2.1, employers should really compare the costs of STD/LTD and group health at their organizations to those of WC to identify opportunities for cost savings, more standardized and shared protocols for case management, and return to work (RTW), early intervention opportunities.

Figure 2.1

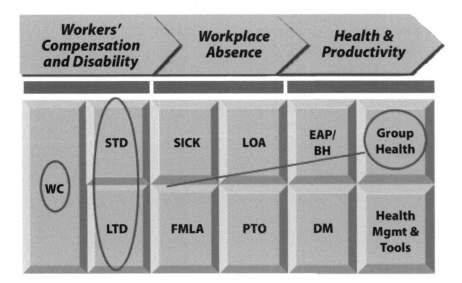

Source: Spring Consulting Group, LLC

Further, compliance with the Family and Medical Leave Act (FMLA) should not only be focused on the concurrency of STD and FMLA but routinely extended to WC claims as well. Similar to STD, WC claims more often than not also qualify as FMLA claims. Due to the heavy focus on RTW under WC programs, it is very possible that an employer could be going through their paces for managing a WC claim and get to a point where they need to terminate an employee because they are not returning to work according to the employer's policies. If FMLA paperwork was not produced in a timely manner - or at all - the employer could be at risk for violating federal and state job protection laws that have now become somewhat ingrained with STD case management. Since both disability and WC programs have waiting periods before the benefits begin (see Figure 2.2), the use of other paid time off, such as sick days or vacation time, should also be closely managed so that both the employee and employer can ensure that the amount of paid time, FMLA time, and STD or WC time was taken and tracked correctly against an employee's entitlement.

Figure 2.2

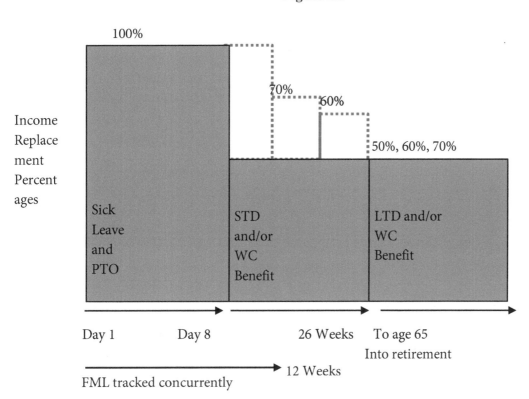

Source: Spring Consulting Group, LLC

It is very important that the health and productivity management programs that employers are making part of the disability management process have the same relation to WC programs. Why shouldn't a WC claimant be told about the EAP program when they are trying to heal from an injury or accident? Why shouldn't they take a health risk assessment so their employer can identify that they should really be enrolled in a disease management program that might not be directly related to their WC claim but that could definitely have an impact on recovery time? Wellness programs that are being rolled out across entire employer organizations are not just for those who are well but should be encouraged for those who may have an illness or injury they need to recover from, and particular programs just might help in that.

Integrated Program Goals and Achievements

Although it makes logical sense — and some employers do integrate disability and WC — today's reality is that WC is not the first program to be integrated. Of approximately 52% of employers that integrate their benefits programs in some way, 8% of them are integrating WC with STD. [xii] Cost savings from these programs vary by employer but typically result in decreased durations, increased return-to-work rates, and decreased employer time necessary to manage these programs. Given employers' goals in integrating their benefits, as noted below, it is not surprising that anywhere from 10% to 15% of direct program savings can be made, [xiii] with probably 5% to 7% of that resulting from what can be done between WC and disability and taking a common approach to return to work. By reporting these claims through a single intake process, a redundant intake and call center activity and cost can be removed. An employee's satisfaction with the process is improved as a degree of complexity and confusion has been decreased or eliminated. Tracking both occupational and nonoccupational absences through one process can eliminate duplication of coverage and therefore duplicate benefit payments. Return-to-work rate improvement due to consistent treatment protocols across WC and disability impacts duration and, therefore, costs. As mentioned above, ensured compliance can avoid legal costs due to incomplete or inaccurate tracking of time that should have been job-protected. The impact of preventative wellness, EAP, and disease management programs are very important but may not be easily tracked; however, they do have an impact, as many employer organizations have realized.

Employer Checklist

As you look across your organization and consider the possibility of integrating your WC and disability programs, the checklist below will prompt you to answer particular questions about your workplace environment and determine the level of integration or coordination that could work best.

Key Questions	Yes/No	Comments
Which internal departments currently handle your WC and disability programs?		
Workers' compensation		
Risk management		
Employee benefits		
Other		

Short-term disability		
Risk management		
Employee benefits		
Other		
Long-term disability		
Risk management		
Employee benefits		
Other		
Family medical leave		
Risk management		
Employee benefits		
Other		
ADA		
Risk management		
Employee benefits		
Other		

Do you apply case management across the programs below? And can the philosophy be coordinated across WC and disability?		
WC		
STD		
LTD		

Do your disability and WC policies contain return-to-work incentive wording that can be relied upon in the claims administration process?		
WC		
STD		
LTD		

Do you have formal return-to-work policies and procedures in place for the programs below? And could they be coordinated?		
WC		
STD		
LTD		

Are there health and productivity management programs your organization employs that could be made part of the disability and WC management processes?		
EAP/behavioral health		

Group healthcare		
Disease management		
Wellness		
Other		

Chapter 3: Statutory Disability Plans

Background and Context

For most employers, providing disability income replacement coverage is a choice; however, five states and Puerto Rico have developed minimum disability insurance standards that ensure local employees who are deemed disabled are provided with a minimum compensation based on pre-disability earnings.

Understanding the nuances of these standards is important for integrated programs, as a variety of parties (e.g., states, insurance companies, employers) play roles in their administration. The states, governing statutes, and dates established are noted below.

Table 3.1

State	Governing Statutes	Date Established
California	Unemployment Compensation Disability Benefits Law (SDI) (California Unemployment Insurance Code, Section 2601 et seq.)	1946
Hawaii	Temporary Disability Insurance Law (TDI) (Hawaii Revised Statutes, Chapter 392 et seq.)	1969
New Jersey	Temporary Disability Benefits Law (TDB) (New Jersey Revised Statutes, 43:21-25 et seq.)	1948
New York	Disability Benefits Law (DBL) (New York Workers Compensation Law, Section 202 et seq.)	1949
Puerto Rico	Non-Occupational Disability Insurance, "SINOT" (for its Spanish acronym) (Act 139 of June 26, 1968, as amended; Puerto Rico Laws Annotated, Title 11, Section 201 et seq.)	1968
Rhode Island	Temporary Disability Insurance Act (TDI) (Rhode Island General Laws, Section 28-40-1 et seq.)	1942

Administering statutory plans can increase the operational burden for employers as each state defines varied plan options and funding requirements. Eligibility requirements, waiting periods, definitions of earnings and disability, durations, unique offset parameters, and continuity of coverage also differ among the six jurisdictions. In addition, the way these plans link with a corporate-sponsored disability plan varies, based on the statutory requirements. Nonetheless, employers must remain in compliance with these plans. This chapter is meant to serve as a guide, although specific questions about your employee population should be considered with your internal legal resources and external subject matter experts.

NOTE: California, New Jersey, and Rhode Island also have paid family leave laws, which in many cases are summarized within the same statute. These leave laws are not covered within this chapter.

California Statutory Disability Insurance (SDI)

Plan Options and Funding

Plan Options

California provides for a public, state-administered disability benefit plan, but also allows the option of an approved private plan. Private plans must be self-insured and are referred to as voluntary plans. This terminology simply implies the employer is voluntarily offering a plan that will meet the requirements of the statutory plans.

To establish a voluntary plan, 50% of employees must consent. When a voluntary plan is used, it must afford no less than the state plan and have at least one feature of greater value than the state plan.

Funding

Employee contributions are required, and in California, if the employee is enrolled in the state plan, employer contributions are not required. However, employers are not prohibited from making contributions on behalf of employees for part or all of the statutory plan premiums.

Pretax contributions under Section 125 cafeteria plans are generally not an option for state disability insurance because cafeteria plans must offer a choice between cash and qualified benefits. Since from California's perspective, contributions are required from employees for disability benefits, cash is not an option. Those covered by the state plan in California may contribute different amounts but the statute sets upper and lower limits. The cost can be no less than 0.1% and no more than 1.3% of eligible payroll up to a maximum. See the state's current year annual appendix for the required contributions.[xiv]

Self-employed individuals may be charged a higher rate as they may be required to make the employer's assessment when such is required.

If employers opt out of California's state plan by implementing a private plan, they may not charge employees higher contributions than they would have incurred within the state plan, even though some benefits are enhanced. Although employers with private plans typically do not make contributions to the state plan, they may be assessed a fee if the fund dips below a certain monetary threshold.

Coverage Provisions

Eligibility Requirement

Eligibility parameters exist for both employers and their employees under each statutory plan. In California, employers are considered covered if they have one or more employees whose wages are $100 or higher in the preceding quarter. Agricultural employers are also covered, along with certain nonprofits and hospitals. Public entities and the self-employed are traditionally not covered by the regulation but may elect to provide disability coverage through the state fund or other means. If employees have earned $300 in base period wages and are working for a covered employer, they are eligible for California state disability.[xv]

Waiting Period

The waiting period for statutory disability coverage is the uncompensated time before benefits are paid. California has a seven-day waiting period, which may be waived if the employee is hospitalized due to the condition.

Definition of Earnings While Disabled

All states define earnings differently. California uses the quarter in which the employee had the highest base period wages when defining earnings for disability coverage. The "base period" is the 12 months preceding the disability. Employees are entitled to 55% of these weekly earnings, up to a maximum that is determined annually. See the state's annual appendix for the current year maximum. [xvi]

Definition of Disability

Each state has a similar definition of disability: the inability to perform regular and customary work due to physical or mental conditions. Variations, however, exist. Laws for all jurisdictions require that a disabled employee is under the care of a provider. In California, this includes authorized religious practitioners of the claimants' faith or if they depend on spiritual means for healing.

California, like most statutory plan jurisdictions, excludes benefits for injuries that are self-inflicted or the result of the perpetration of an illegal act. Further, California prohibits pay during incarceration. Most unique is the fact that California provides coverage for elective surgeries that are typically denied by other statutory (and non-statutory) plans.

In addition to a specific definition, California, like all states, requires a certain amount of documentation, including diagnoses, dates of absence, insight from provider regarding limitations, and an estimated return-to-work date. In California, a physician must complete the certification. Physicians, podiatrists, chiropractors, dentists, or accredited practitioners of a church (spiritual healing) may fulfill medical needs; however, the regulation specifies that employees may be required to submit to a medical exam — although they will not be required to submit to treatment.

Consecutive Disability

California has parameters for consecutive or recurrent disability. California will consider multiple claims as one disability if they reoccur within 14 days and are due to the same diagnosis or similar situational circumstances as the prior diagnosis.

Duration

The maximum length of time employees can be on statutory disability is 52 weeks.

Integration Considerations

Offset Parameters

California, like all states with statutory plans, has designed its plan to offset other state programs. Claims are excluded from disability coverage if they are already covered under workers' compensation or unemployment compensation. There are a few exceptions to this, such as when a workers' compensation claim is partial/permanent. In those cases, it may be possible to also qualify for statutory disability, depending on other circumstances.

When employers are establishing voluntary plans, they must give careful consideration as to how that plan will link with other statutory offerings. This is important because the regulations do not offset employer-sponsored coverage; the offset logistics are therefore the responsibility of the employer.

Return to work is not discussed in much detail within the regulations; however, California is leveraging disability guidelines as a means of controlling disability costs for the state plan so would likely permit the use of such guidelines in a private plan.

Post Employment Period of Coverage

California requires employers to continue coverage for most terminated employees for two additional weeks. This is intended to provide coverage for that worker until they become eligible under their new employer.

Administration

California accounts for administrative costs within the fees collected for the plan. When and if these fees are not enough to cover the administration in addition to the fund, additional assessments may be charged to employers.

Failure to comply with regulations results in a fine. In addition, if employers do not compensate their employees appropriately, the state may pay the claim on the employer's behalf and assess that benefit cost back to the employer along with a fee.

In California, the same area that manages unemployment insurance manages the administration of temporary disability benefits, and similar systems and processes are leveraged.

Process

California requires posters noting the employer or employee rights under the regulation must be provided or posted in a conspicuous location. In addition to notice requirements, employers must supply information required to process statutory disability claims when requested by employees or by the plan administrator.

California also requires that employers keep records regarding employee eligibility, including, but not limited to, salary and status information for a minimum of four years, the current year plus the prior three.

New York Disability Benefits Law (DBL)

Plan Options and Funding

Plan Options

New York provides a public, statutory plan but also allows the option of an approved private plan.

All DBL plans are underwritten by an insurance carrier licensed to do business in the state of New York and the plan must provide at least the benefits required by New York's Disability Benefits Law. Carriers may write plans that provide greater benefits which are called "enhanced plans."

Funding

Employee contributions are required in all states, and in New York employers are required to facilitate that process through payroll deductions. New York requires employers to contribute some portion of the cost of the plan. Pretax contributions under Section 125 cafeteria plans are generally not an option for state disability insurance because cafeteria plans must offer a choice between cash and qualified benefits. If the state requires employee contributions for disability benefits, cash is not an option.

New York employers are authorized to make deductions at a rate of half of 1% of the employee's wages but no more than $0.60 per week. Self-employed individuals may be charged a higher rate as they may be required to make the employer's assessment when one is required.

If employers provide an "enhanced plan", they may charge employees more than this amount as long as the amount is reasonably related to the value of the benefits, and employees agree to the additional amount. Such a plan and rates must be approved by New York.[xvii] New York maintains a fund for the payment of DBL benefits under certain circumstances for covered employees who are not employed at the time of their disability. The State of New York can require employers to make contributions to the fund if the balance falls below a certain level.

In addition, if the special fund established in New York (primarily for unemployed workers who become disabled) is running below an established balance, a fee may be assessed to all eligible employers.

Coverage Provisions

Eligibility Requirements

An employee must be covered by an eligible employer. In New York, employers are covered if they employ one or more workers on each of at least 30 days during the calendar year. Public authorities, municipal corporations, and other political subdivisions are not within the regulation but may elect coverage. Employers of domestics may be covered if the work period lasts more than four weeks (40 hours or more per week) and the domestics are employed on each of the last 30 days in the calendar year. Maritime and farm workers are usually excluded.[xviii] Although no monetary eligibility requirement exists for employees, New York employees must have worked at least four consecutive weeks for a covered employer. Employees who change jobs from one "covered" employer to another "covered" employer are protected from the first day on the new job.[xix]

Waiting Periods

The waiting period for statutory disability coverage is the uncompensated time before benefits are paid. New York has a standard seven-day waiting period. There is no waiver of the waiting period, for example, in the case of hospitalization or extended length of disability.

Definition of Earnings While Disabled

New York defines disability earnings based on a formula tied to prior earnings. New York provides compensation during qualified disability of up to $170 per week. The exact amount is calculated based on 50% of the average weekly wage;[xx] a minimum of $20 will be paid weekly. This amount rarely changes; however, check the annual appendix for current maximums.

Definition of Disability

Each state has a similar definition of disability: the inability to perform regular and customary work due to physical or mental conditions. Variations, however, exist. Laws for all jurisdictions require that a disabled employee is under the care of a provider.

New York excludes coverage for injuries that are self-inflicted or the result of the perpetration of an illegal act or resulting from war.

In addition to a specific definition, New York requires a certain amount of documentation, including diagnoses, dates of absence, insight from provider regarding limitations, and an estimated return-to-work date.

In most cases, as in New York, a physician must complete the certification of disability. When it comes to treatment, the services can be delivered by a wider variety of practitioners. In New York, physicians, podiatrists, chiropractors, dentists, or accredited practitioners of a church (spiritual healing) may fulfill medical needs; however, the regulation specifies that employees may be required to submit to a medical exam — although they will not be required to submit to treatment. This is generally the same in all jurisdictions; however, New York specifies this in detail.

Consecutive Disability

New York, like most states, has parameters for consecutive or recurrent disability. Periods of disability with the same 90 days can be considered as the same disability. For a disability to be considered recurrent, it must be due to the same diagnosis and similar situational circumstances as the prior diagnosis.

Durations

The maximum length of time employees can be on statutory disability in New York is 26 weeks.

Integration Considerations

Offset Parameters

New York, like all states with mandatory plans, has designed its plan to offset other state programs. Claims are typically excluded from disability coverage if they are already covered under workers' compensation or unemployment compensation. There are a few exceptions to this, such as when a workers' compensation claim is partial/permanent. In those cases, it may be possible to also qualify for statutory disability depending on other circumstances.

When employers are establishing voluntary statutory plans and/or employer-sponsored plans, they must give careful consideration as to how that plan will link with other statutory offerings. This is important because the regulations do not offset employer-sponsored coverage; the offset logistics are therefore the responsibility of the employer.

Return to work is not discussed in much detail within the regulations; however, at least two states with statutory plans are leveraging disability duration guidelines, so it is safe to assume that New York will likely allow the use of such in private plan administration.

Post Employment Period of Coverage

New York requires employers to maintain employee coverage for four weeks after termination, in accordance with the state's definition of eligibility. This is intended to provide coverage for that worker until they become eligible under their new employer.

NY State DBL Administrative Costs

New York covers for administrative costs within the taxes collected for the plan. When and if these fees are not enough to cover the administration in addition to the fund, fees may be charged to employers.

Failure to comply with regulations results in a fine. In addition, if employers do not compensate their employees appropriately, the state may pay the claim on the employer's behalf and assess that benefit cost back to the employer along with a fee.

Process

New York requires posters noting the employer and employee rights under the regulation must be provided or posted in a conspicuous location. New York also requires a notice of rights that must be sent within five days of an employee disability report. In addition to notice requirements, employers must supply information required to process statutory disability claims when requested by employees or by the plan administrator.

In addition, New York requires that employers keep records regarding employee eligibility, including, but not limited to, salary and status information. New York requires employers to maintain these records for three years.

New Jersey Temporary Disability Benefits (TDB)

Plan Options and Funding

Plan Options

New Jersey provides a public, state-administered disability benefit plan, but also allows employers to provide an approved private plan.

When private plans are used, they are commonly referred to as voluntary plans. This terminology simply implies the employer is voluntarily offering a plan that will meet the requirements of the statutory plans.

When a private plan or voluntary plan is used it must provide for benefits that are no less than the state plan and have at least one feature greater than the state plan.

New Jersey automatically enrolls employers in the state plan once they become eligible. To establish a private plan with contributions, 51% of employees must agree via election (signature). If employees are not required to make contributions, no election is required, only notification.

Funding

Employee contributions are required in New Jersey. The state also requires employers to contribute to the cost of the plan regardless of whether it is the statutory plan or a voluntary one. Pretax contributions under Section 125 cafeteria plans are generally not an option for state disability insurance because cafeteria plans must offer a choice between cash and qualified benefits. If the state requires employee contributions for disability benefits, cash is not an option.

Self-employed individuals may be charged a higher rate.

If employers opt out of the state plan, they may not charge employees higher contributions than they would have incurred within the state plan, even though at least one benefit is enhanced. Although employers with private plans typically do not make contributions to the state plan, they may be assessed a fee if the fund dips below a certain monetary threshold.

New Jersey sets contributions for employees at 0.5% of taxable wages (taxable wage base), up to a maximum that is specified annually.[xxi] Employers pay the differential between this employee contribution and the actual cost of the plan. This ranges between 0.1% and 0.75% of the taxable wage base via quarterly contributions. In extreme situations, rates may be raised up to 1.1% to refresh the state fund and make up for poor experience. For the current contribution rates and maximums, see the annual appendix for the current year.

Coverage Provisions

Eligibility Requirements

Eligibility parameters exist for both employers and their employees under each statutory plan. In New Jersey, eligible employees must be covered by eligible employers.

New Jersey employers are automatically eligible for and enrolled in temporary disability benefits if they are subject to the New Jersey Unemployment Compensation Law. This mandatory enrollment is for most employers, with some government entitles excluded. Agricultural workers and domestic services may or may not be considered covered employers in New Jersey based on a variety of factors, such as the number of workers they employ. In most cases, employers that are not specifically covered by the regulation may elect coverage. Once approved, the employer is required to maintain coverage for a full two years.[xxii]

Employees are eligible if they have earned at least $165 per week for 20 weeks during the base year. If 20 weeks are not available, the employee is eligible if they have earned $8,300 in the 52 weeks preceding the date of disability ("base year").[xxiii] This eligibility requirement may be changed from time to time. See the annual appendix for the current year.

Waiting Period

The waiting period for statutory disability coverage is the uncompensated time before benefits are paid. New Jersey has a standard seven-day waiting period. While there is no provision for the waiver of this period in the event of hospitalization (as in some jurisdictions), New Jersey regulations require the waiting period to be compensable following payment for all or some part of the third week of payments.[xxiv]

Definition of Earnings While Disabled

New Jersey ties benefits to a formula based on prior earnings. Computing disability earnings in New Jersey is done by taking 66 2/3% of the average weekly wage, up to a maximum per week that changes annually. See the annual appendix for the current year's maximum.[xxv]

Please note, unlike other statutory plans, there is no provision under New Jersey rules for payments for a partial week of disability. Disability benefits are paid in weekly amounts.

Definition of Disability

Each state has a similar definition of disability: the inability to perform regular and customary work due to physical or mental conditions. Variations, however, exist. Laws for all jurisdictions require that a disabled employee is under the care of a provider. New Jersey has provisions that would disallow otherwise eligible individuals to participate in the disability program if they depend on spiritual means for healing.

New Jersey excludes benefits for injuries that are self-inflicted or the result of the perpetration of an illegal act.

In addition to a specific definition, New Jersey, like all states, requires a certain amount of documentation, including diagnoses, dates of absence, insight from provider regarding limitations, and an estimated return-to-work date.

In New Jersey, a physician must complete the certificate; however, regulations also allow that a dentist, podiatrist, psychologist, chiropractor, advanced practice nurse, optometrist may certify disabling conditions.

In New Jersey, like most states, physicians, podiatrists, chiropractors, dentists, or accredited practitioners of a church (spiritual healing) may fulfill medical needs; however, the regulation specifies that employees may be required to submit to an exam — although they will not be required to submit to treatment.

Consecutive Disability

New Jersey has parameters for consecutive or recurrent disability. Separate periods of disability will be considered as one disability if they reoccur within 14 days. For a disability to be considered recurrent, it must be due to the same diagnosis and similar situational circumstances as the prior diagnosis.

Durations

The maximum length of time employees can be on statutory disability in New Jersey is 26 weeks.

Integration Considerations

Offset Parameters

New Jersey has designed its plan to offset other state programs. Claims are typically excluded from disability coverage if they are already covered under workers' compensation or unemployment compensation. There are a few exceptions to this, such as when a workers' compensation claim is partial/permanent. In those cases, it may be possible to also qualify for statutory disability, depending on other circumstances.

When employers are establishing voluntary plans, they must give careful consideration as to how that plan will link with other statutory offerings. This is important because the regulations provided by New Jersey do not offset employer-sponsored coverage; the offset logistics are therefore the responsibility of the employer.

Return to work is not discussed in much detail within the regulations; however, at least two states with statutory plans are leveraging disability duration guidelines, so it is safe to assume that New Jersey will likely allow the use of such in private plan administration.

Post Employment Period of Coverage

New Jersey requires employees to continue coverage for most terminated employees for two additional weeks. This is intended to provide coverage for that worker until they become eligible under their new employer.

Administration

New Jersey accounts for administrative costs within the taxes collected for the plan. When and if these fees are not enough to cover the administration in addition to the fund, fees may be charged to employers.

Failure to comply with regulations results in a fine. In addition, if employers with private plans do not compensate their employees appropriately, the state may pay the claim on the employers' behalf and assess that benefit cost back to the employer along with a fee.

In New Jersey, the same area that manages unemployment insurance manages the administration for temporary disability, and similar systems and processes are leveraged.

Process

New Jersey requires posters noting the employer and/or employee rights under the regulation must be provided or posted in a conspicuous location. In addition to notice requirements, employers must supply information required to process statutory disability claims when requested by employees or by the plan administrator.

New Jersey requires that employers keep records regarding employee eligibility, including, but not limited to, salary and status information. These records must be maintained for the current year, as well as four prior years.

Rhode Island Temporary Disability Insurance (TDI)

Plan Options and Funding

Plan Options

Among the states providing for statutory coverage for disabilities, Rhode Island is unique. They have a state plan established to be used by all employers for their employees. There is no option in Rhode Island for any type of private plan. Employers may provide additional coverage if they desire, but even if they do, Rhode Island employees are required to be enrolled in the state plan.

Funding

Plan costs are covered by contributions from employees, and employers are required to facilitate that process through payroll deductions. It is also possible for someone (e.g., the employer) to contribute on the employees' behalf. However, Rhode Island does not require employer contributions that are typically required in the other jurisdictions. Pretax contributions under Section 125 cafeteria plans are generally not an option for state disability insurance because cafeteria plans must offer a choice between cash and qualified benefits. If the state requires employee contributions for disability benefits, cash is not an option.

Self-employed individuals may be charged a higher rate.

In Rhode Island, quarterly contributions are made by employees through their employer. Rates, maximum covered income, and maximum contributions are set by regulation annually. Refer to the annual appendix to determine this year's requirements.[xxvi]

Coverage Provisions

Eligibility Requirements

In Rhode Island, eligible employees must be covered by eligible employers. Rhode Island has employer eligibility requirements in addition to monetary and non-monetary employee eligibility requirements.

Any employer with one or more employees in the state is required to provide temporary disability insurance. Employers must file with the state on or before the tenth day of their eligibility. Federal, state, and some municipal employees, as well as partners and unincorporated self-employed workers, may be excluded from TDI coverage.

Rhode Island employees must earn a minimum in base period wages to be eligible. See the annual appendix for the current minimum base period earnings. The base period represents the first four of the last five completed quarters. If an individual has not earned the minimum in base period wages, they may still be eligible if they have satisfied all of the following:

- Total base period wages of $3,200

- Earned at least $1,600 in one base period quarter

- Total base period wages are at least one and a half times the highest quarter wages[xxvii]

Waiting Period

The waiting period for statutory disability coverage is the uncompensated time before benefits are paid. Rhode Island has no unpaid waiting period, however an employee must be certified as out of work for at least 7 consecutive days in order to be eligible for benefits. Benefits will be paid retroactively to the first day of absence once the absence lasts more than seven days. Absences that do not last at least 7 consecutive days are not covered under Rhode Island TDI.[xxviii]

Definition of Earnings While Disabled

All states define earnings differently, typically based on a formula tied to prior earnings.

Disabled employees in Rhode Island receive compensation in the amount of 4.62% of total high base quarter wages in the base period. As noted earlier, the base period represents the first four of the last five completed quarters. This benefit is subject to a minimum and maximum amount per week, which is determined on an annual basis. See the most current annual appendix for those amounts.

Additional remuneration is provided in the form of a dependent allowance if the disabled employees have dependents. The dependent allowance is the greater of $10 or 7% of the weekly benefit rate for each dependent, up to a maximum of five covered dependents. Rhode Island is the only state to provide this dependent coverage within its temporary disability plan; documentation must be submitted to the directors' satisfaction when required.[xxix]

Definition of Disability

Each state has a similar definition of disability: the inability to perform regular and customary work due to physical or mental conditions. Variations, however, exist. Laws for all jurisdictions require that a disabled employee is under the care of a provider. Rhode Island has provisions that would disallow otherwise eligible individuals to participate in the disability program if they depend on spiritual means for healing.

Unlike virtually all other statutory plans, Rhode Island does not exclude coverage for injuries that are self-inflicted or the result of the perpetration of an illegal act.

In addition to a specific definition, Rhode Island, like all states, requires a certain amount of documentation, including diagnoses, dates of absence, insight from provider regarding limitations, and an estimated return-to-work date. In Rhode Island, a physician must complete the certificate; however, Rhode Island has expanded its list of medical professionals that are able to certify a disability to include midwives, nurse practitioners, physician assistants, physicians, and psychiatric clinical nurse specialists. More recently, licensed clinical social workers and licensed independent clinical social workers may also certify disabilities. Employees dependent upon prayer or spiritual means for healing are exempt from provisions of the act upon filing the prescribed affidavits.

In Rhode Island, physicians, podiatrists, chiropractors, dentists, or accredited practitioners of a church (spiritual healing) may fulfill medical needs; however, the regulation specifies that employees may be required to submit to a medical exam — although they will not be required to submit to treatment.

Consecutive Disability

All states, other than Rhode Island, have parameters for consecutive or recurrent disability. This provision is not as critical in Rhode Island since the benefit waiting period is only required once per year.

Durations

The maximum length of time employees can be on statutory disability is 30 weeks.

Integration Considerations

Offset Parameters

Rhode Island, like all states with statutory plans, has designed its plan to offset other state programs. Claims are typically excluded from disability coverage if they are already covered under workers' compensation or unemployment compensation. There are a few exceptions to this, such as when a workers' compensation claim is partial/permanent. In those cases, it may be possible to also qualify for statutory disability, depending on other circumstances.

With regard to return to work, Rhode Island is becoming more aggressive in its offering and attempting to provide incentives for partial return to work.

On Rhode Island's TDI plan, partial return to work is allowed and encouraged. If employees return to partial duty, they must report all wages (except holiday pay for a state holiday). If these wages are less than the weekly benefit amount earned, employees are entitled to keep the first 20% of the weekly benefit amount without penalty. Any wages that exceed that 20% will be offset dollar for dollar. [xxx]

Linked to this is the state's claim management unit, which leverages disability duration guidelines and allows them to compare durations on TDI claims to expected durations for similarly situated claims (i.e., those with the same diagnosis). Rhode Island leverages nurses within its claim unit and allows for independent medical reviews. Although other states seem to be striving toward this, Rhode Island is ahead of other jurisdictions.

Post Employment Period of Coverage

Continuity of coverage is not a significant concern to employers in Rhode Island, where employees are covered under a state plan that is administered by the state.

Administration

Rhode Island accounts for administrative costs within the taxes collected for the plan. When and if these fees are not enough to cover the administration in addition to the fund, fees may be charged to employers.

Failure to comply with regulations results in a fine in most states.

In Rhode Island, the same area that manages unemployment insurance manages the administration for temporary disability, and similar systems and processes are leveraged.

Rhode Island requires posters noting the employer and employee rights under the regulation must be provided or posted in a conspicuous location. In addition to notice requirements, employers must supply information required to process statutory disability claims when requested by employees or by the plan administrator.

In Rhode Island, the employer must complete paperwork within five days in order to remain in compliance. If the documentation is not returned by the employer, a signed employee affidavit will be accepted for employment information.

Rhode Island requires that employers keep records regarding employee eligibility, including, but not limited to, salary and status information. These records must be maintained for at least four years.

Hawaii Temporary Disability Insurance (TDI)

Plan Options and Funding

Plan Options

Hawaii is unique in that it provides no state-run plan alternative. Hawaii requires employers to establish private plans, which may be insured, self-insured, or approved collective bargaining agreements.

Employer plans must be equal to or better than the statutory description of the minimum plan design, based on actuarial value.

Funding

Employee contributions are required in all states, and employers are required to facilitate that process through payroll deductions. In Hawaii, it is also possible for the employer to contribute on the employees' behalf.

Hawaii allows employers some flexibility in terms of how much an employee can be charged since there is no state-administered plan with a price to compare with employer's plan. However, employee contributions do have upper limits.

For example, the employer must bear at least 50% of the cost of the plan and in many cases more. The employee's portion of the costs may not exceed 50% of the plan costs and in no event can they be more than 0.5% of taxable weekly wages, up to a maximum contribution that is specified annually. [xxxi] See the annual appendix for the current year's maximum employee contribution. Additional costs must be paid as incurred by the employer.

Coverage Provisions

Eligibility Requirements

Eligibility parameters exist for both employers and their employees under each statutory plan. In Hawaii, eligible employees must be covered by eligible employers, which under Hawaiian law, is any employer, including the state, with one or more workers. Agricultural, fishing, domestic businesses, family businesses, and commission-based workers may not be covered; federal employees are also excluded. To be eligible, employees must have 14 weeks of employment (20 or more hours per week) and have earned $400 in the four quarters prior to the first day of disability.[xxxii]

Waiting Period

The waiting period for statutory disability coverage is the uncompensated time before benefits are paid. Hawaii, like most jurisdictions, has a standard seven-day waiting period. There is no provision for waiving this period, for example, in the event of hospitalization or based on the length of the disability.

Definition of Earnings While Disabled

All states define earnings differently, typically based on a formula tied to prior earnings. Hawaii bases disability earnings on an average weekly wage. The benefit for most employees is 58% of their average weekly wage, up to a maximum specified annually. See the annual appendix for the current year's maximum.[xxxiii]

Definition of Disability

Each state has a similar definition of disability: the inability to perform regular and customary work due to physical or mental conditions. Variations, however, exist. Laws for all jurisdictions require that a disabled employee is under the care of a provider. In Hawaii, this includes authorized religious practitioners of the claimants' faith.

Hawaii excludes benefits for injuries that are self-inflicted or the result of the perpetration of an illegal act.

In addition to a specific definition, Hawaii requires a certain amount of documentation, including diagnoses, dates of absence, insight from provider regarding limitations, and an estimated return-to-work date.

In most cases, as in Hawaii, a physician must complete the certificate; however, Hawaii allows that any person licensed to practice medicine, surgery, dentistry, chiropractic care, osteopathy, naturopathy, or practitioners of healing by prayer may satisfy the certification requirement.

Hawaii also specifies that employees may be required to submit to a medical exam — although they will not be required to submit to treatment.

Consecutive Disability

Hawaii has parameters for consecutive or recurrent disability. Hawaii specifies that multiple claims may be considered as one disability if they reoccur within two weeks. For a disability to be considered recurrent, it must be due to the same diagnosis and similar situational circumstances as the prior diagnosis.

Duration

The maximum length of time employees can be on statutory disability is 26 weeks in Hawaii.

Integration Considerations

Offset Parameters

Hawaii, like all states with statutory plans, has designed its plan to offset other state programs. Claims are excluded from disability coverage if they are already covered under workers' compensation or unemployment compensation. There are a few exceptions to this, such as when a workers' compensation claim is partial/permanent. In those cases, it may be possible to also qualify for statutory disability, depending on other circumstances.

Return to work is not discussed in much detail within the regulations; however, at least two states with statutory plans are leveraging disability duration guidelines, so it is safe to assume that Hawaii will likely allow the use of such in private plan administration.

Post Employment Period of Coverage

Hawaii requires employers to continue coverage for most terminated employees for two additional weeks. This is intended to provide coverage for workers until they become eligible under their new employer.

Administration

Given the structure used in Hawaii, administration for its statutory disability plans is paid through general revenues rather than specific assessments.

Failure to comply with regulations regarding plan design and administration can result in a fine.

Process

Hawaii requires posters noting the employer and/or employee rights under the regulation must be provided or posted in a conspicuous location. In addition to notice requirements, employers must supply information required to process disability claims when requested by employees or by the plan administrator.

In Hawaii, employers are also required to complete documentation in one week. If not, the employee may contact investigations for assistance.

Hawaii requires that employers keep records regarding employee eligibility, including, but not limited to, salary and status information. Hawaii also requires employers to maintain these records for five years.

Puerto Rico Temporary Disability Benefits (TDB)

Plan Options and Funding

Plan Options

Puerto Rico provides for a public, statutory administered plan, but allows the option of an approved private plan.

When private plans are used, they are commonly referred to as voluntary plans. This terminology simply implies the employer is voluntarily offering a plan that will meet the requirements of the statutory plan.

When a private plan or voluntary plan is used, the plan must provide at a minimum benefits and features equal to the statutory plan and at least one feature that is greater in design.

Funding

Employee contributions are required in Puerto Rico, and employers are required to facilitate that process through payroll deductions. Pretax contributions under Section 125 cafeteria plans are generally not an option for state disability insurance because cafeteria plans must offer a choice between cash and qualified benefits. If the state requires employee contributions for disability benefits, cash is not an option.

Self-employed individuals may be charged a higher rate as they may be required to make the employer's assessment when one is required.

If employers opt out of the state plan, they may not charge employees higher contributions than they would have incurred within the state plan, even though at least one benefit is enhanced. Although employers with private plans typically do not make contributions to the state plan, they may be assessed a fee if the fund dips below a certain monetary threshold.

Covered employees in Puerto Rico make contributions at a rate of 0.3% of income up to a maximum income amount and there is a maximum annual contribution amount.[xxxiv] The maximums change from time to time. Refer to the annual appendix for the current year's amounts. In no event can employees be required to pay more than 50% of the plan costs.

Employers would then additionally contribute 0.3%, although in some instances, employers may absorb greater than half of the contributions; in this case, employees would still be responsible for some amount of payment for the plan. If the employer does not make the appropriate deduction for their employees, they are liable for the cost. Private plan employers do not contribute to the state plan; however, they may be charged an assessment if the disability benefit fund is deficient.

Puerto Rico does not allow the employee to be charged a higher price for a private plan compared to the state plan, even though it offers increased benefits.

Coverage Provisions

Eligibility Requirements

In Puerto Rico, eligible employees must be covered by eligible employers. Any employer with one or more employed persons in Puerto Rico is considered covered. Although federal and foreign government employees are exempt, other government employees, as well as agricultural and domestic service employees, are typically covered. Employees also have an earnings requirement for eligibility, which is $150 in the base period.[xxxv]

Waiting Period

The waiting period for statutory disability coverage is the uncompensated time before benefits are paid. Puerto Rico has a standard seven-day waiting period, although this waiting period may be waived if the employee is hospitalized following injury.

Definition of Earnings While Disabled

All states define earnings differently, typically based on a formula tied to prior earnings.

Puerto Rico provides a weekly statutory benefit of 65% of weekly earnings. Minimums and maximums are set and differ based on agricultural versus nonagricultural workers. The minimums and maximums are subject to change. Refer to the annual appendix for the current benefit and salary amounts. [xxxvi]

Definition of Disability

Each state has a similar definition of disability: the inability to perform regular and customary work due to physical or mental conditions. Variations, however, exist. Laws for all jurisdictions require that a disabled employee is under the care of a provider.

Puerto Rico excludes coverage for injuries that are self-inflicted or the result of the perpetration of an illegal act. Puerto Rico also excludes disabilities resulting from an abortion unless the abortion was performed for medical reasons and/or if a complication arises from the abortion procedure.

In addition to a specific definition, Puerto Rico requires a certain amount of documentation, including diagnoses, dates of absence, insight from provider regarding limitations, and an estimated return-to-work date.

In most cases, a physician must complete the certificate; however, while many statutory plans allow a degree of leniency in certifying the disability, only chiropractors and physicians appear to satisfy the requirements in Puerto Rico.

Consecutive Disability

Puerto Rico has parameters for consecutive or recurrent disability. In Puerto Rico, two disabilities can be considered as one if they occur within 90-days of each other. For a disability to be considered recurrent, it must be due to the same diagnosis and similar situational circumstances as the prior diagnosis.

Durations

The maximum length of time employees can be on statutory disability is 26 weeks.

Integration Considerations

Offset Parameters

Puerto Rico, like all states that have statutory plans, has designed their plans to offset other state programs. Claims are typically excluded from disability coverage if they are already covered under workers' compensation or unemployment compensation. There are a few exceptions to this, such as when a workers' compensation claim is partial/permanent. In those cases, it may be possible to also qualify for statutory disability, depending on other circumstances.

When employers are establishing voluntary statutory plans and/or employer-sponsored plans, they must give careful consideration as to how that plan will link with other statutory offerings. This is important because the regulations provided by each state do not offset employer-sponsored coverage; the offset logistics are therefore the responsibility of the employer.

Return to work is not discussed in much detail within the regulations; however, at least two states with statutory plans are leveraging disability duration guidelines, so it is safe to assume that Puerto Rico will likely allow the use of such in private plan administration.

Post Employment Period of Coverage

Puerto Rico requires that employers cover terminated employees for an extended period of time, in many cases until they are employed in covered positions; however, there are exceptions to this regulation.

Administration

Puerto Rico accounts for administrative costs within the taxes collected for the plan. When and if these fees are not enough to cover the administration in addition to the fund, fees may be charged to employers.

Failure to comply with regulations results in a fine. In addition, if employers do not compensate their employees appropriately, the state may pay the claim on the employers' behalf and assess that benefit cost back to the employer along with a fee.

In Puerto Rico, the same area that manages unemployment insurance manages the administration for temporary disability, and similar systems and processes are leveraged.

Process

Puerto Rico requires posters noting the employer and employee rights under the regulation must be provided or posted in a conspicuous location. In addition to notice requirements, employers must supply information required to process statutory disability claims when requested by employees or by the plan administrator.

Puerto Rico requires employers to keep records regarding employee eligibility, including, but not limited to, salary and status information. These records must be maintained for five years.

Resources

Source	Description	Website and Contact Information
California Employment Development Department (EDD)	Disability Insurance Branch Employment Development Department 750 N Street, P.O. Box 826880 Sacramento, CA 94280-0001	www.edd.ca.gov 916.654.8198
Hawaii Department of Labor and Industrial Relations	Disability Compensation Division Department of Labor and Industrial Relations 830 Punchbowl, P.O. Box 3769 Honolulu, HI 96812	http://hawaii.gov/labor/dcd 808.586.9188

New Jersey Division of Disability Insurance Services	Department of Labor Division of Temporary Disability Insurance P.O. Box 387 Trenton, NJ 08625- 0387	http://lwd.dol.state.nj.us/labor/tdi/tdiindex.html 609.292.2700
New York Workers' Compensation Board	Disability Benefits Bureau Workers' Compensation Board 100 Broadway- Menands Albany, NY 12241	www.wcb.ny.gov 518.474.6680
Puerto Rico Bureau of Employment Security	Department of Labor and Human Resources Bureau of Employment Security Prudencio Rivera Martinez Building 505 Muñoz Rivera Avenue Hato Rey, Puerto Rico 00918	http://www.trabajo.pr.gov/ (translation required) www.lexisnexis.com/hottopics/lawsofpuertorico (English translation) 787.754.2142
Rhode Island Department of Labor and Training	Temporary Disability Insurance Division Department of Labor and Training 1511 Pontiac Avenue Cranston, RI 02903	http://www.dlt.ri.gov/tdi 401.462.8000

	California	New York
	2016 Annual Appendix and Statutory Plan Overview	
Title	Unemployment Compensation Disability Benefits Law (SDI)	Disability Benefits Law (DBL)
Waiting Period	7 days (waived if hospitalized)	7 days
Maximum Benefit Period	52 Weeks	26 Weeks
2016 Benefits	55% of weekly wage to a maximum of $1,129 and a minimum of $50. Weekly wage is determined by the high quarter of the previous 12 months (base period).	50% of average weekly wage to a maximum of $170 with a minimum of $20.
2016 Employee Cost	0.9% of the first $106,742 of annual wages or $960.67.	0.5% of the first $120 of the employee's weekly wages or $0.60. If a private plan is used, rates may be higher if the plan design and rates are approved by the state.
2016 Employer Cost	Not required but employer may pick up some or all of the cost for the employee. Employers may be required to pay an annual assessment if the statutory plan is running a deficit.	Employers must pick up all costs in excess of the employee's contribution and may be required to pay an assessment depending upon the state plan's performance.
Eligibility	Employees must have received wages of at least $300 from which SDI deductions were withheld during a previous 12-month base period.	Employees who have worked at least four consecutive weeks for a covered employer even if they are not with the same employer.
Vehicle	Public or Private Plan	Public or Private Plan

	2016 Annual Appendix and Statutory Plan Overview (Cont'd)	
	New Jersey	**Rhode Island**
Title	Temporary Disability Benefits Law (TDB)	Temporary Disability Insurance Act (TDI)
Waiting Period	7 days	7 days (only applied once per calendar year)
Maximum Benefit Period	26 Weeks	30 Weeks
2016 Benefits	66 2/3% to a maximum of $615. The weekly benefit rate is calculated based on the average weekly wage during the 8 weeks prior to the week in which the disability commenced. Benefits are payable for the waiting period after benefits have been paid for 3 consecutive weeks.	4.62% of the base period wages to a maximum of $770 per week. The minimum benefit is $84 per week. The weekly benefit amount is based on the base period wages (see "Eligibility"). The waiting period is retroactively compensable if disability continues after the waiting period expires. (See Notes for additional benefits that may be payable.)
2016 Employee Cost	0.20% of the first $32,600 of annual wages or a maximum contribution of $119.78	1.2% of the first $66,300 of annual wages or $795.60 maximum at least until 7/1. (See Notes for additional important information on employee costs.)
2016 Employer Cost	In the first plan year, employer costs match employee costs. The employer costs may vary thereafter based on the employer's benefit experience during its first three years of operation and the condition of the State Disability Benefits Fund. Future rates could vary from 0.10% to 0.75%. (See Notes for additional costs for Private Plan sponsors.)	Not required but employer may pick up some or all of the cost for the employee. Employers are required to withhold and submit payments on the employee's behalf and keep records of such. Failure to do so obligates the employer to pay employee costs.
Eligibility	Employees must have earned $165 or more per week during 20 calendar weeks in the base year; or $8,300 or more during the base year. The "Base Year" period is the 52 weeks immediately before the week in which the employee became disabled. Once eligible, the employee must be covered for a minimum of 2 years.	Employees must have earned $10,800 in base period wages; or $1,800 in one of the base period quarters and total base period wages of at least 1.5 times the highest quarter earnings, and total base period earnings of at least $3,600. A base period is the first four of the last five completed calendar quarters prior to claim or the last 4 completed quarters if needed to meet minimum earning requirement.
Vehicle	Public or Private Plan	Public Plan Only

	Hawaii	Puerto Rico
Title	Temporary Disability Insurance Law (TDI)	Non-Occupational Disability Insurance, "SINOT" (Sp. acronym)
Waiting Period	7 days	7 days (waived if hospitalized)
Maximum Benefit Period	26 Weeks	26 Weeks
2016 Benefits	58% of average weekly wage up to $570.00	65% of the base salary with a minimum benefit of $12 and a maximum benefit of $113 for non-agricultural workers and $55 for agricultural workers. (See Notes for additional benefits that may be payable.)
2016 Employee Cost	The lesser of 50% of the plan costs or 0.5% of the first $982.36 of weekly wages or a maximum contribution of $4.91 per week. Plans may charge higher if benefits are greater than the minimum required if the design warrants the cost. Employees are still limited to a maximum of 50% of the plan costs.	The lesser of 50% of the plan costs or 0.3% of the first $9,000 of annual wages or $27.00.
2016 Employer Cost	Employers must pay at least 50% of the plan cost, but may pay more or all at their discretion.	Employers must pay at least 50% of the plan cost, but may pay more or all at their discretion. Employers may be required to pay an annual assessment based on the performance of the state plan.
Eligibility	An employee must have at least 14 weeks of Hawaii employment during each of which the employee was paid for 20 hours or more and earned not less than $400 in the 52 weeks preceding the first day of disability. The 14 weeks need not be consecutive nor with only one employer.	Employees must have received wages of at least $150.00 in covered employment during the first 4 of the last 5 calendar quarters which immediately preceded the first day of disability.
Vehicle	Private Plan Only	Public or Private Plan

Notes:

1. Additional New Jersey Employer Costs: Private plans are not rated by the state, but employers that choose private plans may be charged an assessment based on the state plan's performance.

2. Additional Rhode Island Benefits: In addition, there is a dependent's allowance, for up to 5 dependents, for the greater of $10 or 7% of weekly benefit amount per dependent child to age 18, or older if disabled. The maximum weekly benefit amount with the maximum number of dependents is $945

3. Additional Rhode Island Employee Costs: Rhode Island announces changes to its TDI benefit amount in July. However, changes to the taxable wage base and tax rate are made in January. So, the previous year's benefit rate continues until at least July of the following year, but the taxable wage base and tax rate may change in January.

4. Additional Puerto Rico Benefits: Death benefits of $4,000 will be paid in addition to regular benefits to dependents of workers who die as a result of an injury or illness covered by SINOT, or who die within 52 weeks of the start of a disability. Dismemberment benefits will be also paid pursuant to a pre-established table, in addition to regular benefits, to workers who are injured in an accident or who suffer an illness resulting in a disability within 52 weeks of the accident or the beginning of the illness.

Chapter 4: Family Medical Leave

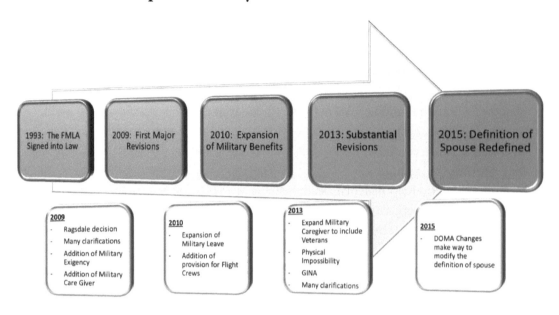

Background and Context

The purpose of the Family and Medical Leave Act (FMLA) was to "balance work and family life and promote economic security of families and serve the national interest in preserving family integrity." With the aging of the Baby Boomers and the influx of more women into the workforce, it was deemed that employers and their employees were not equipped to function effectively when time away from work was needed. Employees were concerned about job security, and employers about maintaining profits and the productivity of skilled workers. The act provides eligible employees with unpaid, job-protected time away from work. This time was granted for an employee's own serious health condition; the birth or care of a newborn child, adoption of a child or foster care; care for a family member with a serious health condition; care for a covered service member with a serious injury or illness; or for qualifying exigencies when a family member is called to active duty as a member of the National Guard or reserves.

Although updated and finalized regulations became effective on January 16, 2009, the FMLA was signed by President Bill Clinton on February 5, 1993, and became effective for most employers on August 5, 1993. Where a collective bargaining agreement (CBA) was in effect on August 5, 1993, the FMLA became effective on the earlier of either the expiration of the CBA or February 5, 1994. Since then, the FMLA has been updated and amended several times, including in 2009, 2013 and most recently in March, 2015.

The standards put forth within the FMLA clearly set a baseline of coverage. Employers are encouraged to provide more robust coverage; however, any leave granted outside of the confines of the act's definitions may not be considered FMLA-eligible absences. States are similarly encouraged to provide more generous regulations surrounding family medical leave, and to date, many states and other jurisdictions have enacted similar statutes. A number of states have expanded job protection to various other types of leave for purposes such as victims of crime, domestic violence, and organ donation. These types of leave will be reviewed in Chapter 5: "Other Leaves of Absence."

Although each state manages its own specific leave laws, the FMLA at the federal level is primarily administered and enforced by the U.S. Department of Labor's Employment Standards Administration. However, some federal and congressional employees covered by the law are under the jurisdiction of the U.S. Office of Personnel Management or Congress. These agencies investigate complaints and may bring action to compel compliance. In addition, employees may bring a private civil action against an employer for violations. Liability and damages for FMLA violations may be imposed upon the employer and individual supervisors or management personnel responsible for committing the violations.

On February 25, 2015, the Department of Labor (DOL) published a"Final Rule" that amended the definition of "spouse" in two fundamental ways. First, the Final Rule changes the regulatory definition of spouse in 29 CFR §§ 825.102 and 825.122(b) to look to the law of the place in which the marriage was entered into, as opposed to the law of the state in which the employee resides. This is better known as a shift from "state of residence" to "place of celebration." Second, the Final Rule expressly includes individuals in lawfully recognized same-sex and common law marriages that were validly entered into outside of the United States if they could have been entered into in at least one state.

On February 6, 2013, the Department of Labor (DOL) also published substantial changes that in large part, (1) amended the FMLA regulations addressing the coverage of military caregiver and exigency leaves; and (2) revamped eligibility requirements for certain airline industry employees. Although the Final Rule will require some changes to most employers' written FMLA policies and forms, it should not result in substantial changes to the way most employers administer military caregiver and exigency leaves.

Summary of the February 2013 Amendments

Employers should note that the Final Rule amends the following:

- Adds a new category of exigency leave for parental care

- Increases the maximum number of days from five to 15 calendar days for exigency leave to bond with a military member on rest and recuperation leave

- Makes effective amendments that extend military caregiver leave to family members of certain veterans with qualifying serious injuries or illnesses

- Clarifies the scope of exigency leave to family members of those in the regular armed forces, which previously were not covered by the exigency leave provisions of the FMLA

- Retains the physical impossibility rule, which provides that, where it is physically impossible for an employee to commence or end work midway through a shift, the entire period that the employee is forced to be absent is counted against the employee's FMLA leave entitlement

- Retains, but clarifies, the existing regulation regarding the appropriate increments to calculate intermittent and reduced-schedule leave

Employers should also be aware that the DOL developed several new FMLA forms and has released new guidance regarding the existing definition of "son or daughter."

Background on FMLA Amendments

The FMLA was amended in January 2008, to provide the following two types of military family leave for FMLA-eligible employees:

- Exigency leave: A 12-week entitlement for eligible family members to deal with exigencies related to a call to active duty of service members of the National Guard and reserves

- Military caregiver leave: A 26-week entitlement for eligible family members to care for seriously ill or injured service members of the regular armed forces, National Guard, and reserves

Congress again amended the FMLA through the National Defense Authorization Act for Fiscal Year 2010 (FY 2010 NDAA), P.L. No. 111-84. In this act, Congress expanded both types of military family leave in the following manner:

- Expanded military caregiver leave to include the family members of certain veterans with serious injuries or illnesses who are receiving medical treatment, recuperation, or therapy if the veteran was a member of the armed forces at any time during the five years preceding the date of the medical treatment, recuperation, or therapy

- Expanded exigency leave to include the family members of those in the regular armed forces but added the requirement that service members be deployed to a foreign country

- Extended military caregiver leave to the family members of current service members with a preexisting condition aggravated by military service in the line of duty on active duty

The FY 2010 NDAA, effective Fiscal Year 2010, therefore by definition the start of the fiscal year for Congress was October 1, 2009. Later in 2009, Congress also passed the Airline Flight Crew Technical Corrections Act (AFCTCA), P.L. No. 111-119, to provide an alternative eligibility requirement for airline flight crew employees. The amendments to the FMLA that were made by both of these statutes were addressed in the 2013 regulatory changes.

Final Rule Relating to Qualifying Exigency Leave

The Final Rule includes a number of changes relating to qualifying exigency leave. It is important to note that in response to concerns raised in the comment period, the DOL reaffirmed that where a qualifying exigency involves a third party, employers may contact that third party to verify the meeting and the purpose of the meeting.

Definition of Active Duty: § 825.126(a), Now § 825.126(a)(1) and (a)(2)

The Final Rule replaces the existing definition of "active duty" with two new definitions: (1) covered active duty as it applies to members of the regular armed forces, and (2) covered active duty, or call to covered active duty, as it applies to members of the reserves.

The new definition of "covered active duty" as it relates to the regular armed forces, requires that the service member be deployed with the armed forces in a foreign country. The new definition of, as it relates to reserves members, requires that the service member be under a call or order to active duty during the deployment of the member to a foreign country under a federal call or order to active duty in support of a contingency operation. While the FY 2010 NDAA struck the term "contingency operations" from the FMLA, the DOL has taken the position that members of the reserves must be called to duty in support of a contingency operation in order for their family members to be entitled to qualifying exigency leave.

Exigency Leave for Child Care and School Activities: § 825.126(a)(3), Now § 825.126(b)(3)

The Final Rule places limits on exigency leave to arrange for child care or attend certain school activities for a military member's son or daughter. Specifically, the Final Rule states that the military member must be the spouse, son, daughter, or parent of the employee requesting leave in order to qualify for the leave. The child in question could be "the military member's biological, adopted, or foster child, stepchild, legal ward, or child for whom the military member stands in loco parentis, who is either under age 18 or age 18 or older and incapable of self-care because of a mental or physical disability at the time that FMLA leave is to commence." The child for whom child care leave is sought need not be the child of the employee requesting leave.

The DOL specifically declined to extend qualifying exigency leave to employees who stand in loco parentis to a child of a military member when that employee does not have the statutorily required relationship with the military member for that leave. For example, while the mother of a military member may take leave to care for the military member's child, the military member's mother-in-law is not qualified for such leave, regardless of her relationship with the child, because the military member is not the spouse, son, daughter, or parent of the employee requesting leave. The DOL also declined to provide a specific category of exigency leave to address educational and related services for disabled children, noting that the current regulations are sufficient to cover meetings about eligibility, placement, and services and meetings related to a child's individualized education plan. The DOL comments make clear that child care and school activity exigency leave does not cover routine academic concerns.

Exigency Leave for Rest and Recuperation: § 825.126(a)(6), Now § 825.126(b)(7)

The Final Rule also increases the maximum number of days from five to 15 calendar days for exigency leave to bond with a military member on rest and recuperation leave, beginning on the date the military member begins his or her rest and recuperation leave. The actual amount of leave provided to the employee should be consistent with the leave provided by the military to the member on covered duty. For example, if the military allows a member 10 days of rest and recuperation leave, the employee is entitled to 10 days. The leave may be taken intermittently or in a single block, as long as the leave is taken during the period of time indicated on the military member's rest and recuperation orders.

New Exigency Leave for Parental Care: Now § 825.126(b)(8)

The Final Rule adds parental care as a qualifying exigency for which leave may be taken. This allowance tracks the child care exigency provision and allows parental care exigency leave for the spouse, parent, son, or daughter of a military member in order to do the following:

- Arrange for alternative care for a parent of the military member when the parent is incapable of self-care and the covered active duty or call to covered active duty status of the military member necessitates a change in existing care arrangements

- Provide care for a parent of the military member on an urgent, immediate-need basis (but not on a routine, regular, or everyday basis) when the parent is incapable of self-care and the need to provide such care arises from the covered active duty or call to covered active duty status of the military member

- Admit or transfer a parent of the military member to a care facility when the admittance or transfer is necessitated by the covered active duty or call to covered active duty status of the military member

- Attend meetings with staff at a care facility for a parent of the military member (e.g., meetings with hospice or social service providers) when such meetings are necessitated by the covered active duty or call to covered active duty status of the military member

The military member's parent must be incapable of self-care, as defined for all family members in 825.113.

Final Rules Relating to Military Caregiver Leave Certification Provisions for Caregiver Leave: § 825.310

The existing regulations limited the type of healthcare providers authorized to certify a serious injury or illness for military caregiver leave to providers affiliated with the U.S. Department of the Defense (DOD) (e.g., a Veterans Affairs facility [VA] or DOD TRICARE provider). The Final Rule eliminates this distinction and allows any healthcare provider authorized under section 825.125 to certify injury or illness under the military caregiver provisions. In doing so, the DOL recognized that private healthcare providers might be unable to make certain military-related determinations to certify that the serious injury or illness is related to military service. Therefore, the Final Rule will allow providers to rely on determinations from an authorized DOD or VA representative on these issues. Because of this change, the Final Rule will allow for second and third opinions on certifications of military caregiver leaves for non-DOD/VA providers. The Final Rule does not alter the prohibition on second and third opinions when the certification has been completed by a DOD/VA authorized provider. The DOL has developed new Forms WH-385 and WH-385-v to help employers meet the FMLA's certification requirements. Although use of the forms is optional, employers may not require any information beyond what is authorized by regulation.

Leave to Care for a Covered Service Member with a Serious Injury or Illness: § 825.127

Military caregiver leave provides a 26-week leave entitlement for eligible family members to care for seriously ill or injured military members. The existing regulations specifically excluded former members of the regular armed forces, former members of the National Guard and reserves, and members on the permanent disability list from the definition of a covered service member. The Final Rule removes this exclusion so that military caregiver leave now applies to former members of the military.

Definition of Covered Veteran for Caregiver Leave: § 825.127

The existing regulations did not define covered service member with regard to veterans. The Final Rule remedies this gap and includes veterans in the applicable definition. Specifically, covered service members include a covered veteran who is undergoing medical treatment, recuperation, or therapy for a serious injury or illness. A covered veteran is defined as, "a member of the armed forces, National Guard, or reserves who was discharged or released under conditions other than dishonorable at any time during the five-year period prior to the first date the eligible employee takes FMLA leave to care for the covered veteran."

Employers need to be aware that the Final Rule excludes the period between October 28, 2009, and March 8, 2013 (the effective date of the Final Rule), from the five-year "look-back" for covered veteran status. This grace period attempts to address complexities stemming from the DOL's position that military caregiver leave did not become effective for veterans until its proposed rules became final. Furthermore, the Final Rule reiterates the DOL's position that leave provided to veterans under this provision before March 8, 2013, cannot be counted against an employee's leave entitlement because companies provided it voluntarily before the effective date of the Final Rule. It is unclear if the courts will agree with this interpretation, so employers should proceed with caution.

Definition of Serious Injury or Illness: § 825.127

The Final Rule clarifies that a serious injury or illness can include a preexisting condition aggravated by military service in the line of duty on active duty. The Final Rule explains that a preexisting injury or illness generally will be considered to have been aggravated in the line of duty where there is an increase in the severity of such injury or illness during service, unless there is a specific finding that the increase in severity is due to the natural progression of the injury or illness. Under the Final Rule, a current member of the armed forces must have a serious injury or illness that renders the member medically unfit to perform the duties of the member's office, grade, rank, or rating.

The Final Rule also defines serious injury or illness of a covered veteran. As is the case in the definition of serious injury or illness for military service, the serious injury or illness of a covered veteran must be incurred in, or preexisting but aggravated by, the line of duty on active duty. The serious injury or illness of a covered veteran also must be one of the following:

- A continuation of a serious injury or illness that was incurred or aggravated when the covered veteran was a member of the armed forces and that rendered the service member unable to perform the duties of the service member's office, grade, rank, or rating

- A physical or mental condition for which the covered veteran has received a U.S. Department of Veterans Affairs Service-Related Disability Rating (VASRD) of 50% or greater, with such VASRD rating being based, in whole or in part, on the condition precipitating the need for military caregiver leave

- A physical or mental condition that substantially impairs, or would do so absent treatment, the covered veteran's ability to secure or follow a substantially gainful occupation by reason of a disability or disabilities related to military service

- An injury, including a psychological injury, on the basis of which the covered veteran has been enrolled in the Department of Veterans Affairs Program of Comprehensive Assistance for Family Caregivers

The DOL noted that while the definition of a covered veteran's serious injury or illness includes conditions that impair the ability of a veteran to work, covered veterans may be employed. The DOL offers the example of a veteran with post-traumatic stress disorder (PTSD) who is able to work because of medical treatment but who may still need care from a family member for other reasons (e.g., to drive the veteran to medical appointments or to assist the veteran with basic medical needs). The commentary in the Final Rule also makes it clear that, although a military member's Social Security Disability Insurance determination is not dispositive of having a qualifying serious injury or illness, a private healthcare provider might consider the determination in his or her assessment.

Special Rules for Airline Flight Crews

Enacted in 2009, the Airline Flight Crew Technical Corrections Act (AFCTCA) closed an apparent loophole in the "hours worked" eligibility requirements for airline pilots and flight attendants whose unique schedules often left them short of the hours required to qualify them for FMLA leave. Under the FMLA, employees must work at least 1,250 hours in the previous 12-month period, which equates to 60% of a typical 40-hour workweek. AFCTCA applies the same concept to airline flight crews, providing that the hours flight crew employees work or for which they are paid — not just those hours working in flight — count as hours of service for purposes of FMLA eligibility.

The AFCTCA provides that an airline flight crew employee will meet the hours-of-service eligibility requirement if he or she has worked or been paid for not less than 60% of the applicable total monthly guarantee (or its equivalent) and has worked or been paid for not less than 504 hours (not including personal commute time or time spent on vacation, medical, or sick leave) during the previous 12 months. Airline flight crew employees continue to be subject to the FMLA's other eligibility requirements. The Final Rule includes provisions to align the existing regulations with the passage of the AFCTCA.

Employers should note that the regulations applicable to airline flight crews in the Final Rule are wholly contained in a separate, newly titled subpart, "Subpart H – Special Rules Applicable to Airline Flight Crew Employees," and are not integrated into the existing regulations by topic.

Hours-of-Service Requirement: § 825.801

Because the AFCTCA established a special hours-of-service requirement for airline flight crew employees, the DOL has adopted new section 825.801, which largely tracks the DOL's 2012 proposal. Airline flight crew employees may become eligible under the FMLA (as amended by the AFCTCA) if they have either the required number of "hours worked" or "hours paid" during the previous 12-month period. The Final Rule provides that an airline flight crew employee can meet the hours-of-service requirement under the FMLA if he or she (1) meets the standard eligibility threshold contained in section 825.110 (1,250 hours/ 12 months) or (2) has worked or been paid for not less than 60% of his or her applicable monthly guarantee and has worked or been paid for not less than 504 hours. For airline employees who are on reserve status, the "applicable monthly guarantee" is defined in new section 825.801(b)(1) as the number of hours for which an employer has agreed to pay the employee for any given month. For airline employees who are not on reserve, the applicable monthly guarantee is the minimum number of hours for which an employer has agreed to schedule such employee for any given month. The Final Rule clarifies that employers have the burden of proof in showing that an airline flight crew employee is not eligible for leave.

Calculation of Leave: § 825.802

The Final Rule allows airline flight crews up to 72 days of leave during any 12-month period to use for one or more of the following reasons: as an employee's basic leave entitlement for the employee's own illness; to care for an ill spouse, child, or parent; for the birth or adoption of a child or placement of a child in the employee's home for foster care; or for exigent circumstances associated with the employee's spouse, son, daughter, or parent on covered active duty. This entitlement is based on a uniform six-day workweek for all airline flight crews, regardless of time actually worked or paid, multiplied by the statutory 12-workweek entitlement. Airline flight crews are entitled to up to 156 days of military caregiver leave.

When a flight crew employee takes intermittent or reduced-schedule leave, the Final Rule requires employers to account for the leave using an increment no greater than one day.

Recordkeeping Requirements: § 825.802

In addition to the recordkeeping requirement applicable to all employers under the FMLA, the Final Rule requires airline employers to maintain any records or documents that specify the applicable monthly guarantee for each type of employee to whom the guarantee applies, including any relevant collective bargaining agreements or employer policy documents that establish the applicable monthly guarantee, as well as records of hours worked.

Other Changes Universal to the FMLA

Increments of Intermittent FMLA Leave: § 825.205

Section 825.205(a) defined the minimum increment of FMLA leave to be used when taken intermittently or on a reduced schedule as an increment no greater than the shortest period of time that the employer uses to account for other forms of leave, provided that it is not greater than one hour. According to the comments of the Final Rule, the DOL intended to emphasize that an employee's entitlement should not be reduced beyond the actual leave taken and therefore added language to paragraph (a)(1), stating that an employer may not require an employee to take more leave than is necessary to address the circumstances that precipitated the need for the leave. This change does not necessitate action for any employer already complying with the shortest increment rule. The DOL further clarified that the additions to section 825.205(a) underscore the rule that if an employer chooses to waive its increment-of-leave policy in order to return an employee to work at the beginning of a shift, the employer is likewise choosing to waive further deductions from the FMLA entitlement period. In other words, if the employee is working, the time cannot count against FMLA time no matter what the smallest increment of leave may be.

The DOL had proposed to remove the language in section 825.205(a) that allowed for varying increments at different times of the day or shift in favor of the more general principle of using the employer's shortest increment of any type of leave at any time. However, the Final Rule does not incorporate this change. Employers who account for use of leave in varying increments at different times of the day or shift may also do so for FMLA leave, provided that the increment used for FMLA leave is no greater than the smallest increment used for any other type of leave. An employer can account for FMLA leave in smaller increments at its discretion.

The existing version of section 825.205(a)(2) included a provision on physical impossibility, which provided that where it is physically impossible for an employee to commence or end work midway through a shift, the entire period that the employee is forced to be absent is counted against the employee's FMLA leave entitlement. The DOL had proposed to either (1) delete this provision or (2) add language emphasizing that it is an employer's responsibility to restore an employee to his or her same or equivalent position at the end of any FMLA leave as soon as possible.

The Final Rule retains the physical impossibility provision with clarifying language that the period of physical impossibility is limited to the period during which the employer is unable to permit the employee to work prior to or after the FMLA period.

The Final Rule also clarifies that the rule stated in section 825.205(c), which addresses when overtime hours that are not worked may be counted as FMLA leave, applies to all FMLA-qualifying reasons and not just serious health conditions. The DOL had proposed to add section 825.205(d), which would have provided a methodology for calculating leave for airline flight crew employees, but noted in the comments to the Final Rule that this language will now appear in section 825.802.

Recordkeeping Requirements: § 825.500

The Final Rule adds a sentence to section 825.500, reminding employers of their obligation to comply with the confidentiality requirements of the Genetic Information Nondiscrimination Act of 2008 (GINA). To the extent that records and documents created for FMLA purposes contain "family medical history" or "genetic information" as defined in GINA, employers must maintain such records in accordance with the confidentiality requirements of title II of that act. The DOL noted that GINA permits genetic information obtained by the employer, including family medical history, in FMLA records and documents to be disclosed consistent with the requirements of the FMLA.

Forms

The regulations will no longer include model forms as a part of the appendices. These forms will remain available on the DOL's website. The practical implication of this change is that the DOL will be able to make changes to the forms without going through the formal rule making process. The DOL has made small modifications to the model forms. For example, Form WH-384 was modified to refer to a military member, use the term covered active duty, and contain the requirement that the member be deployed to a foreign country. The Final Rules also provide new forms for the certification of a serious injury or illness of a covered veteran: Forms WH-385 and WH-385-v.

Eligibility

All public agencies (state, local, and federal), as well as local educational agencies, are considered eligible employers under the FMLA. In addition, the FMLA applies to all private-sector employers who employ 50 or more employees in at least 20 workweeks in the previous calendar year or current calendar year. When employers are considering their employee count, they must include employees who are jointly employed (where two or more businesses exercise some control over the work or working conditions of the employee) and successor employees. Successor employees are employees that worked for another organization and based on a merger, transfer of assets, or simply a contractual change are no longer affiliated with the predecessor company. The FMLA considers the following factors within Title VII of the

Civil Rights Act of 1964 to determine successor in interest as well as successor employees, which includes but is not limited to continuity of the same business; use of the same plant; similarity of supervisory personnel; similarity of products; and services and ability.

An eligible employee must:

- Work for a covered employer

- Have been employed with that employer (or successor employer) for a total of 12 months

- In the previous 12 months, worked at least 1,250 hours

- Be working in a U.S. location where 50 or more employees are employed by the same employer within 75 miles

- Not be considered a key employee

Service Requirements

Service requirements for FMLA eligibility indicate 12 months and 1,250 hours; however, those need not be consecutive. Therefore, employees can accumulate 12 months of nonconsecutive service as long as gaps in service are either under seven years or are the result of some type of protected regulation or agreement (i.e., military leave covered under the Uniformed Services Employment and Re-employment Rights Act [USERRA] or collective bargaining agreements). Individual employee records are used to determine the 1,250-hour requirement. This is based on hours actually worked for the employer, and therefore paid and unpaid leave, including FMLA leave, are not included.

The Final Rule makes clarifications to note that the protections afforded by USERRA extend to all military members, both active duty and reserve, returning from USERRA-qualifying military service. The DOL noted in the comments to the Final Rule that the previous regulation may have been unclear in that USERRA rights apply to employees returning from service in the regular armed forces.

Number of Employees

When assessing the number of employees within a 75-mile radius, the mileage should be based on distance using surface transportation, not linear miles, and their site of employment should be based on the site each employee reports to or, if none, the site at which the work is assigned. Once leave is requested and approved, if the employee payroll count falls below 50 employees within the 75-mile radius, the change in the number of employees will not impact an employee that began an FMLA absence.

Key Employees

Employers do have some flexibility when determining eligibility for key employees or for when a husband and wife both work for the same employer. These limitations help to ensure an employer is able to function and remain profitable during periods of absence.

- When a husband and wife are employed by the same employer and both are eligible for FMLA leave, the employer may limit leave to a total of 12 weeks for the family when the leave is for (1) birth of the employee's son or daughter or to care for the child after birth, (2) placement of a son or daughter with the employee for adoption or foster care, or to care for the child after placement, or (3) to care for the employee's parent with a serious health condition. If the leave is for another reason, they would each be entitled to a total of 12 weeks within a 12-month period.

- A key employee is a salaried employee paid in the highest 10% of all employees in the company whose absence under the FMLA would cause "substantial and grievous economic injury" to the firm. Key employees may be excluded from the rights under the FMLA; however, employers must notify them of their status and explain what it means at the time they ask for leave. At that point, the employee is entitled to a reasonable amount of time to return to work. If that does not happen, an employer may deny job restoration, but many times the leave itself as well as continuation of health care coverage cannot be denied.

For initial cases, it is the employer's responsibility to designate FMLA absences. Employees do not need to articulate the need for job-protected time off or specifically express their desire to use FMLA time; it is the obligation of the employer and its management team to understand the requirements of the regulations and apply them appropriately to their employees. However, if the employee has previously been provided with protected leave under the FMLA, the employee must specifically reference qualifying reasons for the leave and designate the time appropriately.

Leave Entitlement

Covered employers must grant eligible employees 12 workweeks of unpaid, job-protected leave during any 12-month period for any one of the following reasons:

- Birth and/or care of a newborn child of an employee within 12 months after the birth

- Placement of a child with the employee (adoption or foster care) within 12 months after placement

- Care for a family member with a serious health condition

- Employee is unable to work due to their own serious health condition

In addition, through the enactment of the National Defense Authorization Act in January 2008, FMLA was expanded in the 2013 Final Rule to provide military caregiver leave (also termed service member leave) and qualifying exigency leave:

- Military caregiver leave allows 26 workweeks within a single 12-month period to care for a family member or next of kin who is a covered service member with a serious illness or injury that occurred in the line of active duty who is a current member of the armed forces, including the National Guard or reserves

- Qualified exigency leave provides 12 workweeks of unpaid time for qualifying exigencies arising out of the employee's family member being called to active duty as a member of the National Guard or reserves. This goal is to provide families with the ability to manage their affairs while the member is on covered active duty. Qualifying exigencies include: (1) short-notice deployment; (2)

military events; (3) childcare and school activities; (4) financial and legal arrangements; (5) counseling; (6) rest and recuperation; (7) post deployment activities; and (8) other activities agreed to by the employer and employee

- A new qualifying exigency leave category for parental care leave was added to allow eligible employees to take leave to care for a military member's parent who is incapable of self-care when the care is necessitated by the member's covered active duty. Such care may include arranging for alternative care, providing care on an immediate-need basis, admitting or transferring the parent to a care facility, or attending meetings with staff at a care facility.

The airline flight crew leave entitlement defines hours of service requirements as during the last 12 months he or she:

- Has worked or been paid for not less than 60% of the applicable monthly guarantee; and

- Has worked or been paid for not less than 504 hours, not including personal commute time, or time spent on vacation, medical, or sick leave.

For most types of FMLA absences, a family member is defined as a:

- Legal spouse: A husband or wife. A husband or wife refers to the other person with whom an individual entered into marriage as defined or recognized under state law for purposes of marriage in the State in which the marriage was entered into or, in the case of a marriage entered into outside of any State, if the marriage is valid in the place where entered into and could have been entered into in at least one state. This definition includes an individual in a same-sex or common law marriage.

- Legal parent: A biological, adoptive, step- or foster father or mother, or someone who stood in loco parentis to the employee when the employee was a son or daughter. Parent for FMLA purposes does not include in-laws. (note: What may be seen as an exception to this rule, in the event the employee is the spouse of a deployed military member and the individual on deployment would have otherwise been needed to care for a parent who is incapacitated, but in their absence, their spouse can take care of the military members parent …ie. Their in-law….in the same capacity as the spouse / child of the parent would have, should they have been present.)

- Child: Biological, adopted, or foster child, stepchild, legal ward, or child of a person standing in loco parentis who is 18 years or older and incapable of self-care due to a physical or mental disability as defined under the Americans with Disabilities Act

When considering qualified exigency leave or military caregiver leave, a family member includes children of any age, regardless of physical or mental impairment.

Other family members (e.g., parents-in-law or domestic partners) are not considered family members under the FMLA; however, they may be covered within the statutory definitions of other employer-sponsored leaves or under an increasing number of state leave laws.

Serious Health Condition

The term serious health condition includes any illness, injury, impairment, or physical or mental condition that involves:

- Any period of incapacity or treatment in connection with inpatient care in a hospital, hospice, or residential medical care facility

- Continued treatment by a healthcare provider that includes incapacity lasting more than three consecutive, full calendar days, including additional treatment due to the same condition that includes:

    o Two or more visits/treatments with a healthcare provider within the first seven days or within the first 30 days of incapacity

    o One treatment/visit with a healthcare provider within the first seven days and a continued/ongoing treatment plan

- Any period of incapacity or treatment related to prenatal care or pregnancy care; a visit to a provider is not necessary for each absence

- Any period of incapacity or treatment related to chronic serious health conditions that continues over a period of time and requires periodic visits (at least twice a year) to a healthcare provider; a visit to a provider is not necessary for each absence, and if treatment may not be effective, only supervision by a provider is required, not active treatment

- Any absence to receive treatment for restorative surgery for a condition that would likely result in a period of incapacity of more than three days if not treated

- The definition of a serious injury or illness for a current service member is expanded to included injuries or illnesses that existed before the beginning of the member's active duty and were aggravated by service in the line of duty on active duty in the armed forces

- A serious injury or illness for a covered veteran means an injury or illness that was incurred or aggravated by the member in the line of duty on active duty in the armed forces and manifested itself before or after the member became a veteran, and is:

    o A continuation of a serious injury or illness that was incurred or aggravated when the covered veteran was a member of the armed forces and rendered the service member unable to perform the duties of the service member's office, grade, rank, or rating; or

    o A physical or mental condition for which the covered veteran has received a VA Service Related Disability Rating (VASRD) of 50% or greater and such VASRD rating is based, in whole or in part, on the condition precipitating the need for caregiver leave; or

    o A physical or mental condition that substantially impairs the veteran's ability to secure or follow a substantially gainful occupation by reason of a disability or disabilities related to military service or would do so absent treatment; or

- An injury, including a psychological injury, on the basis of which the covered veteran has been enrolled in the Department of Veterans Affairs Program of Comprehensive Assistance for Family Caregivers.

To ensure appropriate care, the FMLA regulations provide guidance around the use of healthcare providers. Providers that may certify a serious health condition include:

- Doctors of medicine or osteopathy authorized by the state in which they practice

- Podiatrists, dentists, clinical psychologists, and optometrists authorized by the state in which they practice

- Chiropractors, limited to treatment consisting of manual manipulation of the spine to correct subluxation as demonstrated through x-ray

- Nurse practitioners, nurse midwives, and clinical social workers performing within the scope of their practice and authorized by the state in which they practice

- Christian Science practitioners listed with the First Church of Christ, Scientist in Boston, Massachusetts

- Healthcare providers recognized by the employer or the employer's group health plan

- Healthcare providers practicing in a country other than the United States, authorized to practice under the laws of that country

- The list of healthcare providers who are authorized to complete a certification for military caregiver leave for a covered service member was expanded to include healthcare providers, as defined in § 825.125, who are not affiliated with DOD, VA, or TRICARE

Defining the 12-Month Period

Employers have a few different options when defining their 12-month period; however, a uniform policy for each group of employees should be adopted. If the 12-month period is redefined at any employer, employees will be eligible for the more generous definition during transition.

An employer can choose any one of the following methods for determining the 12-month period in which the 12 weeks of leave entitlement occur:

- The calendar year

- Any fixed 12-month leave year, such as fiscal year, a year required by state law, or a year starting on the employee's anniversary date

- The 12-month period measured forward from the date any employee's first period of leave under the act begins

- A rolling 12-month period measured backward from the date an employee uses any leave under the act

Types of FMLA Leave

Under the act, leave may be taken on a continuous basis or, in some cases, on an intermittent or reduced-schedule basis.

Intermittent leave includes leave taken in several blocks of time, ranging from a few minutes to several weeks in length. Leave taken on a reduced-schedule leave basis involves the modification of the employee's work schedule for a period of time, reducing the employee's daily or weekly hours of work. If FMLA leave is for birth and care or placement for adoption or foster care, use of intermittent leave is subject to the employer's approval. Be aware, however, that some states require employers to allow employees to take leave on an intermittent basis.

Clarifying language was added that an employer may not require the employee to take more leave than necessary to address the circumstances that precipitated the need for leave and that FMLA leave may only be counted against an employee's FMLA entitlement for leave taken and not for time that is worked for the employer. An employer may limit the increments of leave to the shortest period of time used by the payroll system to account for employee absences, but the regulations state that there can be no incremental limit that exceeds an hour. In addition, it is expected the time under FMLA is tracked in a similar time increment as other leaves. Employers may not require the employee to take more FMLA leave than necessary to address their circumstances that cause the need for leave unless it is physically impossible for an employee to start or end work mid-shift. For example, a flight attendant is not able to leave for an appointment in the middle of a shift; therefore, all time away from work due to their absence will be counted as FMLA-designated leave. Conversely, an employee in a desk job could leave for a physician office visit and return, taking only a portion of a shift off; in that case, the employer cannot force that employee to take more time under the FMLA than required.

When leave is for a planned medical treatment, the employee must make a reasonable effort to schedule treatment so it does not disrupt the employer's operations. If employees need intermittent or reduced-schedule leave for a medical treatment that is foreseeable and does disrupt the employer's operations, the employer may transfer the employee temporarily to an alternative job with equivalent pay and benefits that better accommodates recurring periods of leave. Such arrangements would be subject to the approval of the employee's healthcare provider.

Time taken under FMLA must be time away from work when the employee would normally be working. Therefore, if an employee is working in a full-time, even if it is in a light-duty capacity, this is not considered FMLA leave. Similarly, employers cannot count time against the entitlement if the employee would not normally be at work (e.g., summer break for a teacher).

Calculating Time Taken Under the FMLA

Designated absences under FMLA may be taken in minutes, hours, days, or weeks; however, since the entitlement is based on 12 work weeks, a "work week" is the true basis for calculating FMLA leave. If an employee is regularly scheduled to work five days per week and uses one day for FMLA leave, that would be calculated as one-fifth of a week of FMLA time. However, if the employee were scheduled to work 40 hours in four days, such as a nurse working four, 10-hour shifts, then that individuals "one day" would actually be calculated as one quarter of a week.

If an employee has a varied work schedule, a weekly average of the hours worked over the prior 12 months would be used for calculating FMLA leave.

Employers may also count time that an employee is not available for overtime as FMLA leave if the employee is normally required to work overtime. Voluntary overtime may not be counted against an employee's FMLA leave.

Paid Versus Unpaid Leave

Although FMLA leave is usually unpaid (currently, only three states — California, New Jersey, and Rhode Island — offer paid family and medical leave through state-funded programs), an employee can request, or the employer may require, the overlap of paid leave with family medical leave. When this occurs, FMLA entitlement is deducted based on the time taken, but the employee will be paid for their absence based on the paid leave policy. When those policies run concurrently, it may be termed substitution of paid leave. Examples of this include:

- Paid vacation or personal leave may be substituted for any FMLA purpose.

- Paid family leave may be substituted for FMLA leave for birth, adoption, or foster care or to care for a seriously ill family member.

- Paid sick leave may be substituted for the care of an immediate family member or for care of the employee's own serious health condition.

- Paid disability coverage or workers' compensation coverage may be substituted for care of the employee's own serious health condition.

Under certain conditions, employees and/or employers may choose to run paid leave and family medical leave concurrently to cover some or all of the FMLA leave. An employee's ability to substitute paid leave is determined by the terms and conditions of the employer's normal leave policy. For example, if an employer's sick leave plan does not allow that time to be used for a sick child, then the employer could not require use of that paid time for unpaid FMLA leave to care for a seriously ill child. For most employers, running these leaves concurrently is best practice. It provides compensation to the employee during what may be a difficult time. In addition, it will ensure that employees do not return from a family medical leave of absence and then take additional time off for another paid absence.

If an employee uses paid leave for circumstances permitted under the FMLA, an employer may only require the employee to comply with the employer's requirements for that paid leave in order to receive payment. Additionally, the requirements under the FMLA may only be imposed for purposes of designating the absence as FMLA qualifying. Therefore, an employee who complies with the less stringent requirements of one benefit, may not have the other benefit delayed or denied on grounds that they did not meet requirements that are designed for a different program. For example, if an employer's short-term disability program requires extensive clinical notes in order to determine if the employee qualifies to receive STD benefits, but the employee has provided the documentation that confirms that a serious health condition has been met in accordance with 825.113; the employer may not delay or deny the FMLA while awaiting the receipt of the additional clinical notes.

Job Protection and Benefit Protection

Time away from work on a qualified FMLA leave is considered job-protected and health benefits must be maintained with the same terms as if the employee had continued working. Arrangements need to be made for employees to pay their share of the health premiums while on leave.

The obligation to maintain health benefits under FMLA ends as soon as the employer is informed of an employee's intent not to return to work or the failure of the employee to return to work once leave is exhausted. If the employee is more than 30 days late with their premium payment and the employer has provided written notice with at least 15 days advance notice that coverage will cease if premiums are not received, health benefits may be terminated.

If an employee fails to return to work after an FMLA leave, in some instances, the employer may recover premiums it paid to maintain healthcare coverage.

Benefits must be resumed at the same level as before the leave without any qualifying requirements, such as waiting periods, preexisting condition restrictions, or medical underwriting requirements. The reinstatement is required even if the coverage had lapsed because an employee had not made required premium payments during FMLA leave. Reinstatement must be immediate; the employer cannot require the employee to wait for an open enrollment period to resume coverage.

With respect to pension and other retirement plans, any period of unpaid FMLA leave shall not be treated as or counted toward a break in service for the purposes of vesting and eligibility to participate.

Although earned benefits do not need to accrue during periods of unpaid FMLA (e.g., paid leave, seniority benefits), it may make sense for some to allow elected benefits to continue to ensure the employee will be eligible to be restored to a similar level of coverage upon return (e.g., life insurance). If the employer incurs costs associated with the employee's share of premiums for non-health benefits, they may be recovered once the employee returns to work.

When an eligible employee returns to work after an FMLA leave, they are entitled to be restored to the same position they held when the leave began or to an equivalent position. The only exception is an employee who would have been laid off or otherwise had their employment terminated (e.g., as part of a general layoff), had they continued to work during the FMLA leave period.

According to the regulations, an equivalent position must:

- Have the same pay, benefits, and working conditions, including privileges, perquisites, and status. Intangible, immeasurable aspects of the job (e.g., the perceived loss of potential for future promotion opportunities or any increased possibility of being subject to future layoff) are not covered.

- Involve the same or substantially similar duties and responsibilities, requiring substantially equivalent skill, effort, responsibility, and authority

- Be at the same or a geographically proximate work site where the employee had previously been employed

- Be on the same shift or the same or an equivalent work schedule

- Have the same or an equivalent opportunity for bonuses, profit-sharing, and other similar, discretionary and non-discretionary payments

An employee's use of FMLA leave cannot result in the loss of any employment benefits that the employee earned or was entitled to before using FMLA, nor can it be counted against a no-fault attendance policy. However, if an achievement is based on a specified goal such as hours worked or products sold, and the employee has not met the goal due to FMLA leave, payment may be denied as long as a uniform policy for FMLA leave as well as other similar leaves is applied.

If the employee is unable to perform an essential function of their position because of a physical or mental condition, including the continuation of a serious health condition, the employee is not automatically entitled to another position under the FMLA. Similarly, if their condition requires a medical certification of fitness for duty to return to work, the employer may deny reinstatement without that documentation. In this case, the employer is no longer obligated under FMLA. However, in both instances, the employer's obligations may be governed by the Americans with Disabilities Act; therefore, legal guidance may be required.

Certification of Leave Under FMLA

Serious Health Condition

A medical certification is used to document potential FMLA absences for serious health conditions. An employer can require medical certification from a healthcare provider of an employee's need to care for an ill family member or their own serious health condition. The request for the certification needs to be in writing and must allow a minimum of 15 calendar days for the return of a complete certification.

Most employers provide a certification of healthcare provider form (CHCP) to each employee requesting leave. This is included in their initial packet that also explains their eligibility and rights and responsibilities under FMLA. The onus is on the employee to have the paperwork completed by their provider. In most instances, other appropriate documentation will be accepted in lieu of the CHCP; however, only a clear and completed CHCP is required to make a determination of an FMLA absence. If the employee fails to explain the reason for the leave, the leave may be denied unless the employee provides additional information.

When appropriate, an employer may require the employee to obtain a second and third opinion from a different healthcare provider at the employer's expense. The healthcare provider cannot be one the employer contracts with or otherwise regularly utilizes. A third opinion is final and binding and must be provided by a provider designated or approved jointly by the employer and the employee.

If paperwork from a provider is incomplete or unclear, the employer or its representative may contact the provider directly but only after having first provided the employee with an opportunity to cure the deficiency of the certification. If certification information is considered incomplete or insufficient, the employer must specify in writing what information is lacking and give the employee seven calendar days to cure the deficiency.

To support medical privacy, the employer's representative contacting a healthcare provider must be a healthcare provider, human resource professional, leaves administrator, or management official. In no case may it be the employee's direct supervisor. In addition, the employer may not ask healthcare providers for additional information beyond what is required by the certification form. All contact with a healthcare provider must adhere to privacy standards under the Health Insurance Portability and Accountability Act (HIPAA) and any relevant state privacy provisions. Therefore, it is recommended that the employer require an executed medical authorization from the patient before contacting the healthcare provider.

For purposes of authentication of a certification, such as to validate that the healthcare provider completed the information contained on the form, an employer can request such authentication without the employee's consent.

Non-serious Health Condition Certification

For absences not requiring a medical certification, documentation requirements vary based on employer standards; however, the regulation allows employers to ask for appropriate documentation to prove the leave is eligible under FMLA. Therefore, documentation regarding placement of a foster child or adopted child may be requested, as well as military orders. It is important that employers develop a clear and consistent policy for requesting paperwork, as well as what action will be taken if appropriate documentation is not received.

Recertification Due to a Serious Health Condition

When FMLA is taken for the employee's own serious health condition or for the care of a child, spouse, or parent with a serious health condition, the regulations provide restrictions on when recertification may be obtained.

Generally, employers will request recertification when the time on the certification form elapses. However, when documentation is unclear, employers may request additional documentation no more frequently than 30 days, unless one of the following occurs:

- The minimum duration of the condition is more than 30 days;

- The employee requests an extension of leave;

- There has been a significant change in the circumstances originally provided in the leave request; or

- The employer has reason to doubt either the reason for the leave or the validity of the medical certification.

In any case, an employer may, regardless of the time period indicated in the initial medical certification, request a recertification every six months. This would include a request for the same information previously requested and/or providing the healthcare provider with a record of the employee's absences to determine from the healthcare provider if the need for leave is consistent with the pattern of absences.

The employee must provide the recertification within the time frame requested by the employer (a minimum of 15 calendar days) unless it is not practicable under the circumstances. Any cost related to obtaining the recertification is the responsibility of the employee.

Employers cannot request a second or third opinion for a recertification.

Certification for Leave Due to a Qualifying Exigency

Upon an employer's request, an employee must provide a copy of the covered military member's active duty orders to support a request for a qualifying exigency leave.

In addition, upon an employer's request, a request for a qualifying exigency leave must be supported by a certification containing the following information:

- Statement or description of appropriate facts regarding the qualifying exigency for which leave is needed;

- Approximate date on which the qualifying exigency commenced or will commence;

- Beginning and end dates for leave to be taken for a single continuous period of time;

- An estimate of the frequency and duration of the qualifying exigency if leave is needed on an intermittent or reduced-scheduled basis; and

- If the qualifying exigency requires meeting with a third party, the contact information for the third party and description of the purpose of meeting.

The list of required information for certification for a qualifying exigency leave for rest and recuperation was expanded to include a copy of the military member's rest and recuperation leave orders or other documentation issued by the military setting forth the dates of the military member's leave.

This request may only be made once unless there is a different call to duty or the leave is for a different military member.

Employers may use DOL Form WH-384 for requesting such leave or develop a form that contains the same information; no additional information may be requested.

If a third party is involved in the request for a leave, the employer may contact that third party. Employers may also contact the appropriate unit of the Department of Defense (DOD) to verify certain information.

Certification for Leave Requested to Care for a Service Member

Employers may request certification from an authorized healthcare provider for the seriously injured or ill service member. An employer may also require that the employee provide documentation of the family relationship to the injured or ill service member.

Employers may use DOL Form WH-385 for requesting such leave or develop a form that contains the same information; no additional information may be requested.

Second and third opinions may be required by an employer for military caregiver leave certifications that are completed by healthcare providers, as defined in § 825.125, who are not affiliated with DOD, VA, or TRICARE.

Fitness for Duty and Return to Work

Proof of good health and fitness for duty may be required before an employee is able to return to work. These requirements are usually set forth by employers for employees in safety-sensitive positions or where other regulatory bodies are involved (e.g., Department of Transportation). Employers may enforce a uniformly applied policy or practice as all similarly situated employees have the same requirements for return to work.

Fitness for duty may be applied to all FMLA absences where safety is concerned; this was a change in 2008. Previously, fitness for duty could not be applied to intermittent absences, regardless of the situation.

The fitness-for-duty requirement should be directly linked to the employee's ability to perform the essential functions of their job, and as such, employees should be notified of those essential functions early in the process.

Employer Rights and Responsibilities

Employers are required to provide documentation to employees to ensure they are aware of the FMLA and the rights and responsibilities the act affords them. Notices typically fall into one of the following categories:

- General notice: Explains FMLA at a high level, including where and how to file a complaint

    o Sample: WHD Publication 1420, http://www.dol.gov/whd/regs/compliance/posters/fmlaen.pdf

    [NOTE: at the time of publication, this link downloads the correct file but with an incorrect name that causes the file to appear faulty. This is a problem with the Wage and Hour Division site. To correctly view the file, download it to your computer and change the name of the file from "fmlaen.pdf.html" to "fmlaen.pdf" which should resolve the issue.]

- Eligibility notice: Documents eligibility status when FMLA is requested Also serves as a rights and responsibilities notice: Explains employee rights and responsibilities, including but not limited to, the employer policy on the use of paid time, documentation requirements, and benefit continuation

    o Sample: WH-381, http://www.dol.gov/whd/forms/WH-381.pdf

- Medical certification form: To be completed to certify the absence is valid for a serious health condition of the employee or the employee's family member

- o Sample: WH-380, http://www.dol.gov/whd/forms/WH-380-E.pdf
- Designation notice: Certifies the absence as a qualified FMLA leave and/or documents what additional information is required to assess the absence in more detail
  - o Samples: WH-384, http://www.dol.gov/whd/forms/WH-384.pdf, and WH-385, http://www.dol.gov/whd/forms/WH-385.pdf

The act requires that employers post and/or provide a notice, which is typically referred to as the general notice, to employees of their rights under the statute. This is typically accomplished through the use of a poster within the office site as well as documentation in the employee handbook distributed to new hires. When the workforce includes a significant portion of workers who are not literate in English, employers must give notice in the language in which their employees are literate.

Once an employer has been notified of an employee's need for a leave that may be covered by the act, the employer must provide the employee with notice of the employee's obligations while on leave and the consequences of any failure to meet those obligations. Some employers document this in one packet sent to the employee, but the critical components are usually referred to as the eligibility notice, the rights and responsibilities notice, and the certification of healthcare provider form.

Some of the information the employer needs to include as appropriate is:

- Notification of the employee's eligibility under FMLA and, where appropriate, identifying that the leave will be counted against annual FMLA leave accruals

- The requirements the employee needs to furnish, such as the medical certification of a serious health condition, and the consequences for failing to do so

- Notification that the employee has the right to substitute paid leave, including where the employer requires substitution and the conditions related to the substitution

- Requirements regarding the continuation of health benefits and the employee's responsibility to make premium payments during the leave and the possible consequences of failure to make timely payments

- The requirement that the employee provide a fitness-for-duty certificate to return to work

- Notification of the employee's status as a key employee and the conditions under which job restoration could potentially be denied after FMLA leave

- Explanation of the employee's right to return to the same or equivalent job without penalty after the leave

- Notification of the employee's potential liability for healthcare premiums paid by the employer if they fail to return to work after unpaid FMLA leave

The initial regulation required the communication be distributed within two days after an employer's knowledge of absence; however, based on the 2008 updates, employers now have five business days to provide this documentation. The 2008 clarifications also provide additional insight into what must be included within the notification, as discussed above.

The final documentation requirement is the designation notice that is the result of the certification process. This written documentation may provide information regarding an approval or a request for additional information, depending on the specific situation. This designation must be provided within five business days after receipt of all information to determine qualification under FMLA. Additionally, the designation notice must advise the employee if the employer will require a fitness-for-duty certification and whether that fitness-for-duty must address the employee's ability to perform the essential functions of the job. If the fitness-for-duty must address the essential functions, then a detailed description of the employee's essential job functions must be provided with the designation notice. If no documentation is received as a result of this communication, employers will consider that time as a non-FMLA approved absence; therefore, that time away from work is not job-protected.

Employer Recordkeeping Requirements

An employer is required to keep records that document its compliance with the FMLA, whether or not it has eligible employees. No particular form of records is specified, although records must comply with section 11(c) of the Fair Labor Standard Act. Records must be kept for three years and should include the following:

- Basic payroll and employee data

- Dates of FMLA leaves taken by employees

- Hours of leave, if taken in increments of less than one full day

- Copies of any employee notices requesting leave

- Documents describing employee benefits or employer policies and practices regarding paid and unpaid leave

- Records concerning payment of employee benefit premiums

- Records regarding any dispute between the employer and the employee concerning the designation of FMLA leave

Documents relating to medical conditions or their histories must be maintained as confidential medical records in separate files from the usual personnel files. The recordkeeping requirements are updated to specify the employer's obligation to comply with the confidentiality requirements of the Genetic Information Nondiscrimination Act.

Employee Obligations

To comply with FMLA regulations, employees must:

- Provide notice (verbal or otherwise) of the need for leave. including the qualifying reason for leave, 30 days before a foreseeable leave and as soon as practicable for an unforeseeable leave

- Provide medical certification, including properly completed forms submitted within 15 days of employer's request, and recertification under certain circumstances, unless not practicable under the circumstances

- Provide periodic status reports to the employer regarding status and intent to return to work

- Provide fitness-for-duty certification that the employer may require prior to the employee returning to work

- Pay their share of premiums, if any, for continuing coverages during an FMLA leave, within a 30-day grace period

If the employee fails to provide notice and does not have a reasonable excuse, the employer may delay the FMLA leave until 30 days after the employee provides notice. This requirement is waived for leave for a qualifying exigency.

Absent unusual circumstances, employees must comply with the employer's usual and customary notice and procedural requirements for requesting leave. If the leave is not foreseeable, notice must be provided as soon as practicable. This means either the same day or the next business day. If the employee fails to provide notice as soon as practicable, the ability to delay FMLA leave is based on the facts and circumstances of the situation.

Specifically, employees who need to use FMLA time on an unscheduled basis are subject to the same attendance requirements that are applied to other employees. Therefore, if an employer generally requires that employees must telephone their supervisors at least 30 minutes before their shift starts if they will be out, this standard can be applied to employees using FMLA leave on an intermittent basis.

FMLA and Disability and Workers' Compensation Integration

Given the definitions under the regulation, a clear relationship exists between disability absences and FMLA absences, as well as between workers' compensation absences and FMLA absences. To gain efficiencies and create a positive experience for employees and employers, processes should be leveraged. Where disability and/or workers' compensation services are outsourced, for example, it may make sense to outsource FMLA administration. Similarly, where disability and/or workers' compensation administration is managed internally, economies of scale can be achieved by managing them concurrently.

Care must be taken during management since the criteria for disability and workers' compensation are more stringent than for FMLA, and employees cannot be required to submit the same level of detail to certify an FMLA absence as is required for a disability or workers' compensation absence. For example, if medical information received does not meet the standard of definition for disability or workers' compensation benefit coverage, there may be information to meet the serious health condition standard under FMLA. To that end, FMLA qualification should be evaluated separately in these and similar circumstances.

As with other paid leaves, disability and workers' compensation should always run concurrent with FMLA absences. Some disability claim types (e.g., pregnancy) dovetail nicely from a serious health condition absence to a bonding absence, and linking the plans allows for a smooth transition between the different absence types.

Many coordination and/or integration points exist for FMLA and disability plans from intake through to management to reporting, analysis, and benchmarking of data and information.

Some reasons to integrate the processes are:

- Almost all disability and workers' compensation claims are concurrent with FMLA

- Integration will help protect against litigation by tracking FMLA events

- Streamlined paperwork and approval process

- Reduced duplication in obtaining medical information

- Reduced or minimized absences by utilizing a case manager

Whether an employer decides to outsource the integration or do it on its own, it should conduct the following to maximize effectiveness:

- Verify each disability and workers' compensation claim to see if it is also eligible for FMLA.

- Identify the FMLA absence and advise the employee of their rights under FMLA.

- Run FMLA concurrent with disability and workers' compensation.

- If using an outside vendor, get reports from involved carriers or third-party administrators (TPAs) that will detail the amount of leave granted and the expected date of return.

Sources

The Department of Labor's website was leveraged for all regulatory guidance within this chapter. Information regarding application of the regulation was based on industry experts' experience.

The DOL site includes a significant amount of information regarding FMLA, including overview information, compliance materials, fact sheets, posters, and recordkeeping information, as well as the actual regulatory text. Links to this information are available at: http://www.dol.gov/compliance/laws/comp-fmla.htm#DOL_contacts

The initial FMLA regulation is available at: http://www.dol.gov/whd/regs/statutes/fmla.htm

The Revised Final Regulations under the Family and Medical Leave Act are available at: http://www.dol.gov/whd/fmla/finalrule.htm

A side-by-side comparison of current and final regulations is available at: http://www.dol.gov/whd/fmla/2013rule/comparison.htm

Employer Checklist

It is critical to assess compliance with FMLA on an ongoing basis. Given the changing and updated regulations, auditing your plan is critical. The key questions below are intended to prompt discussion internally and with your outsourcing partners and legal counsel to ensure you are currently in compliance but also pinpoint areas where better processes can be developed to improve the employee, supervisor, and human resource experience as it relates to FMLA absences, as well as their links with other paid and unpaid time away from work.

Key Questions	Yes/No	Comments
Employer Communication Responsibility		
Is a general notice (poster) available, and does it comply with the regulations?		
What is provided to new employees as a general notice, and does it comply with the regulations?		
What is included in the initial packet to employees who request leave? Does it comply with the regulations, and is the timing appropriate?		
What medical certification documentation will be used for serious health conditions, and does it comply with the regulations?		
How are decisions communicated to employees, and does it comply with the regulations?		
Certifications		
Are timeframes for certifications appropriate and in line with requirements?		

Who reviews the medical certification documentation? Are they an appropriate party? If an outbound call is made to the provider, who will make that call? Is this in line with the regulations and respectful of privacy considerations?		
Are uniform policies established for documentation beyond certification of a serious health condition?		
Training		
Do human resource professionals understand the intricacies of FMLA, including overlapping statutory leaves? Are new employees continually trained? Who updates this team on regulatory changes?		
Do supervisors and managers understand their responsibility as it relates to FMLA within your organization? Is a process established to support managers and supervisors when they have questions or concerns? How are new supervisors and managers trained?		
Do employees within your organization understand their FMLA rights and obligations? How are these formally communicated to new hires? Is there a formal process for addressing questions from employees?		
Integration Points		
How are statutory leaves managed? Are processes coordinated where appropriate?		
Are FMLA absences coordinated with disability and workers' compensation absences? If not, it should be considered within a comprehensive review.		

Insource Versus Outsource		
Has your organization considered other sources of FMLA administration?		
If you currently outsource FMLA administration, have you recently explored the market to understand the current landscape and ensure your current partner is the best fit? Even if a change is not made, it is important to ensure your current arrangement is best for your employees, supervisors, and stakeholders.		
If you currently insource FMLA administration, have you considered outsourcing this service to an insurance company, third-party administrator, or specialty firm? This is an important consideration, and examining the benefits and risk of change is very valuable.		
Ongoing Compliance		
Is documentation maintained securely and appropriately?		
Who is responsible for keeping abreast of regulatory updates?		
When is internal versus external counsel used?		

Chapter 5: Other Leaves of Absence

Background and Context

Time-off benefits represent yet another business tool organizations use to attract and retain employees. They contribute to the culture and environment employers wish to foster and affect employee morale, attitude, and overall productivity. Employees, as expected, are very protective of time-off benefits. According to MetLife, paid vacation is cited by 55% of American workers as the most important benefit that employers offer.[xxxvii] In 2010, Mercer found the total direct cost of employee absence to be 12.2% of payroll (including planned time off, incidental absence, and extended disability).[xxxviii] According to BNA, 2013 rates of absence held steady at 0.7 of workdays scheduled, a slightly lower rate than was observed before the recession of 2008–2012.[xxxix]

Original consideration of time-off benefits was guided by labor and a certain level of employee entitlement around sick and vacation time. Holidays have been and continue to be driven by officially recognized (and sometimes regulated) time off and incorporate an organization's philosophy for operating on such dates. Other corporate leave policies are driven by both regulation and employer preference. As for regulation, the Family and Medical Leave Act (FMLA), which established leave-related job protection, and the Uniformed Services Employment and Reemployment Rights Act (USERRA), which excuses employees for military duty, have been paramount to establishing corporate policy, as well as the process for administering these leaves and other company-specific leaves, on a corporate-wide basis. Both require consistent application and tracking across organizations and have highlighted the administrative importance of accurately managing leave.

Today, employers structuring their time-off policies take into consideration the following factors: regulations and process followed; competition in the marketplace and offerings by similar firms; cost of each benefit compared to the perceived value by employees; entitlement mentality and how the policies foster this concept; and communication surrounding the value of these days off. When it comes to integrated programs, employers typically start to integrate some or all of the leave types noted below after they become comfortable with the benefits of bringing disability and family medical leave administration together.

Common Leave Types

Common time-off programs can be categorized as sick, vacation, personal days (often bundled as paid time-off [PTO] programs), holidays, leave types required by law, provisions that have been developed according to organizational preference and policy, and attendance management protocols. Examples include, but may not be limited to, those described below.

Sick Leave

These programs provide a maximum number of days per year that employees may take when they are sick. It is usually closely coordinated with short-term disability, family medical leave, and workers' compensation, as all of these typically require employees to use sick time during the benefit waiting period.

Recently, some local jurisdictions have enacted mandatory "paid sick leave" for employees. (See more information under the "Leave Types Required By Law" section.)

Vacation Days

Usually increasing with the number of years an employee has been with a company, vacation time is often offered in hourly, daily, or weekly increments. Depending on the employer and varied state laws, vacation time may or may not be carried over to the following year. With carryover, many employers have a cap or maximum of how much time can be carried over or accrued. If accrued vacation time is not allowed to be carried over, some employers will reimburse the employee for the unused portion of the leave at the end of the year. Some might even institute purchase programs by which employees can buy additional days. Today, more employers are implementing "use it or lose it" approaches for vacation allotments, when employee forfeiture is permitted by state law. Two common reasons for this include the financial impact to the employer of holding large vacation payment liability on the books, and substantial payouts with employee termination. Today, more employers actively encourage employees to use vacation time as an important time to re-energize away from the world of work, for a healthy work/life balance.

Personal Days

Personal days are to be used at an employee's discretion and may be planned in advance or unplanned and reported on short notice. Employers offering personal days set aside a certain number during the calendar year that can be used in this way. Some view them as a way to make up for holidays that are not standard, such as Washington's birthday, on which children's schools might be closed but the corporation still operates. Others view them as days to recuperate or easily allow employees to acknowledge they need a break or time to take care of personal matters.

Paid Time-Off Plans

Some employers offer paid time-off (PTO) plans that do not distinguish between sick, vacation, and personal days. These plans provide a "bank" of days for the employee to take off. This avoids situations by which employees use sick leave inappropriately as an unscheduled day off, when a day off is desired for personal reasons. With one bank of days, it is often easier for employees to keep track of how many days off they have left when they aren't required to categorize them. Still, many employers use absence management techniques, counting PTO taken "last minute" as an unscheduled absence, which counts against the employee in attendance compliance. Similar to other paid leaves, PTO days available often increase with the number of years the employee has been with the company.

Unlimited, or Flexible, Vacation Plans

A few employers (1%[xl]) have implemented what have been called flexible time-off or unlimited vacation benefit plans. These plans offer "unlimited" time off, with specific vacation or PTO benefit limitations; employee time away is not tracked or monitored. Instead, the philosophy promotes an environment of employee responsibility and commitment to getting the job done and achieving results — not a measurement of time spent at the office. Employers with these programs feel that their employees are well motivated and the best judges of how to spend the time necessary to get the work done. Also, these employers believe (and some studies show) that this approach makes employees more productive and more engaged and fosters less employee turnover. Acceptance of this kind of program is still very small, seen mostly in certain industries and types of corporate cultures, as well as among high-level executive employee groups. Broad implementation over large groups of employees requires significant culture change. Realistically, most employers feel that allocating specific paid time off is a better approach for effective business operations.

Holidays

The majority of employers offer paid holiday benefits. The 2015 Holiday Schedules survey by the Society for Human Resource Management (SHRM) shows that 73% of employers offer between six and ten holidays annually to full-time workers. The most frequently cited holiday schedule is ten days. The most common holidays are New Year's Day, Memorial Day, Independence Day, Labor Day, Thanksgiving, the day after Thanksgiving, and Christmas. The next most prevalent holidays, according to SHRM's survey are Christmas Eve, Martin Luther King Day, Presidents' Day, Good Friday, the day after Christmas, New Year's Eve Day, and Veterans Day.[xli]

The rationale for providing more or fewer designated holidays is often based on business needs, local customs (e.g., Mardi Gras in New Orleans, Louisiana), and direction from management or collectively bargained employees. Some view a designated holiday as less expensive since the entire group is shut down and no replacement workers are necessary. Others view designated holidays as more expensive because without team members working, costs are tied to payroll, lost sales, and sometimes customer satisfaction. Unlike other leaves, the cost of designated holidays is easy to quantify; it is also very expensive. Because of this, employers may designate a minimum number of holidays and provide other paid days off to employees in order to maintain operations on all other business days.

Leave Types Required by Law

Family Medical Leave

As described previously, the Family Medical Leave Act of 1993 requires employers with 50 or more workers to provide up to 12 weeks of unpaid leave for an employee's own serious health condition; the birth or care of a newborn child, or the placement of a child for adoption or foster care; to care for a family member with a serious health condition; to care for a covered service member with a serious injury or illness; or for qualifying exigencies when a family member is called to active duty as a member of the National Guard or reserves. Family medical leave (FML) can be taken on a continuous or reduced-leave schedule, or, in some cases, on an intermittent basis where an employee regularly takes a certain amount of time off at a set time interval. For example, an employee attending physical therapy sessions for two hours once every other week may be able to use intermittent FML time to cover this leave.

Military Leave

Some form of military leave is required by U.S. law. Although no paid leave is required under USERRA, approximately 68% of companies provide a pay differential while on active duty. Of this 68%, 21% provide this benefit for eight weeks or less, and 27% pay for an unlimited amount of time.[xlii] Military policies that provide enhanced benefits typically mirror the level of civic responsibility at an organization.

Paid Sick Leave

Mandatory paid sick leave was first enacted by the city of San Francisco in 2007. Since that time a number of other jurisdictions have enacted mandatory paid sick leave, including the state of Connecticut, and some other cities and counties, including Seattle, Portland, Washington, D.C., Newark, Jersey City, and New York City (2014). Many other jurisdictions have considered or are considering similar laws. These local laws differ from jurisdiction to jurisdiction, but the basic premise requires many or most employers of a certain size or industry to offer paid sick leave to employees who work within the jurisdictional geography. The amount of paid time is usually credited based on hours worked; some jurisdictions also allow for sick leave accrual carryover from year to year. In most jurisdictions, if an employer already offers the same or more time off with pay benefit as sick leave, vacation, or PTO, it is not required to offer additional paid leave days. However, even for those employers that already offer paid leave that qualifies, there is an additional burden of tracking time that has different qualifying factors for pay and different rules for carryover and banking sick leave. For example, some jurisdictions require that the mandatory paid leave can also be used for family illness. As this trend continues to grow, employers who operate in more than one jurisdiction will face significant challenges in setting up systems to track leave entitlement, as well as in educating and monitoring local supervisory staff on differing jurisdictional compliance rules.

Paid Family Leave

As of 2014, paid family leave is offered in only California, New Jersey, and Rhode Island. The leave is funded by an employee-paid payroll tax, using existing state funds (disability and unemployment). More states have discussed implementing this concept but have not moved to enact it as of this writing. Those who oppose paid family leave feel the impact on the employer's business will be significant.

Jury Duty

Similar to military leave, leave for jury duty is based on the sense of civic responsibility of the employer. United States employers are required by law to allow employees to take leave for jury duty; however, they are not required to offer pay during this leave unless otherwise dictated by a specific state law. When employees are compensated, they are usually limited to straight pay based on a standard eight-hour day. Given that most jury duty leaves require limited away time, it is not an expensive benefit, and fraud or management is very limited or nonexistent.

Voting

Although most U.S. states require paid time off on election days for employees to vote, this mandate is only necessary if the polls are not open before or after work hours. Terminology differs by state; however, if polls are open at least three hours before or after an employee's shift, additional time is usually not required as employees should make allowance to vote during those hours. Paid leave for voting, similar to that for military or jury duty, is tied to the civic responsibility of an employer.

Bereavement

Supervisors often find management of this leave to be difficult due to its sensitive nature, and policies are sometimes hard to follow. Most employers provide a fixed number of days for bereavement leave, based on each occurrence, with the average being three days. Alternately, some provide a varying number of days based on the relationship to the deceased. Paid benefits are usually limited to immediate family members such as spouses, children, parents, grandparents, and siblings. Policies typically include both a paid and unpaid component, with the unpaid piece applying to time taken beyond the company-designated paid time for immediate family members or for attendance at services for relatives or friends who were not immediate family members. A few employers seek proof of death and attendance at the wake or funeral; however, this is uncommon.

State-Specific Laws

Many states have their own leave laws that often run concurrently with FML but are also separate and distinct. Employers face difficulties in managing these laws either because they are unaware of them, as some of the state-specific laws are changed and/or added frequently, or because there is no clear guidance on how to manage them. Others might be aware of them but assume they are part of FML administration and, if that function is outsourced, just assume they are covered. Employers need to be aware of these laws as litigation issues can arise if employees if employees feel that their time off that was denied by their employer was actually protected under state law. Common state-specific protected leave types are noted below, but as mentioned, these are continually increasing in number and range:

- Domestic violence leave

- Victims of crime leave

- Civil service leave

- Volunteer/Emergency personnel leave

- School/Parental leave (e.g., for parents to attend their children's school functions)

- Tissue/bone marrow/organ donation leave

- Adoptive parents leave

Other Company-Preferred Leave Policies

Depending on the organization, there may be a need to establish additional leave policies to account for actions employers would like to take for their employees. Examples include:

- Personal leave: Organizations might afford unpaid time off for employees to deal with a personal hardship.

- Administrative leave: Time in addition to other benefits offered may be needed to manage a serious health condition. In such cases, employers may decide to continue benefits so as to minimize the hardship but not necessarily provide job protection.

- Disaster service:
  - For volunteers, most employers offer this type of leave when necessary and on a casual basis; however, a formal policy allows for better communication and more favorable public attention.
    - Eligibility is linked to both employee type as well as circumstances.

- Typical policies would allow for 15 days, 30 days, or more of paid time away to help in support of a crisis with a reputable charitable organization (e.g., American Red Cross).
  - For victims, this would be similar to the volunteer policy but may not be formalized and would likely be implemented in time of distress.
    - Eligibility is linked to circumstance and employee type.
    - Risk for this would likely need to be spread across the organization as a small site may not be able to "self-insure" this exposure.
- Community service:
  - Organ/bone marrow donation: When implemented, this is usually seven to 30 days of paid time.
  - Blood donation: Minimal time is provided to donate blood, usually when a blood drive is sponsored by the employer or held on the employer's premises.
  - Volunteer work: Such work may be part of company-sponsored events or individually selected. The policy will need to not only limit time away but also define voluntary (e.g., volunteer work for which kinds of organizations — churches, schools, nonprofits?)
- Religious leave: In organizations without a paid time-off bank or personal days to be used at the employee's discretion, most employees are required to use vacation time for a religious holiday.
- Sabbaticals: An employer allows an employee paid or unpaid leave for a specific period of time so the employee can pursue a course of advanced training, teach, or perform a public service (more common in the education field).
- Leave for education needs: Such leaves are likely applied by supervisors as needed; however, a formal policy would be valuable (e.g., defining the education need covered, such as to pursue a general education development certificate or an undergraduate or master's degree).

Attendance Management

Many employers have attendance policies as part of their absence management program to minimize unnecessary time off work and maintain employee productivity. Numerous studies have shown that "unscheduled absence" — when an employee calls in sick at the last minute — impacts employer operations more than scheduled absences that can be planned for. When implementing an attendance policy, the employer should explain the importance of employee attendance to the business. Employee attendance notification requirements should be clearly outlined, along with consequences for failure to comply. Attendance management rules are not put in place to punish employees per se, but employers need to recognize that there will always be some employees who will try to abuse and/or manipulate the system. Having firm guidelines in place will help to minimize these actions and protect the employer.

As time off that is subject to an attendance policy is not typically subject to any other leave type, employers must be careful with their tracking mechanisms and communication process. Employers start by defining what qualifies as an occurrence; that is, five minutes late, ten minutes late, or the amount of notice needed for a full-day absence, such as at least two hours before a shift starts. Often, point values are assigned to each occurrence based on its severity. When an employee reaches certain point levels, progressive disciplinary actions are taken. Repeat occurrences or an excessively high point value will often require a face-to-face meeting between the supervisor and employee. Excessive occurrences can lead to suspension and/or termination.

Integrating Leave with Other Absence Programs

Employers' growing concern about employee absence is causing them to take action. Organizations are beginning to think more broadly about what time off means to their organizations and what particular time off and leave of absence policies, outside of those regulated, are appropriate for their particular populations. In doing so, they are making efforts to track employee time away from work, then analyze the data so as to identify the reasons employees are away and what can be done to most appropriately manage them.

This tracking and analysis is being done in conjunction with disability and workers' compensation programs and specifically FML administration as a move toward an integrated approach. Time off is one of the few benefits that employees know, understand, and personally track. To employers, time off is the most costly benefit, second only to direct pay. This is especially true for organizations in which replacement wages must be considered in looking at total time-off costs. Time off is also an administrative burden where consistency in policy and process is critical for employee relations. Program misuse occurs but is often difficult to measure. Employers need to be careful not to react with overly strict policies that inadvertently penalize all employees because of the behaviors of a few.

In setting strategies for offering these benefits, it is important to understand the parameters of best-practice programs and design programs that can positively influence an employer's ability to attract and retain employees while meeting business needs. When employers seek to change their time-off policies, employee reactions must be prepared for, as they can vary significantly by the culture and the use of such policies at an organization. Change can also spur varying reactions from internal management such as Finance, Legal, HR/Benefits, Payroll, Timekeeping, and Communications - all of which play important roles in the process.

Parameters of Best-Practice Programs

Although the goals of best-practice programs are many, key factors are to standardize policy as much as possible and implement processes that allow tracking with ease. They should simultaneously work to reduce absence while maintaining morale and seek to reward all employees fairly and/or equally. The characteristics and administration of time-off programs should be closely linked with the employer's culture so as to reflect its mission and values.

Policies need to consider eligibility requirements; certification and documentation rules (including requests for additional time); notification parameters; and ongoing communication standards and requirements (from employees, supervisors, and HR). They should clearly state what the impact of time away from work has on employment status, benefits, and job reinstatement, as well as how paid versus unpaid time is applied. Although these features call for program formality, employers also need to recognize that time-off plans cannot be so limiting that policy and process cannot be followed.

When it comes to employee recruiting and tenure, employers must balance the sensitive and competitive nature of time-off benefits with the fact that business needs and operations come first. For example, if a generous sick leave policy is in place and highly used by employees, it may be possible that sick leave is being used when other leave types (e.g., personal days) might be more appropriate. If competitor firms tend to combine sick leave into PTO programs and unscheduled absence is causing operating difficulties, it may be useful for the employer to transition from separate sick, vacation, and personal day banks to a PTO program, while retaining an attendance policy that has a penalty for excess unscheduled absence.

Although making this decision sounds straightforward, it does come at a risk of employee dissatisfaction, particularly for the high utilizers of sick leave who will perceive that benefits are being taken away from them. To mitigate this risk and ensure a balanced approach, brainstorming and effective strategy-setting for decisions are essential. Effective communication around the reasons for a change, the value to employees of having a PTO plan, and the value of the employee's entire benefits package is very important.

In addition to setting the strategy and designing the programs, the leading considerations for employers are how time-off programs are aligned with overall corporate goals, administered with or without external resources, communicated across the organization, and appropriately financed and funded.

Alignment

From an organizational standpoint, employers need to ensure that time-off benefits programs align with the overall mission, values, and culture of the organization. While this is part of the strategy setting and program design process previously discussed, it cannot be stressed enough that the amount of paid time off and other types of leaves employers allow should correspond with the working environment, value of employees, and schedules they encourage employees to keep. Time-off programs should be considered part of the overall benefits package and correspond with general employee relations messages distributed company-wide. They should be consistently applied across the organization and allow for concurrent tracking and management of interrelated time, such as sick days with FMLA and use of vacation or sick days before disability or workers' compensation benefits begin. Managers and supervisors need to ensure that time is being reported and tracked according to corporate guidelines and replacement workers are being sought in response. Disciplinary policy and issues must be incorporated into the process so there is clear expectation of what people are accountable for in the process.

Administration

There are many ways to administer time-off programs. The typical approaches are insourcing, outsourcing, or a combination. Insourcing requires an organization to handle (and coordinate) all program administration internally. It involves coordination between Finance, Legal, HR/Benefits, Payroll, Timekeeping, Communications, supervisors, and employees. An advanced database or specialized information systems, with interconnectivity, is valuable to verify eligibility, manage day-to-day leave status, and capture information for management reporting.

With an outsourced approach, administration is handled externally and coordinated with the employer. The vendor provides the majority of services but of course keeps in close contact with key internal resources. Employer roles focus on benefits specialists, managers, supervisors, and other internal advocates to serve as resources for the employees.

In a combination approach, some administration is handled internally and some externally. The distinctions are based on the employer's internal best practices and its outsourced preferences. Internally versus externally provided services are specifically defined to ensure as smooth of a process as possible.

Communication

Once programs are in place, they must be effectively communicated across the organization. This includes explaining the programs, their provisions, and the procedures to access them. The most challenging aspects of communicating benefits programs include the diverse composition of the workforce in terms of educational, financial sophistication and interest levels. Because employee interest is highest in time-off benefits, it is essential that the messages going out to employees are clear, concise, and instructional. The standardization of programs as much as possible is important, as well as the level of interaction required of employees with their supervisors, managers, HR, and other benefits resources.

Financing and Funding Methods

The funding of time-off and leave benefits differs from other programs discussed in that it is generally not an insured expense. Instead, the financial liability associated with employee time-off benefits is either funded through accruals or treated on a pay-as-you go basis.

Typically, the critical element for deciding on funding is the likelihood that the benefit will be paid at some point during employment or pay will be owed to the employee upon termination. There are regulated accounting standards that employer finance departments typically consult in order to determine if funding accruals are needed. How employers account for these accruals internally and through external financial reporting will vary from employer to employer.

From a financial perspective, more employers are now recognizing the direct costs involved with paid time-off benefits, as well as the indirect costs (overtime, cost of replacement workers, hiring new workers, etc.) that are critically important to understanding the total impact of lost productivity due to employee time off work.

Employer Checklist

In considering all of the various leave types that can be offered, it is important for employers to first inventory what they have in place, then move on to an organized feasibility process of what a comprehensive design should look like.

Key Questions	Yes/No	Comments
What parameters does your organization place around the following time-off benefits?		
Sick leave		
Vacation days		
Personal days		

Holidays		
Paid time off		
Family medical leave		
Military leave		
Jury duty		
Voting		
Bereavement		
State-specific		
Domestic violence leave		
Victims of crime leave		
Civil service leave		
Volunteer/Emergency personnel leave		
Parental leave		
Tissue/bone marrow/organ donation leave		
Adoptive parents leave		
Other company-preferred leave policies		

Personal leave		
Administrative leave		
Disaster service leave		
Community service leave		
Religious leave		
Sabbaticals		
Education leave		
Attendance management		
Are the leave types above offered to:		
Management/nonbargained only		
Hourly/bargained only		
Other combination		
Compliance		
Program referrals		
How are the leave types you offer currently managed?		
Insured and handled by:		

Corporate HR		
Mid-level managers		
Direct supervisors		
Other		
Outsourced and handled by:		
Insurance company		
Third-party administrator		
Combination approach		

How well are leave policies perceived to meet your population needs?

Are there any restrictions on changing leave policy within your organization?

Is there any data available to analyze the following:		
Usage: overall and by locations, divisions, etc.		
Costs: overall and by locations, divisions, etc.		

Problem/abuse areas: overall and by locations, divisions, etc.		

Have you been able to take any of the following steps toward program design?	Yes/No	Comments
Compose an internal team and identify stakeholder goals		
Confirm the current state of your sick, vacation, and overall time-off policies		
Gather information to analyze each program		
Review time-off utilization and corresponding financial values and accruals		
Consider benefits programs offered by competing firms		
Analyze and Develop Alternatives		
Review potential plan designs such as: • Standardized leave of absence policies • Comprehensive PTO bank • Attendance tracking • Combination of different plans		
Estimate cost savings and program implementation costs of each option		

Detail communication and training needs to proceed: • Accrual methods • Time increments for utilization • Rollover provisions • Buy/Sell options • Sick employees at work		
Agree on the most effective program for your organization, according to stakeholder goals and objectives		
Create the internal business case for change		
Identify vendor partners (e.g., timekeeping, disability provider, etc.) needed to proceed		
Implementation		
Work with the internal team to finalize plan design		
Design communication and training materials appropriately		
Implement the recommended program		
Provide initial and ongoing manager and supervisor training and employee education		

Chapter 6: Behavioral Risk and Mental Health

Introduction

Investing in employee mental health is one of the most important initiatives that employers can do to reduce absence, increase productivity, and address overall healthcare and disability costs. Incorporating this aspect into an integrated program recognizes the prevalence of human behavior in everything that we do.

This can be accomplished in a number of ways that utilize both current resources (e.g., employee assistance programs [EAPs]) and the development of specialized programs. Addressing these behavioral challenges must be approached as one would with any other risk within an organization; thus, the term behavioral risk is used in this context to define the process and offer proven methods to employ.

What Is Behavioral Risk?

Behavioral risk is a term that was adopted by the DMEC in 2006 to describe a best-practice area of workforce risk management and healthcare cost containment to better understand the underlying behavioral aspects of claims, productivity, safety, and employee performance issues, including:

- Psychosocial and psychosomatic factors

- Productivity losses and presenteeism

- Psychiatric and high-profile claims management (including chronic pain)

- Human resource and labor relations cases

The behavioral risk process proceeds like any risk management process, following these steps:

- Identify and measure behavior-related risk

- Correlate and analyze the loss and risk data

- Take stock of current activities that affect the prevalence of risk

- Introduce risk reduction interventions

- Modify programs over time

What Is Comorbidity?

In medicine, comorbidity describes the effect of all other diseases an individual patient might have other than the primary disease of interest (e.g., heart disease and diabetes). In psychiatry or psychology, comorbidity refers to the presence of more than one diagnosis occurring in an individual at the same time. This can be either a mental-mental or a physical-mental combination. Mental and physical (mental-physical) comorbidity complicates healthcare costs and the perception of disability. For instance, it is has been found that adults with headaches were more likely to rate their health as "fair to poor" (17.9% versus

6.1%), to seek healthcare four or more times a year (43.3% versus 22.7%), and to endorse physical and mental limitations. Health utilization and negative health perception are also more strongly influenced by co-morbid mental disorders than physical disorders.[xliii]

Comorbidity can also influence work behavior and productivity. It has been found that negative emotions are believed to adversely impact health by either directly altering physiologic systems or indirectly leading to harmful health-related behaviors and coping resources.[xliv]

Physical-mental comorbidity (e.g., heart disease and depression) have a significant impact on recovery and return to work. Nearly one half (48%) of patients with heart disease are depressed. Why do heart failure patients display such a markedly elevated prevalence of depression? Is it because they are depressed about having a heart condition? Or is it preexisting? Some researchers believe that the connection may lie in shared pathophysiology, suggesting that physiologic states brought on by depression might hasten the development of heart failure and worsen prognosis. Psychosocial factors may also contribute; for example, depression is associated with medical noncompliance, a higher prevalence of smoking, and lower levels of social support, each of which has been correlated with worse outcomes.[xlv]

What Are Psychosocial Factors?

Psychosocial factors pertain to psychological development in the context of a social environment. Factors include:[xlvi]

- Age

- Gender

- Racial background

- Birth order

- Self-esteem

- Type A personality

- Sensation seeking

- Job dissatisfaction

- Alcohol and drug use

- Education

- Marital status

Psychosocial concerns are the major causes of delayed recovery or work absence. Some factors have a larger impact on return to work and recovery than others:

- Strong effect: age, work dissatisfaction, emotional distress, duration/time off work, financial incentives (litigation), clinical history of back pain

- Moderate effect: pain intensity, perceived health/disability, depression, fear avoidance, catastrophic thinking, pain behavior

- Weak effect: physical demands of work, comorbidity, gender, marital status, education, personality, psychological history, stressful life events, alcohol/drug history

What Is Psychosomatic Disorder?

Also referred to as psychophysiological, psychosomatic illnesses include disorders characterized by symptoms that are caused by mental processes of the sufferer rather than immediate physiological causes. These syndromes are classified as neurotic, stress-related, and somatoform disorders.[xlvii] Although the term has developed a negative connotation, erroneously associated with malingering or delusion, psychosomatic illness has often been attributed to stress, making stress management an important factor in the development or avoidance of psychosomatic illness.[xlviii]

Underlying Behavioral Elements and Their Implications: Current Compelling Research and Surveys

Psychological, organizational, and personal stressors can affect an individual's response to disease, coping, and levels of productivity. Underlying elements that can complicate cases must be identified and clearly understood to avoid protracted absence, delayed return to work, or delayed recovery. Failure to identify and respond to psychosocial factors that can influence productivity and work behaviors can lead to eventual disability, safety hazards, or substandard performance.

To evaluate the importance and necessity for a behavioral risk approach, let's review some background research and statistics that point to the need and urgency for this integrated approach.

National

- Psychiatric conditions, including depression, anxiety, and stress, cost U.S. employers an estimated $525 billion annually in medical costs.[xlix] And this does not take into account lost productivity.

- Mental illness ranks number one among illnesses that cause disability for people age 15 to 44 in the United States.[l]

Mental Health

- 72% of depressed individuals have co-morbid anxiety or substance abuse problems.[li]

- The average time "out of role" for people with major depressive disorders was over 35 days on average which compares with only 15 days for most chronic disorders.[lii]

- Long-term absences appear to be most affected by leadership behavior and social support at work. Over commitment, job control, and job strain were not associated with any of the absence measures.[liii]

Healthcare

- If an individual has anxiety or depression in addition to a physical illness, the anxiety and depression are more predictive of functional impairment over time than the severity of the physical illness.[liv]

Employee Assistance Programs (EAPs)

- EAP use by those with behavioral health issues increases productivity of those reporting difficulty completing work by 70% and decreases missed work in those who reported missing work by 94%.[lv]

- Companies with an EAP utilization of 10% or more had significantly fewer short term disability claims than companies with no EAP.[lvi]

Employer Survey

- Nearly 100% of employers surveyed say that behavioral risk management is an important area of concern.[lvii]

Benefits of Integrating Behavioral Risk Management

As with integration of other benefits programs, one of the key advantages of integrating behavioral risk management is the efficient coordination of resources to ensure a healthy and productive workforce. It also avoids the silo mentality that increases costs and discourages return to work. Other benefits include:

- Early identification of high-risk employees

- Utilization of the most skilled resources

- Efficient use of mental health professionals, especially those employing telephonic case management

- Getting to the underlying psychosocial issues that complicate recovery or delay return to work

- High return on investment (ROI) and low cost (e.g., management fees are reasonable, typically ranging from $200 to $700 per case)

- Good outcomes and cost savings

- Human cost savings and employee satisfaction

- Separation of performance issues from disability issues

- Identification and early treatment of comorbid complications

- Avoidance of cost shifting

In discussing behavioral risk in the workplace, the significant change in the approach over the last ten years has been the interest in the occurrence of comorbidity, specifically psychiatric comorbidity, as a complicating factor. In addition, recognition of psychosocial factors can significantly influence the appropriate treatment, recovery, and return-to-work success of affected employees.

Types of Behavioral Risk Programs

Behavioral risk methods can be employed in a variety of ways, from simple to more complex models, depending on available resources. The underlying element is defined by the use of licensed mental health professionals (psychiatrist; psychologist; marriage, family, and child counselor; social worker; etc.) to clarify and resolve psychological and psychosocial problems that affect job performance and recovery from disabilities and impaired productivity and/or presenteeism. The caveat is that these mental health professionals must be savvy in their understanding of the workplace and the commitment to return to work and optimal productivity. Using trained specialists is critical, because they can provide a variety of unique capabilities:

- Ability to motivate individuals to cooperate and provide information

- Understanding of human behavior

- Training in communication and coping skills

- Facilitation of trust and cooperation with colleagues (peer to peer)

- Unique understanding of both the medical and psychiatric aspects (psychiatrists)

- Ability to formulate opinions on treatment and work restrictions

- Reminding both employees and providers that work can be therapeutic and assist in an employee's overall recovery

- Advocate optimal and urgent treatment if absence from work is needed

Although every employer's program is unique and hybrid programs exist, most programs can be categorized into six major types as described below.

Behavioral Case (or Behavioral Disability) Management

This specialized area of case management utilizes a mental health professional to conduct both case reviews and case intervention. This can occur both telephonically as well as in person. The goal is to review the case for underlying psychosocial or psychiatric comorbidity and to recommend treatment to facilitate optimal case resolution and improvement. Red flags or triggers are identified early in the process by case managers (or even supervisors) as a means to identify candidates. The process then involves a three-point communication between the behavioral case manager and the employee, supervisor, and treating physician.

The approach taken by some specialized case management firms includes the following characteristics:

- Robust interaction with all parties involved with the case

- Early identification of barriers for return to work

- Assurance that a good treatment plan is in place

- Mitigation of workplace stressors (including toxic supervisors and work environments)

- Focus on return to work as the ultimate goal of treatment

Various methodologies can be employed to map the process of behavioral case management. The Disability Management Planning Matrix below is a sample tool for identifying and responding to work performance, physical-mental, mental-physical, and distinct psychiatric disorders.

Table 6.1

Disability Management Planning Matrix: Claims with Significant Psychosocial or Psychiatric Issues					
Type of Claim	Precursors/ Predictors	Degree of Loss and Liability/ Compensability	Treatment/ Restoration	Work Site Accommodation	Work Return Prescription
Work Performance Deficit	1. Objective performance deficits 2. Pattern of absenteeism 3. Pattern of employee health visits 4. Perpetual/ sporadic conflict	1. Lost production 2. Time off work 3. Required overtime or temporary support to cover responsibilities 4. Administrative time	1. Address skill deficits through training 2. EAP referral 3. Conditioning program 4. Goal-oriented medical care and/or personnel intervention	(If necessary and appropriate, given problem) 1. Modify tasks to address skill deficit 2. Short-term assignment 3. Change supervision/style	1. Performance-related improvement plan

Disability Management Planning Matrix:

Claims with Significant Psychosocial or Psychiatric Issues

Type of Claim	Precursors/ Predictors	Degree of Loss and Liability/ Compensability	Treatment/ Restoration	Work Site Accommodation	Work Return Prescription
Physical- Mental (e.g., depression related to a physical condition)	1. Slow or inadequate medical response 2. Feelings of frustration and/or hopelessness 3. Dependent work and life style 4. Inadequate support system 5. Secondary gains 6. Cynical management	1. Job demands analysis: focus on function 2. Assessment of functional capacities 3. Health behavior assessment (e.g., coping skills)	1. Empathic response: peer and supervisor support 2. Transitional work return as soon as possible 3. Adjustment counseling 4. Work conditioning 5. Possible clinical treatment	1. Develop planned accommodation options (what are we capable of?) 2. Flexibility in schedule and job responsibilities 3. Graded work return 4. Focus on achieving "small successes" ASAP	1. Develop coping skills 2. Goal-oriented work return plan 3. Transitional in nature: build in self-monitoring and capacity for fluctuations in performance
Mental- Physical (e.g., migraine headaches)	1. Perpetual conflict 2. Unplanned separation or personnel actions 3. High degree of "at-risk behaviors" (e.g., uniformed personnel, hospital workers, convenience store employees, etc.)	1. Accurate diagnosis 2. Timely and appropriate medical care 3. Clear and equitable process to determine liability/ compensability 4. Functional capacity	1. Address medical condition 2. Risk reduction 3. Modify stressors 4. Enhance coping skills 5. Group support	1. Graded work return 2. Develop planned accommodation pathways 3. Supervisor training	1. Develop coping skills 2. Goal-oriented work return plan: focus strongly on job demands and worker capacities

Type of Claim	Precursors/ Predictors	Degree of Loss and Liability/ Compensability	Treatment/ Restoration	Work Site Accommodation	Work Return Prescription
		exams (FCEs)			
Distinct Psychiatric Disorder (e.g., anxiety disorder)	1. Pattern of absenteeism and/or variable quality work 2. Secondary gains 3. Uncertain economic conditions/ high threat of job loss or responsibility changes 4. High job demands (perceived) 5. Liberal definition of disability	1. Medical examination 2. Complete behavioral review regarding work performance 3. Define stressors and areas of vulnerability in job demands 4. Scope of legal or contractual definition	1. EAP triage 2. Treatment by qualified mental health professional 3. Define job and work site conditions 4. Transitional work return as soon as possible	1. Modify stressors (or the perception of stressors) 2. Temporary flexibility in responsibilities / schedule 3. Verify accuracy and necessity of job demands 4. Review management and/or supervisory style	1. Develop coping skills 2. Graduated work return 3. Transitional in nature: build in self-monitoring and capacity for fluctuations in performance

Source: Leclair Consultation Center, LLC, ©1999. Used with permission.

Management Consultative Services

EAPs and other services can provide management assistance programs to supervisors on performance (including safety) and disability claims. Often the mental health professional (MHP) can facilitate better communication, ease the transition back to work (especially in mental health cases), and educate supervisors about performance expectations. Consultations often result in the recommendation for performance documentation in an attempt to differentiate performance issues from disability symptoms. Other services can include executive coaching, resiliency training, stress management, and interventions.

Warm Transfers

Cooperative programs have been established that encourage interaction between the EAP and the disability carrier or department within an organization. When the claims examiner recognizes that there could be underlying psychological or psychosocial issues affecting the claim, they make a formal or informal transfer to the EAP. These introductions are handled confidentially through either a contractual approval basis or a release signed by the employee.

Behavioral Safety

Repeated safety violations or worker's compensation (WC) injuries are a signal that there may be underlying issues that are causing these events. Organizations can set up key flags to identify these high-profile cases and employ their EAP to assist in finding out the reasons for the high accident rates (e.g., reviewing all cases in which an employee has had one injury per year for five years).

Behavioral Audits

A behavioral audit enables you to quantify your risk exposures and assess your degree of risk. Once you have established the range of your organization's problems, you can determine appropriate solutions to prevent further risk. Data is usually culled from claim files, healthcare utilization rates and costs, employee and management surveys, focus groups, and individual interviews.

Innovative Use of EAPs

Traditionally employed to intervene in substance abuse cases, prevent violence in the workplace, and provide critical incident stress debriefing, a well-designed EAP can also be a proactive business tool. Innovative use of EAPs can help your employees face and overcome life's challenges, while at the same time assist in reducing absenteeism, increasing retention, saving money, controlling costs, and increasing employee productivity. EAPs can also play a central role in helping family members cope with mental health issues, financial concerns, and other life challenges that indirectly affect the employee's performance.

According to the Employee Assistance Professionals Association, the following employers have demonstrated a positive return on investment through the employee use of an EAP:

- Chevron recognized a $50,000 per case gain from reduced turnover and a 50% performance improvement

- Abbott Laboratories reported a 6:1 ROI. Over a three-year period, $10,000 less was spent per case for inpatient medical costs for employees who used an EAP compared to those who did not.

- Virginia Power demonstrated a 23% reduction in medical costs.

- Campbell Soup saved 28% in mental health costs.[lviii]

In addition:

- Caterpillar reduced the proportion of psychiatric disability cases from 33% to 8.1% and reduced the average lost work time from 58 to 32.6 days per year. This included $3.5 million in cost savings in just 18 months.[lix]

- University of Toronto, Johnson & Johnson, Verizon, Canada Post, and other cutting-edge employers have won awards from the Employee Assistance Society of North America for their excellence in terms of partnership with EAP providers to design and integrate a program that enhances employee well-being and enables the company to work toward a healthy and productive workplace.[lx]

Effective Measurement and Sample Practices

How Can Behavioral Risk Programs Be Measured?

Ultimately, the measurement of program effectiveness and bottom-line implications must be addressed in order to establish and implement such programs. Only recently have employers begun to establish meaningful measures of program success. Two excellent examples are both power generating companies: American Electric Power (AEP) and Southern California Edison (SCE).

American Electric Power, with 21,000 employees in 11 states, initiated a behavioral health partnership in 2002. The goals of the program were to begin in-house claims management behavioral training; revise certificates of disability and plan language; require appropriate care, treatment, and stronger documentation; and apply a screening tool for case triage. The results were impressive. In just six years, the number of cases dropped from 30 to two; ROI became $11,000 per case and total long-term disability (LTD) reserve savings reached almost $5 million. Outcomes for the 30 cases included:

- Return to work (19): 64%

- LTD (2): 6%

- LTD pending (1): 4%

- Retire/terminate (6): 20%

- Other/sick pay (2): 6%

In the case of SEC, it measured the difference between annual program results and preprogram benchmarks as a "dashboard" summary of its success in its job coach and warm transfer programs, which were initiated in 2008. Key categories included:

- Number of employees referred

- Number of employees participating

- Percent of employees returning to work on or near the expected date

- Percentage of employees who stayed off work after returning

- Percentage of employees who remained off work

- Percentage of employees with a behavioral health diagnosis

- Percentage of employees who were cross-referred to other resources

As a result of its warm transfer and return-to-work job coach programs, the company experienced improved return to work, enhanced employee satisfaction, and overall improvement in the health and productivity of its workforce. Other measures included cost per claim, change/improvement, and employee satisfaction. Such types of results are the hallmark of a good behavioral approach to disability management, which can be initiated relatively easily and with good outcomes.

Sample Practice: Depression as a Leading Cause of Absence and Lost Productivity

According to the National Institute for Mental Health, approximately 20.9 million American adults, or about 9.5% of the U.S. population age 18 and older in a given year, suffer from mood disorders (including major depressive disorder, dysthymic disorder, and bipolar disorder). In addition, major depressive disorder is the leading cause of disability in the United States for ages 15 to 44.[lxi]

According to an article in the Journal of Occupational and Environmental Medicine, depression can have a significant effect on a person's judgment, attention, decision making, memory, concentration, and motivations — all of which have a direct effect on productivity.[lxii]

Because the median age of the onset of mood disorders is 30 years, these conditions have a significant impact on the peak performance years of workers. Added to that, depressive disorders often co-occur with anxiety disorders and substance abuse, and it is clear that employers cannot afford to ignore the effects that these conditions have on the bottom line.

Fortunately, more than 80% of depressed people can be treated quickly and efficiently. The key is to recognize the symptoms of depression early and to receive appropriate treatment. Many companies are helping employees with depression by providing training on depressive illness for supervisors, EAP, and occupational health personnel. These efforts are contributing to a significant reduction in lost time and job-related accidents as well as marked increases in productivity.[lxiii]

One of the most effective ways to uncover hidden depression is to utilize employee depression screenings. In the 2008 DMEC Behavioral Risk Survey, 35% of employers had expanded the use of depression screenings — up by 26% over 2006.[lxiv]

Signs of depression include:

- Frequent statements about being tired all the time

- Alcohol and drug abuse

- Decreased productivity

- Morale problems

- Absenteeism

- Lack of cooperation

- Safety risks and accidents

- Complaints of unexplained aches and pains

Behavioral risk management is a concept whose time has come. We are now moving to a higher level of sophistication in our understanding and management of comorbid claims. Research demonstrating the biological basis of many mental health conditions, advancements in brain imagining and testing, the passage of mental health parity laws, and the lessening of the sigma have all added to breaking down barriers. No longer are we worried about opening "Pandora's box." We know that if there are underlying psychosocial or psychiatric conditions, it is in our best interest to get those identified and treated. We can now move toward true human integration — the integration of the physical and mental.

Resources

Source	Description	Website and Contact Information
Employee Assistance Professionals Association (EAPA)	Employee Assistance Professionals Association is the world's oldest and largest membership organization for employee assistance professionals, with approximately 5,000 members in the United States and more than 30 other countries. EAPA hosts an annual conference, publishes the Journal of Employee Assistance, and offers training and other resources to enhance the skills and success of its members and the stature of the employee assistance profession.	www.eapassn.org 703.387.1000

Employee Assistance Roundtable (EAR)	The Employee Assistance Roundtable is an organization of internally managed employee assistance programs from both private companies and nonprofit organizations. Members include Fortune 100 and Fortune 500 companies, as well as smaller companies and organizations, and include high tech, banking, railroad, oil, utilities, manufacturing, airlines, telecommunications, aerospace, government and educational institutions.	www.earoundtable.com 216.583.1438
EASNA (formerly Employee Assistance Society of North America)	EASNA is a bi-national association whose members consist of individuals, organizations, employers, and students in Canada and the United States interested in advancing knowledge, research, and best practices toward achieving healthy and productive workplaces.	www.easna.org 703.416.0060
Disability Management Employer Coalition (DMEC)	Employer Behavioral Risk Surveys (2006 and 2008) include best practices in innovative behavioral risk.	www.dmec.org 800.789.3632
National Business Group on Health (NBGH)	EAP Request for Information format and guide, part of An Employer's Guide to Employee Assistance Programs (2008)	www.businessgrouphealth.org 202.628.9320
Partnership for Workplace Mental Health (a program of the American	The partnership advances effective employer approaches to mental health by combining the knowledge and experience of the American Psychiatric Association and its employer partners. One of its offerings is the Employer Innovations Online, a list of employer best practices	www.workplacementalhealth.org 703.907.8673

Psychiatric Foundation)	and recent publications on assessing and managing psychiatric disability.	
Yandrick, Rudy M.	Behavioral Risk Management: How to Avoid Preventable Losses from Mental Health Problems in the Workplace	Jossey-Bass- Managed Behavioral Healthcare Library, 1996
Kahn, Jeffrey P. & Langlieb, Alan M. (eds.)	Mental Health and Productivity in the Workplace: A Handbook for Organizations and Clinicians	John Wiley & Sons, 2003

Employer Checklist

To begin the process of integrating behavioral risk/health into your program, the following questions should be answered. After you have ascertained the need and direction, the above list of resources can assist in taking the next steps toward program development and implementation.

Key Questions	Yes/No	Comments
Do you have an existing EAP program?		
Have you ever conducted a behavioral audit?		
Is management open to including a behavioral aspect to your integrated program?		
Do you have a mental health professional on your integrated team?		

Is your EAP or mental health professional open to exploring innovative uses of their services?		
Are there any cultural issues that would preclude implementing a behavioral approach?		
Is your STD, LTD, or WC carrier/TPA open to assisting in the identification of behavioral red flags in claims?		
Are mental health services provided by your health plan or are they a separate carve-out?		
Do you require employees who take a behavioral health leave to be seen by a behavioral health specialist (psychiatrist or psychologist) as requirement for receiving a company benefit?		
Do you have a work culture that supports early return to work/stay at work through temporary accommodations?		

Chapter 7: Disease Management

Basics of Disease Management

As defined by the Academy of Managed Care Pharmacy,[lxv] disease management is the concept of reducing health care costs and improving quality of life for individuals with chronic conditions by preventing or minimizing the effects of the disease through integrated care. Unlike other healthcare management models focusing on individual patient care, disease management is concerned with treating a patient population that is at risk for, or currently dealing with, a particular chronic condition or illness.

A chronic disease is one that is prolonged and that cannot be completely cured. Conditions such as cardiovascular disease, cancer, and diabetes are among the leading causes of death in the United States. In 2013, heart disease topped the list, accounting for 611,000 deaths. Cancer and diabetes were second and seventh, respectively, accounting for a total of 660,000 deaths.[lxvi]

Figure 7.1

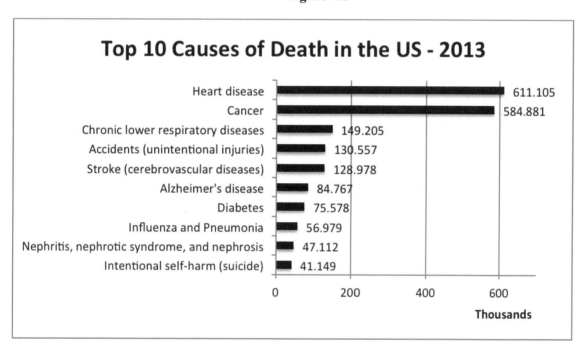

Disease management:

- Supports the physician or practitioner-patient relationship and plan of care

- Emphasizes prevention of exacerbations and complications that utilize evidence-based practice guidelines and patient empowerment strategies

- Evaluates clinical, humanistic, and economic outcomes on an ongoing basis, aimed at improving overall health

Ultimately, the goals of disease management are to:

- Decrease the prevalence of a disease or condition

- Reduce the severity of a disease or condition

- Minimize the risk of medical complications in association with a patient care plan

- Decrease direct and indirect costs associated with a disease or condition

- Decrease the duration of the disease or condition

Assessing the Continuum of Care

Some definitions of disease management imply a focus on managing the disease; therefore, the disease diagnosis is the first step. However, many proponents of disease management would challenge that notion since managing diseases begins with prevention and maintaining health. Therefore, intervention opportunities exist along the entire continuum of care.

Figure 7.2
Healthcare Continuum

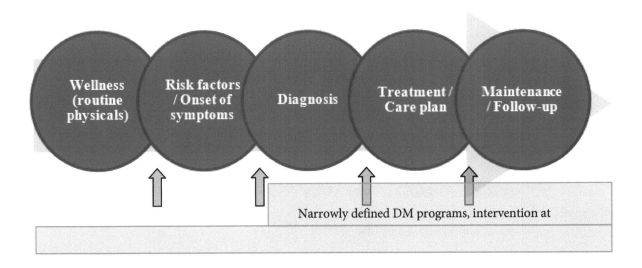

At the beginning of the continuum, techniques such as health risk assessments (HRAs) and predictive modeling are used to identify individuals at risk. This can be done during the wellness state, simply based on certain factors that may not yet be present. When risk factors have been identified but no formal diagnosis has been made, treatment or self-care protocols are established. The ideal result is to reduce the risks and return the patient to a wellness state. If that does not occur, those risks may become a formal diagnosis over time.

At the time of diagnosis, a traditional and aggressive disease management program is engaged to identify self-care initiatives, including provider visits, prescription drugs, treatment plans, and the like. During treatment, patients and provider should routinely be discussing and altering the care plan as appropriate. The treatment plan should reduce the severity of symptoms and allow the individuals to perform at their optimum levels by using evidence-based and clinically driven best practices to increase the likelihood of success.

Evaluating Disease Management Opportunities

Disease management programs were initially designed and developed by healthcare firms looking to contain costs and improve quality of life. Therefore, they identified specific disease states that:

- Have an evidence-based guideline for treatment, thus allowing the opportunity to prevent unnecessary health complications

- Show a high rate of variability in patterns of treatment from patient to patient and from physician to physician

- Disease management seeks to eliminate such variability by applying evidence-based medicine in treating the entire patient population for a particular disease. Care is coordinated across physicians and medical sites to minimize medical errors and ensure continuity.

- Can be managed on an outpatient basis

- Through the use of low-technology, nonsurgical approaches that the health plan can provide, outpatient surgery can be performed at substantially less cost than care rendered on an inpatient basis.

- Yield low rates of patient compliance with recommended treatment

- Intervention programs during treatment of an existing diagnosis can be implemented to ensure compliance.

- Involve a higher rate of preventable complications, some or all of which may result in the use of more costly services, such as emergency department visits and hospital readmissions.

- The biggest opportunity for disease management programs is in avoiding cost escalation through proactive wellness and preventive plans. In its 2007 chronic disease study, the Milken Institute determined that there will be $1.6 trillion in avoidable cumulative treatment costs through 2023 for the seven chronic diseases analyzed.[lxvii] This can be accomplished by reducing or eliminating risk factors such as smoking and obesity.

- Are chronic in nature and are likely to result in high costs over time

- Episodic (one time, infrequent) illnesses could result in high healthcare claims, but these tend not to persist. Chronic conditions, on the other hand, if improperly managed can result in escalating costs as a patient ages and becomes less resilient to disease and/or as additional illnesses arise (comorbidities). Long-term cases not only impact healthcare costs but also disability income claims, prolonging loss of productivity[lxviii]

Over time, disease management has expanded and is now embraced by many organizations, including carve-out providers, health plans, employers, and data warehouse firms. In most instances, they are imbedded or coordinated with the medical plan offering. In addition, economies can be achieved by integrating disease management with other benefits programs, including disability, workers' compensation, family medical leave administration, and other leaves of absence.

The most common disease management programs include:

- Asthma

- Chronic obstructive pulmonary disease

- Congestive heart failure

- Coronary artery disease

- Depression

- Diabetes

- Hyperlipidemia (high cholesterol)

- Hypertension

- Low back pain

- Maternity

- Obesity

- Oncology

Employers usually select a few targeted conditions within their population or subscribe to a global disease management program that covers all disease states within the disease management offering. Generally, small employers opt into an existing disease management offering, whereas mid-sized and large employers may know enough about their populations to identify specific conditions to target those that will have the greatest impact.

Disease management programs are often structured as opt-in or opt-out programs as follows:

- Opt-in: Patients who are targeted receive some type of communication and must actively join the disease management program.

- Opt-out: Selected patients are automatically enrolled in the program unless they actively decline participation.

Proponents of opt-out programs believe it to be best because it targets all patients. Their hope is that even those individuals who are not fully engaged will learn more about their condition and be aware of the resources available, which should have a positive impact over time.

Conversely, those who support opt-in disease management want their program's success to be driven by actively engaged individuals. They prefer not to focus attention and resources (clinical, consultative, and financial) on consumers who will not change their behavior. Although they value education, given that limited resources are available, they want to utilize those resources where they can cause the biggest change in behavior and therefore the disease state.

Regardless of whether the program is opt-in or opt-out, each begins with a communication campaign to targeted members. That communication educates them about their condition and about the tools and support services available. This is usually distributed via U.S. mail to reach the largest audience. From there, users are typically told about any telephonic or online services that support the disease management initiatives. When appropriate, health coaches may be assigned.

Once the communication campaign is received and members identified, the outreach begins. Outreach can be passive (e.g., continued communication pieces) or active (e.g., telephonic call from nurse or personal health coach) and involves both the patient as well as the provider. Depending on the condition and the amount of data tracked, outreach can be triggered by certain events (e.g., office visit, missed prescription refill, hospital visit) or by certain time intervals. Most disease management programs have standard processes in place, but programs can also be customized based on the group.

Critical Components and Barriers to Success

Most successful disease management programs include several key components, which are listed in Table 7.1.

Table 7.1

Components of Disease Management	Examples
Identification of high-cost claims/conditions and high-risk patients	Routine physicals Health risk assessments Screenings
Evidence-based practice guidelines	Institute of Medicine protocols
Collaborate practice models to include physician and support service providers	Provider outreach and education on evidence-based practice guidelines Education on patient self-management Establish partnering relationships

Patient education and empowerment	Health coaching Employee assistance programs Seminars/webinars Literature on preventive programs (e.g., smoking cessation)
Outcome evaluation and reporting	Health informatics Patient-doctor consultations Insurance company notifications and reminders

Great debate exists over the best way to achieve these critical components, but few disagree with their value. Arguably, the three greatest gaps to achieving success are related to: (1) initial identification; (2) patient accountability; and (3) data management.

Initial identification is a challenge for providers, since many patients do not seek care until they experience symptoms. Therefore, in many ways, initial identification is no longer in the hands of primary care providers but instead has been transitioned to employers, who may facilitate annual screenings or HRAs and provide an incentive to participate. Predictive modeling tools, although used by some, do not seem to provide the most effective and actionable results and therefore are usually leveraged after risk factors have been identified in an effort to maintain risks but not truly predict them.

Patient accountability is a struggle for provider and patients alike. Most patients know what they should do to control their risks and/or their disease; however, they may not act on that knowledge. This is easily demonstrated by the prevalence of obesity that exists in this country and abroad, although most understand the value of a balanced diet coupled with moderate exercise.

Data management is also a critical barrier to success. This includes the lack of uniform patient files as well as difficulty assessing the data received from providers to measure results.

The lack of coordinated data poses issues for providers, patients, and employers who value this type of health management. The lack of a uniform standard of tracking and maintaining patient records is a struggle, and although most want to protect patient data, keeping it private is sometimes to the patient's detriment. When providers are not able to easily share information, it can result in over-utilization of care or, perhaps more serious, an underutilization of care.

Many healthcare companies have become experts in data analytics; however, they can only be as effective as the data received. When multiple vendors are used or when additional lines of business are added, employers must often rely on data warehouse firms to coordinate the data appropriately. Without good data, actionable results are not possible; therefore, quality data is critical.

Measuring Return on Investment on Disease Management Programs

The traditional measurement of return on investment (ROI) is in monetary terms. However, disease management challenges the traditional model. Although there are direct and indirect costs that can be used to evaluate the success of disease management, such as healthcare claims, employee absence rates, and disability claims payout, there are also non-monetary variables present, such as a member's behavioral and lifestyle changes. As such, the health industry has been unsuccessful in creating a uniform model. Evidence of success is available, but statistics are not as prominent as stakeholders would like. Therefore, employers and other disease management program sponsors must tailor program objectives and evaluation according to various needs and consider disease management as a long-term investment to attain:

- Decreased direct healthcare costs due to chronic illnesses

- Reduced incidence and duration of disability claims

- Improved return-to-work rates/decreasing absenteeism

- Increased member participation in wellness and preventive initiatives

Disease Management Best Practices

Treatment and care processes for disease management programs vary according to the chronic disease in question. However, all programs should include the following characteristics:

- A holistic approach to patient care. This reinforces the importance of coordinating among various providers and across medical sites as well as managing across the care continuum. Further, a holistic disease management program considers risks presented with comorbidities, when present. Disease management, by definition, standardizes care for a disease across a population, but best-in-class programs recognize the additional risk factors and patient care needs associated with the diagnoses of multiple conditions at the same time.

- Proactive member and provider engagement strategies. The success of disease management requires:

    o Involving employees/plan members and the provider community

    o Aiming for high participation in wellness and preventive programs

    o Providing incentive for completion of health risk assessments

    o Designing health plans to financially encourage wellness visits and screenings

    o Adopting consumer-driven healthcare plan options

    o Structuring provider payment and reimbursement in a way that encourages collaboration

    o Conducting aggressive outreach programs in the provider community

- Analytics. Develop and employ disease modeling to analyze the disease life cycle and determine optimum interventions. Track data over time and establish reporting that provides actionable information. Reviewing data consistently and comparing it against benchmarks assists in tracking global trends as well as progress at the employee level.

Disease Management and Absenteeism

Chronic conditions translate to healthcare costs, disability claims, and loss productivity due to time away from work. In a 2007 research study, the Milken Institute studied seven of the most common chronic diseases (cancer, diabetes, hypertension, stroke, heart disease, pulmonary conditions, and mental disorders) and estimated their direct and indirect costs totaled over $1 trillion in 2003.[lxix]

Although the focus of disease management programs was initially medical costs, studies have proven that absence costs may reap even greater rewards. The links between medical costs and absence costs are easy to identify since employees with non-managed chronic conditions require time away from work due to health issues up to and including inpatient care. However, quantifying the synergy and savings between them is not as simple.

Firms that manage both medical plans and disability plans do support, anecdotally as well as with their data, that a reduction in direct medical costs also has an impact on direct and indirect absence costs. A 2007 study by CIGNA indicated that individuals with integrated medical and disability programs who have taken a short-term disability leave are more likely to return to work. In addition, CIGNA's data indicates that although disability claims make up only about 5% of the population, they represent 37% of the total employee medical costs.[lxx]

In many ways, disease management leverages disability case management techniques but applies them differently:

Table 7.2

Feature	Case Management	Disease Management
Characteristics of patient population	People at high risk for costly, adverse medical events and poor health outcomes	People diagnosed with a specific disease
Methods for identifying patient	Mailed questionnaires; data on use of hospitals and emergency rooms; referrals by physicians using criteria to identify high-risk patients	Data on presence of a particular diagnosis; prescription for certain drugs used to treat a disease; referrals by physicians who treat

		many patients with that disease
Patient education	No standardization of curriculum or educational materials; highly individualized	Standardized curriculum and educational materials for a specific disease
Reliance on evidence-based treatment guidelines	Low	High
Reliance on protocols and standardization	Low	High
Importance of using social support services	High	Low
Importance of engaging family and caregivers	High	Low
Reliance on care coordinator	High	Medium

Source: Based on Best Practices in Coordinated Care (p. 39), by A. Chen, R. Brown, N. Archibald, S. Aliotta, and P. D. Fox, 2000, Contract No. HCFA 500-95-0048 (04). Submitted to Health Care Financing Administration by Mathematica Policy Research, Inc., Princeton, NJ.

Given the direct links, employers should consider the role of disease management within their integrated benefits programs. This may begin with the coordination of data and/or referral services at point of absence intake or during disability or other leave case management. However, building integration through a phased and incremental process is often the best approach.

Employer Checklist

When considering offering a disease management program and linking it to their integrated benefits program, employers should consider the following discussion points and address them systematically.

Key Questions	Yes/No	Comments
Disease Management Priorities		
Does the health plan or plans used by your organization have a disease management program?		
Is the current utilization of your organization's disease management program in line with that of other similarly situated companies?		
Do you feel the existing offering is in line with the level of commitment and desired processes for your organization as it relates to disease management?		
Have employees positively commented on your organization's current disease management program?		
Do you receive data that supports that increased efforts related to disease management will positively impact health costs, disability costs, and/or improve employee wellness?		
Does your organization currently provide any type of risk assessments (e.g., HRAs)? Is an incentive provided for completion?		
Does your current disability plan link with any disease management offering?		
Do you feel your employees would respond positively to a more robust disease management program or one that is part of an integrated benefits program?		

Process Links		
Could your organization's current disability or absence intake process be leveraged to coordinate with disease management? Would this create a more positive employee experience?		
Return on Investment		
Have you attempted to quantify the ROI from a disease management program linked with your health plan or broader integrated benefits program?		
Does your organization's senior management anecdotally agree with disease management and understand its link to health claims and disability incidence/duration?		
Data and Metrics		
Do you currently have health data available to accurately identify target population(s) for disease management?		

Chapter 8: Wellness and Work/Life

Introduction and History

In today's society, where the boundaries between work and home are blurring and employees are finding it harder to find a balance between the two, taking the time to take care of one's self is becoming increasingly difficult. Employers are in a position to help employees achieve a healthy lifestyle through wellness and work/life programs. Encouraging healthy behaviors not only helps employees be more productive and fulfilled in their jobs, but also impacts the morale of the firm, the effectiveness of output, and the overall benefit that an employer experiences.

While wellness programs are still viewed by many as a relatively new concept, they have been around since the 1970s, when the first national conferences on fitness in business and industry were held by the President's Council on Physical Fitness and Sports. Healthcare cost increases over the past decade, however, have spurred wellness program efforts by employers and put them in the spotlight.

Work/life benefits were born out of legislation that offered favorable tax treatment for such programs and are influenced by various social, economic, and demographic trends. The U.S. Revenue Act of 1978 allowed funds for such programs to be excluded from gross income. The various U.S. Internal Revenue Code sections resulted in funding and reimbursement type programs, such as education assistance (IRC Section 127), flexible spending accounts (Section 125), and transportation benefits (Section 132[f]).

Competition has inspired employers to seek ways to help employees work more effectively by providing access to services and tools that allow them to meet personal needs, while minimizing the anxiety that sometimes accompany these activities. Improving overall health has become a similar and coinciding goal, with wellness programs becoming a means to create a positive atmosphere of healthy living. Key concerns causing employers' interest in such programs include a growth in dual-career couples with children, growth in single-parent families, and the projected growth in the share of adults caring for elderly relatives. As work/life demands continue to increase and productivity pressures continue to rise for employers, the value of these benefits is becoming increasingly important.

Program Overview

Wellness and work/life benefits can be defined in many ways and are often explained together, even though they differ in several ways. Wellness programs are health management techniques that promote increased health awareness through employee education and training. Work/life benefits are generally considered extra benefits that employers offer as a way to increase employee economic security and to improve the balance between employee work and life activities. Although the former has more of an educational focus, the latter includes both formal and informal ways of providing compensation other than by salary. Overall, both are viewed as attraction and retention tools, offering methods for employees to not only make their lives easier and healthier, but also to make their time at work more productive.

Recent Developments

Although work/life benefits have been in place for decades, new programs and the infusion of a wellness component are increasing. The concepts of individual health, balance, and improved productivity have become more pronounced. A recent study found that 36% of employers currently offer some sort of wellness program, and of those, 74% also offer one of the following: weight loss programs, gym membership discounts or onsite exercise facilities, smoking cessation programs, personal health coaching, classes in nutrition or healthy living, web-based resources for healthy living, or a wellness newsletter.[lxxi]

When there is an economic downturn, it is important for employers to maintain these programs and resist the temptation to place them in the "luxury" category to be cut. With the added tension in the workplace, it is more important than ever to ensure that employees are at their healthiest and most productive levels, and have tools in place to manage the stress that their environments have brought on to an already "stressed out" population. According to the American Institute of Stress, job stress costs United States businesses an estimated $300 billion per year through absenteeism, diminished productivity, employee turnover, and direct medical, legal, and insurance fees.[lxxii]

In these challenging times, it is important to think of the bottom line: that a healthy and less stressed workforce is a more productive workforce. Doing what you can as an employer to support employees' healthy lifestyles and give them tools to overcome challenges will serve to strengthen your company as a whole.

Strategy for Program Provision

In a time when Americans are working longer hours and technology is forcing 24/7 accessibility while families are still striving to grow, the challenge to balance work and life is becoming more difficult. As the demands on employees add up to high stress levels, employers are adopting programs to help them keep up with it all. By offering an array of programs that range from training programs to commuter benefits to day-to-day convenience services, employers are sending the message that they want to be flexible and help employees to manage their issues. They are also serving their own needs by identifying programs that improve workforce productivity. Other benefits include reduced absenteeism and turnover.

It is first essential for an organization to establish its philosophy around these benefits and then determine where along the spectrum of involvement in work/life programs it falls. On the one hand, certain organizations feel either that the business wins or the personal life wins, but not both. Between these two ends of the spectrum are firms that believe employees and managers need to work together to find ways to meet the needs of both the company and the employee. Management should decide where their balance point lies in that spectrum before designing or selecting programs.

Once an employer acknowledges its position, it should then determine the needs of the employee population in order to develop models and corresponding programs to meet them. Decisions should be based on company available data, focus groups, and/or surveys conducted. They should also incorporate the principles that flexibility is key to any long-term business strategy, and the use of technology, employee self-management, and creative staffing are essential to its success.

Common Program Types and Characteristics

There are many types of wellness and work/life benefits, and, as mentioned, their application can be quite wide ranging. What is most important and most effective for individual employers depends on their particular industry, corporate culture, employee demographics, and competitive nature of recruiting. Described below are some of today's more common programs.

Health Risk Assessments

Often, the first step in determining what kind of programs your workforce requires is to get an idea of their overall current health status. A health risk assessment (HRA) is a questionnaire that can evaluate the health status of individuals and the relative risk of disease, injury, or death associated with specific lifestyle behaviors when combined with specific information about the individuals involved. Some employers have even begun to require that employees fill out an HRA in order to receive certain breaks on their healthcare premiums. A recent survey reported that 33% of firms that have wellness programs provide employees with the opportunity to complete an HRA. That same report indicates that "some" of those employers who request employees complete an HRA offer a financial incentive to employees who complete them. It is difficult to know how many employers are using incentives and/or penalties on their HRAs because of the growing complexity of those incentive programs and the fact they often include other programs in qualifying for an incentive.[lxxiii]

In using an HRA, it is important to make clear to the employees that their information is confidential and is not being used to single any person out as a high-cost claimant or as a potential risk. If employees don't feel sufficiently comfortable to honestly answer the questions provided, then the value of having the HRA in place is lost.

An HRA is a great tool to help employees identify their risks, design a program to address those risks, move forward (often with a health coach or nutritionist, depending on the employer's other wellness offerings), and track their individual progress. Employers also have the potential to use the data on an aggregate basis to get a sense of the health of their employees and then track the progress and financial impact of the specific programs implemented.

Disease Management

Disease management (DM) programs coordinate preventive, diagnostic, therapeutic, and communication measures to provide cost-effective quality care for patient populations who have, or are at risk for, specific chronic illnesses or medical conditions. Since the ideal result of a DM program is to reduce employees' risks and return them to a wellness state, it makes sense that the DM program should work hand in hand with the wellness program. The most common DM programs include asthma, chronic obstructive pulmonary disease, congestive heart failure, coronary artery disease, depression, diabetes, hyperlipidemia (high cholesterol), hypertension, low back pain, and obesity.

Employee Assistance Programs

Employee assistance programs (EAPs) are employer-sponsored services designed to help employees and their families find solutions to personal or workplace problems. These programs can assist with legal or financial issues, childcare or elder care problems, substance abuse, and/or psychological problems. EAPs also address such areas as violence in the workplace and employee harassment. EAP services often are offered online through a website the employee can access and use to call or chat online with service provider representatives for more personalized assistance.

Biometric Screening

Biometric screenings are often offered in conjunction with HRAs, measuring basic health measures, such as blood pressure, body mass index, cholesterol, and blood glucose. Typically, these screenings can be performed with a simple blood test. The test results provide baseline health measurements that can be used to identify risk factors and design a wellness program tailored to the employee. Some employers offer screenings at the workplace either through periodic health fairs, specifically scheduled dates or facility arrangements, onsite health clinics, or some combination of all of these.

Weight Management/Nutrition Education

As most of us are aware, the prevalence of obesity in the United States is high and continues to increase; about 78.6 million adults, or one third of the adult population, are currently obese.[lxxiv] Obesity increases the risks of heart disease, musculoskeletal problems, and many other conditions that also contribute to an employer's claims costs.

Nutrition education programs teach employees the fundamentals of good nutrition and often provide tools, such as food diaries, that employees can use to track their calorie intake as well as other factors to ensure that they are eating healthily. These programs also tailor the plan to an employee's specific health status (e.g., if they are diabetic or have high cholesterol) or even to their lifestyle. If an employee is a vegetarian, requires a gluten-free diet, or just needs healthy meal ideas for themselves and their families that can fit into their busy schedules, assistance is available.

Many companies subsidize such programs as Weight Watchers by paying a portion of the cost to those who participate. Employers can also reinforce participation by tracking meeting attendance and reimburse only those who attend a specified minimum number of meetings.

Fitness Programs

Some larger employers with available space may also be able to provide an onsite fitness facility. Placing this within reach of the employee's workstation definitely creates an ease of use factor and can motivate employees to take action. Many health plans also offer reimbursement for a portion of the cost of a gym membership. Depending on the program, employees may need to provide proof in the form of contracts, payment stubs, or usage reports to verify that they are utilizing their membership enough to receive the reimbursement benefit.

Smoking Cessation Programs

According to the Centers for Disease Control and Prevention, about 42.1 million adults in America smoke cigarettes.[lxxv] Smoking has numerous negative effects on one's health, including increased risk of heart disease, stroke, multiple cancers, and respiratory diseases, as well as pregnancy complications, such as preterm delivery and low infant birth weight.[lxxvi] With taxes on cigarettes continuing to increase, quitting smoking can benefit an employee's fiscal health as well as their physical health.

Personal Health Coaching

Many EAP plans and some stand-alone programs provide personalized coaching in which the employee meets face to face (or over the phone) with a nurse case manager, nutritionist, or other representative who helps them design a program specific to them. Organizations can also hire specialized health coaching services in which the coach meets with the employees initially to develop an all-around individual wellness plan for each employee with periodic check-ins.

Onsite Health Clinics

Onsite health clinics are medical facilities established at an employer work site to help avoid the expense and time off from work incurred by sending employees offsite for routine medical care. In addition to the programs referenced above, they can encompass such services as immediate medical treatment, exams, wellness, job functionality assessment, and return-to-work programs. Providing onsite care does not make sense for every employer, as there would need to be a minimum threshold of employees in a given location to justify the costs of establishing a clinic. Other considerations include the facility itself, buildup and modifications, equipment, and the cost of the medical professionals at the site. Clinic resources and services vary depending on the organization's population and needs. A part-time nurse or dietician on staff might be the best fit for a mid-size organization that only offers health education services to their employees, whereas a jumbo employer providing onsite services to employees and dependents might warrant a full-blown clinic with primary care and pharmaceutical services.

Work/Life Balance

In addition to wellness programs, employers can also offer specific benefits to their employees to help maintain a work/life balance. Some of the more common programs are described below.

Training/Education Assistance

Certain employers offer tuition reimbursement to employees enrolled in continuing education, such as classes leading to undergraduate or graduate degrees or to professional certification or designation. It is not uncommon for these programs to be linked to length of service as well as require supervisor approval for job relevance. They are often offered as a recruiting incentive for new hires as well as a way to increase intellectual capital of the existing workforce. These benefits can be tax deductible as sanctioned under Section 125 of the IRS Code. The code provides for dollar amounts that can be excluded from the employee's gross income and was extended through the Tax Relief Extension Act of 1999 and further through the Ticket to Work and Work Incentives Improvement Acts.

Transportation

Commuter benefits have been rising in importance, especially due to gas price increases, which cause individuals who might otherwise drive to work to consider using public transportation. Part of the U.S. IRS Tax Code Section 132(f) allows employers to offer tax-free benefits for commuting by transit or eligible carpools, qualified bicycle commuting expenses, and paying for commuter parking. Employees can choose the amount to be deducted from each paycheck to pay for their commuter expenses. The deduction is tax free only up to a certain amount, which is determined by the federal government. The amount is set by the employee and can be changed monthly, where the employees are not locked into a onetime elected amount as they are with flexible savings accounts. In 2015, the allowable monthly cap is $130 for transit-related benefits, $20 for qualified bicycle commuting expenses, and $250 for commuter-related parking. [lxxvii]

Flexible Spending Accounts

Governed by U.S. Section 125 of the IRS code, flexible spending accounts (FSAs) allow employees to set aside money for eligible medical, legal, and dependent care purchases. Employees elect a certain amount at the beginning of the year, with the money deducted monthly from the employee's paycheck on a pre-tax basis. As eligible expenses are incurred, employees submit for reimbursement. Some programs offer employees a card that can be used to debit their FSA account, or they can submit their receipts of qualified purchases and co-pays to the FSA manager to be reimbursed later. FSAs are a way of ensuring that employees devote time for getting medical checkups, dental cleanings, and other preventive medical reasons since that money is specifically designated to pay for such things.

Legal Advice and Financial Planning

Employers may offer legal and financial consultative services to help employees plan for needs during their various life stages. These may include legal advice on specific topics (e.g., divorce, adoption, will planning) and financial planning services available through online tools and resources.

Concierge Services

As implied by the name, concierge programs include any kind of convenience service offered to employees. Programs can include flexible schedules, part-time arrangements, telecommuting, errand services (e.g., dry cleaning pickup), and onsite services (e.g., banking), among other things. One situation becoming more common involves employees who are caring for children and an elderly parent at the same time. Concierge programs can provide ways for these employees to continue to work part-time, for example, where they may otherwise have had to quit in order to provide this dual care. Concierge services provide resources and solutions that allow employees to continue their work, while feeling confident that their family issues are being taken care of. Employees gain a sense of security and increased morale from these programs, knowing that employers acknowledge potential difficulties relating to personal and family issues that can take them away from work.

Other programs beginning to be offered more often by employers include dry cleaning and shoe repair; meal services; credit unions; discounted purchasing of computers, cell phones, and travel services; and lactating rooms for nursing mothers.

General Regulatory and Compliance Principles

Wellness programs must comply with ruling 26 CFR Part 54 of the Internal Revenue Code: "Nondiscrimination and Wellness Programs in Health Coverage in the Group Market; Final Rules." Wellness programs that are not subject to these requirements include the following features:

- Reimbursement of all or part of the cost of membership in a fitness center

- Diagnostic testing that provides a reward for participation and does not base any part of the reward on outcomes

- Encouragement of preventive care through the waiver of the co-payment or deductible requirement under a group health plan for the costs of, for example, prenatal care or well-baby visits

- Employee reimbursement for the costs of smoking cessation programs regardless of whether the employee quits smoking or not

- Employee rewards for attending a monthly health education seminar

Wellness programs where "any of the conditions for obtaining a reward [under a wellness program] is based on an individual satisfying a standard related to a health factor" must meet the following requirements to be in compliance with the code:[lxxviii]

- Rewards for other wellness programs, with respect to the plan that requires satisfaction of a standard related to a health factor, must not exceed 20% of the cost of employee-only coverage under the plan.

- The program must be reasonably designed to promote health or to prevent disease.

- The program must give individuals eligible for the program the opportunity to qualify for the reward under the program at least once a year.

- The reward under the program must be available to all similarly situated individuals.

- The plan must disclose in all plan materials describing the terms of the program the availability of a reasonable alternative standard (or the possibility of waiver of the otherwise applicable standard). However, if plan materials merely mention that a program is available without describing its terms, this disclosure is not required.

Selling to Management and Delivery Options

Some employers still find themselves hard pressed to justify the costs of a wellness program without the return on investment to back it up. Every organization calculates and views ROI differently, so it's important to establish what it means for your organization and what information has to be gathered to support an argument for a wellness program. The return on a wellness program is primarily seen in the prevention of future catastrophic costs, and estimating these is not an exact science. Other "soft" savings are seen in increased morale and, while this is hard to measure, the effects could have a significant impact on the productivity of the company as a whole.

As programs become established, more and more statistics are being produced that continue to prove the value of these programs. In Table 8.1 are examples of employer savings.[lxxix]

Table 8. 1

BankOne	Employees who participated in their wellness efforts cost them 18% less in health care expenses than those that didn't.
City of Glendale AZ	While wellness programs were in force, they had practically no rate hikes and three refunds totaling $1 million from the health insurance provider.
Steelcase	Medical claims were 55% lower for participants in their wellness programs over six years.
Standard Telephone	Wellness programs reduced costs for emergency room visits by $23,000 and produced a reduction in health care premiums

Establishing a return figure on the various work/life programs discussed, although important, is less of a focus, as these types of benefits are offered to compete with those of other firms and are viewed as well-justified attraction and retention tools.

In addition to designing effective strategies and corresponding benefits offerings, deciding how to best use technology in the delivery of wellness and work/life programs is important. Likewise, communication of these programs by HR, managers, and supervisors should be strong in order to encourage their use. Ultimately, measuring results and appropriately integrating programs are also key.

Delivery of Services

Technology

Many organizations have implemented online training courses or at least shared educational benefits details available through intranet links. Transportation and FSA account balances can be accessed via the web, thereby encouraging employees to manage their accounts and shifting the administrative burden to the provider. HRAs are often accessed and other services offered are outlined within a firm's intranet, which provides links to the appropriate contacts and resources.

Communication

Part of making these programs available to the workforce is ensuring that employees know about them. Components of an effective communications campaign include frequent and consistent messaging on how to access these programs; clear description of the self-service tools available to employees, managers, and supervisors alike; and an understanding of where employees should go for help. Not all employees are savvy regarding technology-driven programs; therefore, employers need to decide how much to provide in electronic versus hard-copy format. Combining mailing, telephonic, web-based, and manager or supervisor interaction techniques must be sufficient to get the key messages across.

Measuring Results and Integrating Programs

While the employer needs to be tracking results of the program to demonstrate the financial success, the same should be true for the employee to recognize their own success with the program. Seeing reduced risk factors (with the help of visual elements such as charts and graphs) and tracking their progress is often motivation enough for the employee to continue. The employee can see firsthand, in a clear and understandable way, that the steps they're taking toward a healthy lifestyle are paying off.

While wellness programs can prevent many health complications from occurring, a participating employee may already have a disease/condition upon entering the program that is past the prevention point and needs to be managed and monitored. For example, an employee with asthma needs to take steps to minimize asthma attacks by refilling their inhaler prescriptions on time and avoiding or minimizing certain behaviors.

Integrated programs use data gathered in an HRA to design an appropriate wellness plan for the employee and can "soft transfer" directly to the disease management program (including behavioral health and EAPs) for managing that specific condition. Ideally, the wellness and disease management vendors are coordinating and working with the same data to be able to continually evaluate the program to fit the employee's needs.

Best Practices to Consider

In November 2008, DMEC released "Are Your Employees Hitting the Wall?" — an in-depth report addressing the urgent challenges faced by employers to maintain employees' full engagement in their work, while promoting health and wellness and reducing stress. Given economic considerations and job cutbacks that result in high levels of workplace stress, companies need to promote employee health and wellness to maintain optimal productivity — not maximal, which is unsustainable. Employers that fail to meet the challenge risk losing their most precious resource — human capital — to burnout.

In examining the problem of extreme productivity, employers must tailor solutions to their workplace, taking into consideration such factors as the size of the organization, average age of employees, type of work performed, and prevalent health issues.

To mitigate the impact of extreme productivity, companies must be willing to "ask the excellent questions" to discern how best to promote employee health and wellness. For some companies, questions may center on how to build resiliency to help employees handle tough work demands while gaining a sense of control over their lives. For others, it might be how to give employees a greater say in their work and to enhance job satisfaction to reduce turnover and improve morale.

Specific initiatives undertaken by employers representing both large and small companies across several industries showing innovation in this area include:

- GlaxoSmithKline aims to generate optimal productivity while promoting the health of its employees through its Energy and Resilience portfolio of programs and benefits.

- Union Pacific Railroad's comprehensive behavioral health intervention initiative seeks to meet the unique needs of its workforce, a large percentage of which works shifts with irregular hours.

- Crowe Paradis, a benefits advocacy firm, uses a variety of innovative programs to address turnover and motivation within its younger employee base.

- H-E-B Grocery Company, a family-owned retailer, aligns programs and policies with its "culture of caring," which is telegraphed throughout the organization.

- USAA, a financial services company for members of the military and their families, offers the Personal Balance Tool, a web-based resource, to help promote healthier work/life balance.

Regardless of the approach taken, employers of all sizes need to take the initiative to tie the health and productivity of their workforce to wellness and work/life programs that meet the needs of changing demographics and an increasingly supercharged workplace.

Employer Checklist

As employers assess the effectiveness of their existing wellness and work/life programs or seek to expand them as part of their integrated programs, there are several questions they can ask to get started.

Key Questions	Yes/No	Comments
Does your organization offer the following wellness benefits?		
HRAs		
Disease management		
EAP services		
Biometric screening		
Weight management /nutrition education		
Fitness programs		
Smoking cessation programs		
Personal health coaches		

Onsite health services		
Other		
Does your organization offer the following work/life benefits?		
Training/education assistance		
Transportation benefits		
FSAs		
Legal assistance/financial planning		
Concierge services		
Other		
How well are these programs perceived to meet your population needs?		
Do you collect participation data?		
Do you monitor your utilization rates for various services? If so, how do they relate to those of other similarly situated firms?		
Do employees have a way to provide feedback on the programs?		
What is the opportunity to integrate these programs with your disability, workers' compensation, healthcare, and time-off programs currently offered?		
Who are the vendors you currently work with to provide wellness and work/life programs?		

Do any of these vendors also provide or have strategic alliances with your disability, workers' compensation, or group health vendors?		
Do you have the ability to integrate services across other vendors (e.g., disease management, group health, behavioral services, EAPs, etc.)?		
Do you have the capability to run/view reports on usage, costs, or other parameters? Then make key comparative points over time?		

Chapter 9: Group Healthcare

Background and Context

Healthcare financing and delivery systems vary country by country. In most, the main source of funds comes from taxation and Social Security accounts. The majority of the world's developed countries provide universal healthcare coverage, whereby the government holds the greatest share of the responsibility and healthcare is provided regardless of individuals' ability to pay. In the United States, however, employer-based plans are the main source of healthcare coverage for the working population. In 2012, 58.6% of workers aged 18 to 64 obtained health insurance through employers either in their own name or as a dependent.[lxxx] On average, the cost of obtaining insurance is cheaper on a group basis than through the individual market. Group plans take advantage of economies of scale associated with large pools of insured individuals, reducing the cost for each person through risk distribution and greater administrative efficiency. The cost on a group basis, however, is still high and has experienced annual increases in costs that have outpaced the broader cost of living index. Increases in national healthcare expenditure (on a per capita basis) grew 25% for single coverage and 26% for family coverage for the five year period from 2009 to 2014.[lxxxi]

Healthcare continues to be one of the focal points of interest as national healthcare expenditures and the cost of group health plans continue to outpace average inflation. Maintaining the status quo has its advantages, but it is unlikely to curb costs, especially given the current state of the economy and the growing problem of the uninsured. The consequences of medical spending reach far beyond an employee benefit budget line item; they impact an employer's ability to compete in the market due not only to the actual medical costs, which are significantly higher than their global competitors, but also the associated costs of absenteeism and lost productivity when employees are sick and therefore unable to be present and/or productive at work. Medical costs are high profile because they have a clear and undeniable direct cost impact; however, the indirect costs are usually exponentially higher.

History of Employer-Based Group Healthcare

U.S. employer-based health plans find their roots in philanthropy. Hospitals were originally sponsored by religious organizations to provide a service to ill individuals without family. Technological advancement expanded hospitals to treatment facilities and ultimately created the need for prepaid medical care. Born out of the Great Depression, the Blue Cross concept of coverage was originally established for teachers in Texas with a 21-day hospital care benefit linked to Baylor University Hospital. Limitations on wage increases during World War II in the 1940s and the Korean War in the 1950s caused employers to offer benefits in order to hire and retain skilled workers, thus creating the beginning of employer-sponsored benefits. In the United States, Medicare and Medicaid were signed into law in the 1960s, providing care to elderly and indigent patients.

From their start at Baylor, Blue Cross and Blue Shield plans emerged in the 1930s. Blue Cross entities were set up to cover hospital expenditures, while Blue Shield's plans paid for physicians' services on a prepayment basis, with predetermined allowable hospital days or a limit on the dollar amount to be paid for services. Indemnity plans, which reimbursed subscribers for payouts and utilized minimal deductibles and coinsurance, were introduced as supplements to Blue Cross and Blue Shield plans. These were the first form of cost containment, but they failed to avert the escalation in healthcare expenditure over the decades. Costs were driven by a combination of various factors:

- The continual introduction of new technologies;

- New treatments;

- Increased malpractice litigations; and

- Increased frequency and severity in the need for care with the changing demographics and the health status of the population.

In 1973, with the backing of President Richard Nixon, the Health Maintenance Organization (HMO) Act encouraged growth of HMOs and comprehensive care by providing some federal funding. HMOs pioneered the concept of comprehensive benefits with small copayments (e.g., $5) and care management. Prior to HMOs, most plans provided coverage focused on treating illness and disease, not on preventing them. HMOs included preventive health screenings and well visits to primary care physicians at minimal or no cost, in the hope of decreasing illness and treatment needs within a limited network of providers compensated initially on a per-head basis. HMOs and other managed-care derivatives succeeded in providing some relief from cost escalation through utilization review, provider networks, and managed measure of care during the 1990s. This, however, was short-lived, as HMOs gave birth to a consumer detached from the actual cost of care due to the comprehensive benefits provided. Excess utilization continued, as consumers adopted an entitlement mentality that drove demand. Simultaneously, provider contracts under managed care were structured in a manner that rewarded providers for the units of care delivered, as opposed to the quality of care rendered. Various approaches have since evolved (e.g., consumer-driven healthcare and high-deductible health plans), all with an aim of reducing and better managing costs.

History of Non-Employer-Based Group Healthcare

Before the advent of employer-based health, individuals paid for medical expenses out of pocket. In the early 1900s, however, healthcare providers began charging fees at a level that individuals could not easily pay. During his 1901–1908 terms, President Theodore Roosevelt advocated social programs to help the working class pay for healthcare. Roosevelt also made universal healthcare a key component of his 1912 campaign, but as with subsequent proposals for universal coverage, positive backing for the idea withered. The first healthcare financial support for individuals came from privately sponsored, group-based health insurance.

Franklin D. Roosevelt shared Theodore Roosevelt's belief in social insurance programs. Although not leading to universal healthcare, FDR's efforts resulted in Congress passing the Social Security Act of 1935, providing public retirement benefits and unemployment compensation. Upon FDR's death, Harry Truman carried forward FDR's zeal for public health insurance. In 1950, Truman signed an amendment to the Social Security Act, which provided for old-age assistance and served as the foundation for Medicaid. Medicaid has evolved into state-run programs that help low-income families and individuals access healthcare services. Along with Medicare, it was officially enacted as part of the Social Security Amendments of 1965. During the fiscal year 2012, about 16% of U.S. residents were enrolled in Medicaid programs.[lxxxii]

Upon its launch, Medicare provided health insurance to individuals 65 and older. The program was modified in 1972 to include individuals under age 65 with permanent disabilities and people suffering from end-stage renal disease. In 2001, Medicare eligibility expanded further to cover people with amyotrophic lateral sclerosis (Lou Gehrig's disease). In 2011, an estimated 68 million people received healthcare coverage via Medicare.[lxxxiii]

Despite the availability of private health insurance (through employer groups or as individual plans) as well as social insurance programs, a significant part of the U.S. population was not covered. In 2013, 16.6% of the population was uninsured.[lxxxiv] Uninsureds tended to be working-class individuals who did not meet poverty-level definitions (generally defined as earning below the federal poverty level) for Medicaid eligibility, but yet could not afford private health insurance. Uninsureds contributed to the national healthcare expenditure by way of insurance company cost shifting: costs for services provided to uninsured individuals that remain unpaid are redistributed toward pools charged to private payers. Recent reform efforts to the healthcare system are aimed at reducing the numbers of uninsured.

In 2006, Massachusetts enacted a healthcare reform law aimed at reducing the number of uninsured individuals in that state. The law required that all Massachusetts residents have health insurance beginning July 1, 2007, with penalties for noncompliance. To help make this happen, the state's Medicaid eligibility rules were expanded, and the maximum age for dependent coverage was increased up to age 26. The state also made low-cost plans available through the Commonwealth Health Insurance Connector Authority to help eligible individuals pay for certain coverage. Massachusetts served as a case study for reform efforts nationwide. The impact of such legislation to healthcare cost trends remains to be seen.

With the passage of the Affordable Care Act there is consensus that there has been progress in enrolling the formerly uninsured under one of the prescribed plans. However, as with any new social program, the actual number of newly insured is in flux as individuals and local governments learn how to leverage these changes. For example, many who were motivated to enroll in a plan were counted as having moved from uninsured to insured status. However, a significant number of those people were unable to make payments and so have been dropped from coverage. So gauging the actual impact of the ACA is still a "moving target."

Key Features of the Affordable Care Act

Improving Quality and Lowering Health Care Costs
- Free preventive care
- Prescription discounts for seniors
- Protection against health care fraud
- Small Business Tax Credits

New Consumer Protections
- Pre-existing conditions
- Consumer Assistance
- Access to Health Care
- Health Insurance Marketplace.

Benefits for Women
- Providing insurance options
- Covering preventive services
- Lowering costs

Young Adult Coverage
- Coverage available to children up to age 26

Strengthening Medicare
- Yearly Wellness Visit
- Many Free Preventive Services for some seniors with Medicare

Holding Insurance Companies Accountable
- Insurers must justify any premium increase of 10% or more before the rate takes effect

Overview of Plan Options

Medical plan options vary according to the following broad design categories:

- Provider choice and access. Relates to the number, type, and location of the physicians and hospitals contracted by the health plan (its "network"), as well as the degree of ease with which members seek services from any provider of their choosing.

  - Primary care physician (PCP)/referral requirements. HMOs and point of service (POS) plans apply a gatekeeper or referral model, where selection and use of a PCP is required, and referrals to specialists must be obtained from the PCP before a participant is eligible for such benefits. A PCP serves as the main point of contact for all needs relating to an insured member's health, helping to ensure necessity and efficiency of medical treatment and continuity of care. Indemnity and PPO plans do not require PCP selection. The responsibility to coordinate care, therefore, lies with the member.

- Covered services. Most types of plans typically include coverage for the major areas of medical care, such as inpatient, outpatient, emergency visits, skilled nursing, mental illness/substance abuse, and pharmacy.

- Benefit levels. A health plan's benefit design determines how much financial liability the participant assumes in the form of copayments, deductibles, and coinsurance. The greater the degree of a participant's financial liability, the lower the plan's benefit level is considered to be. Copayments, deductibles, and coinsurance liability are to be paid by the participant before a health insurer becomes responsible for the cost of a service. The goal of such cost sharing is to manage a plan's risk, defined by the frequency and magnitude of financial disbursements and the health of its membership population. Copayments are described as fixed dollar amounts and differ for each type of service (e.g., $10 for a routine office visit and $50 for an emergency room visit). Deductibles, also determined as a fixed-dollar figure, are cumulative amounts that can be applied to more than one type of service. For example, a $500 deductible can be applied to inpatient and outpatient treatment, making the member responsible for all charges for these services until the $500 limit is met. Coinsurance is stated as a percentage of total charges (e.g., 20%) and typically does not apply to emergency care. Plans can also apply lifetime benefit maximums, which limit the amount of benefits payable to each insured individual over the course of his or her lifetime.

A summary of the general medical plan designs can be found in Table 9.1.

Table 9.1

Plan Type	Provider Choice and Access	Benefit Levels	PCP/Referral Requirements
Indemnity	No network restrictions	Full indemnification (with minimal cost sharing) of all services	No PCP required No referrals needed
Preferred provider organization (PPO)	Includes coverage for in-network and out-of-network providers	Higher benefit levels are granted for services rendered by in-network physicians and hospitals. Copayments may apply. Out of network includes member coinsurance liability.	No PCP required No referrals needed
Health maintenance organization (HMO)	Strictly defined network, with no benefits paid for out–of-network services	Cost sharing may apply	PCP and referrals required
Point of service (POS) plan	Hybrid of HMO and PPO, in which PCP selection is required, but the plan also provides out-of-network benefits (at a lower level than for in-network). Referrals are required for in-network but not for out-of-network services.		

Open access plan	The newest type of network-based plan. Combines HMO and PPO plan features, in which members are restricted to providers in an HMO or POS network, but PCP selection and referral requirements are removed. Open access plans do not cover out-of-network services.

Consumer-Driven Healthcare

The latest efforts to curb plan costs and address the detachment of consumers from healthcare costs have incorporated consumer-driven healthcare (CDHC) strategies that impose more fiscal responsibility for care decision making onto plan participants. This is primarily done through higher deductibles or larger coinsurance sharing. High-deductible health plans (HDHPs) can be designed on any network platform (e.g., PPO, HMO). The theory goes that with added financial incentive, members will make better and more cost-effective healthcare decisions, thus reducing the utilization of unnecessary services. To support members in the decision making process, insurers and plan sponsors provide education and resources to help ensure that members seek appropriate care. Further, health reimbursement accounts and health savings account can be coupled with an HDHP, allowing members to save and accumulate healthcare funds on a tax-advantaged basis.

While CDHC's prospect for succeeding in managing cost creates optimism, supporters need to be aware of a potential adverse effect it can have on patient health. There is evidence suggesting that patients enrolled in consumer-driven plans are more likely to skip medications, presumably to save money, than those in traditional plans.[lxxxv] When a member's deductible and cost share is set so high that it becomes economically unfeasible, the member may decide to forgo needed services. Such a case could lead to deterioration in the member's health, likely requiring even more (and more expensive) services in the long run.

Coordination with Other Health Offerings

A comprehensive health plan includes coverage for prescription drugs and mental health/substance abuse services. Prescription drugs make up about 15% to 20% of a health plan's overall cost. Benefits are designed to incorporate the same cost-sharing techniques — copays, coinsurance, etc. — as are utilized for medical costs. A plan establishes a formulary, or a list of prescription drugs that are covered under the plan. These drugs are sorted into tier structures: generic versus brand name drugs. (A plan may have three tiers: generics, preferred brand name, non-preferred brand name.) Plan members pay a lesser copay for generics than for brand names as the plan encourages members to utilize the lower-cost prescription.

Other cost-containment efforts include negotiating discounts and rebates with pharmacy benefit managers, using pharmacy benefits administrators, and employing utilization and managed measures similar to the methods of an HMO. An employer or other plan sponsor may also decide to carve out pharmacy benefits and contract with a specialty pharmacy benefit manager that is equipped to more efficiently manage prescription drug costs than the manager of medical claims.

Likewise, the carve-out option is available for mental health/substance abuse services or behavioral health. The prevalence of mental illness has spawned a subindustry of specialized management services. Carve-out plans have been reported to decrease behavioral health costs by as much as 40%. The need for specialized management stems from the growing prevalence of mental illness among the American population. It is estimated that 26.2% of the U.S. population aged 18 and older suffer from a diagnosable mental health disorder, such as depression, anxiety, and schizophrenia, in any given year.

Some health plans may also provide integrated benefits for vision care services. Vision care benefits come in the form of eye examinations and discounts on frames/hardware and lenses. Carve-out vision plans utilize network restrictions. Providers within a plan network include ophthalmologists, optometrists, opticians, and retail stores (e.g., Walmart, LensCrafters).

Dental coverage is common (and is more commonly designed as a stand-alone product than integrated with health): an estimated 156 million Americans have dental insurance. As with prescription drug plans, dental plans tier benefits according to types of services. Type 1 includes diagnostic and preventive services (e.g., x-rays and routine oral examinations); Type 2 includes anesthesia and basic restoration, as in removal of decay and installation of fillings; Type 3 services cover major restoration, including surgery. Orthodontics coverage, considered a Type 4 service, may also be offered. Benefit levels are stated in coinsurance amounts according to the plan's share of the costs; for example, 100/80/50 indicates the insurer will provide full coverage of Type 1 services, 80% coverage for Type 2, and 50% for type 3. A copayment (typically of $25 or $50) can be applied, excluding Type 1 services.

Medical Management in Group Health

Medical management encompasses various strategies and processes that together work toward the goal of ensuring that health plan members receive appropriate, high-quality care in the most cost-effective setting and manner. It seeks not only to treat conditions as they arise, but also, and more important, to identify the risk of disease and implement a preemptive healthcare program to decrease the likelihood or severity of onset. Medical management includes the broad categories of clinical practice management, quality management, and utilization management. The first deals with the parameters of healthcare delivery to plan members. The second, quality management, is the process of measuring and improving the quality of healthcare and services provided to plan members. The third, utilization management (on which we focus our attention), seeks to control the frequency and level of healthcare that members seek to those that are necessary and in the most cost-effective setting (e.g., outpatient setting versus hospitalization).

Utilization Management

Utilization management (UM) incorporates member behavior and decision making, and impacts all types of care services, including primary care, emergency care, specialty care, hospitalization, and pharmaceuticals. UM's primary concern is to manage the supply and demand for healthcare services (reducing the incidence of both over-utilization and under-utilization) as well as the incidence of inappropriate care. Techniques employed by insurance companies and managed care organizations (MCOs) involve plan design requirements that restrict access to services. These include:

- Pre-certification (also known as prior authorization or pre-authorization). Managed care organizations require that a physician or hospital seek permission from the MCO before certain services are rendered. The MCO defines what these services are; they commonly include inpatient hospitalization, behavioral healthcare services, outpatient procedures or surgeries, and home healthcare services. Emergency room visits are generally excluded. Should a request be denied by the MCO, members are generally provided the opportunity to appeal the decision.

- Prospective (utilization) review. In a prospective review, the insurance company or MCO requires that a healthcare provider disclose a patient's recommended inpatient treatment plan to a professional employed by the insurer/MCO in order to analyze the appropriateness of the care recommended and to ensure that it is in line with clinical best practices. Based on the review, the professional may recommend a different course of action and submit these findings to the insurer/MCO.

- Concurrent (utilization) review. When a member is hospitalized, a case manager employed by the insurance company monitors the member's ongoing treatment and care plan to ensure alignment with clinical best practices and cost effectiveness. The review process is conducted by a nurse who, via telephone, may request information about a member from the clinician assigned to the member. It can also be performed by a physician located at the hospital and paid by the insurer/MCO. The physician would be looked upon to coordinate all the elements of a member's care plan to eliminate overlaps and to fill gaps in care, with the goal of influencing a better outcome at the lowest possible cost.

- Discharge planning. When appropriate, an insurer/MCO facilitates a member's transfer from the hospital to an alternative (less costly) care setting. Discharge planning begins once a member is admitted to the hospital and extends from information gathered in the concurrent review process.

- Retrospective (utilization) review. The insurer/MCO may have a review of a patient's treatment conducted after its completion. The main purpose of the retrospective review is to identify variations in the care provided to a member from best-practice guidelines. A high number of incidences of variation attributed to a physician, hospital, or healthcare provider can raise a flag for the insurance company to further investigate the practices of that provider.

Case Management

For a member with high-risk care needs (involving complex or catastrophic illness or injury), high-cost and/or care needs that involve chronic conditions, an insurer/MCO utilizes case management techniques to develop a comprehensive healthcare strategy to meet those needs, coordinate care among all various services and providers involved, and monitor the progress of care delivery. The case management objectives are intended to:

- Improve or stabilize the member's health status by avoiding complications from a given service or medical procedure and alleviating existing conditions and/or symptoms

- Ensure alignment of the care plan with clinical best practices

- Optimize the use of healthcare resources through planning and utilizing the most cost-effective options

- Improve integration among all service providers to minimize error

- Ensure continuity of care

Disease Management

Where case management focuses on an individual patient, disease management (DM) focuses on a patient population diagnosed with, or at risk for, a specific chronic disease. Additionally, DM handles the full continuum of care over time — from risk identification to prevention and throughout treatment, once diagnosed. Case management, on the other hand, applies only to each treatment episode.

The premise of disease management is that a chronic illness can be improved through medical intervention early in the disease process and maintained over the life of the patient. It is a proactive approach to treatment of chronic illness. It is difficult to quantify the total cost of direct medical care for the top chronic conditions because many people suffer from more than one condition. However a 2010 study found that 86% of all healthcare spending was on people with one or more chronic conditions while 71% was on people with multiple chronic conditions.[lxxxvi] The disease management treatment approach uses best practices, clinical practice improvement, clinical intervention, outcomes research, information technology, and other tools and resources to reduce overall costs and improve health outcomes. (Chapter 7 reviews disease management in depth and discusses its role in integrated disability management strategies.)

Developments in Medical Management Efforts

As indicated above, although the rate of increases in healthcare costs has decelerated, the rate still outpaces general inflation. As such, development efforts continue to find ways to contain costs and improve the health of the population. Following are brief descriptions of current developments in pay-for-performance and healthcare transparency initiatives, e-medical records, and predictive modeling.

Pay-for-Performance/Healthcare Transparency

Government leaders, insurance companies, managed care organizations, employers, and other stakeholders recognize that to achieve optimum healthcare quality and truly help the population become educated healthcare consumers, provider incentives must be structured in such a way that a portion of payments to providers is based on predetermined performance standards. The standards reflect actions and metrics that have been determined to be causally related to health objectives; for example, requiring that 100% of pneumonia patients are counseled about smoking cessation. Further, provider performance would be transparent to the population. Methods such as provider rankings for quality in certain surgical procedures can be used by those seeking such services to ensure they receive care from the best.

E-Medical Records

Another solution being pursued to reduce medical error is for providers to develop and exchange patient information via electronic medical records. The goal with e-records is to optimize continuity of care from one provider to the next, offering the most up-to-date information on the patient's history, existing conditions, current medications taken, etc. If successful, e-records can minimize or eliminate duplicate and/or unnecessary care and influence positive health outcomes, thus reducing expenditures in the long run and even saving lives.

Predictive Modeling

Predictive modeling is a tool used to predict a person's risk factor for a certain disease. Modeling systems are utilized by insurance companies, managed care organizations, and large self-insured plans. Modeling systems analyze such information as a person's demographic profile (e.g., age, gender), clinical data (e.g., diagnosis), and health habits/lifestyle information based on available health risk assessments and other data-gathering surveys/questionnaires. By conducting predictive analysis, the insurance company, MCO, or plan sponsor can intervene in the disease path at the prevention stage or post diagnosis to provide the predictive modeling user information that can be used to optimize a care plan for a member.

Trends in Group Healthcare Benefits

To remain competitive in the labor market, employers must keep abreast of the latest trends in group health benefits in terms of types of plans offered by other (peer) companies and the level of employer contributions to plan premiums. There has been a trend in increased employee cost sharing, as illustrated in Figure 9.2 from the Kaiser Family Foundation's (KFF) 2005 Health Benefits Survey,[lxxxvii] which provides average plan deductibles by type of plan, from 1988 to 2005.

Figure 9.2
Trends in Employee Cost Sharing

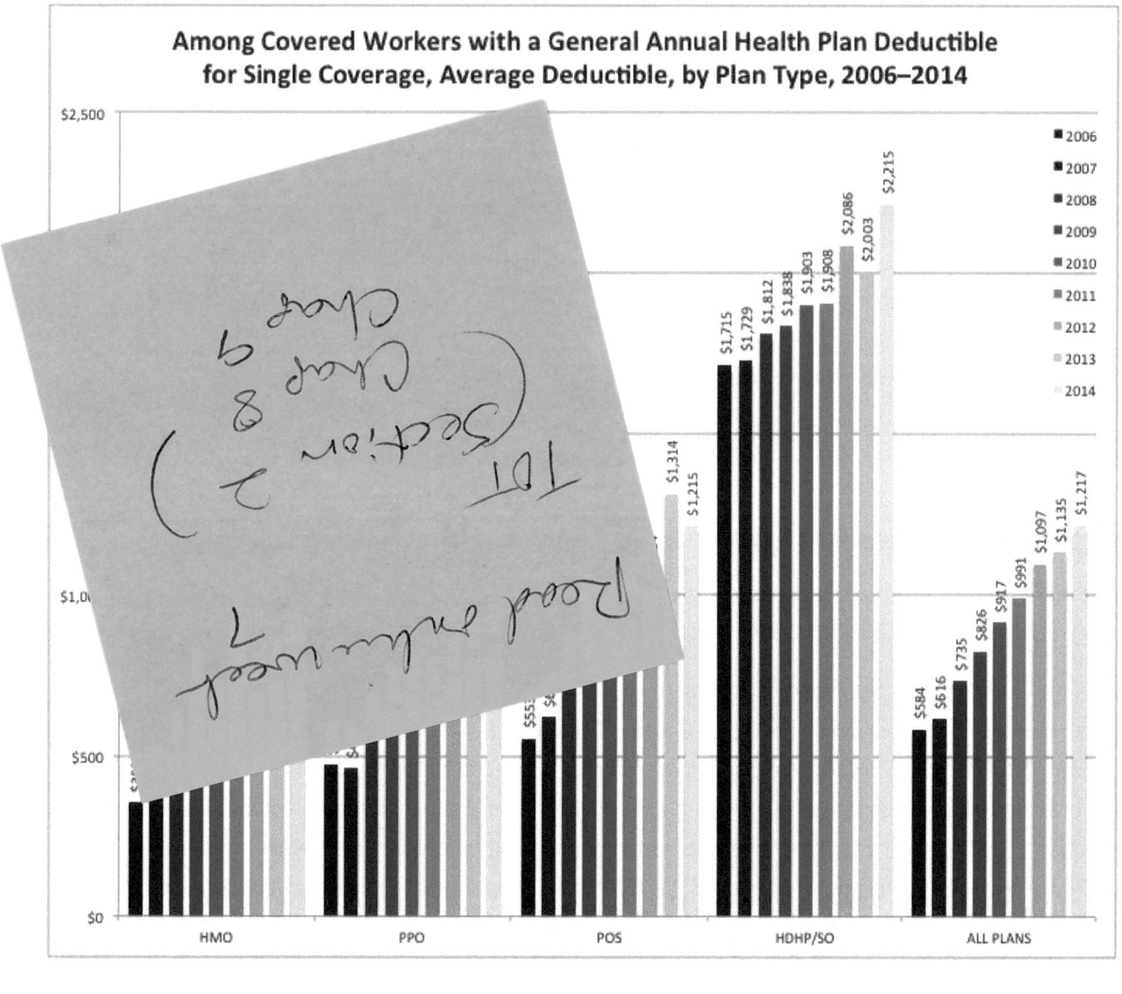

Source: Kaiser/HRET Survey of Employer-Sponsored Health Benefits, 2006–2014

The prevalence of health reimbursement accounts and health savings accounts (with high deductible plans) has also been increasing. In its 2014 annual health benefits survey, KFF reported that 27% of employers surveyed offer an HDHP with a health reimbursement account or HSA. This is a 23 percentage point increase from the prevalence rate in 2005, when just 4% of employers reported that they offered such plans.[lxxxviii]

Work Site Wellness Programs

Employers are increasingly adopting work site wellness programs, such as health risk appraisals/assessments, onsite screenings, health coaches, and smoking cessation, to promote disease prevention, encourage healthy lifestyles, and empower employees as they own more of their healthcare decisions and financing. The top five wellness programs (with 2008 and 2007 prevalence rates) implemented in 2008 are shown in Table 9.3.[lxxxix]

Table 9.3

Wellness Program	% of Companies Offering Program in 2008	% of Companies Offering Program in 2007
Promoting physical activity	68%	19%
Disease management programs	60%	18%
Health risk appraisals	48%	14%
Biometric screening	47%	12%
Telephonic healthcare coaching	46%	14%

The increase in prevalence rates for these programs over just one year is significant and a testament to employers' great concern for healthcare costs. Of course, for wellness programs to accomplish their purpose (ultimately, to decrease healthcare costs), employees must participate. Corporations have looked to financial incentives to drive participation. Approximately 19% of employers have established incentive programs, including health insurance premium reductions (offered by 8% of employers), reduced deductibles (1%), increased contributions to an HSA/HRA (2%), and cash or other gift incentive (offered by 14% of companies). The percentage of companies offering an incentive increases dramatically when only companies with 200 or more employees are counted (36%).[xc] Companies can also drive participation by establishing financial disincentives, such as imposing a penalty for non-participation in the form of a health insurance premium surcharge. In 2012, 15% to 22% of employers utilized penalties, with 36% to 58% of employers saying that they are potentially instituting penalties within the next three to five years.[xci] See also Chapter 8 for more on wellness and work/life.

Expanding Beyond Medical Management: Integration

With the aging population, the current state of the economy, and the increasing competition over skilled employees globally, group health benefits and the size of the national healthcare expenditure will continue to be major topics in the years to come. Expect ongoing growth of consumer-driven healthcare and complementary preventive and wellness programs, further developments in pay-for-performance incentives and healthcare transparency, and enhancements in predictive modeling and other risk assessment tools for identifying opportunities to intervene in high-cost disease paths and implement proactive care solutions for patients/plan members. In addition, prudent employers are examining the synergies between medical costs and other business expenses, most notably absence and productivity.

The employee benefits community broadly accepts the theory that 20% of the population generates 80% of the medical "spend," referred to as the Pareto Principle, or the "80-20 Rule." Therefore, the key in terms of group health management is to pinpoint the 20% and manage their health. Over time, data has supported that this 20% is also significantly impacting absenteeism costs in the form of disability, workers' compensation, family medical leave, vacation or other paid time off, unpaid leaves of absence, and, perhaps most important, missed production. The term health and productivity management can be applied differently by various organizations, but the root is the same: reduced health results in reduced productivity. The two are intertwined and must be analyzed in tandem for the greatest result. As such, employers and vendors are turning to the integration of group health with health management initiatives such as wellness, EAP and behavioral health, and disease management programs. As described in Chapter 1 of this guide, they are then looking to expand their integration by coordinating short-term disability and group healthcare management as a way to impart change.

Given this, employers must have consistent messages within their medical program and disability program, including coordinated referral processes, communication messages, and return-to-work protocols. In addition, claims must be managed with a similar degree of aggressiveness, and vendors should have open dialogues regarding trends. Although results should be realized regardless of data mining, without appropriate data integration, they will be anecdotal.

Value-Based Healthcare

Initiatives such as consumerism, wellness programs, provider transparency, and pay-for-performance, executed in coordination with one another, create a system of value-based healthcare: a model in which patients are encouraged to "shop" for the most cost-effective care option and providers are rewarded under a merit-based system that pays for the quality of the outcome (and not for the volume of services provided).

Debate continues among policymakers, providers, insurance leaders, and advocacy groups with regards to reforming the U.S. healthcare system to tackle its threat on the nation's finances. Healthcare expenditure has been increasing as a percentage of the U.S. gross domestic product, amounting to 17.2% in 2012, up from 15.9% five years earlier and from 13.4% in 2000.[xcii] Healthcare spending under Medicare will exert a great amount of pressure on the national budget as population ages, baby boomers retire, and the general cost continues to rise. Value-based healthcare will minimize waste and unnecessary services, which could contribute to a stabilization in healthcare costs.

While it is anticipated that the Affordable Care Act will have some mitigating effect on either slowing or possibly reducing overall health care costs, it is too soon to tell to what extent that may be true.

Conclusion

Group healthcare involves a complex system of medical, financial, legal, and social components. The historical environment of healthcare has been one that has focused on affordability, beginning with efforts to relieve individuals of the high cost of care first via group plans and then with social insurance. As costs have spiraled, group plan sponsors, such as employers and payers/insurance companies, have sought in earnest ways to contain healthcare expenditure by eliminating unnecessary care and improving health outcomes. During certain periods of the late 20th century, medical management strategies succeeded in decelerating the rate of annual cost increases. Now hopes ride on the effectiveness of consumer-driven healthcare via a combination of financial incentives, outreach, and educational support to extend cost efforts all the way to individual decision makers.

The healthcare picture is further made critical due to the pool of uninsured, which includes children. State reform efforts are centered on ways to extend access to needed care. With the advent and ongoing roll out of the Affordable Care Act, and its growing impact on health care costs, count on healthcare remaining at the forefront of social and economic concern.

Resource

Source	Description	Website and Contact Information
Center for Health Value Innovation	A collaborative community of stakeholders, led by employers of all sizes and sectors, who are improving health status while reducing total cost trends using value-based designs. Members learn and share as a community of thought leaders, as a knowledge resource, and as innovators for new trends.	info@vbhealth.org 12545 Oliver Blvd., Ste. 232 St. Louis, MO 63141

Employer Checklist

To audit your plans, you should consider the following key questions to determine how your group health plan tracks with some of the more recent trends.

Key Questions	Yes/No	Comments
General Structure		
Do you feel your group health offering ties to your overall corporate philosophy for employee benefits?		
Are employees and their dependents satisfied with your organization's group health offering?		
Do you offer enough choices to meet the needs of your organization's employees and their dependents?		
Medical Management		
Has your organization taken any steps to improve your medical management techniques?		
Are your organization's medical management practices in line with peer companies? If not, why?		
Does your organization leverage risk assessments for your population? Do you feel your employees would respond positively to them? If not, what changes could you make in order to net a positive result?		
Data		
Does your organization monitor your utilization rates for various services? If so, how do they relate to other similarly situated firms?		

Is your organization able to collect data to support
health and wellness initiatives? If not, why? If yes,
does the data demonstrate a positive impact on group
health?

Is your organization currently linking group health
data with other employee benefit data? If not, have
you considered this approach?

Integration

Has your organization explored the advantages of
integrating group health with disability
management?

Does your organization currently partner with
vendors that could support an integrated approach?

Chapter 10: Voluntary Plans

Background and Context

Disability benefits provide a major foundation for integrated programs, with approximately 68% of employers offering short-term disability (STD) and 80% offering long-term disability (LTD).[xciii] The nature by which these benefits are offered can vary and is deeply tied to an organization's overall human capital strategy. The most common method is to provide disability benefits on a group basis, whereby the employer offers them as part of the overall benefit package and pays for all or at least part of the premium on behalf of the employee. Another route is to offer them on a voluntary basis, whereby the employer sponsors the program offering, but the employees make the purchase decision and pay the cost with their own dollars. Some employers elect to combine both approaches; for example, providing STD on a group, automatic, and fully employer-paid basis and LTD on a voluntary basis in which employees choose whether to purchase and fund the entire premium themselves. Still other combinations exist, such as coordinating a portion of an LTD program (e.g., 50%) to be offered on a group basis with an additional 20% buy-up available on a voluntary basis. Whatever the strategy, voluntary benefits have grown over the years and are expected to increase, given the continued pressure on healthcare costs and the recent economic downturn.

Voluntary Benefit Plan History and Growth

As healthcare costs continue to increase, employer-paid benefits have become an issue of major concern. In private industry (excluding state and local agencies), employers averaged $9.60 for benefits or 30.6% of total compensation in December 2014 to provide benefits to their employees.[xciv] Many employers are struggling and facing difficulties to remain competitive in offering comprehensive benefit packages to their employees. As we enter period of uncertainty about employer borne healthcare costs, many employers are moving toward passing any increased costs on to employees. Others are turning to voluntary benefits as a means to continue offering differentiated benefits while also maintaining the ability to attract and retain employees without spending a lot of money.

Voluntary benefit plans have been in existence for many years and are becoming more popular as the economy has become more unstable and challenging for both employers and employees. The view of voluntary benefit plans as being "nice to have" has shifted to "strategically necessary." Since 1997, premium dollars spent for voluntary benefit plans have increased significantly. In 2014, premiums amounted to an estimated $6.89 billion, a 3.7% increase from just the year before..[xcv] Figure 10.1 illustrates the growth of voluntary benefit plan premiums spent each year since 2004.

Figure 10.1

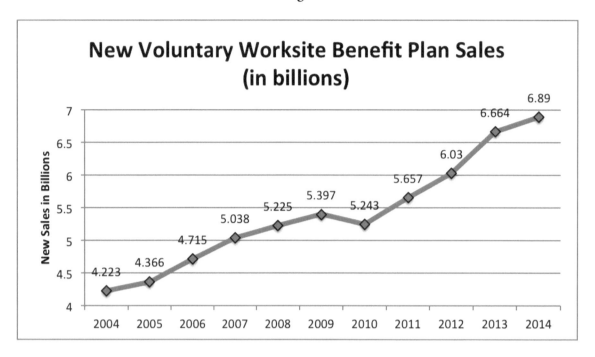

Source: Eastbridge Consulting Group. (2015). Another Good Year for Voluntary Sales. Benefits Selling, June 2015. (http://www.eastbridge.com/news/Artlcle/2015/06.15_What's_Next.pdf)

According to MetLife's study of employee benefit trends, "41% of employers cite providing a wider array of voluntary plans as an important benefit strategy. At the same time, 51% of employees are interested in their companies offering a wider array of voluntary benefits, remaining steady when compared to 52% of employees expressing that opinion in the previous year."[xcvi]

Range of Programs Available

Today, employers are faced with selecting and determining the appropriate voluntary benefit plans for their employees. Voluntary options range from traditional "core" benefits, such as disability, life, vision, and dental to nontraditional, "noncore" benefits, such as long-term care, critical illness insurance, financial planning, auto insurance, homeowner's insurance, pet insurance, and identity theft insurance.

In 2014, the most popular voluntary plan offered by employers was life insurance. Figure 10.2 illustrates voluntary benefit plans offered by employers with the bars and the new sales of voluntary benefit plans with the line. As you can see, with the exception of vision plans, new employers are adding the same voluntary plans that employers now currently offer.

Figure 10.2

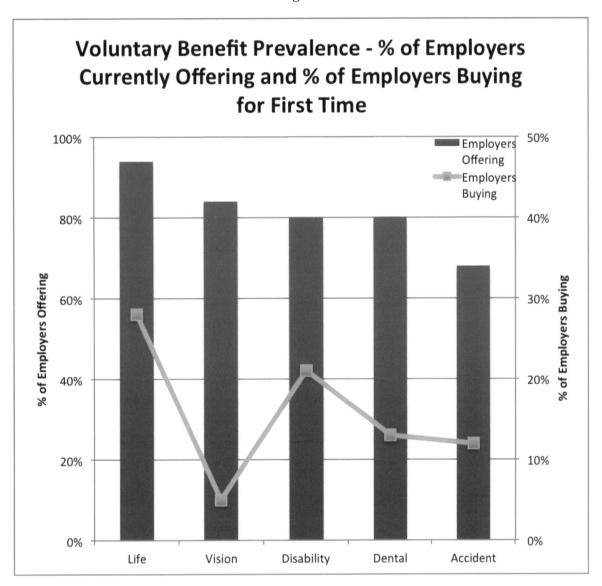

Source: BenefitsPro. (2013). Five Most Popular Voluntary Benefits
http://www.benefitspro.com/2013/08/14/5-most-popular-voluntary-benefits?t=voluntary&page=6 and
BenefitsPro. (2014) "8 things to know about voluntary sales," http://www.benefitspro.com/2014/10/27/8-
things-to-know-about-voluntary-sales

Disability insurance provides a certain level of income to employees who meet the companies' definition of disability. Due to the nature and complexity of each employer, there is no standard definition of disability. If an employee becomes disabled on the job or as a result of a workplace injury, the employer provides the employee with income while they are absent from work. Most frequently, disability insurance covers between 60% and 66% of the employee's base salary. Employees tend to elect voluntary disability insurance to provide additional protection through a "buy-up" voluntary disability program.

Similar to disability insurance, life insurance is a very popular voluntary benefit plan that employees want from their employer. In the case of a predicted or unpredicted accident, income payments are provided to the employee's family or beneficiaries. As with disability insurance, employees tend to purchase additional life insurance through a voluntary benefit program sponsored by their employer.

Vision coverage is considered a traditional voluntary benefit plan that employers offer to their employees. Like all voluntary benefit plans, coverage for the employee is offered at both the individual and family levels. Employers typically package a vision service plan with their medical/health plan and their dental plan. Standard and common vision benefits are defined by a regular eye exam once every 12 months and glasses or contacts once every 24 months. This voluntary benefit plan usually includes an office copayment and annual deductible amount. As you can see from the chart above, vision plans are very popular in the marketplace but appear to have somewhat saturated the market as new sales place it a distant 5th among the top five benefits.

Similar to vision, dental plans are also considered an important and traditional voluntary benefit plan. Standard dental plans are designed to include office copays and an annual deductible amount. Most plans are uniquely structured to include coverage for preventive services, basic restoration services, major restorative services, and orthodontic services.

Not shown, but reasonably prevalent in the marketplace are the following very common voluntary benefits.

Long-term care (LTC) protects individuals of all ages from financial hardships due to chronic, long-term, or non-remedial physical or mental conditions. As the workforce age continues to rise, employees are looking more and more to their employers to purchase long-term care as a voluntary benefit. According to the U.S. Department of Health and Human Services, research shows that at least 70% of people over age 65 will require some long-term care services at some point in their lives.[xcvii] Employees tend to look to their employers to provide a LTC voluntary benefit plan that employees can purchase at a reduced rate rather than going to the market at an individual level.

Critical illness coverage has become another popular, yet nontraditional voluntary benefit plan. Critical illness insurance provides medical benefits for specifically defined illnesses. The terms and conditions of these policies vary with each employer. Typically, coverage must be purchased before any diagnosis is made. Critical illness insurance plans vary from one insurance carrier to the next but can, for example, provide the employee with a lump-sum benefit upon diagnosis of a critical illness or condition. Providing this lump sum allows the employee to make other necessary monthly expense payments.

The need for financial planning has significantly increased as employees have been forced to accept more responsibility for their own financial future and retirement income. Large, medium, and small companies have shifted from defined benefit plans (in which employee benefit amounts are based on a formula) to defined contribution plans (in which employee benefits are specific amounts or percentages), and the establishment of individual 401(k)s has grown from year to year. Employees are searching for additional advice from their employer to help comfort them in a time of uncertainty. Employers typically offer guidance and financial planning voluntary benefit plans in the form of access to financial planners, use of specific financial planning software, or voucher programs that allow employees to seek their own advisors and to have a certain portion of their costs reimbursed. Some employers have resorted to sponsoring seminars and expos on the weekend, which provides an opportunity for employees to educate themselves on the financial resources available.

With auto and homeowner's insurance, employees have the advantage of being underwritten and rated on a group basis. The plans are generally similar to the terms and conditions that an individual is able to obtain; however, carriers are interested in this format because of the direct access to employees as a potential new customer base.

Pet insurance has become available more recently and is usually purchased for an employee's dog or cat. Similar to other voluntary benefit plans, pet insurance is commonly paid through monthly or annual payments. Aetna states that, "More than 60% of American households have a beloved pet and spend approximately $10 billion a year in veterinary care. Insurance provides valuable financial protection, and we know that more than half of the consumers and our own members surveyed find it appealing for us to offer pet insurance."[xcviii] As the economy continues to decline, employees are looking for alternate solutions for savings with their disposable income and their pets. Employees would rather spend monthly premiums over 12 months instead of a one-time four-figure check for an accident.

Employers offer identity theft insurance to provide employees with a sense of security and comfort. Specific features of identity theft insurance include lost wages as a result of time away from work, mailing costs, phone costs, notary costs, fees for loan applications where denials have been made, and additional attorney fees. Identity theft has become a popular voluntary benefit plan as the risk to individual personal information has risen. In 2005, 8.3 million U.S. adults discovered that they were victims of some form of ID theft (including credit card information, social security information, and health, medical, and dental plan information).[xcix]

Voluntary Disability Plan Mechanics

Voluntary disability plans can reflect the same type of benefit percentage options as typical group plans but have a number of differentiating features.

Voluntary benefit plans are employer-sponsored versus employer-provided, which means that employers take the time to research potential companies and work closely with them to design and develop specific products to cater to their employees. Employers look to provide their employees with reputable and financially strong companies and proactively measure the success of their programs every 12 to 24 months to ensure employees are getting the most out of the sponsored plans. Employees feel confident that their employers have properly screened these carriers before implementation and are thus made comfortable purchasing the voluntary benefit plan.

Most of the time, voluntary benefit plans are focused toward full-time benefit eligible employees. However, as employers deem necessary and appropriate, they offer voluntary benefit plans to part-time and temporary employees as part of their strategy to secure ad hoc employment within their workforces.

As voluntary benefit plans have evolved, the shift from large employers to medium and small employers has become more evident since every organization is faced with an unpredictable market and economy. Voluntary benefit plans have become more defined and complete over time, and the theory of a "one size fits all plan" has provided increased flexibility with voluntary benefit plans.

Voluntary programs may be incorporated into an employer's normal open enrollment process but are more often than not conducted off cycle and through a focused effort. Employers invite their selected carriers to hold group meetings with their employee base in order to describe the products and provide an advisor to answer questions before employees make their selections. Other enrollment methods include one-on-one telephone calls between employees and benefits experts, and web-based enrollment and resources.

When it comes to payment, the employer collects premiums from the employee by way of payroll deductions. Because employee payments are made on a pre-tax basis, the benefit received by the employee is not taxed. The employer in return pays the insurance carrier a lump sum or a monthly premium, depending on how the program is designed and structured.

Voluntary disability plans, although offered to individuals, are typically underwritten on a group basis. Rates are traditionally based on the size of the employer and its respected industry, thus resulting in affordable and group rates. The insurance carrier does not collect health information or financial information on the individuals purchasing the coverage. Therefore, certain employees who may not have been eligible to purchase coverage on their own will be offered it through their company's voluntary program at a reduced rate.

Last, but very important, most voluntary benefit plans are portable. In this sense, individuals who are covered can continue their coverage after leaving the company. Employees find portability an important feature when employers are determining the structure of the voluntary benefit plans.

Integrated Program Considerations

Voluntary benefit plans play an important role for employers when attracting and retaining key employees. Smaller companies are being driven to offer more voluntary benefit plans to attract and recruit employees from the larger and medium-sized companies. Organizations of all sizes are considering methods for shifting overall costs, and voluntary plans are a way to do that. Disability is one of the most commonly purchased voluntary benefit, so it is not surprising that a voluntary disability plan should be part of an integrated structure.

When integrating and operating a voluntary program, voluntary disability plans can be just as successful as group programs. The plans can be designed with similar provisions and features as group plans and can also follow the same methods of intake, communication, and reporting if designed and structured appropriately. The biggest challenges posed are the number of carriers involved and the resulting participation rate by employers. If voluntary plans are involved as a buy-up method, there may be one carrier on the base plan and another carrier on the buy-up. Similarly, different carriers can be involved on the STD and LTD programs, which makes coordination and process links more challenging than if carrier assignment were the same. As far as participation levels, employers' efforts to improve productivity can only be followed if employees are part of the plan. Processes created to keep people healthy at work may not be applicable to the entire population and could therefore result in disjointed activities.

On the other hand, voluntary plans can be seen as a motivating force for some populations. In addition to attracting and retaining key employees, employers use voluntary benefits as another way of increasing morale and loyalty to the company. As you can see in Figure 10.3, the number of benefit plan options that an employer offers affects employee retention. When an employer offers fewer than 5 benefit programs, the percentage of employees who do not intend to stay with that employer is almost double the percentage of those who do. For those employers who offer 11-15 benefit programs, those percentages reverse. Overall, employers feel that by offering voluntary benefit plans to the aging workforce, it directly impacts the employee's perception of job satisfaction and loyalty. As illustrated in Figure 10.3, one could make an argument that as employers add voluntary benefit plans, employees' satisfaction, loyalty, and, therefore, productivity increases.

Figure 10.3

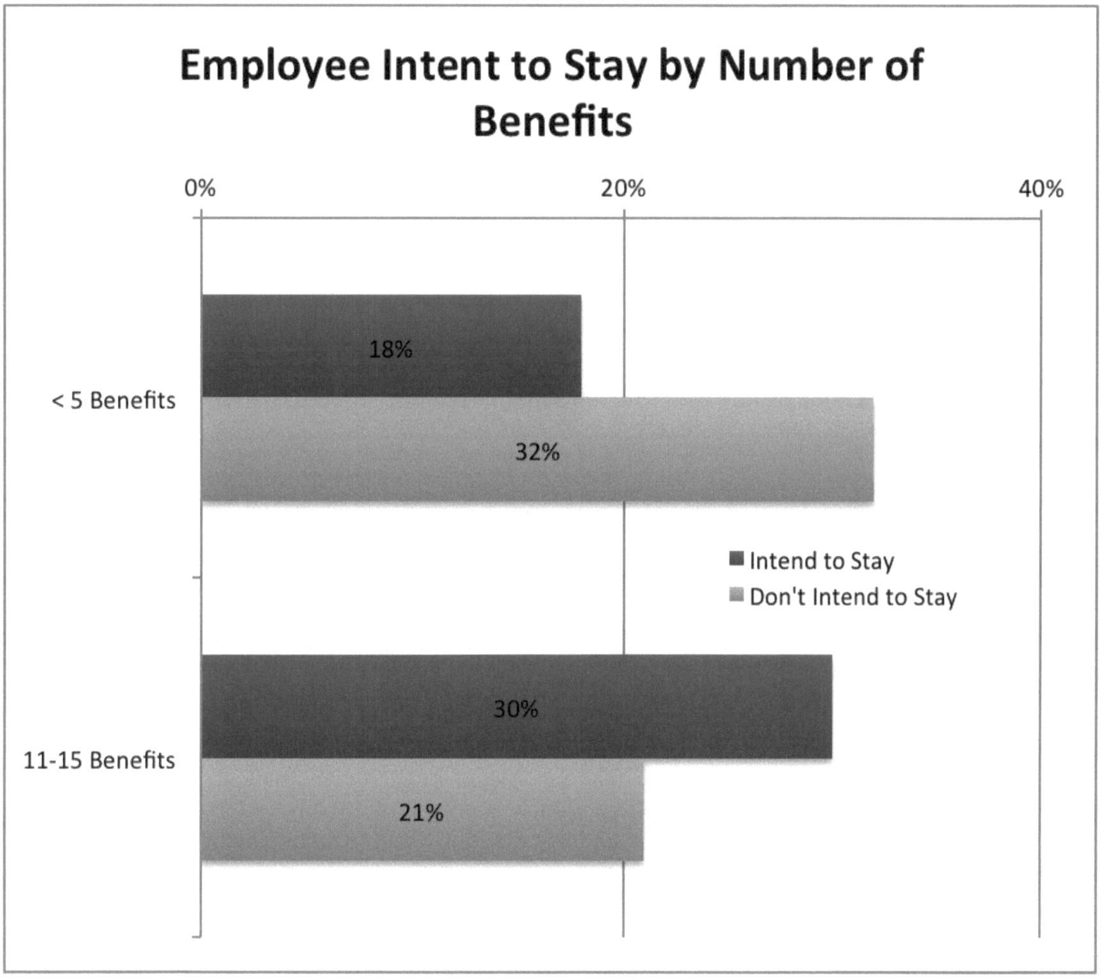

Source: MetLife. (2014). Tenth Annual Study of Employee Benefits Trends, Findings from the National Survey of Employers and Employees.

Figure 10.4
Perceived Advantages of Voluntary Benefit Plans

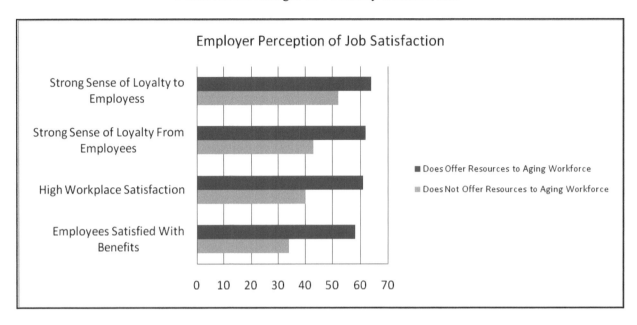

Source: MetLife. (2008). Sixth Annual Study of Employee Benefits Trends, Findings from the National Survey of Employers and Employees.

It is no surprise that the top industries associated with voluntary benefit plans are the healthcare/social assistance (31%) and the manufacturing/construction industries (22%). Both of these sectors represent complex and strenuous environments for employees, not to mention traditionally strong competition for the attraction and retention of workers. Figure 10.5 outlines one carrier's voluntary book of business by industry. Although any industry can be involved in integrated benefits, data does show that manufacturing and service environments, and other industries with high concentrations of employees, can benefit most from integration.

Figure 10.5

Voluntary Policies by Industry

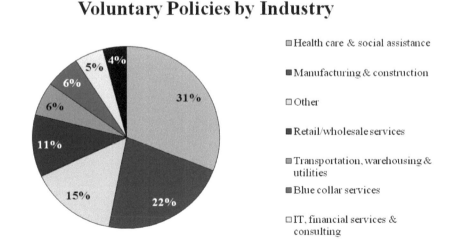

Source: Unum. (2008). Buyers Study: The Trends Employers Are Facing and the Plans They Are Buying.

In times of economic recession, employers may choose to offer voluntary plans as a way to satisfy employees. As recently as 2009, nearly 82 million U.S. workers had the opportunity to enroll in voluntary benefits.[c] Given the extraordinary growth in the prevalence of voluntary benefit plans since then, that number has obviously grown significantly. The employer's ultimate goal is to develop an overall benefit plan package that meets the needs of all employees. Employers are aiming at helping their employees manage their disposable income and provide affordable and necessary benefits that offer increased job satisfaction wherever possible.

Resource

Source	Description	Website & Contact Information
Council for Disability Awareness (CDA)	The Council for Disability Awareness is a nonprofit group formed in 2005 to help the American workforce become aware of the growing instances of disability and its financial consequences. Its online tool "What's My PDQ?" can help individuals calculate their chance of becoming disabled and take the necessary steps to manage risk.	www.WhatsMyPDQ.org

Employer Checklist

The checklist below is provided as a tool to determine which voluntary benefit plans might be suitable for your organization. The key questions prompt high-level thought as to what employers currently offer their employees on a voluntary basis as well as what can be strategically desirable to offer in the future.

Key Questions	Yes/No	Comments
Which of the following voluntary benefit plans do you currently offer your employees?		
Disability insurance		
Short-term disability		
Long-term disability		

Life insurance		
Group universal life		
Supplemental life/Optional life		
Dependent life		
Vision insurance		
Dental insurance		
Long-term care insurance		
Critical illness insurance		
Financial planning		
Auto insurance		
Homeowner's insurance		
Pet insurance		
Identity theft insurance		
Other		
Have you or could you take the following actions to determine which voluntary benefit plans would be of interest?		
Workforce evaluation		

Survey employees for demands and needs		
Benchmark market data and industry trends on most common benefits and variation by generations		
Plan design review		
Compare available voluntary benefit plans to current or competitive group plans for the following characteristics:		
Coverage definitions		
Participation eligibility		
Full-time employee coverage		
Part-time employee coverage		
Temporary employee coverage		
Conversion provisions		
Portability provisions		
Funding analysis		
Cost of coverage combinations		
Employee likelihood of purchase		
Necessary participation levels		

Expected program stability		
Vendor/Carrier availability		
Strength(s) of current vendors/ carriers		
Willingness to provide for employer industry and demographics		
Estimated rate differentials		
If you have moved to voluntary offerings, or plan to, has your organization considered the following implementation aspects?		
Enrollment methods		
Online enrollment		
Telephonic enrollment		
Group meetings		
Combination/Other		
Payment methods		
Payroll deduction		
Annual lump sum		
Monthly premiums		

Communication protocol		
Through external carrier/vendor		
Involves benefits department		
Using various methods including automated emails		
Flyers and brochures via mail		
Intranet sites and links		
Program review		
Internal benefit team review		
External certified employee benefit specialists review/Consultant		
Once every year		
Once every two years		

Section Three

Key Processes and Regulations

Chapter 11: Intake and Call Center Management

Background and Context

One of the foundations of a successful integrated program is the use of a single source of intake to report illnesses, injuries, and/or absences. The selected single source should be able to collect all the necessary and initial claim/absence information from the employee and/or the employee's supervisor for the programs to be integrated. Ideally, an employer develops a set of methods that employees and supervisors can choose from (e.g., telephonic, web, interactive voice response [IVR]), and consistently communicates the options to their workforce in a straightforward and simplified manner. Specific rules and protocols are created to support the process, and corporate managers and supervisors are trained in its usage so they can reiterate the instructions as needed. Developing a consistent and unified intake approach yields several advantages to employers, including, but not limited to:

- Decreased employee confusion and increased employee satisfaction with the overall process

- Reduced time commitment of managers and supervisors in explaining the process and subsequently increased time to do their "real jobs"

- Decreased reliance on the employee in determining what type of claim they have and related reduction in coverage duplication. Timely communication to appropriate parties about the claim/absence, resulting in decreased lag time and increased opportunity for early intervention

- Management's ability to plan proactively for absence and make the "present" team as productive as possible

This chapter will help employers understand the range of intake options that are available to them and prompt thought with respect to how they might design their processes and procedures to be most effective within their particular organizational environments.

Methods and Options

Although old-fashioned, paper and fax reporting of incidences still exists and remains a method used by some companies, a combination of telephonic and web intake has become the norm for integrated programs. In fact, some service providers and employers do not accept information any other way. IVR is also an option and definitely has its place, depending on the types of programs and organizational cultures involved. Regardless of the combination used, best practice is to leverage employee eligibility data via an electronic feed so that the selected single intake source uses existing and available claimant information to make the phone call, web, or IVR interaction with the employee as efficient as possible.

Telephonic Intake

Employers utilizing this option typically provide a toll-free number to their employee population that connects callers to a "live" intake representative or require that they select from a series of IVR options to get to the appropriate party (e.g., press 1 to report a new claim, press 2 to obtain information on an existing claim). This phone number can be linked to an existing internal or external benefit service center already in use for an employer, or it could be a new number that is designated or even specifically branded (e.g., 1-800-RUA-TWRK) for the program at hand. Usually the number is operational during the organization's regular business hours. Depending on the time zones involved for an employer's workforce, however, these could be expanded on both ends of a core set of hours (e.g., 8 a.m. Eastern time to 5 p.m. Pacific time). In addition, workforces that operate on a 24/7 basis may require around-the-clock intake. When workers' compensation (WC) First Report of Injury (FROI) is involved, 24/7 becomes a necessity as the Occupational Safety and Health Act requires it in cases where employees die from a work-related incident, or employees are hospitalized as a result of a work-related incident, and/or an amputation or the loss of an eye occurs.[ci]

Other important features of telephonic intake include support for the hearing impaired, language translation services, and the ability to respond to calls in rapid fashion (e.g., 30 seconds or less wait time). How important or essential these are will vary by employer but should be considered part of the overall process.

Web Intake

Reporting via the web can be accomplished in a variety of ways and should be consistent with other means of access offered to an employer's population. If use of an intranet site is common and an acceptable practice, web intake can become a part of the existing employee portal (a web interface with data, reports and tools for employee use) or structured as a link from the intranet site to the selected intake source. Whatever the case, web reporting by nature is available on a 24/7 basis and, to the extent possible, reflects the same questions that a "live" intake representative would ask in order to begin the process. Once web intake is complete, the information is fed to the integrated program application(s) or system(s), ideally on a real-time basis, so that immediate action can be taken.

Use of IVR

An IVR option tends to be most effective when an employee calling in has limited information to share. For example, sick days can be reported this way by prompting employees to simply type in the date of their absence. Tracking of intermittent absence can also be done effectively through an IVR when the employee's absence has already been certified and they are simply calling in to report the actual timing. Similarly, return-to-work dates — either expected or actual — can also be captured through this type of mechanism. Key criteria for successful IVR use include clear and understandable instructions for the caller, combined with an opt-out feature, so an individual doesn't have to call back in if they are confused. For employer populations that operate 24/7, IVR can be a method of reducing cost of intake staff. For those with multilingual employees, it can only be as effective as the number of languages offered.

Messaging and Script Usage

Once an employee has reached the point of intake, either by way of a toll-free number, a web portal, or an IVR, messaging across all options must be consistent and the wording to the individual clear and concise as to what they are supposed to do and what information they will need to share. The overarching goal in structuring the messaging is to keep the call, or web input time, to a minimum, while capturing the key data needed to move the intake information, whether manager notification or claim processing information, to the next level.

As mentioned, an eligibility data feed should populate the system(s) screens that the intake representative or web portal is using. From there, individuals are asked to verify demographic information about themselves (e.g., address, phone number, location worked) instead of having to explain it to the phone representative or input their personal information into the web portal themselves.

A specific script should be used by the intake representative so that all callers are asked the same questions, as relevant to their situations, and essential data elements are captured to populate the system and give appropriate parties the information they need to proceed. The questions included in the script should reflect the specific situations and benefits that are part of the employer's integrated program. The questions should also be well thought out to avoid duplication and to make them as meaningful as possible to all parties.

As mentioned above, the script used for telephonic intake should be mirrored through the web portal and should even include the same opening and closing remarks so that the caller gets a sense of consistency every time they call or log in. Depending on the programs being integrated, this can include both nonoccupational and occupational absences and can fulfill WC FROI requirements, if the latter is involved. If family and medical leave (FML) administration is one of the programs being integrated, the single source of intake helps comply with state and federal laws of notification and certification while leveraging short-term disability (STD) and WC information. For employers coordinating efforts across STD and group healthcare, a verbal medical release is another aspect of what can be included so that effective case management can begin immediately in compliance with Health Insurance Portability and Accountability Act and employee privacy concerns.

Technology Platforms and Capabilities

Technology plays a significant role in the success of integrated program intake as the telephone systems, web portals, and IVR applications must link to the claim systems that are used to manage the illnesses, injuries, and/or absences being reported. Best practice is for one system to be able to handle all aspects of reporting, but, more commonly, there are sets of systems and technology platforms that feed data to and from each other to successfully move claims and absence reporting from one point in the process to the next.

Although it is not the intent of this chapter to provide the information systems requirements for success, it is important for employers to understand the basics behind the various types of systems used and prompt examination of what is available to them on both an internal resource and external vendor basis.

Phone Systems

Employers must estimate the frequency and timing of the employee absence calls in order to obtain an understanding of the capacity needed for successful telephonic intake. For example, if the majority of calls normally occur on Mondays between 6 a.m. and 8 a.m., the telephone system must be able to successfully accept the surge of calls. The phone system should have the capability for employee verification before the call is routed to a queue or live intake. This allows only eligible callers into the system. Again, employee eligibility data is critical to ensure a successful transaction by eliminating the need for the employee to provide personal data multiple times and to allow the intake provider (vendor or employer) the capacity to handle calls more efficiently.

Web Portals

There are several considerations for employers considering web-based portal applications for employee absence reporting. Where the portal will reside is the first consideration: within the employer's or vendor's firewall? The need for and amount of IT requirements to sustain the solution are based on the answer to this question. Employers must be able to provide employee eligibility data so that the web application is quick and easy for employees to use while obtaining the same information as would be obtained through live or IVR intake. Employers need to assess their employee populations' access to and comfort level with technology when considering a web intake solution.

Web applications are still relatively new to employees for absence reporting and have a smaller percentage of employee use than live telephonic intake and IVR applications. Employers may wish to consider the web as another avenue for intake for both employee convenience and to mitigate costs. As with all intake methods, reporting of employee activity is critical.

IVR Applications

IVR solutions are economical and could be considered in addition to live intake and web-based solutions. Once again, the employee must be able to use a telephone keypad to input their information for eligibility verification. Employers should consider designing this type of solution to address the highest volume of transactions that may be accomplished without live intake intervention. An example would be reporting an approved intermittent FML leave, with the employee reporting an identification number, claim number, date, and time of the absence via the keypad of a telephone. Considerations for this solution must include the employer's ability to provide employee eligibility data, the number of IVR options and placement of the most frequently accessed options, the culture of the company and the employee populations' acceptance of this method, options for transfer to live intake, and reporting requirements.

Mobile Technology

Smartphones are now the norm, and employer supervisors, HR staff and employees expect more real-time access to claim and certification status, approval and payment information. This demand will only continue to grow, and providers will continue to expand their offerings. Consider issues of cyber security while contemplating 24/7 real-time data, integrated with claim systems. Immediate notice to supervisors and employees via email, text messages or even fax can improve communication and even help reduce phone calls for updates. Consider how many ways you can answer, "have you received my cert form?" or, "has my claim been approved?"

Claim Systems

If the employee absence information is processed and administered by someone other than the employer, there must be integration between the intake application(s) and the claims systems. In addition, the employer should have provided employee eligibility information as well as time entry information, when available. If the absence administration involves pay, it may be necessary for claims and benefit payment data to be provided to the employer's payroll. The employer and the vendor must agree upon the timing of data feeds, protocols, reports, and employee communication.

Communication of Process

The process for reporting an absence or claim should become part of an employer's set of policies and should be communicated regularly. It commonly becomes part of a new hire packet, a training structure provided to managers and supervisors, and a daily process reference by human resources and benefits managers.

When an integrated program is newly designed, the intake process forms the foundation for a communications campaign that includes change management when it differs from the current state of affairs.

Preferred methods of communication can vary significantly by employer but can include any or all of the following:

- Letters or mailers sent to employee homes

- Memos provided to managers and supervisors

- Table tents used for introductory and training purposes

- Payroll stuffers to indicate timing of change and instructions

- Postcards to home and/or work as friendly reminders

- Text or email reminders and instructions

- Links on corporate intranet sites

- Other communication used by managers and supervisors to indicate change

- Vendor communications to the employee, such as claims approval letters

Keys to success in this area include finding the right balance in the messaging to improve employee understanding of the process and the new requirements being expected of them, but not encouraging them to be absent or finding ways to take advantage of the systems and processes offered to them. Because this is a difficult balancing act to achieve, it is not surprising that employee use of absence programs almost always increases with the new implementation of an integrated program. This pattern does tend to slow down over time, as employees accept it as the norm and incorporate it into their daily routines only as necessary.

Call Center Management

Call center management is a challenge requiring constant monitoring to ensure that practices are being followed consistently and that opportunities for improvement are identified on a continual basis. Some employers use internal call center resources to handle the intake of integrated benefit programs, while others use an external vendor.

Call center employees face unique absence and productivity issues. Not only are call center employees the frontline for callers who are often unhappy and need to report claims, illnesses, and absences, but they also tend to have a high level of absence themselves. Call centers are intense environments in which employees are monitored through the telephone system as soon as they log onto their phone. They are required to be available to take calls, answer calls within a certain time period, provide succinct responses, log their after-call notes, and be available for the next call. Many calls are monitored by the employee's manager. Employees have limited freedom to do simple things such as get a drink of water or take a restroom break. As such, high employee turnover, high incidence of FMLA and request for job accommodations (e.g., extra breaks, sit/stand desks, lighting changes), and mental and nervous disability claims are common.

The 2005 Call Center Leadership Series, co-sponsored by the Disability Management Employer Coalition and Liberty Mutual, brought together call center experts, risk managers, and benefit managers to discuss what drives call center absence costs and the best ways to manage them. Summarized below are six key challenges the group identified, as well as high-level solutions to address them.[cii]

Best Practice 1: Hire and prepare the right employee for the call center representative role.

Finding and hiring the right employees for call centers critically impacts future absence and lost productivity costs. Assess employee knowledge and clearly convey the call center environment and job requirements to identify appropriate candidates.

Best Practice 2: Allow for flexible, creative scheduling to accommodate changing service needs, including seasonality.

Fluctuating call volumes can make predicting staff scheduling needs and maintaining service levels difficult to manage. Consider software, employee input, and incentives to facilitate scheduling and maintain service levels.

Best Practice 3: Use non-monetary recognition to reward exemplary performance, motivate employees, and increase morale.

Maintaining employee morale contributes to a productive and healthy staff; competitive rewards are integral to employee motivation and satisfaction. Use non-monetary incentives, performance reviews, and mentoring programs to improve motivation and recognize and reward employees who consistently surpass expectations.

Best Practice 4: Support the unique physical needs of the call center representative role.

The call center environment and its high stress, sedentary nature places unique physical demands on employees. Encourage the use of stretch breaks, ergonomics training, and injury-reducing accessories to provide employees with safe, comfortable work environments.

Best Practice 5: Communicate regularly with employees about absence, disability, and benefits.

Regular, meaningful communication between managers and employees about work and benefits issues can dramatically reduce disability incidence, frequency, and severity. Train managers to communicate confidently with employees and to take a proactive role in disability/absence management.

Best Practice 6: Leverage internal and external resources for improved return-to-work outcomes.

Providing employees who have suffered a disability with the resources and support necessary to return safely to work is critical to successfully managing absence and reducing disability costs. Involve healthcare professionals, supervisors, and other internal advocates to develop and implement successful return-to-work programs.

Employer Checklist

Determining the method(s) of intake most effective for an employer's population depends on the programs involved, existing and successful processes that can be leveraged, and whether internal resources or external vendors are used. Technology plays an important role, as the methods are only as good as the systems and platforms behind them. The following questions are intended to serve as a high-level checklist to understand your current state, so that you can design a set of options that will achieve your integrated program goals.

Key Questions	Yes/No	Comments
Does your organization currently use a single source of intake for any of the following programs?		
Short-term disability		
Long-term disability		
Family medical leave		
Sick leave		
Leave of absence		
Paid time-off programs		

Workers' compensation		
EAP/Behavioral health		
Group healthcare		
Disease management		
Wellness		
Attendance or performance management		
Other		
Which of the following methods is your organization currently using for intake? And for which programs?		
Paper reports/forms		
Telephonic reports		
Web portal input		
IVR input		
What are the hours of intake required by your employee population?		
Regular business hours in one time zone		
Extended business hours to cover several time zones		

24/7 availability		
Other		
Does your organization have any of the following resources that can be leveraged?		
Internal benefits service center employees already familiar with intake		
Dedicated toll-free phone number currently used for specific programs (e.g., STD, WC)		
Corporate intranet site or web page employees routinely access		
Other		
Which vendors is your organization using for any of the following?		
Telephonic intake		
Web portals		
IVR applications		
Claim systems		
Which internal resources do you need in order to work within your organization to incorporate your integrated program intake into an already existing method?		
Service center		

Information technology		
Communications		
Public relations		
Other		

Chapter 12: Event Management

Background and Context

Once an absence has been collected and documented through the intake process, the next step is to manage the event in accordance with the processes and procedures set forth by the employer. This begins with triaging the call to the appropriate resource, then working through the process to:

- Determine eligibility for the benefit type
- Notify employees and managers of their rights and responsibilities
- Collect and analyze medical and otherwise necessary documentation
- Arrive at a decision to approve or deny the claim

Whether this process is outsourced to one or several insurance companies or third-party administrators (TPAs) or handled by an employer's own personnel and systems, the goal is to manage events in a consistent manner, ideally driven by well-thought-out business rules within a solid technology and well-documented framework.

This chapter provides guidance on the key aspects of event management employers need to consider so they can review them against the programs they have decided to integrate, as well as the processes and systems they currently have in place.

Eligibility and Triage

Best-practice intake processes structure the questions and interaction in a way that decreases reliance on the employee in determining the claim type. In other words, the intake questions asked and answered are supported by eligibility information and predetermined business rules that lead the managers to the appropriate coverage, rather than the employee requesting a certain type of absence.

As much as possible, this decision tree approach is supported by automated eligibility determination, which is based on an electronic data feed provided by the employer and the business rules within the system. This allows the absence to be set up in the system(s) to appropriately reflect the initial facts obtained from the caller. Communications, such as letters and information packets to employees and emails and reminders to supervisors, are distributed to document rights and responsibilities and to specify the information and corresponding forms that need to be supplied. Timing and specifications can be an important factor as certain leave types, such as those associated with the Family and Medical Leave Act (FMLA), require eligibility decisions and notification timing within a certain number of business days.

Figure 12.1 is designed to give employers a sense of how the steps work collaboratively within a very short amount of time.

Figure 12.1

Triage and Flow for Employee or Manager Initiated Intake Call

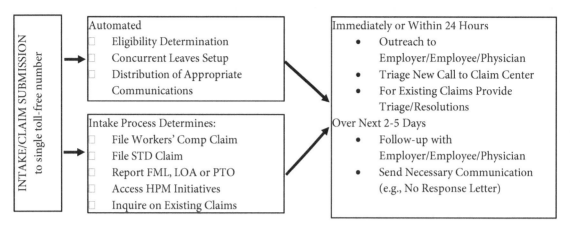

Part of the system setup is not simply to establish the record, but also to assign the absence to the appropriate case management resource on the team. For example, a disability claim might be assigned to an adjustor or a nurse, whereas a military leave claim might be assigned to a leave specialist. Depending on the circumstances, the assigned resource makes an outreach to the employee, the employer, and the employee's attending physician (often called three-point contact) to verify the initial information received, clarify any outstanding questions, and establish a rapport and process that will be taken forward.

This early interaction can be crucial to successful management since early intervention provides the opportunity to engage the right resources at the right time. Other expert resources, such as employee assistance programs (EAPs), behavioral health, and vocational rehabilitation, should be brought into the team to identify potential strategies as early as possible.

Absence Certification and Case Management

Before an absence can be certified, the employee or the physician must provide the required documentation requested from them. In obtaining this information, it is important to consider the confidential nature of the documentation, specifically employee medical information. It is suggested that employers require employees to sign a standardized form to authorize the release of medical and other information as part of the intake and event management process. The party collecting the information must ensure a secure exchange of that information and limit access only to those with a "need to know."

Once the information has been received, the assigned case manager continues to review the employee's specific medical and job information that has been collected. They work to understand the absence situation from many different perspectives and start setting expectations for the duration of the absence. Identification of return-to-work opportunities and additional clinical, vocational, or leave-related resources is an important step for providing additional insight. Further, the case manager should look to coordinate with other benefits programs that are offered by the employer (e.g., state disability, employer supplemental plans, EAP), which might be applicable to an employee's situation.

The steps a case manager can take and the resources they have available to them are highly dependent on the specific employer and available benefits plans, the laws of the jurisdictions involved, and the cultures or nuances of the employee locations. The goal is to provide the necessary resources to promote accurate absence tracking, employee recovery, and/or return to work in a safe and timely manner, regardless of the absence type.

Decisions and Appeals

A case manager's decisions to approve or deny claims are based on all of the information noted above and the specific time frames and protocols established for the types of absence. They must be timely, accurate, and clearly communicated to all of the parties involved, including the supervisor and the employee, as well as the timekeeping or payroll administrators, other benefit plans, and providers that play a role in the process.

An appeals process must be established for each of the absence types included in the employer's integrated program and resources established to support the process in accordance with the appropriate timing and protocols. If the benefit involved is subject to ERISA, a maximum of two levels of review should be afforded. The claim must be reviewed by someone new who looks at all the information submitted and consults with qualified medical professionals if a medical judgment is involved.[ciii] Although often misunderstood, FML claims are not subject to regulatory guidance for appeals. Therefore, some employers choose not to follow a formal process. Rather, recourse is sought through a complaint process that can prompt a more formal re-review or reconsideration protocol. For other leaves of absence, routine review is essentially nonexistent.

Additional information that can be helpful in a case manager's decision making is any historical absence information that has been taken over or supplied by the previous provider, file documentation and case notes by all resources that have interacted with the claimant, and recordings of calls with the claimant that might be on file.

Communicating openly and often with the employee will avoid any surprises experienced with the ultimate decision and make sure the employee's supervisor is aware of any denials before they occur, which may be absolutely critical depending on the employer environment.

Documentation and Communication

Several points of interaction with the employee, the employer, the attending physician or the treating healthcare provider, and the various claim resources must be made as part of an integrated program and documented in a consistent and timely manner. The protocol for doing so is dependent on the type of absence involved and the specifics of the integrated program, but can be thought about in terms of Table 12.1.

Table 12.1

Interaction Point	Initiating Party/Resource	Example Timing	Documentation	System of Record
Intake	Employee, employee's representative or supervisor	Immediately upon knowledge of absence	Phone record	Intake system
Eligibility	Employer	Immediately if data feed populates system screens	Employer data file; system business rules; potential outreach to employer	Intake and claim system
Rights and responsibilities, forms and information	Intake unit or case manager	Sent to employee within 24 hours via U.S. mail (can also include an email copy); sent to supervisors immediately via email	Letters, forms and information to employees; emails to supervisors	Claim system
Outreach	Case manager	Three-point contact within 48 hours to employee, employer, and attending physician	File notes for results of three-point contact made	Claim system

Forms and information	Employee or attending physician	Returned to case manager within 15 to 25 days (for FML); typically 30 days for STD; and various for other absence types	Completed forms	Claim system
Case management	Case manager	Ongoing as needed and depending on absence type	File notes for ongoing communication	Claim system
Decision	Case manager	Within certain number of days of receiving complete information (e.g., five days for FML); various for other absence types	Confirmation email or letter to supervisor; letter sent to employee	Claim system
Appeals rights and responsibilities, forms and information	Case manager	Sent to employee with denial letter	Letters, forms, and information to employees	Claim system

Appeals forms and information	Employee or attending physician	Returned to case manager within specified number of days	Completed forms	Claim system
Appeals decisions	Case manager	Within certain number of days of receiving complete information	Confirmation email or letter to supervisor; letter sent to employee	Claim system

While this likely goes without saying, all letters, emails, forms, and information must be established prior to the implementation of an integrated program. If an employer's integrated program is outsourced to a third party, that third party must have a communications library already equipped with templates and samples that can be shared with the employer for consideration. It should be set up to respond to all of the different leave scenarios an employee might have (e.g., concurrent disability and FML, standalone FML to care for a family member, disability that transitions into a personal leave, healthcare claim that involves an EAP). The selected or potential communications must be reviewed by all the resources involved in the absence management process to ensure that they are clear, concise, and correct, as well as reflect the tone and branding that the employer wants to project. Prior to finalization, they should be tested within the intake and claims systems to make sure that they trigger according to the business rules set for each of them and that they meet all expectations for timing and interaction with the various benefits programs the employer offers.

System Links and Diary Tasks

There are a number of systems that can be involved with integrated programs. The number and type depend on the level of insourcing or outsourcing undertaken and on the number of insurance companies or TPAs involved. It is important to ensure that all intake and claim information is documented thoroughly, and that employees are paid appropriately, in accordance with the compensation and benefits program.. There are laws and benefits structures, and policies that require time keeper and payroll system coordination and the individuals that input, monitor, and process information in the HRIS on a day-to-day basis must be linked to the process.

This means that the business rules guiding the process must be embedded in the appropriate locations to trigger the appropriate actions taken by case managers. It also means that decisions with regard to eligibility, claim acceptance, and denial must link back to the benefit plans and policies in place at the organization. Finally, it means that communications must be released in accordance with the timing and format established by absence type as agreed between the employer and their service providers during the implementation process.

Figure 12.2 gives a sense of the number of systems that can be involved and how they interact as far as feeding data to and from one another.

Figure 12.2

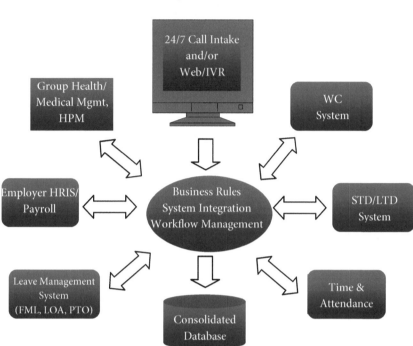

In an ideal situation, data feeds among all systems involved are in real time. However, more common is daily batch processing (overnight) or variances between real-time, daily, weekly, and monthly, depending on the system involved.

For the case manager, specific workflow management and diary tasks are behind the day-to-day activities. For example, many systems can automatically generate tasks as different actions are taken within the system. Case managers have their own task lists containing action items for their specific employee claimants. Once a task is complete, it can either be automatically removed from their list or marked as complete. Tasks can typically be reassigned among case managers if needed, and a process for escalation can be built into the protocol. Audit trails with times stamps, date stamps, and identification for which case manager performed each action can also be automated. Finally, and very important, systems should have the capability to track task lists by case manager so that the manager(s) of the resource teams can monitor and audit performance as necessary.

Due to the potential complexity and process nature of integrated programs, all of the areas mentioned within this chapter are the focus of detailed and continuous training that integrated program managers undergo and should be routinely expanded upon to reflect the changing regulatory and employer positioning environment.

Employer Checklist

To ensure consistent management among absence types that are part of an employer's integrated program, an employer can consider the checklist below to identify the specific management functions and system interactions that need to be established, monitored, and continuously improved.

Key Questions	Yes/No	Comments
How is your organization able to provide employee eligibility information?		
Electronic data feed		
Real time		
Daily		
Weekly		
Monthly		
Other		
Excel file		
Real time		
Daily		
Weekly		
Monthly		
Other		

Other mechanism, describe:		
For which of the following programs has your organization established business rules as part of your integrated program?		
Short-term disability		
Long-term disability		
Family medical leave		
Sick leave		
Leave of absence		
Paid time-off programs		
Workers' compensation		
EAP/Behavioral health		
Group healthcare		
Disease management		
Wellness		
Attendance or performance management		

Other		

Does your organization have the following standardized communications in place to support your integrated program?		
Letters to employees		
Emails to supervisors		
Medical release/authorization form(s)		
Attending physician statement for disability		
Certified healthcare provider form for family medical leave		
Other, according to absence type		

What are the names of the systems in place at your organization to handle the following functions in support of your integrated program?		
Payroll		
Human resources information system		
Time and attendance		
Short-term disability		
Long-term disability		

Family medical leave		
Sick leave		
Leave of absence		
Paid time-off programs		
Workers' compensation		
EAP/Behavioral health		
Group healthcare		
Disease management		
Wellness		
Attendance or performance management		
Other		
Is there a workflow management tool embedded within your organization's integrated program system(s) that can help case managers with the following?		
Daily task generation		
Specific to each employee claimant		
Automatic removal or completion		

Reassignment functionality		
Supported by audit trail		
Overall reporting and case manager specifics		
Has training been established at your organization to strengthen the delivery of your integrated program?		
For intake and case managers		
For internal administrators and supervisors		
Other		

Chapter 13: Return-to-Work Program Development and Stay-at-Work Philosophy

Introduction

When an employee is injured or becomes ill, their absence, recovery, and subsequent return to work directly impacts the organization's productivity. The direct costs of an injury or illness include disability payments; medical treatment; decreased productivity; claim administration; damaged materials and equipment (for work-related injuries); and management time lost in manpower planning, hiring, training, etc. When injury or illness does cause time away from work, the best strategy is to gain control over the costs. One such way is to implement a return-to-work (RTW) program.

The employee's ability to perform the duties of their job may be limited by the physical impairments of the employee's medical condition. However, the purpose of a return-to-work program is to find a way to get the employee back in the workplace to perform productive work within their abilities. This return-to-work philosophy is a win-win for both the employer and the employee.

Purpose

The objective of any RTW program is to assist employees returning to the workplace with a planned reintegration process that ensures a safe and sustained return to productivity. Return-to-work programs establish realistic expectations for employees and managers and acknowledge the value of an employee's capabilities. They provide a transition process to return to active work for those in the organization who have lost time from work due to illness or injury, are disabled for any reason (regardless of whether the disability is the result of an on-the-job or off-the-job injury or illness), and are capable of returning to work at modified duty or with specified restrictions. Second, they provide guidelines for those with responsibilities for the successful functioning of the workers' compensation (WC) and disability programs and claims reporting at the company. Finally, and very important, RTW programs can form the premise for stay-at-work (SAW) programs, which utilize tools, processes, and protocols to prevent employee absence from occurring in the first place or, once an employee has returned, work closely with them to ensure they stay on the job.

Focus

To determine optimal employee productivity, the focus should be on their physical capabilities. Which physical capabilities has the employee retained and how can they be applied to meaningful work? In other words, by simply shifting the emphasis to the positive, the employee is no longer defined by his or her limitations or restrictions to perform certain duties — defining what the employee "can do" versus what they "can't do." Thinking in terms of capabilities versus restrictions helps find meaningful modified duty as well as arrive at job modifications that allow the employee to return to work. In turn, this speeds the recovery process and returns the employee to their regular duties as soon as possible.

Benefits of Return-to-Work Programs

The benefits of the RTW program for most organizations are simple. The employee is assisted in making a smooth transition back to their regular duties in a timely manner and the company realizes reduced costs associated with injury or illness. In addition, since an illness/injury can create problems in the employee's personal life, the RTW program should be prepared to address not only the physical effects of injury or illness, but also to provide the emotional support that may be needed initially and on an ongoing basis. Helping an employee through this sometimes frustrating and difficult period builds strong relationships between the organization and its employees and can serve as a motivating factor in itself for employees to stay at work.

Return-to-work program outcomes include the ability to:

- Minimize employee wage loss
- Reduce workers' compensation costs
- Reduce short-term and long-term disability costs
- Accelerate recovery from an injury or illness
- Improve employee morale
- Improve employee and management relations
- Control treatment of injury for work-related absence
- Coordinate everyone's efforts to achieve a better outcome
- Coordinate with other leave programs, such as family medical leave
- Create awareness of safety concerns
- Maintain optimal employee productivity
- Accomplish necessary tasks in the workplace
- Minimize negative effects on the injured/ill employee's personal life
- Provide a positive workplace atmosphere
- Encourage employee productivity and staying at work over the long term

Steps for a Successful Return-to-Work Program

Development of a successful return-to-work program includes the following steps:

1. Determine the Impact of Lost Time on the Organization

An important element of the RTW program is determining the cost of lost time to the organization. To seek and obtain senior management support for the RTW program, the current costs are the benchmark on which to build the potential return on investment for the organization. Justifying the costs and resources required to implement the RTW program is critical to garner support.

Costs of lost time may include:

- Sick pay
- Salary continuation
- Short-term disability
- Statutory disability
- Long-term disability

- Workers' compensation

Other costs to consider that have a disability component:

- Life insurance programs
- Retirement programs
- Union agreements

The costs of healthcare may also be included as a benchmark if desirable and available. It can be beneficial to segregate the associated medical expenses of employees who are out of work for a medical event.

Another area that requires major consideration is the cost of lost productivity. The ability to capture this element can be critical in getting senior management buy-in, as it targets the indirect costs of disability for the organization.

Variables contributing to the lost-time calculation can include but may not be limited to:

- Number of employees
- Average annual wages
- Payroll load (benefits as a percent of payroll)
- Annual paid time (40 hours x 52 weeks = 2,080 hours as a default)
- Vacation time per employee in hours
- Short-term disability incidence rate (claims per 1,000 employees)
- Short-term disability average duration (in weeks)
- Family medical leave (hours per employee per year) for other than the employee's own health condition
- Workers' compensation (hours per employee per year)
- Sick time (hours per employee per year)
- Paid time off (hours per employee per year)
- Other (personal days, jury duty, bereavement leave, etc.)

2. Determine Corporate Interest and Readiness for a Formal Return-to-Work Program

A critical success factor in developing a return-to-work program is determining the readiness of your organization for this type of program. The areas of potential review include assessing what currently exists in your organization and the impact of your business and corporate culture on the potential success of an RTW program and identifying the barriers to success, as well as the strengths and weaknesses present within your organization.

Questions to be addressed may include:

- Are employees required to perform at 100% of capacity in order to return to work?
- Do you currently have any of these options for return to work?

  o Part-time job schedules

  o Jobs in other departments/job banks

       o   Temporary jobs

       o   Modified work schedules

       o   Work-at-home opportunities

Identify whether options are only available for one type of absence, such as workers' compensation, short-term disability, or long-term disability.

- Does your company have a written RTW policy?
- Is there currently a company resource assigned to facilitate and coordinate RTW efforts?

  - o   If so, is this function centralized?

- Do you have functional job descriptions that include the physical demands of the job?

  - o   Who are the potential stakeholders in the RTW efforts, and do they support the RTW philosophy?

- Do managers and supervisors have incentives to return employees to work? What are they?

- Are your employees represented by collective bargaining agreements (CBAs) and unions? If so, do the CBAs address return to work?

- Is information available on absence rates?

- Do your current plans/policies support return to work?

- What percentage of your workforce is covered under statutory disability plans?

- What is the current level of interest in developing or enhancing an RTW program, and is there a willingness to commit from senior leadership?

Responses to these questions will assist in determining the readiness and interest in developing a return-to-work program while also determining barriers to success and where key players stand on moving forward.

3. Recognize and Plan for Development Barriers/Challenges

As you move forward in developing and implementing a formal RTW program, you may face obstacles and challenges to your program's success. Table 13.1 outlines some of the most frequently occurring challenges and recommendations for overcoming them.

Table 13.1

Potential Challenge	Potential Solution
Senior management resistance: • Bottom-line orientation • Unknown program • Change to organization	Present business case: • Lost-time costs • Expected outcomes • Potential ROI • Get sign off
Turf issues: • Disagree with the concept • Perceived threat to their authority • Don't want employees back until they are 100%	During the program development: • Form a multidisciplinary team • Present benefits of the program
Bargaining unit: • Contracts may contain RTW criteria • May resist RTW in other job classes • Seniority issues may exist	At all stages: • Include union representative on the team • Articulate reasons for having program • Outline benefits to employees • Enhance the organizations' success
Lack of commitment: • Inability to maintain the vision • Inconsistently seek modified-duty options	Maintain focus on: • Disability costs being out of control • The need for productive employees improves the organizational output • Saving money and company assets • It's the right thing to do

Potential Challenge	Potential Solution
Employee resistance: • Employer programs are seen as negative • Entitlement mentality exists • The longer they are disabled, the more comfortable they are staying at home	Communication is the key to success: • They are valuable to the employer • They can get a higher benefit when in an RTW program • Resuming full employment is beneficial to the employee's well-being
Physician cooperation: • Employee is the customer • Employee provides job information • Not trained in disability	Provide the right information: • Job functions • Focus on abilities • Bring them in for a visit to the facility • Communicate the RTW philosophy
Financial concerns: • Program funding • Budgeting concerns for returning employees	Provide: • Funding options • Potential ROI • Impact on company output
Production management issues: • Concerns that modifying jobs will slow down production • Employees not at 100% will slow production	• Include line management in the program development process • Educate managers as to the benefits of having trained employees and the impact on productivity
Claim processing: • Time delays and limited information can delay or inhibit RTW plans due to inadequate or lack of medical information	• Educate the claims management staff about the RTW process, contacts, and setting RTW expectations with ill/injured employees • Communicate the employer's RTW program when communicating with attending physicians

Risk aversion: • May create employee unrest • May expose the company to potential litigation	• Educate the organization management on research that supports no increase in WC injuries when returning employees to work in transitional jobs • Present positive employee responses to RTW efforts
Apathy • Lack of sustained interest in returning employees to work	• Be persistent and share results and information about the benefits of RTW with the team • Benchmark yourself against competitors and others in your industry
Program coordination • A big task to coordinate vendors, insurers/ TPAs, and internal departments and functions	• Meet with vendors and internal stakeholders, explain the RTW program objectives, and require cooperation

4. Obtain Support from All Levels within the Organization

A critical element of a successful RTW program is obtaining the commitment and support of upper management. The process to seek this commitment is driven by how your company normally makes these types of decisions. Regardless of the venue and presentation process, there are consistent requirements to the information being delivered in making your case.

The purpose of the presentation is to provide an overview of the benefits of an RTW program so that your management team can understand the value to the organization and commit to participating in the RTW program.

Areas to discuss to illustrate the value can include:

- Expense management
- Improved productivity
- Staying competitive
- Effective allocation of resources
- Improved supervisor accountability
- A positive work environment
- Costs of lost time for the organization
- Potential return on investment

5. Identify and Prioritize Changes to Be Implemented and Establish a Time Frame

Based on the data collected from previous processes in conjunction with buy-in from upper management, it is time to choose a team and develop a project plan with deliverables and accountabilities. It isn't necessary to try to take on everything all at once. Choose a starting point that fits the resources available, and create a model that fits your company's capabilities and is expected to best impact your business.

6. Enlist Program Sponsors from Various Departments

Once you have commitment to move forward with developing a return-to-work program, the next step is to build a team of key players within your organization. This team will assist in the development, implementation, and ongoing program management. Depending on the size and complexity of your company, you must select the number of partners necessary to guarantee success of the program based on their:

- Expertise
- Understanding of the RTW concept
- Scope of influence within the organization

The team should include both internal and external stakeholders. Suggested participants might include:

- Upper management
- Supervisors and managers
- Employees
- Representatives from human resources and risk management
- Claims administrators
- Medical and rehabilitative providers
- Ergonomic, safety, and occupational health representatives
- Return-to-work coordinators/counselors
- Employee assistance program representatives
- Bargaining unit representatives

7. Define Specific and Measurable Program Objectives and Scope

Now that you have upper-management commitment and sign-off, the next step is to begin the development process. Here you will establish program scope, time frame, policies, and procedures, and train your staff to support the program effectively and consistently.

A critical resource for the RTW program is the person who coordinates the program. Depending on the size and complexity of your company, you may choose to give an existing person responsibility for the RTW coordination or to allocate one or more full-time equivalents to the role.

8. Create a Structure to Support Employees in Returning to or Staying at Work

Developing an overall company policy that addresses return to work should be written. A policy is completed through human resources, benefits, risk management, or a return-to-work coordinator, and is agreed to and adopted by all levels of management and administration, including labor union(s).

Employees who are continuously out of work for a period of time are clearly candidates for an RTW program. However, there should also be strong consideration in utilizing the program to provide opportunities for job modification to other employees who are unable to perform the functions of their jobs but have not been continuously absent. This could include employees who have recovered from a disabling event and are back to work but may need some follow-up or ongoing support to maintain optimal productivity, as well as employees who are at risk for injury or illness. Employees who face the potential of an altered work schedule to receive treatment or diagnostic procedures could also be candidates to benefit from job modifications in line with their abilities at a given point in time. Finally, whenever the employee is not totally productive due to health issues, this brings the concept of presenteeism into the picture and should be addressed.

9. Build Transitional Work Options from Functionally Based Job Descriptions for Absences

During this phase, your organization will:

- Identify and interact with employees who can benefit from the program, and gain physician approval to ensure their safe return to work

- Establish ways to get employees back on the job and improve their capacity to work, such as schedule changes, modified duty, and job accommodations

Once your program is completed, notify your insurance carrier/TPA and coordinate claim management activities to implement RTW processes.

Return-to-work plans should be individualized to the employee, the job, and potential modifications or accommodations available. In vocational rehabilitation, an RTW hierarchy is followed to assess and plan for keeping or returning an employee with a disability on the job. This approach to return to work must initially look for options within the employee's own job and then follow the hierarchy listed below.

- Same job, same employer
- Same job with modifications, same employer
- Different job, same employer
- Same job, different employer
- Same job with modifications, different employer
- Different job, different employer
- Retraining and education
- Self-employment

This hierarchy is used as a guide to determine possible RTW options for the disabled employee and the employer. They should each be considered while an RTW plan is being developed. For example, an employer and employee should first consider whether functional capabilities impact the employee's ability to stay on their own job or if accommodations are needed.

Making Job Accommodations

If accommodation of an employee in their own job is not possible, consideration should be given to a new position with the employer. Continuing down the hierarchy is recommended until an appropriate, reasonable, and acceptable solution is found that benefits both the employer and the employee.

Job Analysis/Description

An important step in coordinating an RTW program is having accurate job descriptions. A job description is a picture of what the job is, and is used to delineate the essential and nonessential duties and requirements of the job.

Ideally, a job description can be developed as a result of a job analysis. Specifically, a job analysis evaluates and analyzes the physical, cognitive, and psychological aptitudes, temperaments, environmental demands, and requirements of a job. From there, accurate job descriptions are developed and will assist in determining modifications for transitional work assignments going forward.

The key steps in conducting a job analysis include but may not be limited to:

- Visiting the work site and observing the job

- Interviewing the worker and supervisor

- Videotaping the job

- Separating the essential and nonessential tasks

- Describing both the physical and cognitive requirements of the job

Individualized Transitional Work Programs

Transitional work is any job, task, function, or combination of tasks and functions that a worker with restrictions can perform safely, for remuneration, without risk of re-injury or illness or risk to others. It is an interim step in the physical recovery and conditioning of a worker with restrictions. It represents an opportunity for the employer to protect the employability of the employee while reducing disability costs.

Transitional work can result in the following advantages to an employer organization:

- Therapeutic value: work hardening and conditioning

- Minimizes lost time from work

- Promotes early return to work

- Promotes continued occupational bonding

- Reduces financial costs of disability

- Increases employee's ability to return to work in a timely manner

Team Work

Several individuals are essential within organizations in developing, planning, and monitoring transitional work. These may include:

- Employees

- Supervisors

- RTW coordinators/counselors

- Human resources representatives

- Risk management representatives

- Medical providers

- Rehabilitation specialists/disability case managers/occupational health nurses

- Risk and safety personnel

- EAP coordinators/counselors

The team should at least include the employee, supervisor, and the individual charged with the RTW effort. The team must be:

- Knowledgeable about disability, functional capacity, and work-related absence

- Empowered by the employer to make decisions

- Able to create and maintain solid working relationships and lines of communication

- Able to balance the needs of the employee and the business needs of the employer

Many employers are currently creating a specific RTW coordinator/counselor position within their companies to oversee and coordinate all occupational and nonoccupational disability and RTW issues.

Basic guidelines for transitional work plans include:

- Specific start and end date

- Ability to change to accommodate variations in functioning

- Agreed-upon therapeutic goals

- Team approach

- Allows employee to be productive even if not 100%

- Have specific expected results (e.g., return to work, own job, full-time schedule)

Either the transitional work plans team or an individual (such as a risk manager, disability or RTW coordinator/counselor, or occupational health nurse) develops most transitional work programs with the employer.

Working with the Medical Provider

The physician or treatment provider should be:

- Educated about the nature of transitional employment

- Understand how the program works

- Provided a copy of transitional work job descriptions

- Work with the team to suggest or endorse transitional work assignments

- Involved in the monitoring of transitional work assignments and approving gradual changes in plans as needed

Communication with the employee is essential. Specific and clear documentation of what the individualized transitional work program is and what is expected is necessary. The letter should document and provide the specific job description with physical and cognitive demands, the goals of the transitional work program, start and end dates, periodic monitoring dates, and, if necessary, salary information. It should also include directions for the employee regarding who to go to for questions and problems.

Monitoring Transitional Work

While the employee is involved with the transitional work program, constant evaluation (ideally, at least once-a-week feedback and communication) is necessary with the employee, supervisor, and RTW team.

When Transitional Work Doesn't Work

No matter how committed an employer, employee, or supervisor is to the RTW process, sometimes RTW efforts do not succeed. There are many reasons for breakdown in a transitional work program. Some examples include:

- Decrease in functioning related to disability

- Employee dissatisfaction with transitional work

- Behavior problems

- Transitional work program not meeting business need

When transitional work doesn't work, the best course of action is to reconvene the transitional work team for that employee and revisit the original planning to find out what went wrong. In most cases, there are adjustments that can be made and the transitional work plan can be "rebooted". However, in many cases where an employee has either re-injured himself or herself or attempted to return to work too soon (i.e. without sufficient work capacity to support the transitional duties) the best course of action may be to allow the employee to go back out on leave until sufficient work capacity is recovered.

In any event, the key is to stay engaged with the employee, his or her supervisor, and the other members of the transitional work team unless and until it becomes clear that there is no suitable pathway to return to work and the only possible outcome is to help the employee find another line of work.

10. Educate All Levels of Employer Stakeholders, Training Supervisors, Managers, and Employees

The next step is to develop a training plan to deliver to your employees, supervisors, and managers. You should also consider compiling all of the RTW program documentation into an administrative manual for the program. The administration manual can be maintained in a paper form or centrally housed on a website.

Educating everyone involved with an RTW program is imperative. Employees, supervisors, and managers need to know what is expected of them. Here are some suggestions to promote understanding and support of your RTW program:

- Hold training sessions for employees, supervisors, and managers for your policy and program.

- Distribute written copies of your program or make policies available via internet or intranet link.

- Make the RTW program part of a new employee's orientation information.

- Train supervisors and managers on their role and responsibilities in the RTW program, disability policies, reasonable accommodations, and transitional return to work.

- Make RTW and disability awareness literature and media readily available.

11. Define Internal and External Roles and Responsibilities

Although the owner of the RTW program is the employer, external assistance can be helpful in constructing program design, evaluating and modifying existing policies and practices, and coordinating efforts among departments to expedite development.

Internal resource skills necessary to best support the RTW program may include:

- Exceptional understanding of the world of work and the impact of disability on individuals and employers

- Knowledge of RTW best practices and principles, and disability early intervention strategies

- Knowledge of both occupational (WC) and nonoccupational disability benefits

- Knowledge of employment and disability employment laws (ADA, FMLA, etc.)

- Communication and functional skills as a team leader with physicians, treatment specialists, supervisors, managers, employees, and human resources, risk and safety, and benefits and insurance claims staff

- Ability to gather and interpret functional, medical, and related information to determine work-related impairments

- Knowledge and ability to evaluate functional demands of jobs (job analysis)

- Capability to synthesize job demands and functional limitations to develop permanent job accommodations and transitional work assignments

- Identification skills for potential transitional work program opportunities with the employer

- Writing/development experience with transitional work programs

- Education and training skills with employees, supervisors, and managers about disability and RTW efforts

- Identification and coordination interfaces with community resources to ensure RTW program success

- Ability to monitor and evaluate RTW programs and individual transitional work assignments

- Case management and organizational skills

- Data and analysis capability to be used in program evaluation and business planning

Resource requirements for these programs varies by employer but are generally recommended to include:

- Human resources and disability (occupational and nonoccupational) professionals

- Bachelor's degree in rehabilitation, nursing, allied health (physical therapy), or related field

- Experience in workers' compensation, disability benefits, or medical case management

Other external resources can be helpful in order to:

- Assess current RTW culture: What is in place within existing policies, procedures, and practices for return to work? Are there disincentives imbedded in performance plans to deter RTW efforts? Is attendance addressed in staff performance reviews?

- Provide a needs assessment as a foundation for program objectives and scope

- Assist in identifying internal resources

- Facilitate the prioritization of program development activities by key stakeholders

- Draft RTW policy based on organizational input

- Develop RTW standards — criteria for application of the return-to-work program, written procedures for managers and staff, guidelines for employee follow-up, manager training, and involvement and coordination of other departments and services

- Coordinate job demand analysis and writing of job descriptions based on essential job functions, including scheduling completion in manageable steps

- Establish a database of modified and alternate work

- Update policies and procedures to reflect RTW program objectives

- Maintain communication about the RTW program within the organization

- Identify key components of a successful RTW intervention, and develop tracking mechanisms to evaluate results with the employer and employees

12. Establish Benchmarking Philosophy

Before the RTW program has been implemented, a method to measure the program's performance and judge its success must be developed. To measure the success of a program or practice, three questions must be answered:

- What will be measured?
    - Input
    - Output
    - Both

- In what units will measurements be taken?
    - Costs
    - RTW rates
    - Disability payment amounts

- How will variables that can impact the results be controlled?
    - Employee demographics
    - Program details
    - Economic barriers

Benchmarking was developed as a way to respond to these measurement problems, but it also addresses the additional goal of continuous process improvement. In its simplest form, benchmarking can be defined as a way to find and implement best practices that accomplish the goals of the program or function of interest. It is a process not only of measuring results, but also of improving results over time. At its most fundamental level, benchmarking is a way to manage change over time because it:

- Identifies operations that need to be improved

- Points out ways to improve them

- Provides statistics for measuring progress

- Helps persuade managers that there is a need for improvement

- Helps build and strengthen teamwork

13. Report Results

To track the RTW program's results, the coordinator should collect information from various sources to compare the results to program goals. Suggested measures follow:

- Aggregate claim costs by coverage type (e.g., STD, state disability, LTD, and WC)

- Overall utilization and cost patterns (e.g., incidence, number of claims, number of days, employee demographics, FT/PT status, EAP utilization)

- Days/hours saved from guidelines or previous durations

- Financial reports (e.g., claims paid, feeds, premiums, other expenses, summary of LTD claims paid, and Social Security award offsets)

- Supervisor activity (e.g., employee anticipated and actual return-to-work date, return-to-work status [transitional, accommodated, full duty, permanently restricted], accommodations discussed, accommodations implemented, and reasons for noncompliance return-to-work rates)

- Cost trend reports (i.e., benefits costs per employee, cost per claim, benefits as percent of payroll, aggregate costs by diagnosis, top five categories by incidence, STD and LTD incidence rates, average claim duration, overtime costs, replacement costs, Americans with Disabilities Act accommodations costs, employee turnover, and EAP costs per utilization)

The benefits to the employee include shorter recovery time, improved morale, and an increased perception of being valued by the organization. Employer benefits include reduced lost-time costs, improved workplace productivity, shorter STD durations, improved incidence rate on LTD, ability to return to work, increased productivity, and minimized activity disruption.

Conclusion

Overall, a successful RTW program is attainable within any work setting and can combat the total cost of absence, which is estimated at almost 9% of payroll for unplanned or extended absences and 35% of payroll for planned absences.[civ] It can also impact presenteeism, which is defined as "lost productivity that occurs when employees come to work but perform below par due to any kind of illness."[cv] As with any strategic business decision, program development requires an investment of time and resources, but the results speak for themselves: an ROI of bottom-line dollars, improved employee retention, morale, and productivity.

The program must focus on the medical situation or condition, not whether it occurred at or outside of work. To maintain employee productivity at its highest level, it is best to draw on any and all programs available. These could include any or all of the following, which are described in other chapters of this book:

- Health and wellness

- Employee assistance

- Disease management

- Safety

- Onsite medical facilities

Particularly important are programs that can positively affect the eight conditions responsible for the most lost time per full-time equivalent: depression, fatigue, allergies, back/neck pain, sleeping problems, anxiety, headache, and arthritis. For these conditions, presenteeism typically accounted for two and a half times more lost work time than from absence alone.[cvi] The challenge becomes how to identify and potentially reach out to appropriate candidates and to create a simple, user-friendly process to seek effective interventions, create and implement an employee specific plan, and track compliance and outcomes. Integration of the available programs and global recognition of the impact of improved productivity can be the ultimate result.

Resources

Source	Description	Website & Contact Information
DMEC's Foundation for Optimal Productivity: The Complete Return to Work Program Manual (2nd ed.)	A step-by-step approach for the implementation of a modified duty return-to-work program. The tools and processes are designed for application, regardless of the causation associated with the impairment or disability, including by small employers.	www.dmec.org
Job Accommodation Network (JAN)	The Job Accommodation Network provides free consulting services for all employers, regardless of the size of an employer's workforce. Services include one-on-one consultation about all aspects of job accommodations, including the accommodation process, accommodation ideas, product vendors, referral to other resources, and ADA compliance assistance.	http://janweb.icdi.wvu.edu 800.526.7234

Employer Checklist

As your organization sets out to establish a new and/or revised RTW (and/or SAW program, which uses most if not all the same tools and strategies), the following checklist can serve as a useful guide.

Key Questions	Yes/No	Comments
What is your organization's purpose for establishing a return-to-work/stay-at-work program?		
Have you determined the impact of lost time on your organization?		
Is corporate interested in a return-to-work program?		
Does your organization have a process to determine RTW program readiness?		
Are you able to plan for potential barriers or challenges and set strategies to overcome them?		
Does support exist for the program at all levels of the organization? Are program sponsors appropriately committed?		
Has your organization established specific and measurable program objectives and approaches to RTW? SAW?		
Does your organization have a structure to turn to for managing your RTW and SAW program, including the use of job descriptions, job analysis, and transitional work?		
Is training available with respect to the RTW program, and is it frequently updated to account for change?		

Chapter 14: USERRA and Employee Reintegration

Background and Context

In today's current work environment, it is probable that some portion of an employer's population will need to take military leave. In 1994, Congress enacted the Uniformed Services Employment and Reemployment Rights Act (USERRA). USERRA protects service personnel's reemployment rights when returning to the workplace after a certain period of time in the uniformed services. The purposes of USERRA are to encourage non-career service in the uniformed services, minimize disruption in the lives of people who enroll in the uniformed services and return to society, and prohibit discrimination by employers toward employees leaving for duty by choice or obligation.[cvii] USERRA applies to almost all U.S. employers, regardless of size;[cviii] including a U.S. employer of a foreign entity.[cix] Therefore, employers not only need to cope with the task of covering an employee's position while he or she is absent and insuring that position is open upon return but also addressing the reintegration of the employee in the workforce following possible physical and psychological injuries. USERRA is included in the U.S. Code at Title 38, chapter 43 (sections 4301 through 4335) and preempts state laws providing lesser rights or imposing additional eligibility criteria.[cx]

This chapter provides specific background on the governing law for employers whose employees are leaving for the uniformed services. It covers general rules for government and private employers. Also included in this section are special notes for consideration, possible costs, and organizational and employee impacts.

Eligibility, Employer Requirements, and Employee Rights

Uniformed service (Army, Navy, Air Force, Marine Corps, Air Force Reserve, Army National Guard, the National Guard, commissioned corps of the Public Health Service, and any other category of persons designated by the president in time of war or national emergency) includes active duty, active duty for training, inactive duty training (e.g., drills), initial active duty training, fitness examination for determination of duty, and funeral honors duty performed by National Guard and reserve members.[cxi] Nearly all employees are covered by USERRA, including part-time and probationary employees.[cxii] Nonpermanent employees taking leave are entitled to the unexpired portion of the work term in the remaining reemployment appointment period.

Employees must provide written or verbal notification to their employer prior to taking leave. However, if notification is deemed impossible or unreasonable, or if giving notice was precluded by military necessity, the employee is not required to give notice.[cxiii] The cumulative length of time an employee is absent also must not exceed five years. There are certain exceptions surrounding length of time for initial active duty exceeding five years for particular military programs, call-ups during emergencies, reserve drills, and annually scheduled active duty for training. Persons dishonorably discharged from service are not protected under USERRA. The employee must also report back to work in a timely manner or submit an application indicating timely return. During the period of time between training and call for duty, the employee is expected to return to work. If an employee is injured during military service, the definition of "timely return" may, in certain circumstances, be extended. If the employee is unable to make an application to return by the end of the recovery period, it will be extended for the minimum amount of time necessary for the employee to recover to the point where he or she can make an application to return to work, depending on the specific circumstance and time needed for recovery.[cxiv]

Information

Employers are required to notify employees of rights, obligations, and benefits under USERRA. A simple way to provide this information is to distribute to employees, in addition to posting, the USERRA rights poster available from the Department of Labor (go to http://www.dol.gov/vets/programs/userra/poster.htm or see resources at the end of this section). Employers can choose to provide this information in such cost-effective ways as electronic mail.[cxv] Another source of information is the Employer Support of the Guard and Reserve (ESGR), which is a free resource for employers and employees covering rights and obligations under USERRA, which can be found at www.esgr.org.

Employee Benefits

Employers must allow affected employees to elect their employer-sponsored health coverage for up to 24 months, beginning on the day on which the employee's leave begins.[cxvi] However, employers may require that individuals protected under USERRA pay up to 102% of total premiums for the elective coverage. An employee who serves in the uniformed services for less than 31 days may not be required to pay more than the normal employee share of the premium.[cxvii] Upon reemployment, employers must also reinstate any healthcare coverage to the employee without any waiting periods or exclusions.[cxviii]

Pension benefit plans offered by the employer, whether defined benefit or defined contribution plans, must be maintained while the employee is in the uniformed services. An employee re-employed under USERRA is not to be treated as having a break in service for their time in the uniformed services.[cxix] That is, each period served by an employee in the uniformed services is considered as service with the employer-maintained plan upon reemployment. The employer is responsible for funding any pension obligation and making employer contributions to the plan as if the employee were any other employee in the company. However, if an employee is absent on service for 91 or more days, the employer may delay making retroactive payments until it receives the appropriate documentation.

Rights and Responsibilities

In addition to providing notification to the employer, employees must return to work within a certain time frame. The required time between service and reemployment is dependent on duration in the uniformed services. Days of rest commence after the end of the calendar day of service duty and travel time to return home safely. Employees in the uniformed services for fewer than 31 days of service have an 8-hour rest period; those with 31 to 180 days have 14 days of rest; and those with more than 180 days have 90 days of rest. If the employee has suffered a service-connected injury or illness, they are allotted up to two years of rest.[cxx] If the employer deems the days of rest are impossible or unacceptable, the employee is then required to resume employment as soon as possible. No notification for restoration of employment is necessary.

If an employee specifies in writing that they are not returning to work, they are not entitled to rights and benefits under USERRA. However, it is the employer that has the burden of proving that a person knowingly provided clear written notice of intent not to return to a position of employment after service in the uniformed services and, in doing so, was aware of the specific rights and benefits to be lost.[cxxi] It is best for the employer to err on the side of caution to avoid potential legal battles, should the employee's situation change and they try to argue that they should have been reinstated.

On the other hand, regardless of whether the employee does or does not specify to the employer that they are leaving for the uniformed services, the employer must keep the position open upon the employee's return and place the employee on leave-without-pay status (LWOP-US) during the length of their service. To process an employee on LWOP-US status, an SF-52 form (see resources at the end of the chapter) must be filed.

During the employee's absence, the employer cannot demote the employee. Upon reemployment, the employee is entitled to seniority and other benefits provided to them since the date of commencement in the uniformed services. If the employee applied for a promotion while on LWOP-US and was approved, the promotion must be processed upon return as if the employee were never absent. Conversely, some employers may institute a reduction in force while the employee is on LWOP-US. If that is the case, the employee would not be included in the reduction in force. If the employee's position were eliminated, they would be entitled to retain a position of like status and pay. Reintegration emphasizes that the employee should return to the position of employment in which they would have been employed had it been continuous employment.

Employers are entitled to ask for an employee's discharge papers, leave, and earnings statements, school completion certificate, endorsed orders, or a letter from a proper military authority.[cxxii] However, if the employee does not provide this information in a timely manner or if the information does not exist, reemployment cannot be delayed or denied.[cxxiii]

If an employee incurred an injury while in service and became disabled, they are treated as any other employee under the Americans with Disabilities Act (ADA). The employer must provide accommodations and alternatives if possible. Information about the ADA and the more recent ADA Amendments Act (ADAAA) can be found in the next chapter.

Employer and Employee Impacts

Employer Impacts

As with any other labor-related act, there are many impacts to the employer. It is crucial for the employer to understand any effects of USERRA so that they will be prepared, should a situation arise. An unprepared employer can suffer legal or financial consequences.

Some of an employer's advantages in having USERRA in place include:

- Definition of reasonable is flexible: The employer can define what is reasonable and unreasonable in the instance of reemployment under USERRA. The employer can deem reemployment "impossible" in some circumstances and in accordance with their workplace specifics.

- Terms and conditions are clearly defined: It is clear to employers and employees what the circumstances of leaving for the uniformed services entails. Potential legal problems can be avoided due to the existence of USERRA.

- Outside experiences can be leveraged: The employee may bring back a wealth of experiences learned as a result of their service. The employee may be able to apply skills, such as leadership, directly gained from the uniformed services to the workplace and their peers upon reintegration.

Some of an employer's disadvantages in having USERRA in place include:

- Added responsibility: The employer bears the burden of providing all information to the employee. The employer must inform the employee of any forfeiting benefits, should the employee provide written notification that he or she is not returning upon honorable termination from the uniformed services.

- More resources required: The employer must keep employer-sponsored plans available to employees who leave for the uniformed services. Health plans must be offered to the employee for up to 24 months while on leave. Upon reemployment, no waiting periods or exclusions can be administered on the health benefits. Pension benefit plans must be maintained with employer-sponsored portions allocated to the employee's account while the employee is on leave. More administrative work must be executed to ensure a smooth transition from the employee working to taking LWOP-US. The employer may need to hire experts, such as lawyers, benefit administrators, actuaries, or accountants, to handle the process in detail.

- Continuation of jobs: The employer must keep the service member's position open for reemployment, despite the uncertainty of how long the employee will be absent and regardless of whether someone else must be hired to fill the position. For a person in a more senior position in the company, it may be difficult to find an individual to fill the role with a similar level of expertise and experience.

- Reduction in force requirements: If an employer experiences a reduction in force while the employee is on LWOP-US, the employee on leave is excluded. Even if the employer would have laid off the employee during the reduction in force had the employee been working continuously, USERRA protects the employee from such action. The employer must reinstate the employee to a job of similar status and pay upon reemployment if the employee's job was abolished during the reduction in force.

- Reintegration difficulties: It may be difficult to integrate the employee back into their position and work with other colleagues after circumstances have changed at the workplace and the employee's military experience has resulted in physical or psychological damage. Extended time away from work can cause an employee to be unfamiliar with the firm's current practices and technologies. In turn, this affects the worker's productivity and possible value to the company.

Employee Impacts

USERRA also impacts employees. It is in both the employer's and employee's interest to understand this impact and to make reintegration into the workforce as effective as possible. Some of the employee advantages of USERRA include:

- Encouragement and incentive: The employee is encouraged and has an incentive to commit to non-career uniformed services. They can leave work with the peace of mind that a position will be there for them when they return from military service.

- Protection from discrimination: The employer cannot deny initial employment, reemployment, retention in employment, promotion, or any benefit of employment while the employee is protected under USERRA.

- Healthcare and benefits continuation: The employee has the right to elect the employer-sponsored health and pension plan. For the health plan, employees can elect the coverage for themselves and any dependents for up to 24 months while absent from work. Upon reemployment, the employee is entitled to be reinstated into the health plan without waiting periods or exclusions, except for service-connected illnesses or injuries. Pension benefits are offered continuously with no break in service.

Clearly defined terms and conditions: It is clear to employees and the employer what leaving for the uniformed services will entail.

Barriers to using USERRA for employees are few, as the act sufficiently protects them and gives them ample opportunity for success at their employer prior to their departure. One challenge to note, however, is that of nontransparent discrimination. The employer may try to avoid hiring or interviewing candidates who are inclined to depart employment for military services. The recruiting process is often not evident enough to differentiate the reasons behind hiring decisions; thus, this situation is very subjective and difficult to prove.

Employer Cost of USERRA

There are many costs associated with USERRA, whether they are benefits-related, administratively driven, or connected to physical resources. Even though the level of military leave and USERRA reliance is unknown, the employer must be prepared to support it. Following is a list of possible costs that employers might experience.

Cost of Resources

Numerous resources must be utilized while fulfilling the requirements dictated by USERRA. The extra transition from having a working employee to having an employee taking LWOP-US status requires paperwork, possible expert advice, and time. Employers are also required by law to distribute any necessary information regarding USERRA to employees. The poster is a possible piece of information that may require extra time and handling.

Cost to Staffing

While the employee is on LWOP-US status, the employer may need to hire a temporary worker to fill the employee's position. Extra costs can be attributed to the time and effort needed to hire another person, train and familiarize the new person with the practices of the firm, and provide benefits to them. Should the employer decide not to hire an additional employee, the company is faced with the challenges of extra work for remaining staff, balancing workloads, payment of overtime, and decreased productivity.

Cost of Expertise

In addition to losing an employee to the uniformed services, the employer may lose particular expertise that the employee may have. This experience may not be easily replaceable, even if a temporary worker is hired. The employee may have years of experience and other valuable knowledge crucial to the company. Since USERRA applies to all employees, from caretakers to CEOs, the range of intellectual capital lost can be vital to the business.

Cost to Keep Benefits for the Employee

As mentioned above, the employer is responsible for any employer-sponsored benefits to the employee while they are enrolled in the uniformed services. Employees can choose to elect health benefit coverage for dependents and themselves for up to 24 months. Pension benefits must be given to the employee as if the employee were any other person working in the company; that is, the employer must fund the employer-sponsored portion of the pension benefit as if the employee had no break in service. The rule applies to both defined benefit and defined contribution plans. The cost to maintain benefits for the employee can be substantial, depending on the generosity of the plan.

Cost of Failing to Comply

Noncompliance with USERRA can be very costly to an employer. Monetary damages can total up to twice the accrued back wages and benefits as well as any costs associated with legal action.[cxxiv] In some states, such as Tennessee, it is a felony to refuse to hire or terminate an employee due to participation in the uniformed services.[cxxv] The employer who refuses to reemploy a veteran who served in the uniformed services may also face negative publicity. It is in the best interest of the employer to have a team in place, including disability assistance, to help a veteran of the uniformed services reintegrate into the workplace.

Cost of Complying

Complying with USERRA, although not without cost, can be manageable from an economic standpoint, as long as the employer is prepared and plans ahead. A study to determine employer costs associated with USERRA was conducted by the Institute for Defense Analyses (IDA) for the Office of the Secretary Defense in 2008.[cxxvi] The study incorporated survey responses from non-representative employers regarding costs. Respondents noted that hiring, pay, and training costs for replacement workers, costs of benefits, workplace dislocation, and lost business or revenue were incurred by complying with the act. The majority of the respondents, however, reported no costs from reservist activation (Figure 14.1). Less than 10% derived gains from reduced salary costs. Between 20% to 35% of employers (state and local government agencies and large for-profit businesses) reported net costs of workplace adjustment, and median cost varied between $2,320 (for nonprofit establishments) and $1,880 (government agencies), with small businesses ($2,001) and large businesses ($1,920) falling somewhere in between.

Figure 14.1
Employer's Workplace Adjustment Costs per Activated Reservist

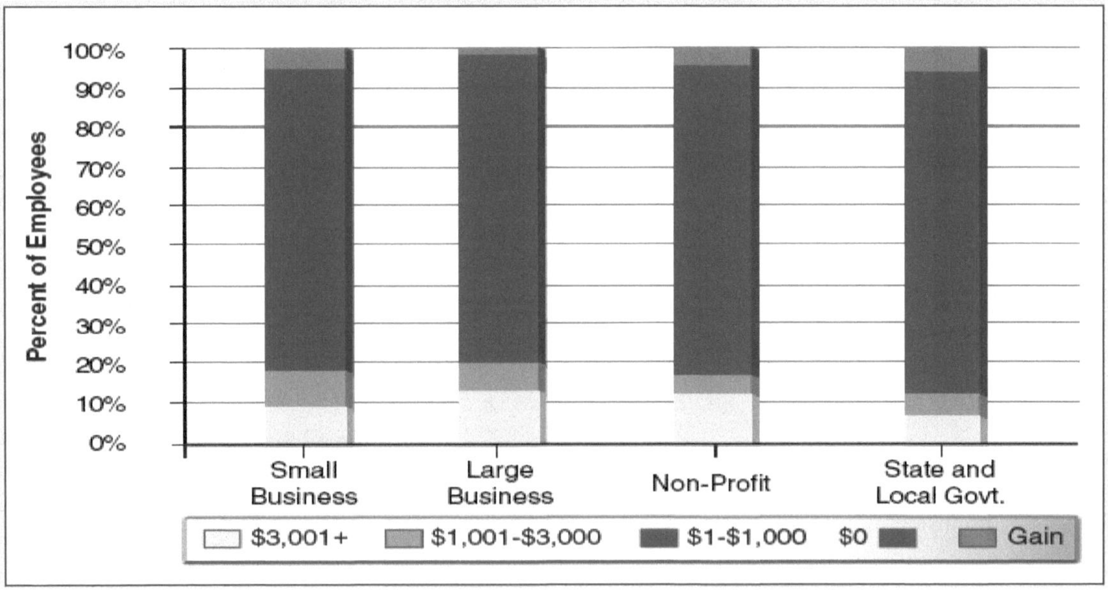

Source: Doyle C. The effects of reserve component mobilizations on employers. IDA Research Notes. (Fall 2008): 11-12.

A relatively small percentage of employers in each category experienced larger costs from reservist activation (Figure 14.2). Seventy-five percent of employers impacted by the act reported workplace costs of less than $5,000, but costs for the other 25% were in some cases much greater. Small businesses incurred costs of over $30,000, and some government agencies' workplace costs approached $40,000. A large fraction of the costs were attributed to training and distributing overtime pay to the remaining personnel.

Figure 14.2

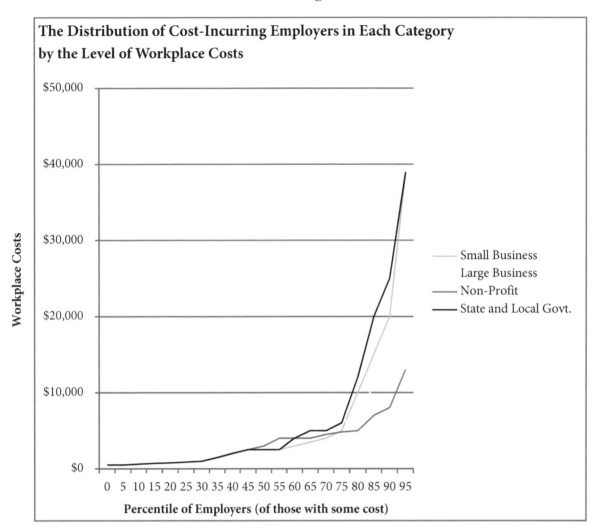

Source: Doyle C. The effects of reserve component mobilizations on employers. IDA Research Notes. (Fall 2008): 11-12.

A full survey conducted by IDA asked employers whether they had lost business. While only a small percentage of large firms reported any loss of business, more than 20% of small businesses did so (Figure 14.3). [cxxvii]

Figure 14.3

For Profit Employer Losses from Reservist Activation

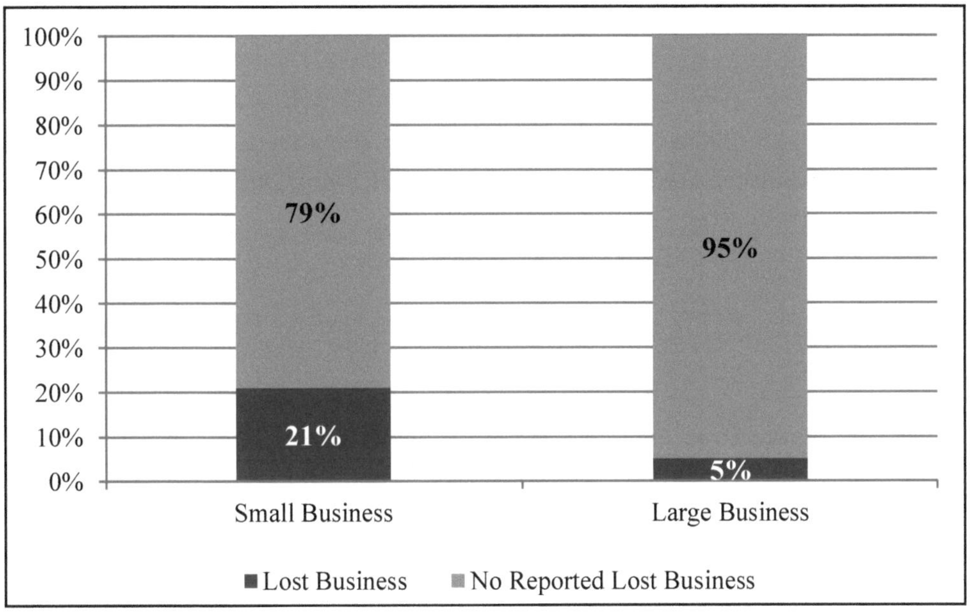

Source: Doyle C. The effects of reserve component mobilizations on employers. IDA
Research Notes. (Fall 2008): 11-12.

Employee Reintegration and Connection to Integrated Programs

Employee reintegration can be a difficult challenge for both the employer and employee. However, in
recognizing potential reintegration difficulties beforehand, the employer can benefit by being prepared to
address the legal and behavioral aspects of an employee's reintroduction to the workforce.

In addition to providing documentation of USERRA to the employee, the employer can also consider
providing extra resources and support to individuals, such as employee assistance programs (EAPs) and
other wellness or work/life balance programs. The addition of resources and support can lead to
successful reintegration of employees, especially those who have suffered physical or psychological
impacts during the course of their service. EAP can address mental health, family, and personal issues as
well as mentor employees as they transition back into the workplace.[cxxviii] Wellness and work/life plans can
encourage healthy behaviors and provide assistive services (e.g., daycare, financial planning) that can be
immediately put to use.

For larger companies, deployment may not cause as much of an issue as it might for a small company.
Larger corporations are more likely to have procedures in place in terms of filling the open position
temporarily while the service member is deployed. However, smaller companies may not have a plan of
action and face a greater burden trying to fill an empty position with either a new hire or allocating more
work to other employees on a temporary basis. Whatever the course of action, compliance is key;
therefore, employers of all sizes must be prepared from a legal and procedural standpoint when employees
return to work from service. Extended time away from work may cause an employee to be unfamiliar with
the firm's current practices and technologies, also potentially affecting the productivity and profitability of
the firm.

If an employee returns with a disability — physical or psychological — the employer must provide the same level of support it would to any other employee. This is not an unlikely scenario as recent military actions have produced a multiple number of soldiers wounded for every soldier killed. For example, data from Iraq, Afghanistan, and other areas in the Middle East indicates at least eight to 16 soldiers are wounded or physically disabled for every soldier killed in combat.[cxxix]

It is crucial that employers understand the behavior of an employee undergoing reintegration. Several best practices outlined by the Disability Management Employer Coalition 2007 Think Tank include:[cxxx]

- Establishing a military leave and return policy

- Conducting performance appraisals pre-deployment to establish a baseline for the returning employee and their manager

- Maintaining contact with the employee and their family during deployment and offering support to employees whose family members or other loved ones have been deployed

- Offering sensitivity training to managers, supervisors, and coworkers on issues and challenges faced by citizen soldiers during deployment and post deployment

- Providing mentoring programs to link returning citizen soldiers with veterans in the workforce

- Evaluating EAP for its ability to identify and address post traumatic stress disorder and other behavioral health-related issues

Further, military leave and employee reintegration should not be considered in a silo, but rather be viewed as part of an employer's broader integrated benefits strategy. Military leave can tie closely with family medical leave, depending on an employer's circumstances. Disability management will often be part of an employee's reintegration considerations and how accommodations can be made according to regulations such as ADA, ADAAA, and OSHA. Return-to-work policies employers already have in place contain valuable processes, practices, and checklists that should be consulted for best practices and ideas that can be translated to individual situations.

If an employer outsources its integrated benefits program, the outsourced provider can take on much of the communication and paperwork processes associated with reintegration. It can also work closely with the employer to provide effective case management, return-to-work services, and access to other important programs, such as EAPs, that are key to successful reintegration.

Resources

YOUR RIGHTS UNDER USERRA
THE UNIFORMED SERVICES EMPLOYMENT AND REEMPLOYMENT RIGHTS ACT

USERRA protects the job rights of individuals who voluntarily or involuntarily leave employment positions to undertake military service or certain types of service in the National Disaster Medical System. USERRA also prohibits employers from discriminating against past and present members of the uniformed services, and applicants to the uniformed services.

REEMPLOYMENT RIGHTS

You have the right to be reemployed in your civilian job if you leave that job to perform service in the uniformed service and:

- ✂ you ensure that your employer receives advance written or verbal notice of your service;
- ✂ you have five years or less of cumulative service in the uniformed services while with that particular employer;
- ✂ you return to work or apply for reemployment in a timely manner after conclusion of service; and
- ✂ you have not been separated from service with a disqualifying discharge or under other than honorable conditions.

If you are eligible to be reemployed, you must be restored to the job and benefits you would have attained if you had not been absent due to military service or, in some cases, a comparable job.

RIGHT TO BE FREE FROM DISCRIMINATION AND RETALIATION

If you:

- ✂ are a past or present member of the uniformed service;
- ✂ have applied for membership in the uniformed service; or
- ✂ are obligated to serve in the uniformed service;

then an employer may not deny you:

- ✂ initial employment;
- ✂ reemployment;
- ✂ retention in employment;
- ✂ promotion; or
- ✂ any benefit of employment

because of this status.

In addition, an employer may not retaliate against anyone assisting in the enforcement of USERRA rights, including testifying or making a statement in connection with a proceeding under USERRA, even if that person has no service connection.

HEALTH INSURANCE PROTECTION

- ✂ If you leave your job to perform military service, you have the right to elect to continue your existing employer-based health plan coverage for you and your dependents for up to 24 months while in the military.

- ✂ Even if you don't elect to continue coverage during your military service, you have the right to be reinstated in your employer's health plan when you are reemployed, generally without any waiting periods or exclusions (e.g., pre-existing condition exclusions) except for service-connected illnesses or injuries.

ENFORCEMENT

- ✂ The U.S. Department of Labor, Veterans Employment and Training Service (VETS) is authorized to investigate and resolve complaints of USERRA violations.

- ✂ For assistance in filing a complaint, or for any other information on USERRA, contact VETS at **1-866-4-USA-DOL** or visit its **website at http://www.dol.gov/vets**. An interactive online USERRA Advisor can be viewed at **http://www.dol.gov/elaws/userra.htm**.

- ✂ If you file a complaint with VETS and VETS is unable to resolve it, you may request that your case be referred to the Department of Justice or the Office of Special Counsel, as applicable, for representation.

- ✂ You may also bypass the VETS process and bring a civil action against an employer for violations of USERRA.

The rights listed here may vary depending on the circumstances. The text of this notice was prepared by VETS, and may be viewed on the internet at this address: http://www.dol.gov/vets/programs/userra/poster.htm. Federal law requires employers to notify employees of their rights under USERRA, and employers may meet this requirement by displaying the text of this notice where they customarily place notices for employees.

U.S. Department of Labor
1-866-487-2365

U.S. Department of Justice

Office of Special Counsel

1-800-336-4590

Publication Date—October 2008

Standard Form 52
Rev. 7/91
U.S. Office of Personnel Management
FPM Supp. 296-33, Subch. 3

REQUEST FOR PERSONNEL ACTION

PART A - Requesting Office *(Also complete Part B, Items 1, 7-22, 32, 33, 36, and 39.)*

1. Actions Requested	2. Request Number
3. For Additional Information Call *(Name and Telephone Number)*	4. Proposed Effective Date

5. Action Requested By *(Typed Name, Title, Signature, and Request Date)*	6. Action Authorized by *(Typed Name, Title, Signature, and Concurrence Date)*

PART B - For Preparation of SF 50 *(Use only codes in FPM Supplement 292-1. Show all dates in month-day-year order.)*

1. Name *(Last, First, Middle)*	2. Social Security Number	3. Date of Birth	4. Effective Date

FIRST ACTION

5-A. Code	5-B. Nature of Action
5-C. Code	5-D. Legal Authority
5-E. Code	5-F. Legal Authority

SECOND ACTION

6-A. Code	6-B. Nature of Action
6-C. Code	6-D. Legal Authority
6-E. Code	6-F. Legal Authority

7. FROM: Position Title and Number

15. TO: Position Title and Number

8. Pay Plan	9.Occ. Code	10.Grade or Level	11.Step or Rate	12. Total Salary	13.Pay Basis	16. Pay Plan	17. Occ. Code	18.Grade or Level	19.Step or Rate	20. Total Salary/Award	21. Pay Basis

12A. Basic Pay	12B. Locality Adj.	12C. Adj. Basic Pay	12D. Other Pay	20A. Basic Pay	20B. Locality Adj.	20C. Adj. Basic Pay	20D. Other Pay

14. Name and Location of Position's Organization

22. Name and Location of Position's Organization

EMPLOYEE DATA

23. Veterans Preference			
1 - None	3 - 10-Point/Disability	5 - 10-Point/Other	
2 - 5-Point	4 - 10-Point/Compensable	6 - 10-Point/Compensable/30%	

24. Tenure	25. Agency Use	26. Veterans Pref for RIF
0 - None 2 - Conditional 1 - Permanent 3 - Indefinite		YES NO

27. FEGLI	28. Annuitant Indicator	29. Pay Rate Determinant

30. Retirement Plan	31. Service Comp. Date (Leave)	32. Work Schedule	33. Part-Time Hours Per Biweekly Pay Period

POSITION DATA

34. Position Occupied	35. FLSA Category	36. Appropriation Code	37. Bargaining Unit Status
1 - Competitive Service 3 - SES General 2 - Excepted Service 4 - SES Career	E - Exempt N - Nonexempt		

38. Duty Station Code	39. Duty Station *(City - County - State or Overseas Location)*

40. Agency Data	41.	42.	43.	44.

45. Educational Level	46. Year Degree Attained	47. Academic Discipline	48. Functional Class	49. Citizenship	50. Veterans Status	51. Supervisory Status
				1 - USA 8 - Other		

PART C - Reviews and Approvals *(Not to be used by requesting office.)*

1. Office/Function	Initials/Signature	Date	Office/Function	Initials/Signature	Date
A.			D.		
B.			E.		
C.			F.		

2. Approval: I certify that the information entered on this form is accurate and that the proposed action is in compliance with statutory and regulatory requirements.

Signature   Approval Date

CONTINUED ON REVERSE SIDE
52-118

OVER

Editions Prior to 7/91 Are Not Usable After 6/30/93
NSN 7540-01-333-6239

PART D - Remarks by Requesting Office

(Note to Supervisors: Do you know of additional or conflicting reasons for the employee's resignation/retirement?
If "YES", please state these facts on a separate sheet and attach to SF 52.)

☐ YES   ☐ NO

PART E - Employee Resignation/Retirement

Privacy Act Statement

You are requested to furnish a specific reason for your resignation or retirement and a forwarding address. Your reason may be considered in any future decision regarding your re-employment in the Federal service and may also be used to determine your eligibility for unemployment compensation benefits. Your forwarding address will be used primarily to mail you copies of any documents you should have or any pay or compensation to which you are entitled.

This information is requested under authority of sections 301, 3301, and 8506 of title 5, U.S. Code. Sections 301 and 3301 authorize OPM

and agencies to issue regulations with regard to employment of individuals in the Federal service and their records, while section 8506 requires agencies to furnish the specific reason for termination of Federal service to the Secretary of Labor or a State agency in connection with administration of unemployment compensation programs.

The furnishing of this information is voluntary; however, failure to provide it may result in your not receiving: (1) your copies of those documents you should have; (2) pay or other compensation due you; and (3) any unemployment compensation benefits to which you may be entitled.

1. Reasons for Resignation/Retirement (NOTE: Your reasons are used in determining possible unemployment benefits. Please be specific and avoid generalizations. Your resignation/retirement is effective at the end of the day - midnight - unless you specify otherwise.)

2. Effective Date	3. Your Signature	4. Date Signed	5. Forwarding Address *(Number, Street, City, State, ZIP Code)*

PART F - Remarks for SF 50

Employer Checklist

The following checklist is meant to serve as a guide to help employers evaluate their current structure to support USERRA and what might need to be changed to facilitate effective employee reintegration.

Key Questions	Yes/No	Comments
Does your organization have a checklist available to assist in determining eligibility under USERRA? If so, does it include the following categories?		
The Armed Forces including: the Army, the Navy, the Air Force, the Marine Corps, the Air Force Reserve, the Army National Guard, the Air National Guard, commissioned corps of the Public Health Service, and any other category of persons designated by the president in time of war or national emergency, active duty, active duty for training, inactive duty training (such as drills), initial active duty training, fitness examination for determination of duty, and funeral honors duty performed by National Guard and reserve members		
Full-time, part-time, or probationary worker		
Cumulative service is five years or less (exceptions for service with a minimum requirement term)		
Employee is discharged honorably; dishonorable discharged employees are not eligible		
Employee returns to work in a timely manner (exceptions exist for employees with disabilities)		
Does your organization have the following processes in place?		
Ability to notify employees of rights, obligations, and benefits under USERRA		

Process for employees to elect employer-sponsored health coverage for up to 24 months (beginning on day employee's leave begins)		
Protocol for maintenance of employer-sponsored pension benefit plans for USERRA-eligible employees		
Ability to ensure employees have or have not forfeited USERRA rights and to notify employees of potential benefits forfeited (employer has the burden of proving the employee provided written notification that they do not plan on returning to work after service)		
Does your organization have experts within the following areas who are prepared to assist with administration of the various aspects of USERRA?		
Payroll		
HR/Benefits		
Legal		
Administrative		
Insourced		
Outsourced		
EAP		

Chapter 15: Americans with Disabilities Act

Background and Context

Employers had few legal restrictions or parameters when managing injured or ill employees before Congress passed the Americans with Disabilities Act (ADA) and the Family and Medical Leave Act (FMLA). Within a little more than one year, these two laws dramatically altered the legal landscape for employer efforts to enforce consistent standards concerning employee leave, attendance, and productivity.

The ADA's full impact was just starting to be realized when the ADA Amendments Act (ADAAA) was passed. The ADAAA was signed into law on September 25, 2008, and became effective on January 1, 2009. The Equal Employment Opportunity Commission (EEOC) then released Final ADAAA Regulations, which became effective on May 24, 2011. The ADAAA dramatically expands the number of medical conditions that constitute ADA "disabilities," opening the door to many more situations in which employers must consider "reasonable accommodation" requests. In reality, many of the most interesting ADA legal issues have yet to be decided because so few individuals were found "disabled" before the ADAAA. The ADA's complexity will become increasingly apparent as more ADA cases make their way through the courts. Employers must be prepared for this new legal environment.

As explained below, the ADA is the beginning, not the end. Employers must also consider state and local leave laws and varying standards for proving "disability," "reasonable accommodation," and other ADA concepts under state and local law. These laws also must be integrated with Genetic Information Nondiscrimination Act requirements and employer benefit programs. This integration effort requires considerable knowledge of the law and practical insight into how the law applies to daily employment and benefit decisions. This chapter aims to provide both.

Overview of the ADA

The ADA was enacted on July 26, 1990. President George H. W. Bush hailed the passage of the ADA as an "independence day" for people with disabilities, declaring, "With today's signing of the landmark Americans with Disabilities Act, every man, woman, and child with a disability can now pass through once-closed doors into a bright new era of equality, independence, and freedom."[cxxxi]

The ADA prohibits discrimination based on a disability in employment, public accommodations, and other areas. Additionally, employers must make reasonable accommodations for disabled employees' disabilities, unless the accommodation creates an undue hardship on the business. The anticipated changes were so dramatic that Congress gave private employers two years, or until July 26, 1992, to prepare for its implementation. Small employers with 15 or more employees were not covered until four years after enactment, or July 26, 1994.

Most expected the ADA would eliminate the "patchwork" of protections for individuals with disabilities under state law. The ADA's definition against discrimination was and remains broad and includes a failure to provide reasonable accommodations to qualified individuals with disabilities unless doing so poses an undue hardship on the employer. Individuals with disabilities are protected if they are qualified, meaning they can perform, with or without reasonable accommodations, the essential functions of positions sought or held. Disabled individuals also must satisfy any "qualification standards" for positions, including a qualification standard that individuals employed not pose a "direct threat" of harm to themselves or others in the workplace.

When enacting the ADA, Congress defined disability the same way it defined handicap under Section 504 of the federal Vocational Rehabilitation Act. Under the Vocational Rehabilitation Act, the definition of handicap was very broad. In 1984, a federal district court noted that in ten years, only one court had found a plaintiff not to have a "handicap." In 1987, the Supreme Court in School Board of Nassau County v. Arline [cxxxii] stressed the reason for such a broad definition for handicap. It noted that Congress included individuals who are regarded as being impaired in addition to those who are actually physically impaired because society's myths and fears about disabilities are "as handicapping" as actual physical limitations.

Against the backdrop of Arline, Congress enacted the ADA and issued findings that it would protect an "insular minority" of 43 million Americans with disabilities. [cxxxiii] The ADA defined disability (42 U.S.C. § 12102 [2]) [cxxxiv] as: [cxxxv]

> (A) A physical or mental impairment that substantially limits one or more major life activities of such individual;

> (B) A record of such an impairment; or

> (C) Being regarded as having such an impairment.

The ADA's intentionally flexible definition of "disability" opened the door to claims by individuals with relatively minor or temporarily disabling conditions. As the number of potential ADA plaintiffs began to grow, the Supreme Court reviewed several cases involving plaintiffs with medical conditions that arguably were less severe than those initially foreseen as part of the "discrete and insular minority" protected by the ADA.

Faced with claims by individuals with correctable vision, monocular vision, high blood pressure, and carpal tunnel syndrome, the Supreme Court tightened the reins on who was disabled under the ADA. This series of decisions was later rejected through the ADA Amendments Act.

As noted above, the ADAAA became effective on January 1, 2009, and it expanded the ADA's protections by explicitly rejecting the Supreme Court cases that narrowly construed the ADA's disability definition. The ADAAA states in Section 2(b)(5): "[I]t is the intent of Congress that the primary object of attention in cases brought under the ADA should be whether entities covered under the ADA have complied with their obligations, and to convey that the question of whether an individual's impairment is a disability under the ADA should not demand extensive analysis." Therefore, the ADAAA expressly provides in Section 4(a)(4)(A) that the "definition of disability . . . shall be construed in favor of broad coverage of individuals . . . to the maximum extent permitted by the terms of [the ADA]" and directs the Equal Employment Opportunity Commission (EEOC) to draft new regulations requiring a less demanding standard for an individual to establish a substantially limiting physical or mental impairment.

The ADAAA removed the original congressional findings in the ADA regarding the number of Americans with disabilities (43 million) and the finding that individuals with disabilities are "a discrete and insular minority." The Supreme Court had used these two sections to limit the ADA's scope. By removing these findings, Congress eliminated an historical basis for construing the ADA narrowly. The following summarizes in more detail the ADAAA's changes.

The Concept of Disability Under the ADAAA

As stated above, while the ADAAA retains the ADA's definition of disability, it says that term "shall be construed in favor of broad coverage of individuals . . . to the maximum extent permitted by the terms of [the ADA]" (Section 4[a][4][A]). The ADAAA also clarifies that "[a]n impairment that is episodic or in remission is a disability if it would substantially limit a major life activity when active" (Section 4[a][4][D]). The ADAAA's congressional findings and purposes state the EEOC's existing regulations interpreting the term "substantially limits" are "inconsistent with congressional intent, by expressing too high a standard" and express "Congress' expectation that the Equal Employment Opportunity Commission will revise that portion of its current regulations that defines the term 'substantially limits' as 'significantly restricted' to be consistent with [the ADA]" (Section 2[b][6]). Overruling the Supreme Court's Sutton v. United Air Lines decision, the ADAAA prevents courts and employers from considering mitigating measures an individual may be using when determining whether the individual is disabled. The only exceptions are ordinary eyeglasses and contact lenses. [cxxxvi]

While careful to state that an individualized assessment is always required, the Final Regulations allow that some impairments involve "predictable assessments" that, in "virtually all cases," will result in a finding that they are covered by the ADA. The Final Regulations seek to provide a "predictable, consistent, and workable" framework for ensuring more generous coverage and application of the ADA's discrimination prohibition. Impairments that should lead to "predictable assessments" include deafness, blindness, intellectual disabilities, partially or completely missing limbs or mobility impairments requiring the use of a wheelchair, autism, cancer, cerebral palsy, diabetes, epilepsy, HIV infection, multiple sclerosis, muscular dystrophy, major depressive disorder, bipolar disorder, post-traumatic stress disorder, obsessive compulsive disorder, and schizophrenia.

While it is unclear precisely how courts will interpret and apply the ADAAA's standard for disability, the congressional direction "that the question of whether an individual's impairment is a disability under the ADA should not demand extensive analysis" will certainly make it easier for applicants and employees to show they fall within the class of individuals protected by the ADA. This will make it much more difficult for employers to obtain court dismissals on this basis, which, in turn, will turn the spotlight in ADA cases on employer decision making — whether and how they individually assess if individuals with disabilities are capable, with or without reasonable accommodations, of performing essential job functions.

The ADAAA lowers the standard to prove an employer discriminated against an individual whom it regarded as having a disability. Traditionally, individuals claiming they were "regarded as" having disabilities had to prove the employer mistakenly regarded them as having impairments that substantially limited a major life activity. Under the ADAAA, an employer will now be liable under a "regarded as" theory if individuals can prove discrimination because of an actual or perceived physical or mental impairment, whether or not the impairment actually limits or is perceived to limit a major life activity.

The ADAAA clarifies that "regarded as" claims cannot be based on transitory and minor impairments where the impairment is expected to last less than six months. Also, employers are not required to provide a reasonable accommodation to individuals who are regarded as disabled, an issue over which the federal courts of appeals were previously split.

Employer Implications and Accommodation Realities

For years, many employers delayed exploring reasonable accommodations with injured or ill employees until they were determined to have long-term or "permanent" disabilities. Such thinking, born out of the Supreme Court decisions that narrowed the scope of the ADA's disability definition, is no longer applicable under the ADAAA. Employers who continue to view the ADA's disability definition narrowly likely will find themselves with considerable ADA exposures.

In reality, employers would be well advised to consider most individuals with injuries or illnesses lasting longer than a few weeks or months to be potentially protected under the ADA or state disability discrimination laws. As a practical matter, there is little downside to exploring reasonable accommodation with individuals who, in retrospect, may not be entitled to the ADA's protections. Keeping individuals at work through reasonable accommodation efforts, in fact, may reduce the need to administer increasingly complex medical leaves. For example, if, through reasonable accommodation, an injured worker remains fully employed, there would be no need to provide FMLA or other forms of job-protected leave and incumbents in positions would not be forced to work longer hours, be paid overtime, or exposed to fatigue that could lead to other work-related injuries. Obviously, ADA exposure and the accompanying legal costs also would be limited by more aggressive pursuit of reasonable accommodations.

The changes to "regarded as" theory could be the most significant of all of the ADAAA's changes. Every time employers make adverse employment actions because they believe individuals, due to injury or illness, are not qualified to perform their essential job functions safely or successfully, they must be prepared to confront a "regarded as" claim. Even if physical or mental limitations are not considered "substantial limitations" (and thus deny individuals the protections of the first prong of the ADA's disability definition), the expanded notion of "regarded as" protections may provide individuals a vehicle to attack the appropriateness of the employer's judgment that they are not qualified.

ADAAA and State Law Versions

As stated above, the impact of the new ADAAA is state specific. In states that do not have their own statutory protection for individuals with a disability or that have statutes that define disability analogously to the original ADA, the impact of the ADAAA should be significant as more individuals will be entitled to reasonable accommodations and protection from adverse employment action based on disability. Some states, however, including California, New York, New Jersey, and Connecticut, have already defined disability broadly for purposes of their anti-discrimination statutes.

For example, courts in these states have already interpreted the statutory definitions of disability under these states' anti-discrimination statutes as not requiring that an impairment "substantially limit" a major life activity. In addition, some states still go beyond the protections the ADAAA provide. In California, for instance, workers in the "regarded as" condition must still be offered reasonable accommodation, a protection not required under the ADAAA. Whether the ADAAA will cause courts to further liberalize the interpretation of "disability" under these state laws remains to be seen.

Interface with Other Statutes and Regulations

FMLA

The FMLA becomes a consideration in integrated disability and absence management programs when employees need leave due to injuries or illnesses. Section 102 of the FMLA is entitled "Leave Requirement." Section 102(a)(1) is labeled "Entitlement to Leave" and should be read literally as imposing just that — an entitlement to leave unless one of the exceptions provided in the law or regulations is met. In relevant part, that FMLA provision states "an eligible employee shall be entitled to a total of 12 work weeks of leave during any 12-month period . . . (D) Because of a serious health condition that makes the employee unable to perform the functions of the position of such employee." Section 102(b)(1) provides an entitlement to take leave intermittently or on a reduced leave schedule "when medically necessary" and further states that "the taking of leave intermittently or on a reduced leave schedule pursuant to this paragraph shall not result in a reduction in the total amount of leave to which the employee is entitled under subsection (a) beyond the amount of leave actually taken."

Section 104 of the FMLA provides for "employment and benefits protection." Section 104(a), entitled "restoration to position," states that "any eligible employee who takes leave under section 102 for the intended purpose of the leave shall be entitled, on return from such leave-- (A) to be restored by the employer to the position of employment held by the employee when the leave commenced; or (B) to be restored to an equivalent position with equivalent employment benefits, pay, and other terms and conditions of employment." Considered together, Sections 102 and 104 remove discretion from most FMLA leave situations. Accordingly, regardless of the impact on operations, employers generally must provide this leave.

The FMLA covers injuries or impairments that are considered "serious health conditions." A serious health condition is an illness, injury, impairment, or physical or mental condition that involves either an overnight stay in a medical care facility or continuing treatment by a healthcare provider for a condition that prevents the employee from performing the functions of the employee's job. The continuing treatment requirement may be satisfied by a period of incapacity of more than three consecutive calendar days combined with at least two visits to a healthcare provider within 30 days of the first day of incapacity (unless extenuating circumstances exist) or one visit and a regimen of continuing treatment. In both cases, the first in-person visit with the healthcare provider must occur within seven days of the first day of incapacity. Continuing treatment could also be established if any period of incapacity (as compared to the "more than three consecutive calendar days" referenced above) was due to pregnancy or prenatal care or a chronic condition. Continuing treatment also covers a period of incapacity that is usually permanent or long-term due to conditions for which treatment may not be effective or any period of absence to receive multiple treatment for restorative surgery following an accident or injury or a condition which, in the absence of medical intervention or treatment, likely would result in incapacity of more than three full consecutive calendar days (such as cancer [chemotherapy, radiation], severe arthritis [physical therapy], or kidney disease [dialysis]).

FMLA leave is available to "eligible employees." To be an "eligible employee," an employee must: (1) have been employed by the company for at least 12 months (which need not be consecutive); (2) have been employed by the company for at least 1,250 hours of service during the 12-month period immediately preceding the commencement of the leave; and (3) be employed at a work site where 50 or more employees are located within 75 miles of the work site.

HIPAA

The privacy provisions of the federal Health Insurance Portability and Accountability Act of 1996 (HIPAA) apply to health information created or maintained by healthcare providers who engage in certain electronic transactions, health plans, and healthcare clearinghouses. The HIPAA Privacy Rules specifically exclude from the definition of a "health plan" any policy, plan, or program to the extent that it provides, or pays for the cost of, excepted benefits, which are listed in Section 2791(c)(1) of the Public Health Service Act, 42 U.S.C. 300gg-91(c)(1). See 45 C.F.R. Section 160.103. As described in the statute, excepted benefits are one or more (or any combination thereof) of the following policies, plans, or programs:

- Coverage only for accident, or disability income insurance, or any combination thereof

- Coverage issued as a supplement to liability insurance

- Liability insurance, including general liability insurance and automobile liability insurance

- Workers' compensation or similar insurance

- Automobile medical payment insurance

- Credit-only insurance

- Coverage for onsite medical clinics

- Other similar insurance coverage, specified in regulations, under which benefits for medical care are secondary or incidental to other insurance benefits

State and Local Disability Discrimination Laws

While the ADAAA lessens the need to rely upon state and local laws to bring a viable claim of disability discrimination, some state laws impose a more onerous burden on employers to initiate an interactive dialogue about reasonable accommodations. Many state or local laws also offer employees potentially broader damages than the ADA. It is important, therefore, that employers consider state disability discrimination laws as they develop integrated disability and absence management programs.

State Leave Laws

In addition to the FMLA, some states potentially require that employers provide leave under workers' compensation laws, pregnancy disability leave laws, or family and medical leave acts.[cxxxvii] Unlike the FMLA, leave obligations under these laws may exist without regard to an employee's length of service or the number of individuals employed in the state or at a specific work site. Before even considering leave obligations under company policy or as a reasonable accommodation under the ADA or a state or local disability discrimination law, employers should identify any state laws providing leave "entitlements." For employers maintaining operations in multiple states, that task is onerous but critical to a successful disability management program.

Remedies for violating these state laws vary greatly. Most provide a right to file complaints with state agencies charged with enforcing the laws and/or to file a lawsuit for damages caused by a violation.

Wage and Hour Issues

The Federal Fair Labor Standards Act (FLSA) generally impacts integrated disability and absence management programs in two ways. First, its provisions requiring a minimum wage set a floor for any wage rate paid to employees performing transitional work assignments. Second, when employees who are classified as exempt from the FLSA's overtime provisions return to work with their hours or duties restricted, employers generally must still pay them their regular salary. Failing to do so could jeopardize the FLSA exemption for that employee and potentially others in the same job classification, opening the door to potentially significant liability for unpaid overtime. Employers may be entitled to reclassify employees, either temporarily or permanently, into a different job classification to avoid this FLSA risk. Most states also have wage and hour laws that contain provisions similar to the FLSA; however, state wage and hour laws might differ from the FLSA in important ways.

National Labor Relations Act

Unionized employers must always evaluate whether they have the right, under a collective bargaining agreement, to implement leave or accommodation programs. If the right to implement such a program is not covered by a collective bargaining agreement, it generally would be viewed as a mandatory subject of bargaining under the National Labor Relations Act.

Many union contracts indirectly impact integrated disability and absence management programs. Seniority provisions, for example, might provide employees with a right to certain job openings, thereby restricting an employer's ability to return an injured employee with less seniority to work in that position. The impact on a collective bargaining agreement is one factor to be considered in determining whether a reasonable accommodation is an undue hardship under the ADA.

Integrated Program Considerations

Employers and counsel must be mindful that ADA leave obligations are only one piece of the leave puzzle. Before analyzing ADA obligations, which are infused with discretion and judgment about what is reasonable or an undue hardship, employers must first provide all the leave affirmatively required under federal, state, or local law. As noted above, the federal FMLA and state leave laws must be considered. Thereafter, employers also ought to provide any additional leave granted under company policy. In effect, the question of whether employees are entitled to additional leave as an ADA reasonable accommodation is the last of three distinct inquiries. Employers proceeding to analyze ADA leave obligations before considering statutory leave entitlements or company leave policy commitments may unwittingly miss important leave obligations. Conversely, as employers increasingly outsource FMLA, short- or long-term disability, and workers' compensation programs, special care must be taken to ensure that absence management programs integrate ADA leave analysis into FMLA or disability benefit programs.

A key element of doing so is identifying the essential functions of jobs and the physical demands traditionally associated with performing such job functions. While many employers identify physical demands—such as the ability to lift a specified amount of weight or to squat, crawl, or bend—as essential job functions and courts frequently fail to challenge such assertions, employers need to be wary of the potential perils of doing so. The ADA's concept of "reasonable accommodation" is specifically intended to force employers to explore creative ways to overcome barriers faced by individuals with disabilities. Many individuals with physical disabilities obviously encounter difficulty engaging in physically demanding activities such as lifting, bending, and squatting.

If such demands are considered "essential job functions," they need not be compromised because, to be qualified, an individual must be able to perform essential job functions. For this reason, it is more appropriate to regard the goal sought to be accomplished when engaging in these physical activities as the essential job functions. For example, rather than characterizing the ability to lift 100 pounds as an essential job function of a warehouse employee, one might describe the essential job functions as "transporting boxes from trucks to shelves." If functions are described in this manner, it also is very useful to communicate the traditional physical, mental, sensory, and environmental demands associated with performing such functions. Together, knowledge of both function and traditional physical demands needed to perform functions sets the stage for an interactive dialogue about alternative ways (i.e., reasonable accommodations) that allow individuals to accomplish a job's function despite physical or mental limitations.

While the ADA does not require employers to develop job descriptions, job descriptions accurately prepared and periodically revised will be an invaluable tool to supervisors and managers who must assess the abilities of applicants and employees on a daily basis. In addition, the EEOC states that if written job descriptions are prepared before advertising or interviewing applicants, they will be considered evidence of the essential functions of the job. Accordingly, properly written job descriptions can be an invaluable tool to ensure ADA compliance efforts and likely will place employers in a favorable posture to defend most ADA claims.

The fundamental elements of a functional job analysis under the ADA can be gleaned from the EEOC's ADA Regulations and Policy Guidance. We use the word fundamental because the degree of analysis engaged in by a company will depend on a number of factors, including the financial and/or human resources available to perform the analysis, the number of positions to be analyzed, and the nature and complexity of the positions. At the very least, however, employers who are seeking to identify what functions are essential should consider the factors referenced by the EEOC. Those factors generally require employers to answer the following questions about each job function:

1. Are all employees in the position actually required to perform this function?
2. Did previous employees perform this function?
3. Does the position exist to perform this function?
4. Would the demands of the business prevent other employees from performing this function if the incumbent could not?
5. Does performance of this function require a special expertise or skill?
6. Would removing this function from the list of duties required to be performed fundamentally alter the position?
7. Would failure to perform this function have significant consequences?
8. Does the incumbent spend a significant portion of his or her workday (week) performing this function?
9. Does a collective bargaining agreement require or prohibit the performance of this function?
10. Do current or past job descriptions list the function as a requirement of the position?

Employers should review the answers to these questions plus any other relevant evidence and determine whether each function is essential or nonessential. As a general matter, affirmative answers to these questions tend to show that a function is essential. Employers should obtain input from supervisors, employees, union representatives, and other individuals familiar with the position as they answer these questions. Employers should document their efforts, noting specifically the date or time frame when they analyzed the position. Since the analysis of existing positions may take some time, many employers choose to start with those jobs that raise concerns about threats to employee health and safety.

Employers also must be careful to avoid rigid limitations on the length of medical leaves of absence. Such practices run counter to the currently accepted ADA requirement that additional job-protected leave be considered as a reasonable accommodation. The EEOC, in particular, likely will find fault with any leave policy that does not, on its face, communicate a willingness to consider extensions of medical leaves as potential reasonable accommodations for individuals with disabilities. Employers need to examine leave policies to ensure they do not mandate termination of employment if employees are unable to return to work after a stated period of medical leave.

Conclusion

The ADA is primarily concerned with preventing discrimination and allowing working opportunities to those with disabilities. The requirements of the ADA should be considered in coordination with integrated disability, absence management, and overall health and productivity management programs offered by the employer. Accommodations made in compliance with the ADA may assist in returning disabled employees to work, thereby reducing the costs of disability, workers' compensation, and overall integrated programs.

Additionally, the experience of assisting currently disabled employees under ADA may ease the process of reintegrating newly disabled employees back to work. For example, the employer may have already installed ramps or other access devices that will be needed or may have best practices established for assisting with a disability. If a newly disabled employee is reluctant to return to work, the presence of current employees working with a similar disability would strengthen the employer's case that the employee can indeed return to work.

Employer Checklist

As employers work to comply with the ADAAA and ensure they are following the ADA, they should work closely with their legal counsel to confirm their actions are appropriate. As part of their preparation, the following issues should likely be considered:

- More people will likely be eligible for reasonable accommodations under the ADAAA. Those reasonable accommodations could include such things as telecommuting, working from home, and modified work schedules. Employers must be prepared to document if providing such requested accommodations would be an undue hardship to the employer.[cxxxviii]

- "Regarded as" claims are likely to be much more common and formidable. This highlights the importance of documenting the legitimate, nondiscriminatory reasons for employment decisions and the objective factual evidence about jobs, such as essential job functions reflected in current and accurate job descriptions, which formed the basis for evaluating workers.

- Employers should focus on defining the levels of performance and productivity that are required in the essential functions of the job.

- Adequate documentation will be very important. Employers should consider designating individuals responsible to review denials of reasonable accommodation requests and training them on ADA and ADAAA standards.

- As regulators come to terms with these changes it is likely that employers can count on more scrutiny of the interactive process that they engage in with their employees. Employers will now need to think beyond the "definition of disability" stage. Instead, employers must focus on the specific employment action, including requests for accommodation and the accommodation process.

- Training of frontline managers and supervisors will aid compliance. Many supervisors withhold from management medical information that employees communicate casually or "confidentially," believing this is necessary to protect an employee's privacy interests. Because such information frequently triggers employer obligations to explore reasonable accommodations and/or administer FMLA leave, employers should consider training managers and supervisors on the potential legal significance of employee medical information they may receive and internal procedures for communicating confidentially such information.

- Ensure ADA and other protected absences are not considered in annual performance reviews and/or performance-based promotion or compensation decisions. Even if employers do not discipline employees under leave or no-fault attendance policies, they must guard against attendance or leave being considered in promotion or performance-based compensation decisions. Training of managers and supervisors will help reduce exposure of these claims, as will periodic audits of decisions impacting individuals who are known to have a history of medical absences protected by the ADA, FMLA, or state law.

- Develop written policies that communicate a willingness to consider excusing absences under the ADA and other similar laws. Policies should, on their face, communicate to employees the intent to consider excusing absences on a case-by-case basis as a form of reasonable accommodation under the ADA.

- Ensure internal systems to track the reasons for occasional absences. Compliance with ADA, FMLA, and state law absolutely requires a robust record-keeping system. Employers should reevaluate whether they have the tools to comply effectively with these increasingly burdensome laws.

To address the above issues and other needs, the employer's internal policies, procedures, and checklists that are already being used should be updated based on the most current EEOC guidance. The following summary checklist can help employers work in the proper direction.

Key Questions	Yes/No	Comments
Is your human resources staff informed that they may not discriminate based on disability when hiring?		
Is your human resources staff informed of the definition of disability as updated under ADAAA, and do they understand they must interpret it as broadly as possible when in doubt?		
Is there a procedure for a disabled employee to request reasonable accommodations and for these accommodations to be reviewed for undue hardship to the employer?		
Is there a policy for reviewing claims under short- or long-term disability to see if ADA applies?		
Is there a policy for reviewing claims under workers' compensation to see if ADA applies?		
Is there a policy for reviewing claims under FMLA to see if ADA applies?		
Is there a policy for reviewing claims under other leaves of absence (e.g., personal leave) to see if ADA applies?		

Resources

EEOC website: http://www.eeoc.gov/facts/fs-ada.html

Text of ADAAA: http://www.eeoc.gov/laws/statutes/adaaa.cfm

DMEC, Navigating the Waters.

Chapter 16: Workplace Safety and Regulatory Management

Introduction

The goal of an effective workplace safety program is the development of a long-term plan that succeeds in protecting people from injury and death, complying with regulations, and controlling the associated financial costs of loss. At its core, its objective is to save lives, prevent injuries and illnesses, and protect the organization from harm.

Core Regulatory Requirements

Sound safety leadership results in the prevention and control of employee injuries, exposures to toxic substances, and other unhealthful conditions that can produce work-related illnesses. Effective workplace safety systems produce lower costs, higher productivity, reduced waste, and improved employee morale. The Occupational Safety and Health Administration (OSHA) is the federal agency responsible for worker safety in the United States. States either operate their own safety and health regulatory plan (state plan) or engage the federal government (federal plan) to oversee OSHA enforcement [cxxxix] (see www.osha.gov/dcsp/osp/index.html for plan information).

Regardless of the title of your workplace safety program, the managers or supervisors involved in safety at your organization, or the state in which you operate, your written workplace safety program must contain these core elements:

- Management commitment and responsibility (how managers, supervisors, and employees are responsible for implementing the program and how continued participation of management will be established, measured, and maintained). This section delineates management's commitment (in writing) to safety and health.

- Employee involvement (and how safe work practices and rules are enforced). This section discusses ensuring compliance among the workforce regarding codes of safe practice and any other safety and health procedures designed to safeguard their welfare.

- Work site analysis (the methods used to identify, analyze, and control new or existing hazards, conditions, and operations)

- Hazard recognition and resolution (how workplace hazards are recognized and resolved, and how incidents are investigated and corrective action implemented). This section also includes incident investigations and procedures for conducting the investigations and taking action on the findings.

- Training and education (how the plan is communicated to all affected employees so that they are informed of work-related hazards and controls). This section provides for internal communications that highlight workplace hazards and applicable safety and health procedures.

- Record keeping (maintaining injury and illness, safety training, and inspection records)

Management Commitment and Responsibility

Management participation and commitment is crucial to the success of the workplace safety program. Employees and supervisors need to be given the authority to identify and correct hazards; the budget to purchase new equipment or make repairs; the training necessary to work safely and to recognize hazards; and systems in place to get repairs made, materials ordered, and other improvements accomplished.

Management establishes the importance of the workplace safety program, both by the priority given workplace safety and health issues and by the example set by initiating safety and health improvements, correcting hazards, enforcing safety rules, rewarding excellent performance in safety and health, and following all safety rules. Safety and health programs are similar to quality improvement and other efforts that organizations engage in to continually improve performance, customer service, competitiveness, organizational culture, and so forth.

Employees reflect the safety attitudes of their leaders and managers. If the organization is not interested in preventing employee injuries and illnesses, employees will probably not give safety and health much thought. For example, think about the message it sends when the boss walks through the shop without safety glasses when everyone else has to wear them. Therefore, it is absolutely essential that organizational leaders and managers demonstrate at all times their personal concern for employee safety and health. An organization's actions and policies must clearly demonstrate that safety is an intrinsic company value.

Workplace safety programs must describe how everyone in the organization, whether management, first-line supervision, or labor, is responsible for making the program work. These duties should be clearly laid out. Everyone in the organization should be able to explain what their role is in creating a safer, healthier workplace.

To help employees engage in a sense of ownership and responsibility for creating a safe workplace, they should be provided with the training, equipment, resources, and assistance to carry out their roles. Employees and supervisors need to know where to go to obtain assistance to resolve issues of safety and health concerns and to get questions answered. Most important, they need to know how to correct safety and health hazards in the workplace as the hazards are identified.

Enforcement of Workplace Safety Programs

Responsibility for safety and health exists at all levels in an organization. Owners, managers, supervisors, and employees should all know what their duties are to create a safe and healthful workplace, and they must follow all safety rules. All employees must know and understand what they need to do and not do to make the workplace safer for themselves and their coworkers. Workers must be trained about safe work practices, proper use of engineering controls, and personal protective equipment (PPE). Additional strategies to enforce safety include:

- Coaching employees to correct unsafe actions and disciplining them if violations continue. Safety procedures should become a key part of the daily routine.

- Enforcing safety rules. Supervisors are responsible for ensuring that engineering controls and PPE are correctly used and that procedures are followed correctly. Supervisors should be taught basic skills in being an effective supervisor.

- Supporting and encouraging supervisors who attempt to enforce the rules fairly and equally. Safe work practices rules are only effective if they are enforced. Typically, OSHA holds the employer responsible if the organization does not enforce its own rules. Many supervisors do not like to discipline employees, especially if the employees are generally good workers. Others may not feel that management backs them when they take disciplinary action against employees. If workplace rules are not enforced, they cease to have meaning.

- Enforcing safe work practices. Such enforcement should be fair and consistent throughout the organization and based on an established policy.

- Setting and obeying the same rules as the rest of the workforce. Management and supervisors should be conscious of the examples they set for the workplace.

- Recognizing exceptional workplace safety and health performance.

Employee Involvement

Leaders and managers can demonstrate their depth of safety commitment by involving employees in the planning and delivery of workplace safety. Employees who are involved in the identification and resolution of safety and health problems bring unique insights and energy in achieving the organization's safety goals and objectives. Doing this also creates employee safety buy-in and safety ownership. Employees are among the most valuable assets you have, and their safety, health, and goodwill are essential to the success of the business. Asking employees to cooperate with you in protecting their safety and health not only helps to keep them healthy, but also makes a manager or supervisor's job easier. Here are actions to consider that engage a workforce:

- Hold a meeting with all employees to communicate the workplace safety policy and discuss objectives for safety and health.

- Ensure that all leaders, managers, and supervisors follow all safety requirements that apply to all employees (e.g., if an area requires a hard hat, safety glasses, and/or safety shoes, everyone in management must wear them when in the area, even if only briefly). Presidents and owners of large companies have been known to become personally involved (supportive) when a person has suffered an injury.

- If you run an administrative office or department, practice good ergonomics.

- Take advantage of employees' specialized knowledge and encourage them to buy into the program by having them make inspections, conduct safety training, or investigate incidents.

- Make clear assignments of responsibility for each part of the organization's safety and health program, and make sure everyone understands them. The more people involved, the better. A good rule of thumb is to assign safety and health responsibilities in the same way production responsibilities are assigned.

- Make working safety a part of everyone's job.

- Provide those with safety and health responsibilities enough people, time, training, money, and authority to fulfill their role.

- After assignments are made, make sure the jobs get done.

- Recognize those who do well and correct those who don't.

- Review accomplishments and reevaluate whether new objectives or program revisions are needed at least once a year.

- Institute an accountability system in which all employees are held accountable for safety.

In certain companies, some employees may be part of an informal safety committee in which they participate in various safety activities and responsibilities. However, some states require all employers with more than a certain number of employees (or at a certain injury rate) to establish a safety committee (also known as joint labor management safety committee). Check your state's OSHA regulations (www.osha.gov/dcsp/osp/index.html) to determine if safety committees are required.

Work Site Analysis

Employers are encouraged to use a needs assessment tool/checklist (a sample is provided at the end of this section) to help identify physical hazards and unsafe work practices.

It is management's responsibility to know which workplace items or substances could harm people in the organization. Work site analysis is a group of processes that helps you understand what's needed to keep workers safe. Items to consider may include:

- Requesting a consultation visit from the state onsite consultation program covering both safety and health to get a full survey of the hazards that exist in the workplace and those that could develop.

- Contacting your organization's workers' compensation insurance carrier. Some companies offer a safety and health walk-through and provide recommendations.

- Contracting services from expert private consultants.

- Establishing a way to obtain professional advice when you make changes to procedures or equipment to ensure that the changes are not introducing new hazards into the workplace.

- Finding ways to stay current on newly recognized hazards in your industry (associations, newsletters, and online groups).

- Periodically reviewing with employees each job, analyzing it step-by-step to see if there are any hidden hazards in the equipment or procedures.

- Setting up a self-inspection system to check hazard controls and evaluate any new hazards.

- Making sure employees feel comfortable in alerting you when they see things that look dangerous or out of place.

- Learning how to conduct a thorough investigation when things go wrong. This will help you develop ways to prevent recurrences.

- Reviewing your company's injury and illness records from previous years to identify patterns that may help you devise strategies to improve workplace safety and health. Periodically review several months of records to determine if any new patterns are developing. In small companies, there may be no injuries for review; however, there may be "near misses" (those events in which injury or property damage does not occur but could have if conditions were different) or hazards that can be identified.

Hazard Recognition and Resolution

Hazard recognition and resolution is another core aspect of workplace safety. It includes hazards that currently exist in the workplace and those that may occur due to future changes, such as the introduction of new equipment, processes, or materials, or revision of existing procedures.

Hazard Recognition

Organizations can use several methods to identify hazards. Some rely solely on walk-around inspections by supervisors, management, or safety committees and employees. Others involve formal hazard analyses of different parts of the operation or use a combination of methods. Regardless of the methods used, the best hazard identification methods combine expert opinion about safety and health hazards with input from either a cross-disciplinary team or at least one employee who works directly with the process or equipment in question. At least some of the individuals involved in hazard identification should be trained in hazard recognition.

Inspections should be made on a regular basis to identify both newly developed hazards and those previously missed. In certain environments, you should also consider the value of periodic industrial hygiene monitoring and sampling for hazardous substances, noise, and heat.

A checklist is one of the more common tools used for hazard identification. It can serve as a good starting point to help employers and employees identify workplace hazards. One disadvantage of using a checklist is that it focuses an inspection on certain specific hazards and can cause other hazards not on the checklist to go unnoticed. This is particularly true of generic checklists that are not site- or process-specific.

A method often used to identify workplace hazards is job hazard analysis (JHA), also known as job safety analysis (JSA). Job hazard analysis is a step-by-step method of identifying the hazards associated with a particular task or job. It is important to involve the employee who normally performs the job in the development of the JHA. Steps involved in creating a JHA include:

1. Listing all job steps or tasks that the worker must perform to complete the job. Create this list by watching the employee perform the operation in question, recording each step of the process, and reviewing the list with the employee for completeness.

2. Reviewing each step to determine what safety and health hazards are or could be present; these should be listed as well. Further observation may be necessary to ensure all possible hazards are identified.

3. Determining which measures, if any, can eliminate or lessen the risk of injury or illness to the employee from the identified hazards. These measures can include engineering controls, such as guarding or ventilation; work practices; administrative controls, such as job rotation; and PPE.

Some employers feel there is benefit in having a professional from outside the organization inspect or audit a facility's workplace safety program. This person may have more specialized knowledge in the safety and health field than others in the organization. An outsider may also recognize hazards you have overlooked. Sources for onsite help with occupational safety and health issues include consultants from governmental assistance offices, private firms, insurance company loss control representatives, and occupational safety practitioners.

In any event, there is a Job Hazard Analysis Checklist provided in a following section on documenting workplace safety.

Hazard Resolution

After hazards are identified, they should be eliminated or abated to the degree it is feasible. Both OSHA and best practices principles promote a hierarchy of control measures. At the top of the hierarchy are engineering controls, which include tactics such as machine guarding, guardrails, ventilation, and raw material substitution. All reasonably feasible engineering controls should be exhausted before other measures are taken.

Work practice improvements, another technique for employee protection, involves modifying tasks and jobs to reduce employee exposure to hazards. These include measures such as wetting down areas to keep airborne dust levels to a minimum, or replacing lids on solvent degreasing tanks when not in use. Administrative controls, such as job rotation, are other tools employers sometimes use to reduce employee exposure.

PPE, such as respirators, gloves, and safety glasses, should be used only as a last resort, after all feasible engineering and administrative controls and work practice improvements have been implemented.

Employee input regarding abatement techniques is highly recommended as they may be able to provide insight about equipment and work procedures or have their own ideas about how to abate the hazards. They often are familiar with the history of the process and what measures have been tried in the past. Employees are also more likely to use the control measures and incorporate safe work practices if they feel some ownership in their development. Consider giving employees the authority and ability to correct hazards themselves whenever feasible.

Regular preventive maintenance of equipment is also important to prevent the occurrence of safety and health hazards. Among the items that require regular inspection and maintenance are ladders, forklifts, hoists and slings, exhaust fans and belts, and pressure vessels.

Whenever possible, hazards should be eliminated. Sometimes that can be done through substitution of a less toxic material or engineering controls. When hazards cannot be eliminated, systems should be established to control them. Consider each of the following:

- Set up safe work procedures based on an analysis of the hazards in the workplace and ensure that employees understand and follow them. Involve employees in the analysis that results in those procedures.

- Be ready to enforce the rules for safe work procedures. Ask employees to help establish a disciplinary system that is fair and understood by everyone.

- Where necessary, ensure that PPE is used and that employees know why they need it, how to use it, and how to maintain it.

- Provide for routine equipment maintenance to prevent breakdowns that can create hazards.

- Ensure that preventive and regular maintenance is tracked to completion.

- Plan for emergencies, including fire and natural disasters. Conduct frequent drills to ensure that all employees know what to do under stressful conditions.

Incident Investigation

Incident investigation (also known as accident investigation) is a key component of a safety and health program. The goal of an incident investigation is hazard identification and prevention. It should not affix blame. All events that cause injuries or property damage should be examined. When possible, all near misses should also be investigated.

Incident investigations should be started as soon as possible. Precautions should be taken to control any remaining hazards in the area before the investigation begins. OSHA programs describe three cause levels of incidents:

- Direct causes: The immediate causes of the injury, illness, or damage. Direct causes are the hazardous material(s) or energy (e.g., electrical energy, potential energy, or heat) that caused the injury or damage.

- Indirect causes: Unsafe actions and conditions that caused the hazardous materials or energy to exceed safe limits.

- Basic causes: Those that contribute to the creation of the indirect hazards. These can include poor management policies, personal factors, or environmental factors.

Incident investigations should be a team effort, including supervisors; it's best to involve someone familiar with the process or equipment involved in the incident. Incident investigations are used to identify the causes of incidents and to determine how to eliminate one or more of these causes to prevent other incidents. Investigators need to ask questions such as:

- Who was involved in the event?

- Who witnessed the event?

- What happened?

- What was abnormal or different before the incident occurred?

- When did each event in the incident occur?

- Where did the hazard first occur?

- How and why did an event take place?

The investigation process should include:

- Incident site examination

- Witness interviews

- Documentation (including notes, maps, sketches, and photographs)

- Process information (e.g., flow charts, chemical properties, equipment diagrams, normal operating limits, maintenance records, and job hazard analyses)

- Development of a sequence of events leading up to the incident

- Review of operating procedures

Each contributing factor must be traced back to its root cause. A written report that describes the incident, its causes, and recommendations for corrective action and prevention should be prepared.

The ultimate goal of the investigation is to determine the root causes of the incident as well as appropriate corrective action so that it does not happen again. Simply attributing an incident to "employee error," without further consideration of the basic causes, deprives the organization of the opportunity to take real preventive action. Engineering controls, improved work practices, and administrative controls should be considered to help employees do their jobs safely. Management practices should also be considered as a possible causative factor. If there is managerial or supervisory pressure to increase production or cut costs, employees may take unsafe shortcuts in work procedures or necessary preventive maintenance may be delayed or skipped.

Injury and Illness Care and Treatment

It is imperative that leaders and managers work with their workers' compensation carrier and/or insurance agent or broker and medical provider to help develop an occupational medical program that fits the organization's workplace. Here are a few key points:

- Get to know the best workers' compensation doctors in the area. Not only should they be medically qualified, but they should also understand the nuances of the WC system.

- Directly pay for occupational ("first aid") cases when doing so is financially and regulatory appropriate. Ask the organization's insurance agent or other professional to conduct an analysis to determine the best course of action.

- Involve nearby doctors and emergency facilities by inviting them to visit the workplace and help plan the best way to treat employees in case of injury or illness.

- Ensure ready access to medical personnel to offer advice and consult on matters of employee health. (This does not mean that your company provides expert advice on healthcare; however, the company must be prepared to deal with medical emergencies or health problems connected to the workplace.)

To fulfill these requirements, consider these steps:

- Develop an emergency medical procedure to handle injuries, transport ill or injured workers, and notify medical facilities. Don't let injured workers drive to the doctor; have someone in the company (such as a supervisor) provide transportation.

- Post emergency numbers.

- Survey the medical facilities near your organization and make arrangements for them to handle routine and emergency cases. (Cooperative agreements may be possible with nearby larger workplaces that have onsite medical personnel and/or facilities.)

- Consider connecting with a local doctor or an occupational health nurse on an as-needed basis for advice on medical and first aid planning.

- Ensure that procedures for reporting injuries and illnesses are understood by all employees.

- If an organization is remote (including construction work sites) from medical facilities, the company is required to ensure that adequately trained personnel are available to render first aid. First aid supplies must be readily available for emergency use. Arrangements for this training can be made through the local safety council (American Association of Safety Councils or National Safety Council), Red Cross chapter, WC insurance carrier, and others.

Training and Education

An effective workplace safety program requires proper job safety performance from everyone in the workplace. Leaders and managers must ensure that all employees know about the materials and equipment they use, known hazards, and how to resolve/control the hazards. You might be able to combine safety and health training with other training, depending on the types of hazards in the workplace. Each employee needs to know that:

- No employee is expected to undertake a job until he or she has received job instructions on how to do it properly and is authorized to perform that job.

- No employee should undertake a job that appears unsafe.

- Employees have been trained on every potential hazard that they could be exposed to and how to protect themselves.

It is imperative that employees really understand the information being taught. Pay particular attention to new employees and to employees who are moving to new jobs. Be sure to conduct a new hire orientation and include safety topics. Train supervisors to understand all the hazards faced by the employees and how to reinforce training with quick reminders and refreshers or with disciplinary action, if necessary. And, as we discussed at the beginning of this chapter, you must communicate safety to employees in a language they understand.

A written workplace safety program is just words on paper if management, supervisors, and employees are not aware of it and don't understand it. Observing employees' understanding of safe practices is a more efficient measure than employees simply telling you or saying that they understand.

Employees cannot follow safety rules, identify hazards, use correct work procedures or protective equipment, or work to achieve goals if they do not have the necessary knowledge to do so. Furthermore, if employees are afraid to discuss safety and health concerns with management or have no clear method of reporting their concerns to management, safety and health hazards can go undetected. Uncorrected hazards can adversely affect employee morale and productivity, even if an incident, injury, or illness does not occur as a result.

While communication regarding safety and health issues should be a continual process, there are times when it is especially critical, including:

- The beginning of an employee's new job assignment

- Whenever materials, processes, or procedural changes are implemented

- Whenever the employer notices deficiencies in safe work practices

Communication

The best safety programs exceed the minimum training requirements set by OSHA regulations. Some key points when incorporating training are:

- Engage employees directly in the training delivery by using pictures, video, and multimedia. It is okay to use generic or core training materials; making them applicable to the specific work environment, however, will lead to the best effect.

- Supervisors should receive at least as much safety and health training as frontline employees, if not more.

- Training content should be directly applicable to the hazards, procedures, and equipment the employees encounter on the job.

- Employees are more receptive to training if they see how they can apply the training to their work.

- Training content must cover emergency procedures as well as normal, day-to-day activities.

- Because individuals learn in different ways, a variety of training methods should be used to help communicate the material to be learned. Changing an employee's role (having him or her conduct training) will positively and perhaps forever change their safety behavior.

- Some trainers develop games to review material, especially for refresher training.

- There should be a way to check that employees understand the course content to ensure transfer of the training to the workplace. Methods often used include class discussion, written tests and quizzes, demonstrations, and on-the-job observations.

- Supervisors can lead the majority of safety training sessions; however, it is imperative that frontline employees also lead safety meetings.

- Supervisors can observe and coach their employees by correcting unsafe work practices as they occur and positively reinforcing the use of safe work practices.

- Employees can be encouraged to work with each other to reinforce workplace safety. Experienced employees should teach newer employees safe work practices rather than risky shortcuts.

- Other methods of communicating job safety and health information include posters; employee handbooks; and handout materials, including one-page fact sheets or booklets, computer-based learning, and safety promotional activities.

- If posters are used, they must contain a clear message and be located in areas in which employees are likely to see them, such as near the time clock or in the cafeteria. It is highly recommended that you incorporate your employees in the posters (think of how some retail stores incorporate their employees in print ads), rather than using generic "be safe" posters. With the availability of digital cameras and color printers, it is a small investment with a big payoff. Posters should be rotated regularly.

- Relying exclusively on written materials can be ineffective for the following reasons:

  o Many working adults may lack basic reading skills. To avoid embarrassment and humiliation, they will often hide this from their supervisors and coworkers. Due to the growing diversity of today's workforce, some of your workers may have limited English speaking and reading skills.

  o It is common for a person to set aside reading material "for later, when I have time" and never pick it up again. These problems can be addressed at least partially by having the employees complete worksheets or quizzes about the written material and submit them to their supervisor or the safety coordinator for grading.

- Increasing numbers of businesses are turning to computer-based learning as a training method. Computer-based learning can combine video, sound, and text in an interactive format to test employees for completion and understanding. Several standardized programs are available in this format, and many employers are developing their own.

- Safety promotional activities, such as fairs, dinners, and safety stand-downs, can also be effective for communicating the importance of workplace safety to employees. Employers must be careful, however, that "incentive programs" do not send the wrong message. For example, some programs (based on the number or frequency of lost-time injuries) have resulted in the underreporting of injuries by employees.

- One of the strongest methods of communication is by example. Managers and supervisors must model their actions for employees by working safely and following all safety and health rules.

Effective communication flows in two directions. Employees must feel free to discuss their safety concerns with their supervisors without fear of retaliation. They should know the proper procedures for reporting safety and health hazards in the workplace so that the hazards can be corrected or they can have their questions answered. Supervisors should know whom to contact for assistance in addressing safety issues and have the authority to take appropriate corrective action. You must ensure that communication is occurring on all levels of the organization.

Recordkeeping

To ensure compliance, you must document activities from all elements of the organization's workplace safety program. Essential records, including those legally required for workers' compensation, insurance audits, and government inspections, must be maintained as long as the actual need exists or as required by law. Keeping activity records on policy statements, training sessions, safety and health meetings, information distributed to employees, and medical arrangements made is greatly encouraged.

Maintaining essential records also demonstrates sound business management such as proof of credit applications, showing "good faith" in reducing any proposed penalties from OSHA inspections, and insurance and other audits. Good records also aid efficient review of the organization's current safety and health activities for better control of operations and to plan improvements.

Records of sales, costs, profits, and losses are essential to all successful businesses. They enable the owner or manager to learn from experience and to make corrections for future operations. Records of incidents, related injuries, illnesses, and property losses can serve the same purpose, if they are used in the same way. The primary purpose of OSHA-required recordkeeping is to retain information about incidents that have happened to help determine the causes and develop procedures to prevent recurrences.

Injury and Illness Records

OSHA rules for recording and reporting occupational injuries and illnesses affect 1.4 million establishments. Small businesses with 10 or fewer employees throughout the year may be exempt from most of the requirements of the OSHA recordkeeping rules. Some industries, such as service, finance, insurance, and real estate, may be exempt or classified as low hazard. Detailed information about OSHA recordkeeping rules can be found at www.osha.gov/recordkeeping/index.html.

Basic OSHA recordkeeping requirements address only injuries and illnesses; many organizations expand their records to include all incidents, including those that resulted in no injury or illness, such as near misses. This information can help pinpoint unsafe actions, conditions, and/or procedures. Safety councils, insurance carriers, private consultants, and others can assist you in instituting such a recordkeeping system.

Exposure Records and Others

In addition to injury and illness records, certain OSHA standards require records of toxic substances and hazardous exposures, physical examination reports, inspection records, safety committee meeting minutes, safety training records, and employment records. As you identify hazards and steps toward hazard resolution, you will be able to determine whether these requirements apply to your workplace. Records should be used in conjunction with the control procedures and the self-inspection activity. They should not be considered merely as bookkeeping.

Safety as a Company Value

It is strongly suggested that you make employee safety and health an intrinsic company value (i.e., workplace safety is not just a "program" but also a way of doing things). Ideally, safety and health programs should correspond with and become part of the organization's overall mission or business plan. Every employee should know what the goals of the organization's safety program are and how they are to be achieved.

Safety must be integrated as an intrinsic company value (not just a priority) by every leader, manager, and employee in the organization. Safety should be viewed as a value just like honesty, working hard, and showing up to work on time. Values are embedded while priorities can change. Making safety a company value leads to building a workplace safety culture.

A workplace safety culture is created by (1) making safety part of the performance appraisal process; (2) practicing "active caring" techniques; (3) engaging employees at all levels; and (4) having company leaders, managers, and employees commit to being safe. An organization should expect its leaders, managers, and employees to make safety a value.

A safe and healthful workplace depends on effective management to ensure that hazards are identified and that effective physical and administrative protections are established and maintained. Business owners and managers must recognize that their role is essential to the establishment and implementation of an effective safety and health program. Management must:

- Establish and communicate policies.

- Guide their subordinates to set safety and health goals and objectives.

- Provide needed resources, including money, machines, materials, methods, staffing, and time. They must also motivate personnel through active participation in, and support of, safety and health activities.

- Recognize that although traditional safety programs have been geared toward WC programs, nonoccupational and other employee benefits programs must be incorporated into the process.

Developing a strong safety culture has the single greatest impact on injury reduction of any process. For this reason, developing a safety culture should be a top priority for all businesses.

What Is A Safety Culture?

According to OSHA's Creating a Safety Culture fact sheet:

Safety cultures consist of shared beliefs, practices, and attitudes that exist at an establishment. Culture is the atmosphere created by those beliefs, attitudes, and so forth that shape our behavior. An organization's safety culture is the result of a number of factors, such as:

- Management and employee norms, assumptions, and beliefs

- Management and employee attitudes

- Values, myths, and stories

- Policies and procedures

- Supervisor priorities, responsibilities, and accountability

- Production and bottom-line pressures versus quality issues

- Action or lack of action to correct unsafe behaviors

- Employee training and motivation

- Employee involvement or buy-in

In a strong safety culture, everyone feels responsible for safety and pursues it on a daily basis; employees go beyond the call of duty to identify unsafe conditions and behaviors, and intervene to correct them. For instance, in a strong safety culture, any worker would feel comfortable reminding the plant manager or owner to wear safety glasses. This type of behavior would not be viewed as forward or overzealous, but rather would be valued by the organization. Likewise, coworkers routinely look out for one another and point out unsafe actions and conditions to each other....

Over time, the norms and beliefs of the organization shift focus from eliminating hazards to eliminating unsafe actions and building systems that proactively improve safety and health conditions. Employee safety and doing something the right way take precedence over short-term production pressures. Simultaneously, production does not suffer but is enhanced due to the level of excellence developed within the organization. [cxl]

Safety Culture Process: Getting Started

Again, taken from the OSHA site itself on building a safety culture, "People tend to focus on the accomplishment of tasks, that is, to train everyone on a particular concern or topic" (e.g., implement a new procedure for incident investigations). Companies that maintain their focus on the larger process to be followed are far more successful. "They can see the 'forest' from the 'trees' and thus can make midcourse adjustments as needed. They never lose sight of their intended goals, therefore, they tend not to get distracted or allow obstacles to interfere with their mission. The process itself will take care of the task implementation and ensure that the appropriate resources are provided and priorities are set." [cxli]

Mainly based on OSHA guidelines, [cxlii] following are the major processes and milestones needed to implement the safety culture process successfully. Note that the list focuses an organization on the process rather than on individual tasks.

- Get ownership and management buy-in. This is the very first step that needs to be accomplished. Owners and managers must be on board; if they are not, safety and health will compete against core business issues such as production and profitability. As companies become more safety successful, organizational barriers, such as fear and lack of trust — issues that typically get in the way of all of the organization's goals — are diminished. Most people place a high value on their own safety, and, if you are sincere in your approach, employees will view your safety efforts as those that are truly being done for them.

- Continue building buy-in. Create an alliance or partnership among management, the union (if one exists), and employees. Spell out a compelling reason for the change for everyone. People have to understand why they are being asked to change what they normally do and what success will look like.

- Identify key personnel to champion the change. If it is only you, make yourself visible and articulate reasons for the changes. The reasons must be compelling and motivational. People frequently respond when they realize how many of their coworkers or subordinates are being injured (or potentially could be injured).

- Build trust. Trust is a critical part of accepting change. Trust occurs at different levels within the organization.

- Conduct self-assessments/benchmarking. To get where you want to go, it is essential to know where you are starting from. Use self-audit mechanisms, visits to other successful companies, and safety perception surveys to measure the strengths and weaknesses of the safety culture.

- Provide initial training of management and supervisory staff, union leadership (if present), safety and health committee members, and key employees. This training may include safety and health training, and any needed management, team building, hazard recognition, or communication training. By training these people, you have a core group to draw from as resources. Training also gets key personnel on board with needed changes.

- Establish a steering committee (in larger companies). A steering committee made up of management, employees, union (if present), and safety staff should be established. This group's purpose is to facilitate, support, and direct the safety culture change processes. To be effective, the group must have the authority to get things done.

- Develop a company safety vision. The company safety vision should consist of key policies, goals, measures, and strategic and operational plans. These policies provide guidance and serve as a checklist that can be used to see if the decision being made supports or detracts from the organization's intended safety and health improvement process.

- Align the organization. The organization must be aligned by establishing a shared vision of safety and health goals and objectives. Ownership and management must support the workplace safety program by providing resources (time, training, and equipment) and holding managers and supervisors accountable for doing the same. The entire management and supervisory staff must set the example.

- Define specific roles. Define roles and responsibilities for safety and health at all levels of the organization. Safety and health must be viewed as everyone's responsibility: working safely is not a choice. Clearly spell out how the organization deals with competing pressures and priorities (e.g., production versus safety and health).

- Develop a system of accountability. A system of accountability should be developed for all levels of the organization. Everyone must play by the same rules and be held accountable for their areas of responsibility. The sign of a strong culture is when the individuals hold themselves accountable.

- Develop measures. Develop measurable objectives and measure the number of:

  o Hazards reported or corrected

  o Safety walk-arounds

  o Equipment checks

  o Safety meetings conducted

  o Employees leading a safety meeting

  o Completed job safety analyses

- Develop Policies for Recognition, rewards, incentives, and ceremonies. Again, reward employees for doing the right things and encourage participation in the upstream activities. Continually reevaluate these policies to ensure their effectiveness and to ensure that they do not become entitlement programs.
- Awareness Training and Kick-off for all employees. It's not enough for a part of the organization to be involved and know about the change effort - the entire site needs to know and be involved in some manner. A kick-off celebration can be used to announce it's a "new day" and seek buy-in for any new procedures and programs.
- Implement Process Changes via involvement of management, union (if one is present), and employees using a "Plan To Act" process Total Quality Management (TQM).
- Continually Measure performance, Communicate Results, and Celebrate Successes. Publicizing results is very important to sustaining efforts and keeping everyone motivated. Everyone needs to be updated throughout the process. Progress reports during normal shift meetings allowing time for comments back to the steering committee opens communications, but also allows for input. Everyone needs to have a voice, otherwise, they will be reluctant to buy-in. A system can be as simple as using current meetings, a bulletin board, and a comment box.
- On-going Support - Reinforcement, feedback, reassessment, mid-course corrections, and on-going training is vital to sustaining continuous improvement.

Workplace Safety and Regulatory Management

In 1941, President Franklin Roosevelt called on every citizen to lead a "concerted and intensified campaign against accidents." As a direct result of FDR's national call and in the ensuing years, business professionals, union leaders, and working people from every job description rallied to establish effective ways to prevent injuries and illness in the workplace. Companies have been successful as injury rates have been decreasing ever since. [cxliii]

Documenting Workplace Safety

Much has been written in the past 20 years about methods to improve workplace safety. Perhaps the greatest single lesson learned is that there are many ways to create successful workplace safety programs. Foremost among them is that to achieve workplace safety successes, a first step has to be taken. Whether an audit or best practices review, a foundation must be constructed and plans drafted. The more your safety efforts truly relate to your employees and the specific hazards they face, the better outcomes you will experience. Following are two checklists designed to help benchmark your workplace safety program and help identify hazards in the workplace.

Job Hazard Analysis

According to OSHA, "A job hazard analysis (JHA) is a technique that focuses on job tasks as a way to identify hazards before they occur. It focuses on the relationship between the worker, the task, the tools, and the work environment. Ideally, after you identify uncontrolled hazards, you will take steps to eliminate or reduce them to an acceptable risk level." [cxliv] A JHA is considered one of the best ways to determine and establish proper work procedures and to create an ongoing effort.

Table 16.1

Job Hazard Analysis

Specific Job/Task:		Location(s):	JHA #:
Date Prepared:		Preparer:	

Description of Job/Task (List of Steps)	Potential Occupational Safety/Health Hazard	Safe Work Practices	Required PPE

Description of Job/Task (List of Steps)	Potential Occupational Safety/Health Hazard	Safe Work Practices	Required PPE

Page:	of		Original date:
Approved by:			Revision date:

Employer Checklist

Before an organization can take stock or assess the needs of its workplace safety program, it must know how its program is structured. Using a needs assessment tool such as the Taking Stock Checklist [cxlv] allows the organization to:

- Analyze the program as it exists today

- Recognize where improvements need to be made

- Deploy or enhance a workplace safety program that includes elements focused on the recognition of actual hazards, from both unsafe acts and conditions, and how best to control them

Each of us has a responsibility to make every effort to create a safe workplace for our employees, coworkers, and associates. We're confident that with some effort, teamwork, and critical thinking, your efforts to save lives, prevent injuries and illness, and make the workplace a safer place will be successful.

Taking Stock Checklist

Scale: Poor: 0-31; Fair: 32-95; Good: 96-143

Category	[0-1+] Poor	[2-5+] Fair	[6-8+] Good	[9-10] Excellent	N/A	Total	Comments on Rating
1. Injury and illness prevention program							
2. Standard operating procedures or risks (JHAs)							
3. Safety responsibilities							
4. Group safety talks							
5. Inspections							
6. Training							
7. Accident reporting and investigation							
8. Housekeeping							

9. Emergency procedures							
10. Safety committees							
11. Equipment/Tool use & maintenance							
12. Personal protective equipment							
13. Material handling							
14. Chemical safety/hazard communication							
15. Noise control							
16. Fleet operations							
Note: No points assessed for A-J; they are used as differentiators in 1-16.							
A. Employee handbook							
B. Interview/Back ground check/Drug screening							

C. Employee orientation and placement							
D. WC leave/FML coordination							
E. Injured employee communicatio n/documentati on							
F. Harassment prevention training (>50 employees)							
G. Return-to-work program							
H. Supervisor safety responsibilities							
I. Employee safety responsibilities							
J. First aid							
Total points							

Discussion/Comments:

Section Four

Program Establishment

Chapter 17: Building an Integrated Team and Marketing the Program to Management

Background and Context

Employers who seek to introduce integration for the first time or to take the next step in furthering their benefit program integration need to coordinate an appropriate team of stakeholders and prepare a business case or marketing strategy to gain the support and approval from top management within their organizations. Fundamentally, employers seek changes to their benefits programs or administration in response to market trends and internal needs; however, responding to those needs thoughtfully and translating the market trends to reflect a best-practice approach for the organization are critical. To achieve this desired outcome, a diverse team must be engaged in developing the key messages that grab and hold the attention, commitment, and leadership of senior management.

The Team

A team working to design and develop a new integrated benefits program or improve a less-than-seamless absence management program delivery system requires the following:

- A diverse knowledge base and skill set

- Different styles of thought

- Various levels of the organization

In addition, and perhaps more important, the team must be engaged with clear goals and flexibility to change while being accountable to each other and senior leadership.

Given that integrated programs link across many areas of a firm, the best teams are cross functional in terms of their current roles and background. A cross-functional team approaches employee health and productivity more effectively since they consider various aspects of the program to include care coordination, return to work, injury prevention, and implementation. For example, including both occupational and nonoccupational expertise is of paramount importance. Even if the initial goal is to develop an integrated program with only an occupational focus, the nonoccupational team members add value. Therefore, bringing together the various areas and promoting cooperation across business functions and enhanced communication among all groups should be a core premise of the project. Current expertise as well as past experience must also be considered when assessing knowledge and skill set, particularly because lessons learned from similar projects or efforts can be valuable.

Within each organization, tactical and strategic thinkers exist and should both be engaged for a project of this scope. Strategic thinkers challenge assumptions and make strides considering the long-term vision that will set the course. However, tactical and task-oriented team members are required to translate the vision into action. When coordinating the team, both styles of thought are essential, ideally with one project manager assigned to hold the reins of the project. Many organizations are tempted to overlook the project management function; however, teams without an assigned coordinator struggle to succeed. Project managers are usually not the business leaders or decision makers, but rather they ensure consistency and documentation, which are both important during a project of this magnitude with the links to various areas of the business.

Another consideration is the tenure and seniority of the team. Unbiased and fresh ideas ensure a forward-thinking approach that is instrumental, given the challenges that can exist when and if change is introduced. Having said that, experience within an organization can benefit the team immensely and cannot be overlooked. Therefore, success is likely more attainable if the group has seasoned members as well as some newer associates. Those with tenure may represent champions of the cause who can easily gain the trust and ear of their colleagues, whereas newer associates bring a fresh perspective. Another important consideration is to solicit team members who have facilitated change at the current organization or in other organizations in the past. Their experience is invaluable for a project of this magnitude.

When coordinating the team, each organization has unique characteristics to consider. For example, multisite firms may want to consider a core team at their headquarters with additional leadership throughout the disparate sites and locations. Participation with the entire team takes place via conference calls and in person at various intervals. If this model is used, the team should consider pilot sites that they could implement in advance to ensure the right messages are communicated and the overall firm is prepared for the level of change required.

Any team engaged to implement or extend their integrated program will bump against established practices, processes, and territories resistant to change. The lack of support can be fierce as you try to combine business function and responsibilities. Early on, frequent and clear communication fosters better cooperation and diminishes the fear of transition.

To ensure success, the team engaged must have clear roles, responsibilities, and goals. Some would argue those are more important than the team members themselves. Establishing the stakeholders is the first step in identifying roles and responsibilities. From there, each individual role should be documented, and goals can be highlighted in a living team charter. In addition, the team must feel as though they have a supported foundation and periodic checkpoints with senior leaders to keep the project on task.

Diverse teams that are not motivated inevitably create disjointed programs that will not provide the best results for your organization. To combat motivational issues, ongoing organizational meetings should be facilitated with a project plan and clear documentation of immediate actions and progress to date. Subgroups should be created when appropriate to avoid bottlenecks.

Table 17.1 lists stakeholders and therefore team members recommended for organizations seeking integration.

Table 17.1

Stakeholders and Team Members	
Human resources/benefits	Risk management
- Disability and absence management program managers	Health and safety
	Ergonomics
- Health management program leaders (e.g., EAP)	HR operations/other technology partners
Legal	Information technology/data exchange
Employee relations	Communications
Finance	Field representatives
Payroll	Union representatives
Onsite medical (occupational or nonoccupational clinics)	

Specific roles and responsibilities of these stakeholders vary, with some needed to attend and facilitate team meetings, others to review key deliverables, and yet others to make final decisions. The listing below provides a more comprehensive view of this range, which should be applied and communicated to all stakeholders once determined:

- Meeting attendance

- Data gathering

- Input and review

- Scenario planning and testing

- Peer review

- Final decision making

Although the majority of your team should be made of internal representatives, do not underestimate the value that your current providers and vendors may bring. In addition, if your team docs not have the appropriate depth of experience in all areas, working with a consultant or other vendor partner with that subject matter expertise is usually worthwhile. Experts in the area of integration can assist in the detailed work and/or provide advisory support to audit progress and share lessons learned.

Throughout the course of the project, the scope and resulting team needs may change. Therefore, it will be important to continually keep a pulse on the goals of the project, as well as on the demands of your company. Frequently, you may want to add one of the following to assist in the development of an integrated team:

- The employee on leave

- The manager of the employee on leave

- Finance/payroll

- State/Federal agencies

- Unions or other employee representative groups

- Third-party vendors

The Business Case

At the end of the day, the business case represents your deliverable to senior management, which may be in the form of a firm recommendation or perhaps a strategy to take forward. It may be fixing a problem or creating a proactive solution. In either case, employers should approach the development of a business case by first gathering the data during the initial assessment phase to clearly define what is working and what is not working or where underperformance exists within the current structure. A high-level or thorough gap analysis can assist in this regard, as management may need specific examples of how your organization's current approach compares to industry and best practices. From there, the business plan will identify the changes needed and the expected results of those changes. That deliverable should demonstrate successes where they exist, but also focus on where improvements will be made. The analysis and results should include qualitative and quantitative findings.

In discussing what is working and where improvements exist, it can be helpful to categorize the areas of the plan into the following segments:

- Plan design features that encourage or motivate absence (e.g., high income replacement percentages, generous benefit durations, and nonexistent or ineffective return-to-work incentives), as well as those that create integration opportunities

- Processes, such as reporting protocols, claim approval, denial and appeals processes, staffing levels, and benefit calculation errors

- Legal compliance, including issues that may be identified if there are not enough resources to keep track of federal and state leave regulations. Inadequate staffing or lack of legal oversight could result in compliance steps missed or managed inconsistently.

- Inadequate customer service/vendor capabilities, especially those that directly impact satisfaction levels, including decision timelines and response time to claimants and other stakeholders. Limited reporting capabilities, inflexible operating processes, and outdated technology platforms should also be assessed.

Building the case for change must first focus on defining what works at the organization, advantages to the firm achieved by the current state, and progress made to date. This sets a baseline for senior management and educates them on the current underpinnings. Status quo is usually based on earlier priorities and business focus; therefore, it helps to consider why the organization chose the current product, program, and process, and treat that as a control group compared to the improvements suggested in the business case.

Once the current state is examined, a qualitative and quantitative analysis must be facilitated to determine what is not working within the program, in essence, what the product, program, and process should look like as an end state. If a phased approach is suggested, several end states may be discussed. Benchmarking to peer firms is usually incorporated, and it is common to seek assistance from a subject matter expert who can describe best practices leveraged in the industry. Your vendors and current partners can also provide insight while this is being contemplated.

After the current and future states are described, senior leadership expects a gap analysis demonstrating the variance between the two and the benefits of closing that gap. Although the specific areas are derived on a case-by-case basis, many firms have been successful at looking at the benefits of cost reduction and missed opportunity. For example, where inefficient processes have been identified, the root-cause analysis can show that procedures for reporting an absence differ by division or region within the organization. This causes inconsistent management and confusion among employees, supervisors, and vendors that results in additional and unnecessary costs. The recommended change may be a new process to eliminate or substantially mitigate the underperformance. In this instance, the business case reflects a proposal to introduce a single, standard policy and a process for reporting absences across all lines of business. Another example is identifying a lost opportunity due to an ineffective return-to-work program. In this instance, a cost-benefit analysis can be done based on industry-standard return-to-work statistics compared to your group using benefit payments and replacement wages as the incurred costs.

A cost-benefit analysis typically involves measuring the total expected cost of change against the expected benefit, outcome, or result. This can be shown as a tangible cost and/or estimated cost avoidance. All assumptions should be clearly outlined and based on sound references or examples the team can relate to.

Each integration opportunity has its own set of benefits and challenges, and the priorities of your organization and its particular management style will drive the format that works best for you. Table 17.2 illustrates how a large firm made their business case to senior management; however, the following concepts can serve as a baseline in developing your own specific story:

- Identify administrative cost savings and efficiencies as well as improved accuracy and timeliness of reporting due to a single source of intake.

- Estimate how early intervention positively impacts (and reduces) absence duration.

- Demonstrate how data can be consolidated, integrated, and analyzed in a more comprehensive manner.

- Explain how absence patterns can be identified and the root cause managed.

- Illustrate how supervisors and managers benefit from early notification of absences and better workforce planning.

- Describe how consolidated claims data can be used to develop targeted, more effective disease management programs.

- Provide examples of early intervention opportunities among program administrators with complex absence cases such as depression or stress.

- Detail the employee experience and how that can be improved:

    o More streamlined access to report absences

    o Common or consistent case management

    o Programs that reflect a company's desire to improve workforce health and productivity

Table 17.2
Making the Business Case

Driving Issues
<ul><li>STD and LTD claims growing at a higher rate than employee population</li><li>5% of workforce absent at any given time</li><li>75% of absences occurring in key service areas</li><li>Process confusing to employees and causing additional work for managers</li><li>Estimated annual cost of employee time away from work: $25M</li></ul>
Recommended Approach
<ul><li>Single source of intake</li><li>Coordination of all disability (occupational and nonoccupational) and leave events</li><li>Early intervention to facilitate recovery and return to work</li><li>Maximum electronic communication</li><li>Ability to integrate and analyze data</li></ul>

Return on Investment		
Current STD, WC, LTD claim costs:	$10,000000	
Expected STD, WC, LTD claim savings:		$1,350,000
Estimated lost productivity savings:		$3,050,000
Total direct and indirect savings:		$4,400,000
Increased spending for vendor services:		
Return on investment:	$500,000	9:1

Expected Outcomes
☐ One-stop shopping for the employee
☐ Head count reduction of 4.50 Full Time Equivalent Employees
☐ Expected annual savings of $4.4M (9:1 ROI)
☐ 30% reduced time commitment for managers
☐ Process to manage claim duration, recovery, and return to work
☐ Electronic connectivity to share appropriate information
☐ Identification and proactive management of loss causes

Barriers and Challenges

The greatest struggle for most firms is arriving at a return on investment (ROI) calculation. Depending on the position of your firm, the formula for those savings estimates varies. Program administrators, health plans, brokers, and consultants can assist with developing potential investment returns on any number of opportunities. If data for your firm is not available, benchmark data can serve as a proxy to prove the cost or benefit of implementing integration steps.

Even if data exists, that may not be enough to support the decision to integrate a program. If the qualitative and quantitative analyses support integration, it may be necessary to engage one senior management team member who will likely have greater success in advancing receptivity to change among top management. Another positioning tactic is to educate senior management regarding the commitment to the project. This involves detailing the approach for overall project management, team members involved, milestones with associated dates, and mechanism for managing, tracking, and measuring in the future. This not only ensures that the integrated strategy, structure, process, and technology are appropriately aligned, but it also demonstrates the group's desire for success.

Employer Checklist

When establishing your integrated program team and subsequently making the business case to management, the following checklist can serve as a guide in planning and overall project management.

Key Questions	Yes/No	Potential consideration(s)
Have stakeholders and therefore project team members been selected from the following areas within your organization?		
Human resources/benefits		
Legal/compliance		
Employee relations		
Finance		
Payroll		
Onsite medical		
Risk management		
Health and safety		
Ergonomics		
Human resources operations		
Information technology		

Communications		
Field representatives		
Union representatives		
External vendors and consultants		
EAP		
Have stakeholders' roles and responsibilities been clearly defined, communicated, and agreed to by all parties, such as the following?		
Meeting attendance		
Data gathering		
Input and review		
Scenario planning and testing		
Peer review		
Final decision		
Has your organization taken the following steps to make the business case for change?		
Identify what is working well		
Determine future state and overall goals		

Conduct gap analysis against current and future states		
Perform a cost-benefit analysis or expected ROI calculation		
Define metrics/measures of success and methods for collecting necessary data		

Chapter 18: Funding Options and Determinations

Background and Context

Ever since employee benefits gained widespread recognition as an important talent retention and attraction tool, employers have faced the challenge of containing benefit costs while maintaining a competitive benefit package. One cost-saving strategy that does not reduce benefits and yields substantial savings involves re-examining the benefits program funding approach.

Summary of Options

There are four broad categories of funding approaches: fully insured, self-insured, a hybrid combination, and captive arrangements. These categories can all be applied to disability, workers' compensation (WC), and/or group health benefits. This chapter will review these funding options and discuss the characteristics of each option as they apply to various lines of coverage and integrated programs. The reader should keep in mind that benefits integration is often undertaken as a cost-containment measure; additional savings, beyond those typically achieved through integration, may be gained via funding strategy modification. Figure 18.1 explains the relation between funding approaches and program types discussed in this chapter. It also distinguishes between terms commonly used in the employee benefits and property and casualty (P&C) industries.

Figure 18.1

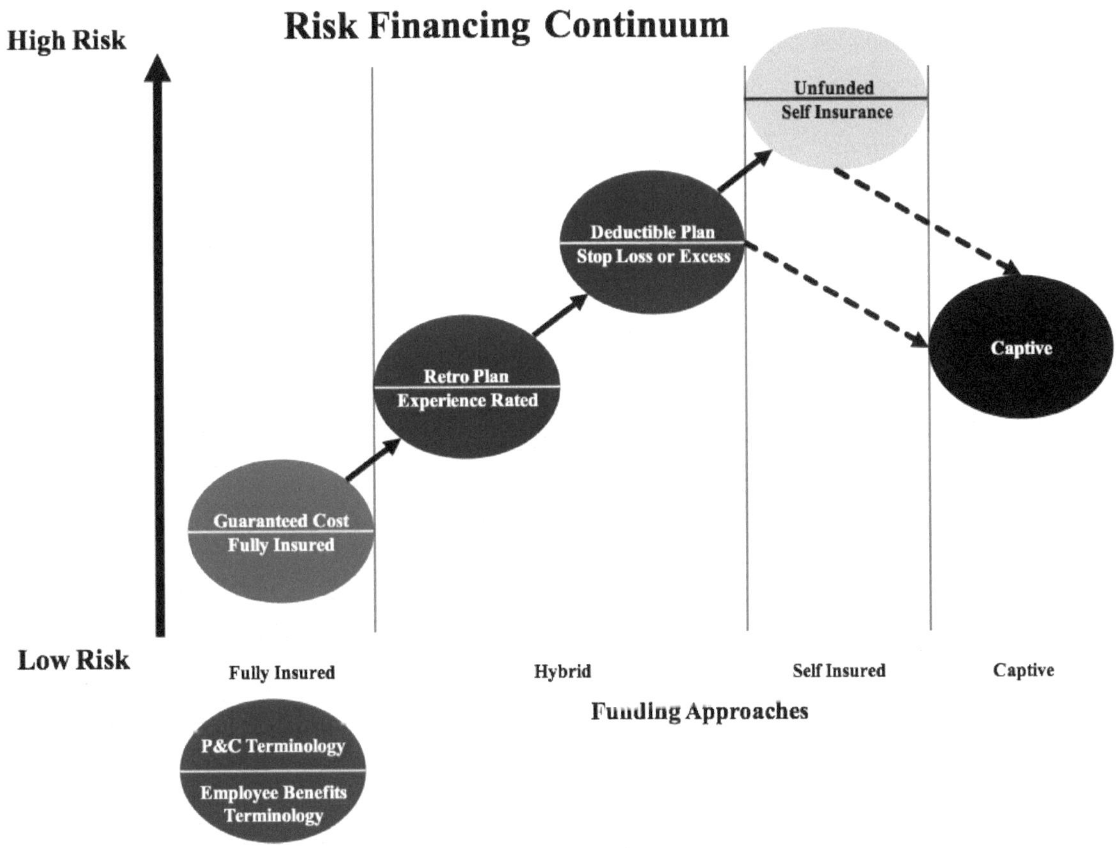

Risk Financing Continuum

High Risk

Low Risk

- Guaranteed Cost / Fully Insured
- Retro Plan / Experience Rated
- Deductible Plan / Stop Loss or Excess
- Unfunded Self Insurance
- Captive

Fully Insured — Hybrid — Self Insured — Captive

Funding Approaches

- P&C Terminology
- Employee Benefits Terminology

Key Differentiators to Consider

Fully Insured Arrangements

In a fully insured (guaranteed cost) program, the employer pays a premium to a commercial insurance carrier in exchange for coverage. The amount of the billed premium is generally commensurate with the exposure unit covered and the risk exposure transferred from the employer to the insurance company.

Risk exposure is typically determined using the expected number (frequency) and amount (severity) of losses. Historic claim frequency and severity are extrapolated to obtain these premium pricing parameters. In cases where loss history of the group is insufficient for adequate contract pricing, the insurer charges a premium, called a manual premium, which is based on loss history of other similarly sized groups with comparable risk characteristics. As the insured group generates claim history, the insurer adjusts the premium to better reflect past experience. Adverse experience (high claim frequency and/or severity) typically results in increased renewal premium, and positive experience (low claim frequency and/or severity) can result in decreased renewal premium. The modification of the premium for experience is referred to as experience rating.

The initial arrangement may require no evidence of insurability from the group's members at the inception of the insurance contract; experience rating is applied going forward. This group underwriting method considers the group's loss experience as a whole versus the individual losses of group members to set renewal premiums. The premium is renewed at regular intervals subject to the contractual rate guarantee period, which typically ranges from one to three years. While loss history plays a central role in determining an adequate premium level, a number of other factors influence the price of a fully insured contract and are discussed below.

Premium Taxes

Insurance companies pay state premium taxes based on the state of the policyholder (employee). Premium taxes are included in the fully insured premium and typically cited as a percentage of paid premium.

Claims Administration Expenses

Claim administration expenses are fees for claim handling, which includes investigating, case management, processing, issuing payment, and other claimant account maintenance. These fees depend on the complexity of claim handling (insurance products that require involved claim management may have a substantial portion of premium allocated to claims administration) and the size of the insured group (larger insured groups are expected to have more claims than smaller groups under the same insurance plan, so the claim handling fees for the former are usually higher than for the latter).

Commissions

Commissions are brokerage service fees. Brokerage firms act as independent agents or advisors who help the insurance buyer (employer) find an insurance plan that best addresses the buyer's risk profile and insurance needs. Initially, the broker coordinates with insurers to obtain insurance quotes for comparison shopping. Typical plan selection criteria are cost and features. Following plan selection, the broker interacts with the insurer on behalf of the insurance buyer in all matters involving maintenance of selected coverage, including renewal and plan amendments (if needed). Broker commissions are typically stated as a percentage of the fully insured premium.

Catastrophic Risk Charge

Typically, a portion of the fully insured premium is pooled with catastrophic risk fees from other policyholders' premium contributions into a single catastrophic contingency reserve. The size of this charge varies based on overall risk and size of the group. This reserve is maintained to cover low-frequency, high-severity losses — large, unexpected claims that could be due to a natural disaster, terrorist attack, pandemic, or other catastrophic events.

Additional Benefit Coverage Charges

Additional benefit coverage charges include fees for expanded plan coverage allocated through endorsement or riders, depending on the coverage at hand. The number of additional features depends again on the nature of the insurance product and the employer's specifications.

Other Policy Administrative Expenses or Surcharges

A portion of premium is used to cover actuarial, legal, audit, and/or several other policy maintenance services. These fees can be set as a percentage of premiums but are usually charged as a fixed amount. These charges may vary among coverage periods if service offerings are modified, usually at the discretion of the employer. Policy administrative expenses generally do not benefit from economies of scale: most employee groups require similar services, regardless of size. A more important factor in determining these charges is plan or coverage design. For certain lines, regulatory requirements and/or benefit structure may require additional support, which may result in higher policy expenses.

Workers' compensation surcharges and assessments come in many forms. Some states apply expense constants, which are designed to cover expenses for policy issuance, recordkeeping, auditing, etc. Residual market loads can be passed on to purchasers of retrospectively rated plans. Other WC surcharges may be applied when insurers feel additional contribution is needed to cover claims and other policy expenses. Surcharges are typically charged to high-risk groups with volatile claims (e.g., industrial workers). Employers should request documentation and methodology behind any surcharges levied on their WC policy.

Profit or Surplus Charges

A fully insured premium includes a charge for a profit margin to generate desired returns to the insurer's shareholders. Mutual insurance companies typically refer to this fee as contribution to surplus. Should a mutual insurance company cease operation, its policyholders will be able to participate in the distribution of net assets and company surplus.

Self-Insured Arrangements

In a self-insured arrangement, the employer is responsible for all benefit payments specified in the contract. The employer effectively retains the risk exposure associated with providing employees with coverage and typically outsources claims handling to a third-party administrator (TPA) and other administrative functions (e.g., actuarial) to appropriate service providers as needed.

While employers under self-insured arrangements bear most, if not all, of the substantial financial risk, they avoid many of the frictional costs (e.g., profit loads, commissions) associated with fully insured arrangements, as discussed in the previous section. Under a self-insured framework, the employer has four main plan costs: claims, policy administrative expenses, surcharges, TPA fee, and other administrative fees. Additional factors self-insureds typically take into account are discussed below.

Stop Loss

Many employers purchase stop loss coverage from an insurance company to protect themselves from higher than expected frequency and catastrophic losses they are subject to under a self-insured arrangement. Typically, the employer can purchase two types of stop loss: specific and aggregate coverage. With a specific stop loss contract in place, the insurer agrees to cover the amount of incurred claims above a specified limit during the coverage period (typically one year). This cap can be a set dollar amount or expressed as a percentage of expected claims. The specific stop loss contract can be applied to an individual's claim costs (e.g., covering any amount above $75,000 in claims for each of the members of the covered group) or as an aggregate coverage cap (e.g., covering any amount above 125% in aggregate group claims) over the expected level of total claims for the period of the stop loss contract.

Stop loss settlements are offered on paid (also called reimbursement) or incurred (also called advance funding) bases. Under a paid contract, the stop loss cap is applied only to claims paid during the coverage period. Claims incurred but unpaid are factored out of the stop loss reimbursement. Under the incurred claim settlement, all claims incurred within the coverage period are considered reimbursable under the stop loss policy. Incurred claim settlement is more appealing from a cash flow perspective and is generally more expensive.

Claims Handling

Claims processing can be performed in-house by designated and trained claims administrative personnel or, more often, outsourced to a TPA or insurance company as part of an administrative services only contract. Neither the TPA nor the insurance company assumes any financial risk associated with the administered benefit plans. Instead, the benefit payments are made from the employer's funds. These funds are either the employer's general assets or assets specific to benefit plans from an employer-sponsored trust.

General Asset Funding

If an employer chooses to pay program expenses from general assets of the company, these payments can be managed and reported much like other company expenses. As mentioned previously, self-funded short-term disability (STD) and wage continuation plans often make use of the payroll system, with the payments taxable to the employee like regular income, depending on the employer/employee contribution structure. While accounting and reporting involved in general asset funding are relatively simple, plan asset accumulation is not tax deductible unless the liability has been paid. This, in effect, limits the general asset funding approach to pay-as-you-go benefits such as paid time off (PTO), STD, and other wage continuation plans. Another disadvantage of general asset funding is its dependence on company welfare.

Extended cash flow requirements of long-term disability (LTD) and other plans with long claim tails (e.g., WC) may become an onerous burden during times of poor company performance or economic downturns.

VEBA Trust

A more proactive approach to funding of benefit lines is through a tax-favored voluntary employees' beneficiary association (VEBA) trust. A VEBA is an employer-sponsored and/or maintained pre-funded trust whose assets are used to pay employees' claims. A VEBA trust can be used to provide welfare benefits such as life, health, disability, and accident protection to employees, retirees, and their dependents. The main advantage of a VEBA trust over the pay-as-you-go method is the immediate tax deductibility of contributions as expense items. This deduction is subject to the qualified asset account limit, which is an actuarially determined amount necessary to meet claim obligations that have been incurred but unpaid, in addition to any administrative expenses involved in settling such claims within a taxable year. Also, benefit plan assets, with the exception of post-retirement medical funding, enjoy tax-free treatment of investment income.

VEBA tax exemption requires IRS approval. Trust setup is further contingent upon fulfillment of numerous other regulatory conditions, including:

- Membership restrictions. Eligible classes include employees, retirees, and their dependents.

- Nondiscrimination requirement. The plan may not discriminate in favor of officers, shareholders, or highly compensated individuals. The amount and type of benefits must be homogenous across all covered employees and should be based upon a fixed multiple of salary.

- Independent oversight. VEBA operations must be overseen by either participating members or a participant-selected trustee with fiduciary responsibilities.

- Payment constraints. VEBA funds can be used solely for the benefit of employees to disburse specified life, health, sickness, and other eligible expenses.

Both the initial setup and maintenance of VEBA trusts require considerable administrative and operational effort, which may act as a deterrent to some employers.

Self-Funding Considerations

Self-funding is predominant among organizations providing benefit plan coverage to large groups of employees because employers can rely on credibility of loss data (loss frequency and severity are statistically stable in the long term due to the size of the covered group). The most commonly self-funded benefits are health and STD, as well as some portion of the employer's WC exposure. STD is especially popular, as it involves short-term claims payouts (typically up to six months), which are usually issued through the payroll system. The Employee Retirement Income Security Act (ERISA) preemption allows self-funded plans greater plan design flexibility than fully insured plans bound by state requirements. With the passage of ERISA in 1974, self-funded arrangements have been declared separate from insurance business and, as such, exempt from state insurance laws and governed by less arduous ERISA regulations instead.

The primary advantage of self-funding, aside from the direct savings resulting from the elimination of premium loading, is the opportunity for the employer to benefit from favorable loss experience. Stable claim behavior lends itself to accurate rate setting and loss forecasting, and is imperative for successful self-funding implementation and sustenance. Plans experiencing high claim frequency and low claim severity (such as medical, dental, STD) are best suited for self-funding. Large groups that generally enjoy a steady, predictable claims pattern and relatively low loss ratios in fully insured scenarios may also be good self-funding candidates for LTD, WC, and possibly other benefit plans.

Hybrid Arrangements

As the name suggests, a hybrid framework combines a fully insured arrangement with elements of self-funding. The primary objective of utilizing a hybrid arrangement is to postpone or minimize benefit plan payments associated with risk transfer and/or outsourced administrative functions. Direct savings are obtained through premium reduction, and indirect savings are achieved by minimizing certain expenses. The most common hybrid setup involves a risk-sharing arrangement as discussed below.

Participating Arrangement

For employee benefit plans, a participating insurance contract is a common example of a hybrid plan, combining a fully insured framework with experience-driven risk sharing. The employer purchases a group insurance contract whereby both the insurer and the employer share in the ensuing losses of the group. If the paid premium exceeds claims incurred in a policy period (typically one year), the insurer offsets the future claims amount with the surplus amount. If the loss experience is unfavorable and the paid premium is insufficient to cover policy period losses, the insurer records a deficit balance, which is determined as the difference between plan costs and received premium. The insurer offsets deficit balances with future surpluses, if any. The employer is also usually not obligated to repay deficit balances in the event of contract termination. The extent of employer participation is determined based on the spread of risk and predictability of losses.

Loss Sensitive Plans

For WC programs, participating contracts are better known as loss sensitive plans. One option is a retrospectively rated agreement in which surplus and/or credits are assessed based on group experience, much like in a fully insured experience rated contract. Unlike participating arrangements, where deficits are deferred indefinitely and offset only by ensuing surpluses, the retrospective surplus/credit assessments are applied directly to premiums. Favorable experience results in lowered policy premium, and adverse experience results in increased policy premium. Retrospective plans provide a strong incentive for employers to control WC claims in both the short and long term via workplace safety initiatives and other loss-containment activities. Another WC funding option is a large deductible program, which may require collateralization of the expected losses in the deductible layer. This funding method eliminates premium taxes on the deductible amounts found in retrospectively rated agreements. The deductible layer naturally reduces the insured premium and functions as a self-retention component in an otherwise commercially insured arrangement.

Key components of well-run risk sharing plans are discussed below.

Spread of Risk

Spread of risk refers to pooling unrelated risks, including a large number of individual risks, to reduce the impact that low-frequency, high-severity claims have on the insured group's overall loss experience. Larger groups are able to absorb a few high-severity claims without significantly affecting the expected loss scenario. In this case, large claims are dispersed among participants filing smaller or no claims, often resulting in actual experience conforming to expected losses. Smaller groups are more sensitive to adverse loss experience, as the group premium is often not large enough to cover unexpectedly high claims. Insurance companies require that group plans sustain an adequate spread of risk prior to enrolling the employee group in a participating arrangement.

Predictability of Losses

As discussed in the self-funding section, long-term stable loss behavior can be extrapolated to obtain reasonably accurate future group claim estimates. From an insurer's perspective, plans such as health and STD typically experience high-frequency, low-severity claims and are most optimal for participating arrangements; plans experiencing low-frequency, high-severity claims, such as LTD, typically exhibit volatile loss patterns and are thus less desirable. WC groups can get to a level of predictability quickly.

Employer's Extent of Participation

The insurance company sets the employer's participation using individual pooling points (IPPs) and/or actuarial analysis of claim experience. The objective is to cap the dollar amount included in the participating experience of the plan. In some cases, any amount up to the cap is included in the risk sharing arrangement and any amount beyond the cap is treated like a claim in a fully insured arrangement. In other cases, the employer and insurance company share in the risk equally. A quota share arrangement, for example, can be expressed as a fixed dollar amount or as a percentage shared. The cap and/or risk sharing amounts are set based on the covered group's underwriting characteristics (including size, claim history, spread of risk, and loss stability) and may be changed at plan renewal.

Captive Arrangements

Captive insurance is an alternative funding approach that allows employers to minimize frictional costs, benefit from favorable loss experience, and, depending on the setup, enhance plan design/coverage and overall program efficiency.

A captive insurance company is a special-purpose insurance company owned and operated by the sponsoring employer or group of employers. Historically, captives were established by large employers wishing to fund risks that were either too expensive (such as general liability) or uninsurable (such as medical malpractice) in the traditional insurance marketplace. Captives started in the 1950s and gained prevalence in the 1970s. They were traditionally used to insure property and casualty (P&C) lines (e.g., WC, professional liability). Currently, captives are also used to underwrite various other lines, including warranty and credit insurance, and more recently, employee benefits.

Department of Labor (DOL) approval is often required before welfare benefits programs can be funded through the employer's captive. In these transactions, the DOL requires that a fronting carrier be involved in captive transactions, insuring ERISA-based employee benefit risks. The front is a commercial insurer that essentially acts both as the direct writing insurer and an administrative interface between the captive and the covered group. The front insures the group benefits and then reinsures, either in part or in full, these risks with the captive. In addition to the portion of the premium retained by the front when the risks are only partly reinsured with the captive, the front will charge claims settlement and other administrative expenses (similar to an ASO contract), premium taxes, and a fronting charge reflecting the insurer's profit and surplus loading. These fees are typically much lower than the set of expenses charged in a fully insured arrangement and do not include some large charges such as commissions and reduced profit margins.

Adding employee benefits to a captive writing primarily P&C coverage can ensure additional spread of risk, while improving the tax efficiency of related-party P&C premiums. Economies of scale and loss volatility can be improved since employee benefit losses are generally more stable over time than P&C losses. In a recent IRS revenue ruling, the IRS maintains a safe harbor rule that if a captive currently insuring P&C lines underwrites at least 50% of unrelated risk, the P&C premiums may be tax deductible to the sponsoring employer. [cxlvi]

Captive Transaction for WC

As mentioned above, WC is one of the P&C programs that has been funded through a captive for years. Although the logic for captive funding of WC and employee benefits is the same, WC is not subject to ERISA. Instead, it must meet federal and state law requirements, particularly those of self-insurance, which include taxes, surcharges, and assessments. WC captive transactions may or may not include a front and could be established to fund deductible levels within a larger program context.

Captive Capitalization

Regulations and captive domicile laws typically require that the captive is well capitalized and thus able to fulfill its claim obligations in case of an adverse loss scenario. The capital and surplus requirements of a captive can be handled in a number of ways. These requirements can be met with a cash deposit, or because the employer may not wish to issue a large cash outlay to fulfill this requirement, the captive is most commonly capitalized using a line of credit (LOC) from a reputable bank approved by the captive domicile. Banks have historically charged low rates for these instruments, typically less than 1% of the LOC face amount annually; however, this charge is increasing due to economic pressures. The LOC face amount is released by the bank in case of captive insolvency to cover any necessary expenses.

This collateralization results in improved plan member security: claim payouts are ensured by the captive and further backed by the bank providing the LOC. Despite the fact that the captive reinsures most or all of the risk, the ultimate responsibility for claim payments lies with the fronting insurer. In effect, this setup essentially provides several levels of comfort to the covered employees.

Captive administration is provided to the captive insurer and not the plan directly to run the captive insurance company. Normally, this is commonly performed by a third-party captive management firm. Actuarial and legal services can be performed in-house but are also typically outsourced to a consulting or specialty service firm.

The main function of a captive manager is captive bookkeeping and accounting. In addition to handling reporting and associated accounting, captive managers also offer such services as underwriting, policy management (including claims handling), and captive cash flow management. Captive managers may be affiliated with a brokerage firm, insurance company, or be an independent firm.

Employers may contract with a captive manager for a subset of their services (as opposed to the full range of offerings) and pay commensurate fees. Fee increases at contract renewals are typical but should be reviewed critically if substantial (which can be as low as a 5% increase in fees) to ensure that services are added and/or streamlined to justify the increase.

Long-Term Considerations for Underwriting Employee Benefits

It is no longer true that only large employers can make effective use of a captive funding vehicle; many mid-sized employers now own P&C captives and may already be funding their WC programs. Captive transactions benefit from risks similar to those most desired for self-funding: larger groups with high-frequency, low-severity claim patterns. Captive funding offers the opportunity to capture favorable loss experience and minimize operational costs and even eliminate larger fees (such as commissions) charged in a fully insured arrangement.

Because captives are regulated much like a traditional insurance company, the requirements add an extra layer of plan member security. The captive regulations, however, are less stringent than those for traditional insurers, which allows for greater plan design and benefit offering flexibility. Other advantages of captives include broader coverage capabilities and increased control over premium levels.

Impact of Integration

For employers offering disability benefits, funding can often be a catalyst to integration. Employers wanting to take a common philosophy toward risk can look to what they have been doing more traditionally on the WC side and try to apply it to their STD and LTD plans. For example, if an organization is self-insuring its WC risk, it may make sense to handle STD and LTD in this way. If a captive is involved, WC and LTD (not typically STD, due to its short-tail nature) are the prime candidates for consideration. Self-insured and captive structures offer a common approach across WC and disability. This causes an employer to treat the risk more similarly, work toward common definitions and measurement points, and analyze the results for common, repetitive, and complex claims for management.

From a savings perspective, alternative funding options can produce an additional 10% to 15% of cost reduction over and above the (up to) 15% on average costs employers can achieve by integrating plan design, process, and technology aspects of their benefits programs. This, of course, is dependent on the risk pool and risk tolerance of the employer organization, as well as its current funding mechanisms and level of program integration.

Resources

Source	Author/ Editor	Print/ Electronic
The Handbook of Employee Benefits, 5th edition	Jerry S. Rosenbloom	Print
Employee Benefits, 6th edition	Burton T. Beam, John J. McFadden	Print
Insurance and Risk Management Institute risk financing and workers' compensation manuals		Print
Leveraging Risk Management Techniques for Additional Savings	Teri Weber	Print
http://www.assetprotectioncorp.com/vebafaqs5.html		Electronic
http://www.mwe.com/index.cfm/fuseaction/publications.nldetail/object_id/92793D21-483B-4277-9845-AB2D0CC6BE35.cfm		Electronic

Employer Checklist

The right funding strategy can help employers not only minimize their costs but also see the bigger picture of employee benefit and WC programs in general and how integrated programs can benefit organizations. The checklist below highlights the key areas employers should consider in reviewing alternatives to their current status.

Key Questions	Yes/No	Comments
Which of the following best describes your organization's current funding approaches — fully insured, self insured, hybrid combination, or captive arrangement — for the following lines of coverage?		

Short-term disability		
Long-term disability		
Workers' compensation		
Group healthcare		
How would you describe your organization's level of risk tolerance?		
Minimal: risk averse		
Medium: risk conscious		
High-risk assumptive		
Which of the following actions has your organization taken to review your program funding options?		
Conducted an actuarial feasibility study to consider various funding approaches		
Currently operates a captive for P&C or other risks		
Reviewed the following prefunding vehicles for various benefit lines:		
General assets		
VEBA trust		

Compared various TPAs and insurers offering ASO contracts		
Services covered		
Thorough breakdown of fees		
Contract flexibility		

Chapter 19: Requests for Proposals (RFP) and Vendor Selection

Background and Context

Vendor selection can be a tedious and arduous process but one that is necessary and often revealing. Whether you have decided to consider a new broker, change third-party administrators, or select a new insurance carrier, the process requires time and commitment. Although it may seem difficult to manage, selecting a new vendor or determining whether your current vendor is the best choice for you is critical for the success of your integrated program. Without facilitating a bidding initiative in the form of a request for information (RFI), request for proposal (RFP), or other format, it is difficult to know how the services you receive compare to the offerings available from other organizations. Also, competitive bids allow your firm to validate the current cost structure and reduce potential waste from both a hard dollar and a process efficiency perspective.

Your vendor partner(s) should provide a service that is best in class, based on your specific needs. This includes balancing choice, flexibility, pricing, and customer service as well as other priorities for your organization. Best in class or best practice is defined differently by all buyers, and as such, competitive bids are facilitated for many reasons, including but not limited to:

- Dissatisfaction with current program and/or services
- Testing the market to ensure competitive positioning and pricing
- An internal requirement to bid coverage
- Change in the plan or process that warrants examining options in the market
- Lack of capability by current partners

Regardless of the reason, a systematic approach is always best and should include a qualitative and quantitative analysis. Setting a framework for the entire process at the onset will ensure biases are reduced. That framework should include an assessment for current needs as well as potential future considerations. The latter are imperative to include as they will require your internal stakeholders to think more broadly and position for a longer term partnership. This is valuable because the cost of an RFI or RFP is significant and therefore a longer term relationship (i.e., three years or more) is ideal.

Most RFP or RFI initiatives include four primary steps: (1) preplanning, (2) proposal process, (3) analysis, and (4) selection. From there, implementation of a new vendor or perhaps re-implementation of your current vendor will begin. All of the information gathered during those four steps of the bidding initiative will be used as the catalyst for a smooth implementation or re-implementation.

The graphic below provides an overview of the four main stages of the RFP process and the steps that should take place during each stage.

Figure 19.1

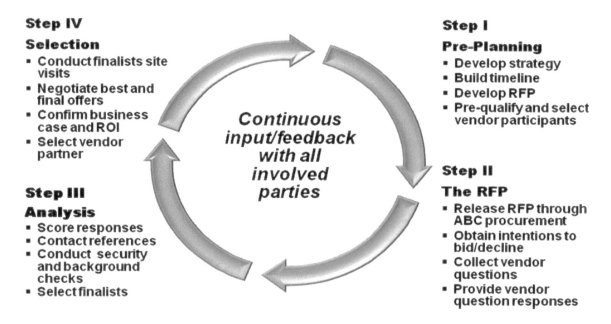

Step IV

Selection

- Conduct finalists site visits
- Negotiate best and final offers
- Confirm business case and ROI
- Select vendor partner

Step III

Analysis

- Score responses
- Contact references
- Conduct security and background checks
- Select finalists

Continuous input/feedback with all involved parties

Step I

Pre-Planning

- Develop strategy
- Build timeline
- Develop RFP
- Pre-qualify and select vendor participants

Step II

The RFP

- Release RFP through ABC procurement
- Obtain intentions to bid/decline
- Collect vendor questions
- Provide vendor question responses

Source: Spring Consulting Group, LLC.

Step 1: Preplanning

The preplanning process typically requires four primary steps, including (1) establishing goals, (2) building the business case, (3) setting the team and timeline, and (4) prequalifying participants. The scope of these will vary based on the organization as well as the services being included in the RFP. As is the case with most large projects, careful planning predicates success, and if internal subject matter experts do not exist, it will be important to leverage external support.

Establishing Goals

To establish goals for the project, you must first identify the various customers impacted by the bidding process as well as the internal stakeholders. Ensuring that all key stakeholders provide insight regarding their goals for the RFP initiative will better position the project. When multiple stakeholders are involved, it may make sense for round tables to occur in order to engage all parties to promote exchange of ideas and facilitate development of goals. It is likely that during these discussions, goals and objectives above and beyond the RFP will also be discussed, and it will be critical to capture those goals so they are not missed once a vendor is selected. With various "customers" providing feedback, conflicting goals may be raised. A process to resolve these conflicts should be established in advance.

Documentation is a critical part of the RFP process, as topics discussed will evolve over time and decisions made will impact other decisions. Therefore, it is always best to have a project manager assigned during the preplanning process who can manage this project through to implementation. Documentation should begin at these round table discussions, keeping all parties informed through meeting minutes, action item logs, decision logs, project plans, and the like.

If in determining your goals you discover that you merely want to gather market information, you may want to consider an RFI, as opposed to or as a preliminary step to an RFP. An RFP is typically more formal than an RFI; however, both may contain the same level of detail. In some organizations, the RFI is linked to the "business needs," whereas the RFP is derived from the "system or information technology needs." Other organizations establish an RFI as a precursor to an RFP as a way of prescreening potential vendors. Regardless of terminology, the goal is to use the most efficient method to achieve your desired results.

Building the Business Case

Feedback from goal setting will position the core team to begin building the business case. Similar to the goal-setting process, requirements for establishing the business case will vary considerably depending on the organization. Some groups will require a business case for the RFP itself, mandating management and other internal stakeholders agree to the RFP and any spending and/or staffing it requires.

Other groups use this step to plan their own internal business case for changing vendors and therefore identify requirements for potential providers as well as advantages and disadvantages of their current plan in order to solidify their needs for the future. The remaining groups may hope to accomplish both within this task.

When senior management approval is required for the RFP, it will be important for the core team to clearly lay out not only the costs involved but also the anticipated savings or other benefits that will result from the RFP process.

Setting the Team and Timeline

To establish the core team, you need to consider the departments directly involved and any that might be affected by a change in vendor. Often it is helpful to have one individual from the organization (e.g., project manager) spearheading the effort. Some organizations leverage a broker or consultant in this capacity; others utilize the broker/consultant as primarily a subject matter expert. More and more, employers are turning to internal procurement teams to play this role. Either way, clearly defined roles will enable everyone to operate efficiently and avoid duplicative efforts.

Beyond the core team, it will be necessary to identify other stakeholders that may need to be pulled in from time to time for certain pieces of the implementation process. Even if a certain group's involvement won't be needed until further along in the process, it is important to identify them up front so that there are no surprises down the road. Deciding how and when to communicate with other stakeholders will be important as well; they may want to be up to speed on the project status but will probably not need to know the level of detail that the core team will be involved in. Therefore, it is critical to have a forum to address questions and solicit feedback. This can be a monthly conference call or meeting, depending on the group. For disability and absence management bids, typically human resources, risk management, occupational health and safety, information technology, payroll, legal, and communications are directly involved. In addition, procurement may be considered a contributing team member.

In setting the timeline, the core team will need to consider other important dates and deadlines impacting the project and its stakeholders, such as enrollment dates and board or budget meetings. Depending on the size and scope, the bidding process can range from a few months to a year. Implementation can vary widely, including some phased implementations that may range over years, but anywhere between three to nine months is common for most programs. Once the team has an implementation estimate, it can then work backward from the set deadline, usually an enrollment date, and add time in for the RFP process, including development, distribution to the vendors, time to respond to vendor questions, and the time involved in vendor selection, which may include additional meetings and/or site visits.

Inevitably, some bidding initiatives take longer than originally planned. Especially as it relates to leave and absence management providers, attention to detail is critical. Therefore, truncating the timeline for a bidding effort is ill-advised without revising the scope. Timelines could be restructured by adding additional resources, including subject matter experts, decreasing the number of bidding vendors and the like; however, a timeline should not be cut without understanding the risks involved. Given the expense of the bidding process (including direct and indirect costs, including time) it is almost always best to revise the timeline based on the required scope than the reverse.

Prequalifying Participants

Identifying who will receive your request to bid can be laborious. If a broker or consultant is involved, it should have a list of prequalified vendors that fit your needs. Without an advisor, it is suggested that you consider trade publications, membership organizations, and research tools to assist in prequalifying participants. High-level conversations should be held with all potential bidders to ensure they understand the requirements.

Unless the situation with the current provider is dire, the incumbent provider should be included in the bidding process. This will allow it the opportunity to demonstrate any revised capabilities since your last marketing initiative, as well as give a strong comparison point.

During this phase, it is also important to understand what, if any, contractual obligations will be required of bidders. It is considered optimal to have bidders sign nondisclosure agreements to ensure they keep the content of the RFI or RFP confidential.

Step 2: The RFP

The RFP itself is designed to meet specific company criteria and should be organized into key categories. Some categories to consider in developing an RFP are:

- Background and fit

- Functional requirements

- Corporate standards

- Customer service

- Performance and pricing

Background and Fit

This section gives the vendor the opportunity to describe its organizational experience and reputation. The vendor should also detail its staffing and training capabilities and provide information on its team's experience and years of service, as well as average length of employment, geographic closeness of claims staff to company locations, and average caseloads per claims administrator.

Functional Requirements

It is very important that the RFP be tailored to the company's specific needs as it relates to requirements. The employer needs to be clear in what it is asking the vendor to describe, as this information will likely be where the bulk of the decision making comes into play: the core team will need to be certain that the selected vendors can in fact provide the requested services. It will be important to compare each vendor's capabilities within each of these specific areas and their flexibility within these categories:

- Intake

- Claims administration

- Leave administration

- Information technology and interfaces

- Reporting and data

- Proactive consultation

Corporate Standards

Depending on the employer's organizational structure, the vendor may be looked upon to provide guidelines around compliance. Contractual and legal issues should be identified up front, such as who will bear fiduciary responsibility. Data security and integrity of information should also be outlined and clarified. For some organizations, this will link directly to information technology and interface discussions. For other organizations, the focus is tied more closely to confidentiality. Defining confidentiality and pinpointing what information will be shared within the organization and at what level is critical. At the core, a vendor partner should have policies that are in line with the employers' policies. This would include but not be limited to its interpretation of the Health Insurance Portability and Accountability Act, which does not apply to disability or leave programs but may have some philosophies or standards that could be leveraged.

As more information is exchanged, data protection and rules regarding data transfer and permission levels are becoming increasingly vital. The vendor should also be asked to detail its quality assurance processes and how it goes about ensuring the validity of its data and systems, preventing errors, and dealing with issues that may come up.

Customer Service

The account management section should provide information on the vendor's structure, whether there is a designated team, and if the implementation team will differ from the account management team moving forward. The size of the account out to bid may determine the level of customer service put forward by the vendor; this will be an important point of comparison between the service providers.

At the end of the day, the employer needs to be comfortable with the vendor's implementation and account managers and know that they are up to the task of developing and successfully managing a program for the company. The involvement level of the employer will vary, so the vendor needs to be flexible in its role. Some organizations prefer to work hand in hand with the vendor throughout the process, whereas others look to the vendor to take a leadership role.

Performance and Pricing

The performance and pricing section of the RFP will likely be frequently referenced further down the line, potentially even after choosing a vendor and implementing a program with it. Performance guarantees will be dependent on the employer's organizational structure. In going forward with a vendor, there is usually a series of negotiations around these before all parties are in agreement. The employer and vendor will need to agree on measurement and amount of fees to put at risk. The pricing structure should be provided in a clear and understandable way.

As vendors work through the material shared, questions will be raised. A format to address questions should be established well in advance. Whenever possible, answers should be shared with all bidding providers to keep the messaging consistent. Tardy questions may or may not be addressed, but if they significantly alter the positioning of the proposal, every effort should be made to provide responses. Following suit, responses to bidder questions should be timely as well. Typically, a two- to three-day turnaround is ideal. If communication issues arise, a conference call can be scheduled in which vendors are able to pose questions without revealing their identity to the other parties on the call. This may or may not prove valuable, depending on the circumstances.

Some firms are leveraging online software systems or proprietary procurement tools for RFPs. While those tools do provide efficiencies, they also have limitations. Great care must be taken to ensure responses are as detailed as necessary for an absence management program. Forcing bidders to respond yes or no may provide a quicker analysis but not a quality analysis. Details are important. Therefore, it may or may not be advantageous to use online tools for this type of procurement initiative. Consider the employer, broker, consultant, and bidding providers when determining the best tools for your bidding process.

Step 3: Analysis

Analyzing responses may be difficult, depending on both the RFP format and the quality of the responses received. Considering the proposal analysis within the preplanning phase will make this smoother and less time-consuming. Absence management bids must be reviewed from both a qualitative and a quantitative perspective. Therefore, to ensure a consistent process, answers should be compared side by side. In addition, engaging multiple team members to review the responses is helpful as it allows for various perspectives as well as strong peer review.

Perhaps the most important aspect of the analysis is to ensure bidding vendors are compared appropriately (i.e., apples to apples). Great care must be taken to weigh responses that are uniform and, when necessary, follow up with providers to gather responses that are comparable. If the proposal considers both current and future needs, the analysis should separate those and provide two different reviews. This will ensure that the team understands which providers are the best fit given the current state and which providers are equipped to support anticipated needs. In addition to reviewing detailed responses, it will also be important to assess cultural fit. Based on the cultural fit and the detailed responses, two to three finalists should be selected for additional review.

Step 4: Selection

Once finalists are selected, a more in-depth review of the vendor may be warranted. Steps to consider include finalist site visits, reference checks, performance guarantees, final financial proposals, and understanding each provider's commitment to the overall business case, including return on investment.

Finalist Site Visits

At this point, all information shared to date should be reviewed and discussed with team members who will attend site visits. In many ways, the intangibles become very meaningful in the selection phase as the margin between finalists may be small. The site visit team should include internal stakeholders from various areas within the organization. If a system is being purchased or links with a system are needed, a representative from the information technology team is critical. The site visit will give the team time to get a "hands-on" feel for the vendor's operations and observe how the organization is run on a daily basis. Ideally, the group will be able to meet some key team members who would be leveraged if the business were placed with that provider and make an overall assessment of the cultural "fit" between the working groups. After the site visits, optimally the same day, each team member should complete an assessment of that vendor. Those assessments will be helpful if multiple site visits are made, as over time it may be hard to recall details of the visit.

Reference Checks and Performance Guarantees

To validate the team's findings during the site visit process, it is customary for the finalists to provide at least two references and ideally three — two current customers and one past customer — to provide confirmation of the capabilities and expertise the vendor presented during the procurement process. The team will strive to understand what went well in these relationships and what didn't, and why the one reference might have terminated the vendor's services.

At this time, another round of performance guarantee discussions might take place to assess the vendor's overall commitment to the pending employer relationship. As performance guarantees can be quite detailed and specific to an employer's situation and some vendors may not share specific guarantees in their initial proposal, it is often more productive to discuss them with a smaller group of finalists than with a larger group of potential partners at the onset of the RFP process. This is a very important point of comparison, and although final details can wait until the contract, discussions on performance standards are critical to have before a vendor is selected.

Final Financial Proposals

The final financial proposal must consider more than the core pricing. It should also detail any out-of-scope fees, since such charges will be likely over the course of the relationship, as well as any assumptions inherent in the costs. It should also adjust for any specifics uncovered during the site visit and really serve as the vendor's best and final offer. In conjunction with the performance guarantees, fees at risk should be clearly stated. In addition, the team should understand how issues and miscommunications will be resolved and how pricing for those will be managed. Essentially, your team will want to be assured that if your vendor makes an error, it will assume the cost for correcting that error and if new needs are discovered during implementation, there is a process to account for them.

Decision Making and Selection

Selecting a vendor may not be easy and can require a lot of internal analysis and discussion, depending on the organization. Senior management, or at least the initial team that agreed to the business case, will likely be involved or at least interested in the outcome. The original goals and objectives set out by the team will need to be compared to the proposal of the preferred vendor, and the anticipated return on investment validated or even improved upon from the process. If the decision involves a change in vendor, there may be political ramifications for the team to consider.

Once a decision has been reached, a communication plan should be established so that all internal stakeholders are aware of it and the corresponding rationale behind it. The chosen vendor should then be notified, followed by the incumbent vendor and any other finalist providers. The communication timeline may need to be varied in some situations, but it is important to communicate directly to both vendors and internal parties as quickly as possible to avoid them learning about your decision from other sources.

If bidding providers request feedback, it should be given candidly and constructively. This feedback will help them as they prepare for other proposals and will help your organizations maintain a good working relationship for future needs.

Whether the decision is to remain with your incumbent provider or to change vendors, care must be taken to implement or re-implement according to your needs. Set reasonable timelines and clearly identify roles at the onset. It will also be important to continually tie back to the program goals set forth in the RFP. During implementation, refer to the RFP and consider it the selected vendor's commitment. It should be adhered to unless a change in strategy is mutually agreed upon.

Employer Checklist

Key Questions	Yes/No	Comments
Are you required to bid your plan at specific intervals?		
Does your current provider fulfill the needs of your integrated program?		
Have situations arisen that have made you question your current vendor's commitment to your organization?		

Have you considered where your plan will be in three years? Will your current vendor be able to meet those needs?		
Does your team have the capacity and subject matter expertise to support a marketing initiative?		
If no, do you have a trusted advisor to turn to?		
Have you determined the timing for your RFP initiative?		
Have you set a budget — both internal and external — for the process?		
Have internal stakeholders in the following areas been identified?		
Human resources		
Risk management		
Information technology		
Payroll		
Legal		
Communications		
Other		
Has the business case, at least at a high level, been made so your team can begin the process in an orderly manner?		

Section Five

Program Management

Chapter 20: Integrated Reporting and Metrics

Data Integration and Why It Is Important

Data integration allows employers to unify data from multiple sources into one cohesive system and create useful information to support and direct important decisions. The integrated, employee-specific model monitors both employee-level and provider-specific outcomes and assesses the impact of incentives and changes in contractual relationships between the worker and the provider. For example, when an employee has more than one benefit activated, such as a workers' compensation (WC) and a short-term disability (STD) claim, the elimination period enforced by one vendor (as a form of employee cost-sharing) might be rendered useless if the second vendor provides payment during that time. An integrated model is able to uncover these discrepancies.

Yet too often, employers combine data using the same calculations that have not changed over the years. The use of information technology (IT) is commonly relegated to simple calculations, such as total cost and number of claims. Evolving trends show more sophisticated approaches, such as using employee-level data to better define trends and address productivity.

Although employers prepare for employee absence by creating specific benefit plans to give staff the ability to take time off from work without suffering serious financial detriments, the complexity and increasing health- and absence-related costs require a more sophisticated model of analyzing and evaluating benefit plan designs and employee absence. Complicating factors driving the absence costs include: the aging workforce, the variable levels of eligibility for different employee types (union, salaried, hourly), increased pressures of productivity in an effort to remain competitive in a global economy, and a tumultuous economy that adds considerable physical and psychological stress and strain on employees, as well as employers.

The Value of Integrating Data

To fully understand the big picture and address the complexity of integrated disability, absence, and health management programs, data integration is necessary. Specifically, data integration can address issues such as:

- Highlighting duplication

- Identifying employee migration from one benefit to another

- Limiting variation in the ways benefit plans are managed

- Detecting moral hazard responses

- Formalizing risk identification

- Assessing the effectiveness of a program

- Recognizing Pareto groups

- Reviewing the cost of workers' compensation and disability claim overlap

- Coordinating return-to-work programs

Ultimately, the value is expressed through cost effectiveness, increased efficiency, increased knowledge, and better productivity throughout the organization.

What types of data or metrics are required for the level of reporting necessary to achieve real cost savings?

The concept of a Pareto group states that 20% of claimants are responsible for 80% of costs. Identifying the Pareto group across all benefit types requires integrated data. Without it, Pareto groups can only be identified for each benefit type. Additionally, when claimants use more than one benefit type (such as using both STD and WC or disability and family medical leave [FML] time), integrated data allows employers to accurately identify the group of claimants who are responsible for the most significant costs or usage.

Chevron, a global energy company, reduced STD claims by 15% and saved nearly $9 million in program costs over a three-year period after implementing an information sharing and reporting system based on an integrated database model.[cxlvii] Specifically, Chevron provided the disability carrier with FML, payroll, absence eligibility, STD, long-term disability (LTD), and WC leave data. It integrated the payroll system and the absence data, and was able to identify employees who had leaves extending beyond five days and were not in a case management program. In an effort to maintain equal treatment for all employees on leave, Chevron and the disability carrier were able to redirect resources to manage the employees who were out more than five days and did not have a support system in place.

The value of an integrated claims system is more than a financial consideration; it is a productivity and efficiency issue as well. L.L.Bean outsourced its STD claims processing in 2001. In 2005, in response to the level of difficulty in managing absences from numerous data sources, it outsourced its STD check processing and switched to telephonic claim filing. Between 2002 and 2007, L.L.Bean experienced a 35% reduction in lost-time claims.[cxlviii]

Figure 20.1
Integrated Database Components

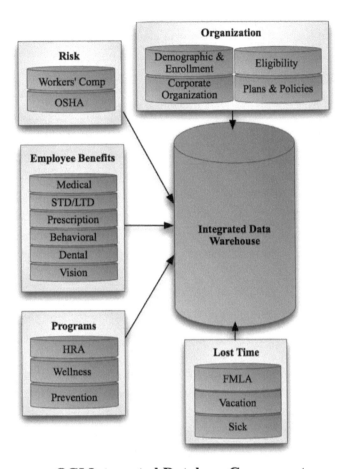

OCI Integrated Database Components

Source: Optis, Inc.

Another study demonstrated that an employer improved upon its decentralized absence management system through the use of a comprehensive, online system in which managers received updates and a list of activities that needed to be completed in order to manage each claim at any given point of the day. The system not only contributed to improving manager productivity but also established a standard of uniformity and compliance with the company's best practices.

Getting Started

To move toward an integrated data management approach, employers should start with what they can handle from a scope and cost perspective. It is critical that a baseline for your program is established. An iterative approach is highly recommended because your organization is unique, and, as such, your risks, productivity, benefit plans, integrated reports, data, and metrics will not match those of any other organization. In addition, you will learn many new things about your organization as you review your variables through the "data looking glass." You need to be able to adapt to what you learn at each juncture and apply that to your metrics and reports.

Although data integration can become sophisticated and complex quickly, the following premises will help you get started in a practical way:

- Build an historical event timeline of changes in the organization, benefit plans, vendors, and laws. This document is an invaluable tool when comparing historical data trends with current snapshots. Make sure you keep this timeline current throughout the life of the database. If you see coming changes in the timeline, you can correlate them to the historical events and adapt early.

- Insist on integration collaboration from your vendors. To keep the request manageable, agree to receive the initial data feeds in their standard format. The data should be summarized at the claim level for closed claims only. You will need a claimant identifier that allows you to connect back to the demographic and organizational data so you can pair that with claims from the other sources. Realize that your disability insurer may not be able to provide claimant-identified data if you insure your program with them. Disability insurers are not held to the Health Insurance Portability and Accountability Act, but they are required to adhere to the Gramm-Leach-Bliley Act, which has stricter requirements regarding employee and claimant privacy.

- Prepare to own the data repository to ease the inevitable competitive concerns among the data sources. This can be accomplished with internal resources or outsourcing to an independent data management group.

- Collect three years of history for each claims and absence source. Provide a matching three-year history from the demographic and organizational sources. Three years is a minimum number of years to establish trends and benchmarking. Three or more years of data helps to avoid misleading trends influenced by an abnormal year. Again, claims data should be collected at the claim summary level for closed claims only. Open claims substantially increase the complexity of the metric calculations and have no impact on the baseline being established at this point. Without close dates for the open claims, it would not be possible to accurately determine duration without predictive modeling. The lost-time data should match the same three-year time horizon as that of the claims sources. If there was a vendor change during the prior three years, you will need to collect data from all vendors to fill in the timeline and get a complete picture.

Data quality is an important concern when building any database but absolutely critical when integrating data from disparate sources. The maximum data quality in your integrated database needs to be as high as the quality of the source data. Most data sources have quality issues of varying degrees, but that is not within the domain of the integrated reporting project to correct. The concern with data quality in the integrated database is maintaining the integrity of the source data as it moves to metrics and reports so that it matches the source data reporting. Each data source should be assessed for quality with any exceptions noted and reported back to the source system. Under no circumstances should the data in the integrated database be modified. If the source system corrects the data, then it can be reloaded into the database.

- Conduct a baseline analysis to determine areas of concern. A baseline analysis is a high-level summary of the current trends and characteristics of the state of your benefit plans. Benchmarks are established by calculating percentage growths and declines over a period of at least three years or could be based upon one single point in time. These metrics are typically based on financial performance (such as average claim cost per eligible employee or total cost per member per month) and lost days metrics (such as average duration per claim or average number of lost days per employee).

- Monitor the data in the newly created data asset from the top down. Top-level metrics are easier to produce, digest, and adjust. Before investing in a full set of reporting tools and data mining tools, explore what metrics are valuable to your decision-making process and what tools are necessary to calculate the metrics. Given the vast number of analytical software packages that are on the market and their varying level of cost and sophistication, your final choice in software necessitates thorough research and planning. Some software packages require years of experience to navigate and operate efficiently due to proprietary coding language. The choice of software is not only dictated by the employer's budgetary concerns and the software's ability to provide the necessary calculations but also by the literal amount of data that will be analyzed.

Adapt As You Learn

Data integration, analysis, and reporting are part of a learning process. Do not expect to know everything from the beginning. The more data added over time, either in history or from new sources, the more powerful the information. New data leads to the constant and conscious effort to evaluate the value of the existing reports and metrics in accurately describing the overall benefits picture. Add, improve, and revise the package of reports and metrics, as necessary, to provide maximum clarity of your overall data picture.

Enter into the effort with the expectation that you'll know more tomorrow than you do today. Prepare to adapt based on this newly gained intelligence, and you'll find success over the long term with your integrated reporting and metrics solution.

Information Delivery Methods

Once the data asset is operational, your focus should turn toward information dissemination. The information must be relevant, actionable, accessible, and have an impact on the recipients to maximize the value of this newly discovered benefits intelligence. This section focuses on the accessibility of the information. Accessibility is the first hurdle to cross in disseminating information because the decision makers need the information in their hands when the decision points present themselves. Timing is nearly everything in this situation. It is highly advantageous to remain as flexible as possible with your information production and distribution toolset (tools, formats, and vendors) to ensure that your benefits intelligence needs aren't moving faster than your support system can deliver and that your data asset is not the organization's best-kept secret.

When selecting your delivery methods, keep in mind that all information recipient needs are not created equal. With the potential information recipients ranging from individual employees to senior management within the organization and extending to claims managers, plan providers, and health and wellness vendors, the information needs are very diverse. Selecting the appropriate delivery method for each distinct recipient is accomplished by evaluating the appropriate scope of information and the delivery vehicle. If not carefully planned, both dimensions of report delivery can render the information useless. Getting too much (or too little) information to the recipient via the appropriate method is ineffective. For example, providing a corporate STD/WC claims overlap percentage metric to the operations managers who are most interested in their departments is just as ineffective as producing the correct information but never getting it into the right hands. In another example, there is no value in providing the same corporate STD/WC claims overlap percentage metric via an ad hoc data query tool that intimidates your senior managers because they aren't able to access or take the time to understand the tool.

One effective approach is to put basic information into the hands of each recipient, filling the immediate need, and then providing them with tools and proper instruction to dig deeper. This approach is simple to implement and will satisfy the needs of the majority of the audience, while maintaining the capacity for the occasional deep dive into the supporting data.

Fortunately, with the broad set of powerful, commercially available reporting tools on the market today, scoping the information to match the needs of the recipient is much simpler than it was just a few years ago. Generally speaking, the tools allow mass customization by filtering the content on each report at the recipient level. The approach is very straightforward when the report/metric is created as a template. As the report/metric is generated, the security permissions for each user are applied to the data as it is selected from the database to produce the report. This method effectively right-sizes the data to fit the scope of the recipient. The application administrator need only manage the permissions for each user based on the organization structure and related information privileges to ensure that each recipient receives the appropriate level of information.

The next step is to provide a basic set of reports/metrics that have relevance to every user group and present these reports/metrics in a way that keeps the reporting tool out of the way of the information. The reporting tools available today address the full spectrum of recipient distribution needs. Some of these common distribution methods include:

- Push reporting: Completed reports/metrics are delivered via email to the recipient.

    o Pros: No user effort to generate report/metric; delivered through a standard business channel such as email; report creator controls content received by recipients; reports can be mass produced in a batch cycle

    o Cons: Email has limited data security; users don't have to read the report/metric; information is static or may or may not even be viewed

- Pull reporting: Reports/metrics are delivered as requested via an online interface.

    o Pros: Strong data security; real-time drill-down into supporting data; content is controlled by the recipient

    o Cons: Requires knowledge of the reporting toolset; user has to proactively come to get reports/metrics; mass production isn't possible

- Ad hoc reporting: The recipient configures the report selection parameters, output template, and runtime parameters, then runs the report.

- Pros: Recipient isn't limited to data behind canned reports; supports open-ended, "what if" query capability

- Cons: Requires mastery of the content as well as expertise of the query tool

- Data extract: Raw data is produced by the reporting tool for use in another system and/or analytic tool.

  - Pros: Allows the recipient to use the reporting tool of their choice

  - Cons: Output is not user friendly, bypasses all reporting application controls

- Dashboard: Metrics are presented at a macro level with some graphic indicator of performance.

  - Pros: Graphic indicators provide interpretation of the metric; drill-down to supporting data; just the information the recipient needs, no extra filler

  - Cons: Setup and use require a strong data knowledge; macro-level metrics can mask underlying performance issues; impact of micro-level adjustments are impossible to discern using just the macro dashboard metrics

- Alerts: Notices are sent to interested parties when preset thresholds are exceeded. The notice goes out via email or text message. This method combines the other methods into one seamless solution in which the recipient sets up alerts for the areas in which they have concerns and then lets the reporting solution tell them when those areas are in need of attention.

  - Pros: Only alert information is sent (no confidential data); saves time reviewing uneventful reports/metrics

  - Cons: Requires the recipient to engage in digging into the cause of the alert; false alerts can create unresponsive recipients

Most likely, a mix of some or all of these methods may be required in your integrated reporting and metrics implementation. The good news is that you don't have to settle on just one. Your recipients will help you define the most appropriate scope and distribution methods after you initiate the program. Get them started with a basic set of information, don't overwhelm them with the tool, and then ask them what they like, need, and want in the way of information. It is important to give them a basic set of information before asking this question so you can control the conversation within the boundaries of what your integrated solution can support today.

With the information in the hands of the decision makers, it's up the business experts who built the integrated reporting and metrics solution to keep the information relevant and actionable. You'll find that the recipients will help with this evolution, but the original builders or implementers need to guide the group's efforts over time. These business experts know the business best. This expertise, combined with a sound, adaptive integrated reporting and metric solution, make for a very powerful benefits management tool.

Important Insights

Establish and Maintain the Business Case

The integration of information has to be financially viable in order to have longevity in the organization. Evaluate each new opportunity with an eye toward the expected return on investment (ROI) of having that information available at the fingertips of the decision makers. Reserve some of your report/metric development resources to calculate ROI on the integrated data investment.

Keep It Simple

It is easy to fall into the trap of presenting complex data still in its complex form or to get lost in the details. Thus it is suggested to keep the reports/metrics at a high level and concentrate on how the information can positively impact decisions and what value the information brings to the organization. The system should provide insight into why, how, and from where costs are moving and why, how, and which benefit plans are performing without being overly complex. This allows management to focus on problem areas, address the root causes, and make changes to mitigate risks.

Garbage In = Garbage Out

Invest the appropriate amount of resources to establish sound data quality in the integrated database. The phrase "garbage in =garbage out" refers to how inaccurate data leads to inaccurate results and eventually poor decisions. If data quality issues are uncovered during the procurement process, take the time to work with the sources to address concerns before replicating the data problems in the integrated database. However, don't let the quality of a particular source stall the entire project. Continue to build the database with the clean sources while working with the troubled source to improve the quality. After the database is fully operational and receiving updates, make sure to continue to monitor the quality of the data being added.

Socialize Early and Often

The reason for building an integrated database asset is to make better decisions. To provide the value of better decisions, the asset has to be used. Communicate the project to the recipient community early, get them involved, and keep communicating with them.

Conclusion

In conclusion, integrated data opens up the doors to much more sophisticated and useful data analysis that can support and direct managerial decisions regarding plan design, heath and productivity, cost containment, vendor selection, and other benefits-related components in a very focused approach. With proper data collection, insightful metrics, and value-based conclusions, organizations stand to save a considerable amount of cost, decrease absence, increase productivity, and promote a healthy and caring workplace.

Employer Checklists

The following table summarizes data sources that can be included in an integrated database and the recommended variables to collect. All data sources need an employee identifier (common field) that is consistent across all sources to join all data into integrated reports and metrics. A minimum of three years of history is recommended for all sources to establish a reliable baseline. Three years of information provides enough data and measurement points to trend the data accurately as well as to assess the current state compared to historical levels. History is valuable for the payroll and demographic/organization sources to accurately categorize claims and lost-time costs for trending purposes.

Data Source	Associated Variables
Claim Sources	
Short-term disability	Claim summary level: cost, lost days, illness date/type, location, pay percentage
Workers' compensation	Claim summary level: cost, lost days, injury date/type, location
Long-term disability	Claim summary level: claimant, cost, lost days, illness date/type, location, pay percentage
Group health	Service detail level for employees and dependents: service date, cost, place of service, diagnosis, procedure codes, employer and employee paid amounts
Prescription drug	Prescription detail level for employees and dependents: service date, drug name and code, dosage, days supplied, employer and employee paid amounts
Lost-Time Sources	
Family medical leave	Lost days, reason, leave type, dates
Paid time off	Lost days, reason, cost, dates

Integration/Grouping Sources	
Payroll	Compensation types/dates
Demographic/Organization	Hire date, termination date, birth date, organizational structure, work locations

The following table summarizes an ideal base set of metrics to produce from the integrated database. All of these metrics should include current measurement against a baseline value, trending, and period-over-period comparisons.

Metric	Explanation
Integrated	
Pareto group	Analysis of top cost drivers; subpopulation that is incurring the majority of claim cost
Integrated total absence	Historical trend and/or predictive analysis for claim incidence, duration, and cost
Overlap	Analysis of individuals utilizing multiple benefits in a time period (e.g., incurring both STD and WC claims)
Risk identification	Populations of claims that incur the most cost; locations/populations that have higher-than-average costs
Disability Benefits	
Top conditions	Top 10 conditions based on diagnosis (most frequent and most costly)
Average cost	Cost per claim/employee

Reporting lag	Time lags in the claim reporting and handling process
Average lost days	Lost days per claim/employee
Workers' Compensation	
Injury type	Top 10 injuries (most frequent and most costly)
Repeater claims	Multiple use of benefit during the measurement period
Reporting lag	Gap between incurring the injury and reporting the claim; gaps in claim process
Average cost	Cost per claim/employee
Average lost days	Lost days per claim/employee
FMLA Leave	
Type of use	Tracking of personal versus family use
Concurrent claims	Number of FML claims that are also disability- or WC-related
Average time used	Time used in days per claim/employee
Group Health/Prescription Drug	
Average cost	Cost per employee/member
Cost comparison	Place of service comparison (e.g., cost for inpatient versus outpatient or in-network versus out-of-network)

Top conditions	Top conditions based on diagnosis (most frequent, most costly)
Top drug therapy	Top drug therapies based on national drug code (most frequent, most costly)

Chapter 21: Integrated Program Costs, Savings, and Return on Investment

Background and Scope

The top reasons employers implement integrated programs are to reduce costs and increase employee satisfaction. Specifically, they aim to reduce direct costs of benefits but are also focused on decreasing absence rates, increasing return-to-work percentages, reducing lost time for workers' compensation (WC), and decreasing the length of disabilities. Some of the biggest advantages to integrating benefits are easier administration, a better customer experience, better tracking or reporting, consistent administration, and increased control.

Determining the baseline costs of an integrated program, not to mention confirming the level of savings and return on investment (ROI) achieved over time, however, is no easy feat. Employers routinely struggle with their ability, or lack thereof, to collect credible information at the onset of their integrated program implementations that can later be translated into measurable results. In many cases, there is an acknowledgement that the initial data just doesn't exist, for example, in the case of salary continuance programs where they are embedded within regular payroll costs, and industry benchmarks must suffice. In others, and more commonly in today's environment, it becomes a matter of establishing processes to identify, define, and subsequently collect the data. The complexity will vary by employer and the objectives they set out for themselves and their programs.

With the overwhelming statistics released every day about the rising costs of healthcare and the increasing findings that lost productivity related to absence and presenteeism actually dwarfs those costs, employers must continue to quantify their own costs and savings achieved or at least establish initial benchmarks to measure themselves against. As there is often an initial cost in establishing an integrated program, identifying these figures early and often is becoming a requirement and foundation for success.

This chapter will offer background on particular challenges both the industry and employers have faced, discuss how the ability to measure has evolved over time, and point to definitions, models, and methods that are becoming more common and credible as the integrated industry grows and changes.

Industry and Employer Challenges

For some, simply collecting the data is an issue. For most, however, the biggest challenge is in getting management support and cooperation. The silos that exist within most companies are often like fortress towers designed and developed to protect the established processes and practices within them. Measurements and data are the most effective ways a change agent can build support for implementing a successful integrated program. Both the employee benefits industry at large and employers themselves are facing several challenges in their quest to quantify costs, resulting savings, and ROI.

Employers that have problems collecting data might be those who are shifting from unmanaged salary continuance (SC) plans to managed short-term disability (STD) programs that are closely coordinated with long-term disability (LTD) and other benefits programs. As 36% of STD or SC plans are self-insured and self-administered,[cxlix] it is not surprising that many do not have a plan to follow and that internal resources are simply paying dollars out of payroll and not applying any claims administration or tracking techniques that would allow for proper quantification.

Not being able to pull needed data from insurance company and third-party administrator (TPA) providers can also be difficult. Although industry veterans would agree that this capability has improved immensely over time, some provider systems still require manual interventions to produce data, especially if it is in a format that differs from their norm. Specific benefit plans, such as healthcare, can be more problematic than others, as some providers are concerned with employee confidentiality and/or the proprietary nature of insured business and provide only aggregate data as a result. Employer size can also contribute to an organization's frustration, as smaller organizations typically receive the information the provider deems appropriate (citing statistical significance) and don't have enough leverage to require something different.

The biggest challenge with metrics for employers, however, is ultimately not in the data collection and gathering. It is in interpreting and knowing how to use and apply the numbers they have. Data analysis has not been a skill set found within most integrated program professionals, mainly because it used to be a purely outsourced (or in some cases nonexistent) process. As integrated benefits programs have grown, so have the knowledge and ability to identify data that is meaningful to company's executives, management, claims adjusters, and the industry overall.

Measurement Evolution

In response to these challenges and the need of both employers and their provider partners to demonstrate savings and the resulting ROI of their efforts, the industry has been working hard to understand how various benefits fit together and what integrating them from a plan design and process perspective can really do to the bottom line.

Industry Resources

Several consulting and research firms have developed surveys that capture the costs of absence from a number of different perspectives. Nonprofit organizations and institutes have been established solely for the purpose of measuring costs, researching trends, and producing benchmarks employers can rely upon. Insurance companies, TPAs, and other service providers have increased their capabilities and learned how to work together with several sources to provide meaningful results.

For example, specific surveys show that employers report an increasing trend in absence rates due to illness, injury, or family concerns. Incidence rates have increased for STD, LTD, and family medical leave (FML) absences for 24%, 19%, and 38% of employers, respectively while 33% note more intermittent FML leaves. [cl]

Further, industry information tells us that an estimated 4% to 10% of an employer's workforce is "not at work" on any given day. [cli] Nearly half of employees report up to three days of unscheduled absences in six months — not always because they are sick. [clii]

Overall, lost productivity related to absence and presenteeism is proving to be greater than the costs of medical and pharmacy, as illustrated in Figure 21.1.

Figure 21.1

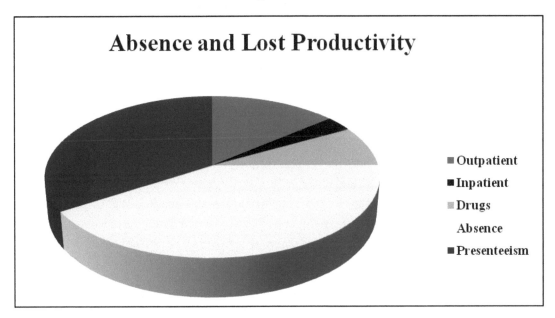

Source: Integrated Benefits Institute. (May 2007). Research Insights: I Don't Have All the Data? Now What Do I Do?

And finally, the industry is moving beyond the historical focus of managing claims after the fact to more of a proactive view of determining how health and productivity risks and costs can be prevented. In fact, preventable factors top the list of health issues affecting business performance, as shown in Figure 21.2.

Figure 21.2

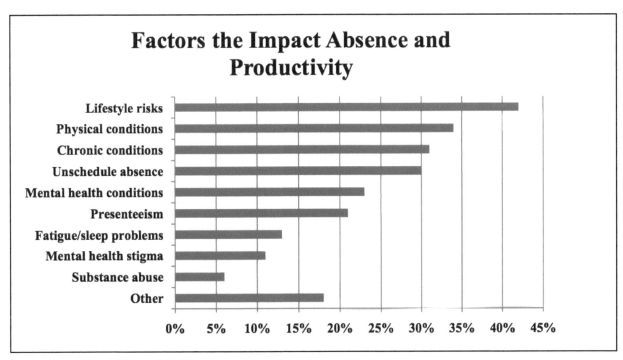

Source: National Business Group on Health and Watson Wyatt. (2007/2008). Staying@Work Report: Building an Effective Health & Productivity Framework.

Providers view FML requests as opportunity for proactive interventions with care management programs before a disability claim, as according to one CIGNA study, "Employees on FML are five times more likely to file a subsequent STD claim (24%) than those who have not requested FML (4.5%). Those who take FML for family reasons are 50% more likely to have a mental health related STD claim than those who take FML for other reasons. Employees on intermittent leave are even more likely to file an STD claim (38%) than those on continuous leave (16%). Employees on intermittent leave, regardless of the reason for the leave, are two times more likely to file an STD claim for behavioral illness than those on continuous leave."[cliii]

Overall, highly effective health and productivity organizations — those with an integrated framework for managing health and injury risks, acute and chronic illness, stress, and disability — have achieved lower incidence and length of disability rates for STD, LTD, FML, other absence, and WC by providing an organized process for employees and family members, which reduced related business costs, boosted worker productivity, and ultimately improved the company's financial performance.

Employer Actions

Because information like this is available to employers as they begin to implement their benefits programs or continue to expand what they have already integrated, employers are better positioned than ever to think about the specific measures and benchmarks that will show their company's management how the desired results are being reached. Although definitely a start, it is not enough to say that an integrated program will save money or reduce absence. Integrated program leaders will be obligated to prove that it can be achieved.[cliv]

The first step employers need to take in this regard is to define the objectives of their integration efforts.

- What is it that the employer wants to accomplish and why?

- What are the specific outcomes that can be associated with the accomplishments and why?

- How can measures be tied to how the program works, how the business works, how finance allocates expenses, who the stakeholders are, how the business defines the language it uses for measures (e.g., revenue, savings, number of production units), who the audience is, and what the potential ROI areas are?

The "what" involved in this line of questioning prompts thought around particular data points that can be measured, whereas the "why" helps to identify where an employer should go to build the ROI.

In general, integrated program leaders should operate under the premises that:

- Almost all integrated program objectives can be measured

- Integrated program objectives must be tied to overall business objectives (e.g., productivity, profit, market share, quality, increased revenue)

- Objectives must acknowledge the past and anticipate the future

From there, it becomes an exercise in determining how the employer is going to use the data. This dictates the particular data elements that need to be collected as well as the method of collection. Compilation of usable data must flow from a collaborative process that first establishes desired outcomes, as mentioned above, and then obtains data specifically targeted at evaluating those outcomes. Usually a combination of several data-gathering strategies is used so a full picture is obtained by the employer. Common methods include but may not be limited to:

- Database queries and specific report variable extraction

- Employer population demographic detail summary and confirmation

- Structured individual interviews of key stakeholders

- Focus group discussions of stakeholder groups

- Surveys and/or questionnaires

- Onsite observations (e.g., meetings, conferences, work processes)

- Benchmark and source identification

The importance of obtaining adequate, objective data in the design of integrated programs cannot be overemphasized. Data that is incomplete or biased can take the program in the wrong direction. It may satisfy the agenda of a specific individual or department but could cause the program to have limited scope and usually will fall short of meeting the business objectives of the program and company. In data gathering, a common mistake is to exclusively look at quantitative "hard" data at the expense of using helpful qualitative "soft" data that can be obtained through some of the methods noted above. The latter often provides insight on the problems or particular areas that need improvement. The combination of both hard and soft data provides the most meaningful view into the full costs of an integrated program and the savings and ROI that can be achieved over time.

Once the data has been collected, measurement and evaluation play the most significant roles in refining and expanding integrated programs. Effective integrated programs result from careful consideration of what is to be accomplished and how it may be best achieved in terms that a particular employer understands. The integrated program leader/stakeholder team plays a key role in helping the organization obtain clarity, while also focusing on initial goals and continually refining strategies over time.

In making a cost-benefit analysis of an integrated program's achievements, the two most common ways to justify costs are:

- ROI methods: These methods take into account how much money the company will spend and its expected return on that money. Defining the amount of expenditure and determining the expected savings levels form the foundation of this calculation. A 1:1 return rate, for example, will produce one dollar for every dollar spent by the employer. It is important to equate this in terms that resonate with the particular employer, such as acceptable level of ROI within the organization and typical units of measurement (e.g., revenue, production unit).

- Break-even calculations: Sometimes projects will not show an immediate profit. It may take some time to see a return. This is especially the case when employers purchase new programs as part of their integrated strategies, so there is actually an additional line item cost that did not specifically exist before. For example, outsourcing FML administration is typically a per-employee, per-month (PEPM) charge to an employer. Although supervisors were administering employee requests prior to outsourcing, many employers do not track manager and supervisor time and expense associated with FML as a separate line item, so the PEPM is viewed as a pure and new cost. Proposing a project that may have a loss during the first few years may require a break-even calculation such as the following:

Table 21.2
Cost/Benefit Example for a New Program

	Costs	Profits (loss)
Year 1	$100,000	($20,000)
Year 2	$100,000	$50,000
Year 3	$100,000	$500,000

Further, some types of program evaluation or assessment that integrated program leaders undertake to continually improve and refine their programs and to identify components that may be missing can include the following:

- Impact assessment: Determining if the program goals were reached and, if so, to what extent from both a qualitative and quantitative perspective

- Efficiency assessment: Reviewing what the program costs were in relation to the benefits that were paid to the employee population

- Coverage assessment: Concluding whether the target employees were served through the processes and protocols developed and taken forward

- Service delivery assessment: Ascertaining if the quality of services provided met the expectations of the recipients, managers, and other stakeholders within the organization

- Fiscal assessment: Revealing what the cost per client or cost per service actually was and how that compared to the initial and overall expectation of the program stakeholders

- Legal assessment: Establishing the degree to which integrated programs address compliance, equity, privacy, informed consent, and so forth within the organization

Common Definitions and Models

It cannot be stressed enough that what works for one employer may not work for another. Data that one organization is able to collect may be foreign or not attainable by another organization. Processes, infrastructure, and technology capabilities differ, and employers must take all these factors into account in determining how they define success at their organizations.

However, the industry has progressed to establish more common understanding around measurement and fully agrees that definitions drive outcomes and that these must be well thought out and clarified when analyzing and presenting results. For employers that look to external guidance either to initially set their goals for integration or to compare their particular outcomes to other industry benchmarks over time, the following definitions, models, and methods have come to be considered standards for integrated programs. Although each serves as a guideline that employers can feel confident in following and there are surely additional credible sources that exist, it is up to the particular employer to determine which of them resonate for their organization and how well they perceive them to match up to their integrated program goals and objectives.

Although the terms direct and indirect are commonly referenced as cost types employers need to be aware of, they do vary slightly from survey to survey and are beginning to encompass more detail than in the past. Further, "administrative" costs must be taken into account and are usually done so outside of and in addition to direct, and indirect costs. Some organizations prefer to reference "hidden costs" as the opportunity cost of lost productivity, but again, it comes down to understanding what an employer is actually measuring, then understanding how that measure relates to the overall program and the relevance of external benchmarks in its consideration.

As far as absence types go, the full range of what an employer can integrate, track, and manage is broad and dependent on employer prioritization, as mentioned throughout this guide. Although several reference points describe the actual benefit program type (e.g., STD, FML) in their compilations, there is also a movement to categorize absence as "unplanned," "planned," and "extended." Lastly, the concept of "presenteeism" has become a concern for employers, and methodologies to understand and manage it have already started taking shape.

Examples for Reference

A 2008 Mercer online survey sponsored by Kronos Incorporated [clv] represented a large-scale initiative to identify the total costs of absences in terms of type of cost and absence. Although not shown in Figure 21.4, it also examined the differences among exempt, nonexempt, and union employees.

Figure 21.4

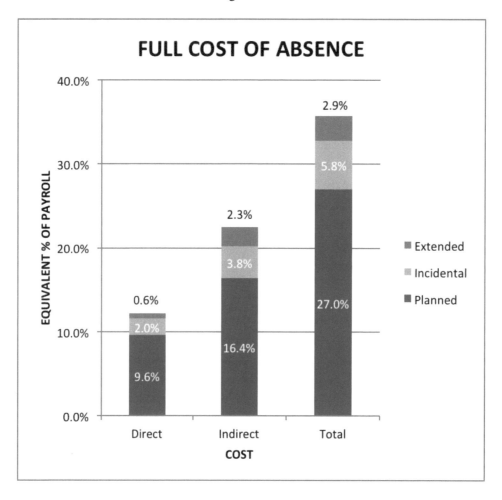

Source: Mercer. (October 2010). Survey on the Total Financial Impact of Employee Absences.

As referenced in Figure 21.4, the direct costs of the three major leave categories — extended, incidental, and planned — total 12.2% of payroll. This figure is similar to the 14.2% of payroll for direct costs that was identified in the 2007 Mercer/Marsh survey on health, productivity, and absence management programs, as well as the 14.4% uncovered by the National Business Group on Health and Watson Wyatt Staying@Work: Building an Effective Health & Productivity Framework survey (2007/2008), illustrated in Chapter 1, Table 1.1 of this book. The indirect costs total 22.5%, which follow the industry rule of thumb that indirect costs range from 150% to 250% of direct costs. The most significant finding in this survey, however, is that when 8.7% total costs for unplanned incidental and extended absences are added to the 27.0% total costs of planned absences, the overall total cost is 35.7% of payroll, or about three times the direct costs for the same plans.

In this survey, direct costs were defined as the pay or benefit provided to an employee for time not worked, while the indirect costs represented replacement labor expenses and net lost productivity value. The total costs summed the direct and indirect costs but netted out the indirect costs using the employee's salary, so as not to double count. Although not included in the calculation, the research stressed that the additional costs an employer bears for internal staff, software, office space, equipment, and outside organizational support to administer integrated programs - otherwise known as administrative expenses - should also be considered.

Types of absence were defined as unplanned incidental absences of five workdays or less, such as casual sick days, where the occurrence was not known and approved ahead of time by the employee's supervisor. Planned absences were short or moderate duration absences, such as vacations and holidays, where the supervisor knows about (and has likely approved) the absence in advance. Extended absences represent absences lasting beyond one week, often unplanned and generally due to short-term disabilities, extended FMLA leaves, and work-related disabilities lasting beyond a week. Finally, unplanned incidental and extended absences or absenteeism is the combination of two of the previous categories representing the kind of lost time that employers try to minimize or at least manage carefully.

From another vantage point, a 2008 study by the Integrated Benefits Institute (IBI)[clvi] examined the cost of absence by going beyond the consideration of only the wage replacement payments of absence cost. It included the opportunity costs of the advantages an employer could have received by not having the absence occur. These costs are particularly relevant as "lost productivity" and represent a commitment of financial resources to replace absent workers that could be used productively elsewhere in the business. The relative costs of each response in the research are shown in Figure 21.5 as per full-time equivalent (FTE).

Figure 21.5

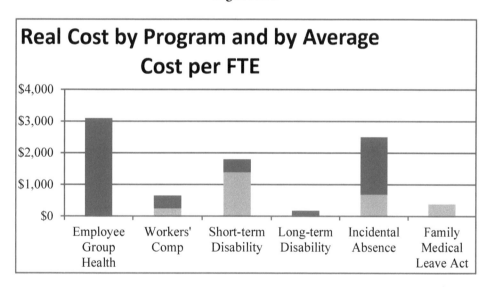

Source: Integrated Benefits Institute. (2008). The Business Response of Employers to Absence. San Francisco: IBI.

Further to this research, a study of CFOs[clvii] documented the ways in which companies respond to absence, which can be tied to the indirect costs and administrative costs mentioned in Figure 21.5—something IBI commonly references as "hidden costs."

Figure 21.6

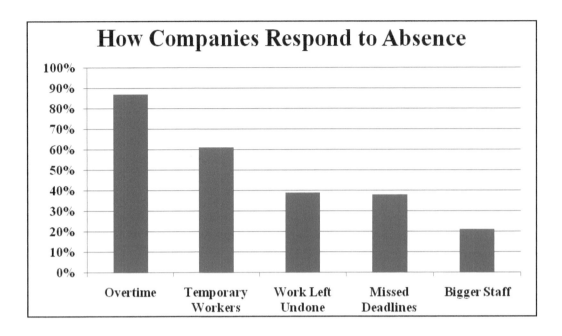

Source: Integrated Benefits Institute. (May 2006). The Business Value of Health: Linking CFOs to Health and Productivity. San Francisco: IBI.

Other Tools and Resources

A number of data integration, metrics, and self-help/self-report tools and resources are available to employers, depending on their budget, need, and degree of sophistication. Nonprofit organizations offering such resources include IBI, National Business Group on Health (NBGH), Bureau of Labor Statistics, National Business Coalition on Health, and the World Health Organization, among the most prominent.

IBI has developed a set of health and productivity measurement resources that contain a range of data depending on what an employer is interested in. Its Health & Productivity Snapshot tool helps employers understand how health may influence absence, presenteeism, and related lost productivity in their company based on a few simple data elements. IBI's Full Cost of Benchmarking Report offers benchmarking of WC, STD, LTD, and FML programs using a very large and detailed database contributed to by employers, insurance companies, and TPAs. The HPQ Select is an initiative for employers that want to set a baseline for their health interventions over time. It includes data on lost time and business relevant outcomes in their analysis of health-related programs and provides information about both the prevalence of health conditions and their effect on lost time and productivity (https://www.ibiweb.org/tools/full-cost-estimator).

Employer Measures of Productivity, Absence and Quality (EMPAQ) was designed by the NBGH's Council on Employee Health and Productivity to provide industry-accepted, standardized metrics and protocols to enable employers and suppliers to determine the effectiveness of their health-related lost-time programs in critical areas such as cost, productivity, outcomes, employee satisfaction, and overall program performance. EMPAQ's standard metrics have been established to allow employers to compare data within their organizations and do some benchmarking against their competition. Specific metrics that EMPAQ provides are around disability (occupational and nonoccupational) and absence (sick leave and FML). In support of the definitions noted above, there is further consensus on definitions around data elements and metrics that employers, insurance companies, TPAs, benchmarking organizations, consultants, and other service providers utilize and expand upon in their quantification and comparison work.

For employers that do not have access to data or resources for their own internal data analysis, the Blueprint for Health tool has been created to help them estimate medical costs, absences, and work impairment (http://blueprint.acoem.org). The concept was developed through a collaboration of members of a development team that included representatives from the Health as Human Capital Foundation, the American College of Occupational and Environmental Medicine, NBCH, Sanofi Aventis Pharmaceuticals, and Riedel and Associates. Access to data, analytical support, and web development was provided by the research team at the Human Capital Management Services Group. The idea evolved following a survey of national decision makers that indicated that the majority of companies lacked access to absence and work impairment data — or had limited ability to analyze it. Therefore, the tool was created to provide approximations when other information is not available. It is not intended to replace data analysis that summarizes a company's actual experience, nor is it intended to be used as a benchmark for cost comparisons.

The Bureau of Labor Statistics and the Occupational Safety and Health Administration make incidence rates, days away, and restricted time rate data publicly available. The National Council on Compensation Insurance provides experience modifiers that can be referenced.

Lastly, but certainly not all inclusively, several employee self-report tools have been created to identify the medical conditions most likely to drive lost productivity and are helping the industry understand, among other things, the impact of presenteeism and what can be done about it. A few examples are the Work Limitations Questionnaire (WLQ) and the World Health Organization Health and Work Performance Questionnaire (HPQ).

The WLQ is a 25-item, self-administered, self-reported questionnaire measuring the degree to which employed individuals have experienced health-related deficits in job performance in the prior two weeks and health-related work productivity loss or presenteeism. The WLQ is available from Debra Lerner, The Health Institute, Tufts-New England Medical Center, Boston MA, USA. WLQ@tufts-nemc.org.

The HPQ includes retrospective self-report questions about such things as time off task and concentration at work over the past week and can be found at http://www.hcp.med.harvard.edu/hpq/info.php. These and other tools have been tested and utilized in a variety of ways and are published in numerous peer-reviewed journals.

Key Considerations and Best Practices

Getting the program objectives and key data points that will be measured right at the onset of an integrated program is crucial to program success. Once an integrated program has been in place for six months or more, they are typically able to demonstrate reduced lost time, decreased incidence, and lower absence rates because the absences the program has the most impact on are absences of less than 6 months duration (incidental, FMLA, WC, and short term disability – virtually all unplanned lost time other than long term disability). Additional break-even analyses are often necessary to prove viability and to ensure senior management that the program is indeed on track.

From an operational perspective, employer ability to effectively track claims and absence and move toward viewing the big picture of how employee behavior is affecting the health and productivity of their workforce is key. Turning to an automated solution that centralizes all of an organization's absence data in one location enabling human resources to compare and contrast absence data across all business units and geographies to discover trends that might have been overlooked is ideal. In reality, however, employers need to gather targeted data elements from the appropriate, and often times numerous, systems to obtain their desired comparators.

Important points for employers to take away from the information shared above are that definitions of data, metrics, and methodologies must be clear and consistently applied over time. Further, if survey, research, or benchmark data is something an employer uses to support its business case, data that can be most closely matched to what an employer can track will be most valuable. Finally, with the breadth and depth of information published in the marketplace today, it behooves employers to consider what other organizations have been able to do and to think about how it can translate to their particular situations.

Following are examples of how American Electric Power (AEP) and Waste Management (WM) evolved to confidently share their costs, savings, and integrated program achievements both internally with a broad range of stakeholders and externally across industry publications, conferences, and events.

The following case studies are included without attribution, based on work done by the Integrated Benefits Institute.

> AEP[clviii] began its journey into integrated disability over 15 years ago, not with data, as you might expect, but with a mandate for change. The industry was going through significant reform and deregulation, and there was a fear that rallied AEP executives to look at new and improved ways of performing the same functions. The silo mentality that had existed was being replaced by centralization and collaboration. Loyd Hudson, Manager of Integrated Disability for AEP, said that integrated disability "was not an option for us. It was a requirement for us to keep our jobs. The philosophy was that if we changed our processes and looked at doing what was right, what made sense, while eliminating duplication and inconsistencies, our cost savings would follow." Measured as a percentage of payroll, by 2009 AEP's costs had decreased by almost 1% from 1997, saving more than $3.7 million each year. Since the latest merger with CSW in 2000, yearly actual costs were down by $10,000,000. According to Hudson, "Measurements are not why we do what we do. Measurements tell us if what we are doing is beneficial. Case managers and companies who are reactive will always be reacting. Companies and individuals who are strategic are looking for ways to detect issues and prevent problems before they occur. Data analysis and audits (detection) are the only way to move from a reactive position to a strategic position."

> Similar to AEP, Waste Management (WM) set an overall strategy for total absence management and workforce productivity about 15 years ago and has methodically taken steps to phase in the management of all of its benefit programs, consolidating vendors, processes, and procedures as

they have made sense. A cross-functional team representing benefits, human resources, risk management, and operations management has been focusing on absenteeism, presenteeism, and health management to target the highest cost drivers within the organization. After confirming that only 10.3% of employees accounted for 80% of health spending and that the average cost for employees in this group was 35 times greater than the average cost for the vast majority of employees, WM created a specialized return-to-work program and deployed occupational health counselors in the field, which has contributed to WM experiencing a 45% reduction in lost time claims and a 40% reduction in lost workdays, leading to millions of dollars in lost time and medical cost savings. Now bringing absenteeism into the mix, WM is able to document that 6.6% of its workforce (or approximately 3,000 of its workers) is absent on any given day. "The programs and processes we have implemented allow us to gather and analyze this data," says David Kasper, WM's Vice President of Benefits. "This analysis then enables us to identify gaps in our programs or policies that require us to take action. Every year WM invests more than $400 million dollars on employees' benefits. Our goal is simple: to help our people and their families get and stay well so that they can lead productive lives both in and out of work. We want that investment to make a real difference in people's lives, and reliable data and analysis of it help us get there."

Acknowledging that employers' integrated programs, experiences, and measurements differ in many ways, the following best practices, as identified by the Disability Management Employer Coalition's 2008 Leadership Series Absence Management Best Practices in Metrics and Reporting, should be taken into consideration.

Best Practice 1: Assess the scope of absence in your environment.

Absence is accounted for by a vast array of explanations, including doctor's appointments, illness, jury duty, FML, STD, LTD, WC, military leave, adoption, bonding, bereavement, vacation time, and so on, and employers need to identify the critical areas they will assess. In doing so, it is important to keep in mind that while larger employers have internal systems to generate and analyze data, smaller organizations and start-ups may ask TPAs to assist or may use proprietary software to initiate and monitor tracking data.

Best Practice 2: Identify metrics to sell the business case for your integrated program to upper management.

Absent explicit support at the upper-management level, integrated programs face much tougher challenges. If workplace safety, employee health and fitness, and supportive return-to-work programs are integral to the culture of an organization from the top down, their likelihood of success on all levels improves dramatically.

Best Practice 3: Partner internally to identify and capture critical information.

An organization need not be a global behemoth nor have tracked employee data for decades for its integrated program to have an excellent chance of success. The critical element is to begin the aggregation of information from every possible source, encompassing as much history as is obtainable.

Best Practice 4: Create benchmarks for your integrated program.

Benchmarking is almost wholly dependent of factors as varied as the nature of the business; the makeup of the workforce; the geographic distribution of employees; local, state, and national laws or regulations; industry regulations; collective bargaining agreements; and a myriad of other factors. Benchmarks that address the needs of one organization may be totally inadequate for another.

Best Practice 5: Make absence management sustainable.

Dollar cost savings may be the first measure of success of an absence management program, but workforce engagement and participation are a secondary, if less precisely measured, component. On a more global scale, innovative return-to-work approaches can lead to real savings measured by the productivity of the affected workers and by employee attitudes toward their environment and the work they do.

Best Practice 6: Partner with TPAs for reports that meet your needs.

TPAs introduce access to a much broader universe of leave and claims data that can be mined in very specific ways — geographic, industry specific, age, or any other demographic — to develop competitive benchmarks. TPAs can help organizations establish standardized metrics for use within the organization and with other providers, as well as assist in the collection and analysis of program data.

Best Practice 7: Use data to fine tune programs.

A variety of factors can affect absence and medical utilization trends. Armed with accurate and timely data, an organization can deploy resources and personnel to ensure that integrated programs are delivering meaningful results.

Best Practice 8: Balance incentives with disincentives.

It is widely recognized that absence is frequently a result of personal behavior and family-related issues, including smoking, obesity, high blood pressure, diabetes, depression, alcoholism, and stress. The role of incentives and disincentives is a subject that integrated programs would be well served to investigate further. They are a low-cost and sometimes even cost-neutral way of reducing absences and increasing productivity, and they are a way to engage employees directly in the process.

Best Practice 9: Keep employees in the loop at every stage.

The active engagement and participation of those whose absences are being managed are critical to the success of any integrated program. No return-to-work program will succeed with employees who wish to extend disability. No employee assistance program or behavioral intervention will counter an employee's stress, depression, or substance abuse without engagement on the part of the employee.

Best Practice 10: Adopt, analyze, assess, adapt — and repeat as needed.

Research supports the potential benefits of integrated programs. Except for the smallest businesses, integrated programs will have an immediate, direct, and significant impact on productivity and costs. Successful employers must track the appropriate data within their own organization.

Resources

Sources	Description	Website and Contact Information
Bureau of Labor Statistics (BLS)	The BLS produces national measures for sectors of the U.S. economy. These are the productivity statistics most often cited by national media.	www.bls.gov
Integrated Benefits Institute (IBI)	The IBI provides employers and their supplier partners with resources for proving the business value of health. IBI is a pioneer, leader, and nonprofit supplier of health and productivity research, measurement, and benchmarking.	www.ibiweb.org 415.222.7280
National Business Coalition on Health (NBCH) and American College of Occupational and Environmental Medicine (ACOEM) – Blueprint for Health	The NBCH is a national nonprofit membership organization of employer-based health coalitions. NBCH and its members are dedicated to value-based purchasing of healthcare services through the collective action of public and private purchasers in communities and markets large and small. In collaboration with the ACOEM, it developed Blueprint for Health, a free, online tool to help companies calculate their total healthcare costs.	www.nbch.org 202.775.9300 http://blueprint.acoem.org

National Business Group on Health (NBGH) and EMPAQ (Employer Measures of Productivity, Absence and Quality)	NBGH is the national voice of large employers dedicated to finding innovative and forward-thinking solutions to the nation's most important healthcare issues. EMPAQ* is a set of standardized metrics and benchmarking tools developed by NBGH to help employers evaluate the effectiveness of their health and productivity management programs.	www.businessgrouphealth.org 202.558.3000 www.empaq.org

Employer Checklist

As you work to identify and measure the costs, savings, and ROI associated with your integrated program, the checklist below will serve as a tool to help you think through the possibilities.

Key Questions	Yes/No	Comments
Have you defined the objectives of your integration efforts?		
What is your organization trying to accomplish and why?		
What are the specific outcomes that can be associated with the accomplishments and why?		
How can the measures be tied to:		
How the business works?		
How finance allocates expenses?		
Who the stakeholders are?		
How the business defines the language it uses for measures?		

Who the audience is and what the potential ROI areas are?		
Which of the following data gathering strategies will be used by your organization?		
Database queries and specific report extraction		
Employer population demographic detail summary and confirmation		
Structured individual interviews of key stakeholders		
Focus group discussions with stakeholder groups		
Surveys and/or questionnaires		
Onsite observations		
Benchmark and source identification		
Other		
Which of the following methods will your organization utilize to justify integrated program costs?		
ROI methods		
Break-even calculations		
Impact assessment		

Efficiency assessment		
Coverage assessment		
Service delivery assessment		
Fiscal assessment		
Legal assessment		
Other		
What definitions will your organization rely on to measure outcomes (e.g., direct costs, indirect costs, hidden costs)?		
Which absence types will you track and measure (e.g., STD, LTD, WC, FMLA, leave of absence)?		
Are there particular surveys or research data against which it makes sense to routinely compare your organization?		
Is your organization able to employ some or all of the best practices noted above in measuring your integrated program?		

Chapter 22: Benchmarking and Ongoing Measurement

Background and Context

Costs of absence for employers far exceed the benefits paid to absent or disabled workers.[clix] Research shows that at a minimum, there are additional wage and benefits costs for a replacement worker. At worst, the products and services will be delayed, deadlines missed, and customer good will jeopardized.[clx,clxi]

So how does your lost-time experience compare to that of your competition? Is your workplace safer? Are your employees more likely to go out on short-term disability (STD)? What about your family medical leave (FML) experience? If you can't answer these questions, then you can't take action to improve your lost-time results or to justify keeping your successful programs. If you can't do that, then your bottom line will have to continue to absorb those additional costs of lost productivity. Employers that can minimize these health-related lost productivity costs will gain competitive advantage in hard economic times.

In a tight economy, an inability to make a business case for a workplace program likely means that program will be cut. This may not seem like a big deal, but depending on the medical condition driving lost time, your lost productivity costs from absence due to the condition are more than two times your medical and pharmaceutical costs to treat it.[clxii] One answer to helping employers make the business case and establish the basis for necessary change is benchmarking.

Scope of Benchmarking

In simple terms, benchmarking is a process used by organizations to measure or compare themselves to others in terms of performance against certain indicators, industry standards, or best practices. It is mostly used for strategic management in which organizations evaluate various aspects of their programs, then develop plans and specific actions to improve them.

Within this context, there are two types of benchmarking: internal and external. Internal benchmarking involves comparing your past experience with your current experience and results from location to location or department to department, and then deciding if you need to take action to better manage the results. For many companies, especially smaller organizations, internal benchmarking of this sort is as far as they are either interested in or capable of going. Often the best benchmark is their own performance, taking into consideration the unique nature of their environment, benefit plan design, and budget constraints.

If the desire is to compare results with the outside community or to keep up with your competition, then external benchmarking is the more sophisticated method to employ. The ability to benchmark aspects of your organization's integrated program performance presents an effective and inexpensive avenue for quantifying any lost-time differences among companies in your industry and for making the business case for effective programs. In addition to helping employers evaluate their program performance, administration, and design against their industry peers, industry-based benchmarking programs are used by insurers and third-party administrators (TPAs) to demonstrate program performance beyond their own book of business.

Benchmarking Sources

Conducting a benchmarking process can be complicated and time-consuming but certainly doesn't have to be. In addition to an organization internally benchmarking against its own experience, the following general sources with progressively higher costs can be consulted:

- Insurer/TPA: Probably the most readily available benchmarks for employers that don't self-administer their integrated programs are performance benchmarks from their insurer or TPA. Offsetting that convenience and availability is the limitation that the comparisons will come from only one supplier and, depending on the size of the book of business of that supplier, may not provide deep enough comparisons within a single industry.

- Industry Nonprofit Organizations: Most employers of any size are likely to be able to internally compare the performance of their own program year to year or from location to location. For those employers seeking broader comparisons, benchmarking for absence and disability is currently provided by at least two nonprofit organizations, the Integrated Benefits Institute and the National Business Group on Health. Costs for those programs depend on membership in the organization and the depth of the detail in comparisons sought. Other, for-profit proprietary programs also are likely available.

- Data Warehousing: For those willing to invest in more costly options that provide powerful comparisons with the potential of integrating data across multiple programs, there are a number of data warehouses that gather and report program performance data for individual employers and multiple clients, [clxiii] and some employers may provide in-house databases across their programs that allow them to view their program performance in an integrated fashion. For more information, see Chapter 21: Integration Program Costs, Savings, and ROI.

This section will focus on basic benefits performance, benchmarking comparisons of absence and disability frequency, duration, and cost, but not the more expansive services provided by data warehouses.

Integrated or Program-by-Program Benchmarking?

Ideally, a benchmarking program should encompass performance across programs in comparing employers, rather than examine and compare performance within each of the benefit silos, employer by employer. The advantage of an integrated comparison is that it can discern whether an employer simply is cost shifting from one program to another or is truly performing better or worse across all absence and disability programs.

Unfortunately, experience has shown that it is extremely difficult to gain the corporate-wide support necessary for an integrated benchmarking initiative that is intended to draw detailed incidence, duration, and cost information for all programs, regardless of who administers the programs, for a sufficient number of employers to provide credible benchmarks (small groups of employers don't provide credible industry-specific benchmarks). The risk manager may have been enthused and willing to submit workers' compensation data but may have had difficulty gaining the same commitment from the STD manager. Perhaps a greater impediment is the relative lack of reporting of essential incidental absence or sick pay. Without such incidental absence information, nothing can be said about companywide results. The information may exist, but it might reside in payroll or operations and not be accessible or accessed for benefits benchmarking purposes.

A recent and growing problem results when employers initiate a paid time off (PTO) program but believe they then can stop keeping track of the reason for the absence in the name of administrative simplicity. Without essential cause information, it is impossible to know whether health-related absence is a problem or to report it separate from vacation or other leave. Without such important information, employers can't get the information they need to justify or focus health-related absence management.

As a result, benchmarking efforts have shifted away from an earlier attempt to collect data across all aspects of integrated programs to focus more on absence and disability only. Further, benchmarking organizations have shifted away from collecting information solely from employers directly or with the support of their program suppliers. Now, benchmarking comparison bases are built principally through working with suppliers. Program-by-program benchmarking has become the focus because of the greater ability of employers, or their insurer or TPA partners, to gather claims-level data for the individual programs they administer. Since much of the data comes from separate programs, by its nature it is not and cannot be integrated. At the same time, data from individual employers also can be accepted, but the comparison databases aren't limited to that data.

When a substantial number of insurers and TPAs provide bulk, blinded claims data, the result is a huge comparison base,[clxiv] with the ability to credibly drill down to more refined comparisons of industry groupings. For example, instead of being limited to STD program comparisons among those in a "manufacturing" classification, a lithographic commercial printing company could drill down three more levels to compare performance with competitors in that limited industry group.

Sometimes the data reported is limited by what is collected by the claims administrators. Relatively few, for example, have consistent information about covered lives, so incidence information (episodes of absence or disability in proportion to the covered population) isn't always available. Nonetheless, the power of the resulting comparison groups more than compensates for such data weakness.

As a result of these impediments and new bulk claim reporting initiatives, and despite the fact that integrated reporting and metrics are core to integrated programs, benchmarking of these programs for most employers is conducted on a silo-based, program-by-program basis, and comparative databases are built on the same premise.

The Law of Large Numbers

Benchmarking isn't for all employers. If an employer is too small, its experience will vary significantly from year to year, reflecting the impact of chance more than the true experience of an employer's benefits structure or program administration. This is particularly true for programs with relatively low incidence (such as WC), where it is not unusual that 5% or less of employees will be affected in a normal year. To gain actionable, representative information from benchmarking, an employer needs to be sure that its annual experience is an accurate and typical reflection of its overall program. While a single, severe illness or injury can be expected to affect overall results of a mid-sized employer, it certainly will have a disproportionate influence on the results of a smaller one.

Although it would take an actuarial analysis to determine what a truly credible size would be for an individual employer in one of the absence or disability programs, a rule of thumb might be that an employer with fewer than 1,000 employees would not be a good candidate for any kind of credible benchmarking comparison.

By the same token, there needs to be an adequate number of employers in any comparison group to ensure that the mean, median, and percentile results for the group are truly representative. Data confidentiality also is a key issue. If a single supplier contributes almost all the employer experience in an industry comparison group, it may be possible to reverse engineer the identity of the contributing supplier and thereby discern that supplier's book of business results.

To protect against such misuse, credibility and confidentiality guidelines for benchmarking reporting are important, such as not including comparison groups with fewer than 30 employers represented in the industry group or not publishing industry groups to which fewer than three suppliers have furnished data.

Programs to Benchmark

Most of the benchmarking comparisons available focus on absence and disability programs including STD, LTD, WC, and FML experience.

Although it is important to benchmark incidental absence results, few employers are able or willing to collect the required data, and most external suppliers of absence and disability management have no access to such results to include in a benchmarking submission of claims data. Thus, incidental absence is not a standard program available outside extensive and powerful data warehouses maintained by relatively few large employers, either internally or through a data warehouse company.

Group health is "top of mind" for most employers and is a program for which employer benchmarks would be valuable. Integrating group health use and cost with absence and disability results would be most useful and telling in demonstrating that the wrong medical treatment and incentives can have a large impact on health-related lost time and lost productivity, but outside a data warehouse, such linkage isn't practicable.

Nonetheless, due to the importance of group health and incidental absence to employers, benchmarking programs must respond in some fashion, even if only to collect nonintegrated program data. A growing number of employers are interested in data from all health-related programs so that they can begin to see the full implications of key health conditions.

The need to include group health and incidental absence data within an absence and disability benchmarking reporting structure can be handled in other ways. Group health comparisons can be incorporated by including group health data in partnership with data warehouses, such as Thomson Reuters MarketScan database. Incidental absence and presenteeism information can be reported based on results from employee self-report surveys and monetized to reflect lost productivity costs. Finally, to offset the limitations of absence and disability claims-level program data, research can be conducted to show the relationship of medical treatment and pharmaceutical benefits to lost time and resulting lost productivity.

Direct Versus Hidden Costs

There may be debate as to the relative importance of hidden costs compared to paid benefits, sometimes referred to as direct costs. However, as recent studies have borne out, the hidden costs that are so often ignored or not measured in fact have a more pronounced effect on an organization's profitability and costs than direct, paid costs.

To demonstrate the importance of including hidden costs, Figure 22.1 shows an example of the relative direct and hidden costs of various employer programs modeled for a 45,000-life manufacturing employer and using a lost-productivity modeling technique incorporating a research-based methodology. Clearly, lost productivity has a substantial impact on total health-related costs for this employer and others.

Figure 22.1

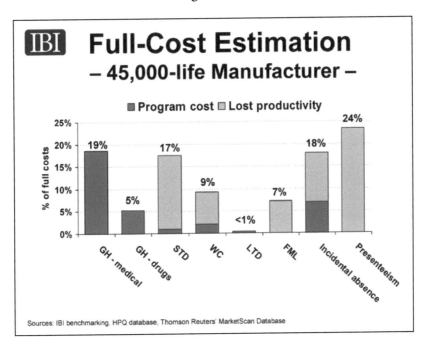

What Metrics to Compare?

Another requirement for benchmarked programs is consensus on the definitions of the data elements to be submitted and the numerator and denominator of the metrics reported. Unless definitions exist that apply to data submitted for benchmarking purposes, it is difficult to compare results from employer to employer and from supplier to supplier.

Fortunately, for the absence and disability programs specified above - STD, LTD, WC, and FML - there is consensus on definitions developed in a partnership between the IBI and the National Business Group on Health. (See also the discussion on other tools and resources in the Integrated Program Costs, Savings and ROI chapter.) The resulting data and metrics set for these programs include basic definitions to which employers, insurers, and TPAs can now turn. The EMPAQ data elements and metrics serve as an important baseline definition and are typically supplemented to meet more sophisticated and expansive benefits performance benchmarking needs.

The metrics actually included in any benefits performance benchmarking program depend on how the program is designed and for what purposes, how credibility and confidentiality are maintained, and how the volume and breadth of data that actually can be reported are reflected. For disability programs, benchmarking efforts commonly collect and report active and closed claims information on:

- Incidence (the proportion of covered employees who file a claim or use the system)

- Severity of claims (cost), including cost per claim and cost per 100 covered full-time equivalent (FTE) workers

- Lost workdays per claim and per 100 FTEs

For STD and WC, benchmarking may track effectiveness of an employer's return-to-work program through utilization of transitional duty. So few suppliers/employers can report such data that it is often difficult to benchmark the use of transitional duty due to limitations for reasons of confidentiality and credibility. For STD, a rough proxy might be the proportion of claims that reach the maximum duration of the STD plan, a metric that commonly can be reported.

WC reports track experience by benefit type (e.g., medical only, indemnity, and temporary and permanent disability). Including benchmarks on the aging of such claims is also critical for employers to get a flavor for how efficiently and effectively their program is processing and managing WC claims.

Federal FML benchmarks include the incidence of use of FML, the proportion of FML claims running concurrently with other benefits, a comparison of lost workdays for continuous versus intermittent FML, and the relative burden of personal versus family leave.

Group health data varies but, as noted above, can be powerful and telling. Incorporating information such as a broad collection of disease types and cutting group health data by industry group and these disease states to access medical condition statistics by prevalence, utilization, payments (inpatient, outpatient, and emergency room), prescription drugs, and comorbidities can provide helpful comparisons.

Relevant Data Cuts

What are the potential drivers of disability lost time and costs? What data cuts can best be expected to demonstrate those drivers?

Industry Codes

Employers always want to know how their experience compares to that of their competition. There are two common industry classification systems in place, the Standard Industrial Classification (SIC) and the North American Industry Classification System (NAICS).[clxv] SIC codes were replaced by the NAICS system starting in 1997, but benchmarking systems still use SIC codes because most disability insurers and TPAs have not yet changed their claims systems to use the NAICS. Both SIC and NAICS classify establishments by their primary type of activity. Benchmarking by SIC codes as the pragmatic approach likely to capture available data and produce credible results, rather than what is most current, is likely to be the decision of choice for the near future.

SIC starts by establishing a single letter code for 10 basic industries (A through J) and then drills down to the four-digit level, gaining granularity of operations with each additional digit. The example used above bears repeating. Instead of being limited to STD program comparisons among those in manufacturing (a single character level), comparisons at the four-digit level allow a lithographic commercial printing company to drill down three more levels to consider performance compared with that of competitors in that limited industry group. Of course, the level of drill-down available should, for any industry group, be limited by considerations of credibility and confidentiality.

Plan Design

Many employers and suppliers believe comparing results by plan design to be of equal or even greater importance than comparing by industry grouping. Certainly the information garnered would be important to making changes in plan design to improve results. One hurdle to comparing results by plan design, however, is the myriad of plan design options available and used, even within a single employer.

Instead of trying to recognize a bewildering variety of plan designs in STD and LTD, absence, and disability, benchmarking programs must find an acceptable alternative to reduce the variation among plan types by creating a limited number of general types of plans reflecting varying eligibility periods and benefit entitlement durations for STD and LTD. Although the fit cannot be perfect for each employer's plans, it can be close enough to give employers and suppliers a sound idea of where their various programs place in the typology without creating an unmanageable variety of plan design comparisons.

Workers' Compensation Jurisdictions

For WC, the SIC groupings substitute for WC classifications, which frequently vary by state. Incidence, cost, and duration experience in WC also varies markedly by state, reflecting its statutory variation. Benchmarking programs should be able to report results by jurisdiction to give appropriate comparisons.

Workforce Age and Gender

The age and gender of a workforce will have a significant effect on benefits costs. However, this information must be gathered from employers individually, as few, if any, insurers and absence and disability managers collect and retain this information in their claims databases (although suppliers do collect information on age and gender for claimants). Since large, credible databases can only be created with claim information, this presents a barrier to widespread inclusion of such comparison categories in any credible benchmarking database.

To accommodate the inability of many suppliers to submit demographic information on behalf of their clients that isn't regularly included in a claims database, at least one benchmarking program permits suppliers that seek client comparisons to enter specific information into the benchmarking database for their clients, such as number of covered lives, payroll, and workforce age and gender composition. If enough employers and suppliers are interested in this comparative data, the system will build itself.

Effective and Useful Reporting

Benefits performance benchmarking, offered broadly to the employer community, began with the premise that employers would submit data on their own behalf and, in return, would receive reports. The thought was that employers could share their reports with their supplier partners to discuss making the changes necessary to improve benefits delivery and performance.

Because of the challenges for employers in reporting data, reports directly back to participating employers are less common than expected, although some do participate in that way. To meet this challenge, a benchmarking program might consider a variety of purposes and uses for benchmarking data, including uses solely for suppliers to help them work with their clients and to encourage their participation in creating a benchmarking comparison base:

- Make industry comparisons available to employers and suppliers regardless of whether they submitted data. Such reports can be used to compare results for whatever parameters an individual employer is able to develop. In addition, suppliers can work with employers, using such industry reports, to bring their results into line with or to exceed industry performance.

- Since many employers are likely to value benchmarking reports, even if they can't submit data, suppliers that submit blinded claims data can be permitted and encouraged to download reports for employers on whose behalf they submitted blinded claims data, using proprietary identifiers. Such reports will include direct comparisons of each employer's own program to the comparison database and be useful for planning changes in benefits management, design, and administration. Suppliers also can use client-specific benchmarking results as a comparison base beyond their own book of business in working with clients.

- Companies can be permitted to submit a customized query to compare results for an employer by specific size, industry, and plan design to others with the same characteristics that are in the benchmarking database.

Report Format

There is, of course, any number of ways to report benchmarks in a way that is clear, useful, and compelling for employers and their supplier partners. Several organizing features may be viewed as important:

- Benchmarking results can be organized around pragmatic responses to relevant questions that an employer is likely to have about benefits performance, whether from a benchmarking organization or internal year to year, location to location, or department to department. For STD, for example: "How often is the program used?" "How severe are the cases?" "How much lost work time is generated by the program?" and "How successful is the program at return-to-work?" (See samples of these types of questions for industry and plan design comparisons in Tables 22.1 and 22.2 which are examples from the Integrated Benefits Institute benchmark database.)

- A dashboard of key results can provide insights at a glance to engage readers in the opportunities they face.

- Online reports, available when desired, are convenient and more likely to be used when available as needed.

- Results for individual employer programs can be arrayed for the comparison group by percentiles (showing where within the range of responses the employer's experience lies) and reporting the mean result (the arithmetic average); the median result (that value above and below which half of the other values are distributed); the number of employers and the number of claims in the comparison group; and, for context, the all-group median. This provides information on the "shape" of the distribution for the metric as well as valuable information to the employer with regard to where its results fit overall and where attention might best be focused.

- Since industry groups may have missing data, the report format should be flexible so as not to include numerous "not available" items that can interfere with an understanding of what actually is presented.

Table 22.1

Sample (not actual employer results) STD report for comparisons within an industry group:

I. Claims Experience -- *How well is the program working?*

How often is the program used by employees?	Your Company	Group Average	Group Median	10th percentile	25th percentile	75th percentile	90th percentile	N ERs	N claims	All-Group Median
New claims per 100 covered lives										
Active claims per 100 covered lives										
New claims as % of active claims										
New pregnancy claims as % of new claims	6.9	7.4	6.0	2.2	4.1	9.3	12.6	196	35692	6.1
How severe are the cases?	8.2	8.6	7.1	3.0	4.8	10.6	15.0	196	35692	7.1
Claims payments per active claim (not incl. payments supple	86.3%	82.9%	90.2%	50.0%	80.6%	100.0%	100.0%	663	154715	92.3%
Claims payments (incl. payments supplementing WC claims	11.2%	27.0%	19.7%	4.0%	8.3%	34.6%	59.5%	414	154715	29.2%
Claims payments (incl. payments supplementing WC claims)	$3,602	$2,683	$2,344	$787	$1,327	$3,517	$5,114	548	75209	$1,978
Claims payments per closed claim	$3,264	$2,149	$1,776	$0	$571	$3,154	$4,798	663	154715	$1,623
How much lost work time does the program generate?	$331	$254	$144	$0	$49	$274	$541	199	35692	$124
Lost workdays per 100 covered lives	$4,183	$3,131	$2,609	$881	$1,526	$3,988	$6,083	535	64071	$2,213
Lost workdays per active claim	338.7	527.2	257.4	77.0	146.5	440.5	723.6	196	34850	268.4
Lost calendar days per closed claim	41.9	40.9	35.4	20.3	27.9	46.9	66.9	651	144915	35.1
How successful is the company at returning employees to w	54.2	78.7	64.1	40.3	49.6	87.0	128.2	650	136526	62.3
Claims reaching maximum benefit duration as % of active cl	7.7%	9.1%	0.9%	0.0%	0.0%	11.5%	28.4%	353	154715	0.0%
What share of STD payments go to support other programs										
STD payments to supplement WC claims as % of all paymer	0.0%	0.4%	0.0%	0.0%	0.0%	0.0%	0.0%	541	154246	0.0%

Table 22.2

Sample (not actual employer results) LTD report for plan design comparisons:

	Plan A	Plan B	Plan C	Plan D	Plan E	Plan F
Plan Characteristics						
	< 90 days	90 - 179 days	180+ days	< 90 days	90 - 179 days	180+ days
	To normal retirement	To normal retirement	To normal retirement	Other duration	Other duration	Other duration
Claims Experience -- How well is the program working?						
How often is the program used by employees?						
Active claims per 1,000 covered lives						
Company value			16.3			14.8
Industry median			7.6			8.1
Industry mean			14.3			14.1
# of employers			1,064			151
# of claims			37,664			9,855
New claims per 1,000 covered lives						
Company value			3.2			2.8
Industry median			2.6			2.6
Industry mean			4.1			4.4
# of employers			1,064			151
# of claims			10,920			2,324
New claims as % of active claims						
Company value	12.8%	14.9%	17.1%			41.8%
Industry median	0.0%	0.0%	0.0%	0.0%		25.0%
Industry mean	19.0%	21.7%	16.6%	12.7%		37.4%
# of employers	176	3,837	5,388	17		820
# of claims	26,012	37,571	83,627	356		13,402
New claims per closed claim						
Company value	0.6	0.7	0.7			0.6
Industry median	0.7	0.5	0.0	0.4		0.7
Industry mean	0.8	0.8	0.9	0.6		1.0
# of employers	101	1,975	2,869	11		482
# of claims	1,178	6,635	8,212	37		1,408

Reaching the "C Suite"

As mentioned in previous chapters of this book, to have the most impact on corporate decision makers, it may not be enough to simply report lost time and the dollar costs of benefits payments. Many in the "C Suite" (e.g., CEOs, CFOs, COOs), without being presented compelling information to the contrary, may view such expenses simply as costs of doing business to be transferred to the workforce, if cost cutting is their major goal. As mentioned above, lost productivity is influenced by how employers respond to absence. The true cost of lost time to employers, moreover, is never limited to the amount spent on benefits.

Information necessary to translate lost time into lost productivity (e.g., wages, benefits loading, occupation mix, net income, gross revenue) typically is not part of a data provider's claims system, but moving to a benchmarking approach can provide valuable information that senior management can rely upon. Research about monetizing lost time to lost productivity now is being published in peer-reviewed journals[clxvi] and developed by researchers into proprietary tools that can be used to supplement benchmarking databases and reports to ensure that the full costs of health-related absence are considered by employer decision makers and their supplier partners. Putting monetized lost productivity into such terms as percent of net income or in proportion to the company's costs of workforce wages and benefits will surely get the C Suite's attention. This is especially true as those costs cannot simply be shifted away from the impact on the employer's bottom line.

Taking Action

Benchmarking results don't readily fall into easily accepted solutions. Sometimes, it is obvious that an employer needs to improve the culture or practice in promoting effective return to work. Or it may be that medical management of lost time needs to be improved or plan designs altered to focus on value instead of creating disincentives that may affect appropriate treatment and worker productivity.

When solutions aren't obvious, a savvy employer, armed with benchmarking results, is likely to be able to tap resources from a disability or WC insurer, TPA, benefits organization, or other benefits partner to craft solutions that improve the employer's standing compared to results for the industry group. Each employer will have a different set of circumstances that calls for a customized approach. Whether the employer benchmarks or not, suppliers may now have industry comparisons available to them that they never had before. These industry reports often will point the way to a problem and potential solutions when compared to the employer's own metrics.

For larger employers with more resources (and higher costs), consulting firms often have a designated practice devoted to integrated programs and routinely incorporate absence and disability benchmarking into their practices. For organizations of all sizes, there are separate and objective benchmarking organizations they can turn to such as the IBI and the NBGH that operate on a nonprofit basis. Specific for-profit and proprietary options also exist. Data warehouses may also be an option, although their cost structures typically limit involvement to only the largest employers.

Employers should consider including benchmarking assistance in their next request for proposal to determine which suppliers (e.g., insurers, TPAs, consultants) are committed to benchmarking and the availability of benchmarking results to help plan improvements in program delivery. They also may want to include a requirement that their claims administrators help them submit claims and demographic data to organizations that offer benchmarking services and to make benchmarking reports and analysis available to the employer as part of their services.

Future Insights

The reality that benchmarking is unlikely to readily develop information on incidental absence was discussed earlier. Further, the significant costs of presenteeism also are beyond the scope of traditional benchmarking. The main issue with both of these "hits to productivity" is the lack of consistent data from employers and vendors which could be used to develop benchmarks. This is unfortunate because the cost of both issues is not an insignificant element in overall absence and lost productivity costs.

To capture these significant costs, employers might consider using one of several employee self-report tools that are available in the market. Depending on the tool used, such surveys can identify the medical conditions most likely to drive lost productivity, show the extent to which those conditions are treated by medical professionals, and demonstrate how much increased revenue would be needed to equal a given level of savings from reducing lost time for its equivalent impact on the bottom line.

These tools have been validated against objective measures as published in peer-reviewed journals. Use of such powerful tools can go a long way to helping employers understand the full impact of their costs of ill health in a way that the benchmarking of siloed lost-time program performance can never do by itself.

Other low-cost, accessible tools are available to help employers model and estimate the full costs of ill health based on a variety of techniques and databases. [clxvii]

Employer Checklist

Benchmarking plays an important role managing benefits programs for absence and disability and is useful for integrated programs. It can help an employer measure its own progress as well as how it compares to its peers within the industry. Determining how to begin is perhaps the most difficult step; thus, the checklist below is meant to serve as an inventory of questions to ask in getting started. Your designs will depend on the depth and breadth of benchmarking sought and how the data is to be submitted. By no means must all the questions be answered in the affirmative to begin to benchmark effectively.

Key Questions	Yes/No	Comments
Which of the following data types are available to you within your organization or from a supplier partner?		
Disability		
Incidence		
Cost		
Lost workdays		
Incidence and duration of days in temporary, transitional employment		
Workers' compensation		
Experience by benefit type		
Medical only		
Indemnity		

Temporary and permanent disability		
Death benefits		
Incidence and duration of days in temporary, transitional employment		
FMLA and state leave programs		
Incidence of use		
Type of use		
Concurrent claims		
Lost workdays		
Group health		
Disease types		
Condition statistics		
Utilization		
Payments		
Prescription drugs		
Comorbidities		

Incidental absence		
Paid time off only		
Health-related, i.e., sick pay		
Employee satisfaction		
Presenteeism		
Direct measure		
Employee self-reports		
Lost time only or monetized to reflect lost productivity costs		
Corporate descriptors		
Average number of full-time and part-time employees, "headcount," U.S. only		
Number of full-time equivalent employees		
Workforce gender distribution		
Total payroll		
Average benefits load		

Net operating income		
Operating revenue		
Total payments for services provided by contract, leased, registry, or other temporary employees' labor		
Is your data credible enough to be appropriately benchmarked against?		
How many employees are in the segment of your organization to be benchmarked?		
Fewer than 1,000		
More than 1,000		
Are there external sources you can leverage for benchmarking information?		
Insurance company		
TPA		
Consultant		
Benchmarking organization		
Data warehouse		
Disease management supplier		

Do your RFPs for insurers/claims administrators include benchmarking analysis and data submission assistance?		
Is there a cost for obtaining benchmarking data?		
What information is important to your integrated benefits team?		
Is all your medical, pharmaceutical, and health-related absence information reported to minimize the effects of cost shifting?		
Do you seek to measure health risks using an assessment with self-reported lost time?		
What information is important to your senior management?		
Is credible information available for your industry group?		
Is information available to monetize lost time to represent full costs?		
Can you get help from the benchmarking supplier to measure incidental absence and presenteeism?		
What benchmarking program is best for you?		

Is credible information available on the industry group most relevant to you?		
Does the program contain a sufficient number of participants in your representative industry comparison group to be credible?		
Did a sufficient number of data sources contribute to your industry group to maintain confidentiality?		
Does the program offer plan design comparisons?		
Does the program work with your suppliers to ease data submission and reporting of your results?		
Is there a cost for participating in the benchmarking program?		
Is the cost based on a membership, and are you a member?		
Are reports available on line?		

Section Six

The Changing Workforce

Chapter 23: Strategies for the Changing Generational Workforce

Background and Context

Currently, four generations make up the vast U.S. workforce: Generation Y (born after 1980), Generation X (born 1965–1980), Baby Boomers (born 1945–1964), and Veterans (born before 1945). Each generation presents a significant impact on employers, and it is vital to focus our attention to the significant cultural differences between generations as they affect disability, absence, productivity, retention, and culture. This chapter provides a brief outline of some of the impacts that employers must anticipate and how they can develop a plan to respond.

Table 23.1

Common Generational Labels

1922–1945	1946–1964	1965–1980	1981–2000
Veterans Silent Traditionalists	Baby Boomers	Generation X Gen X Xers	Generation Y Gen Y Millennial Echo Boomers

Source: Based on Pew Research Center's Internet and American Life Project, 2010.

Generation Overviews

Today there are more evident differences between the four generations than ever before, and so it is necessary for employers to be acutely aware of these differences so that they can create a positive and cohesive work environment. Understanding others and adapting to different work styles is one of the paths to great business performance. To increase productivity and quality, one needs to understand generational characteristics and learn how to use them effectively in dealing with each individual.[clxviii] The chart below lists workplace characteristics by generation.

Table 23.2
Generational Work Styles

WORKPLACE CHARACTERISTICS				
	Veterans (1922–1945)	Baby Boomers (1946–1964)	Generation X (1965–1980)	Generation Y (1981–2000)
Work Ethic and Values	• Hard work • Respect authority • Sacrifice • Duty before fun • Adhere to rules	• Workaholics • Work efficiently • Crusading causes • Personal fulfillment • Desire quality • Question authority	• Eliminate the task • Self-reliant • Want structure and direction • Skeptical	• What's next • Multitasking • Tenacity • Entrepreneurial • Tolerant • Goal-oriented
Work Is…	• An obligation	• An exciting adventure	• A difficult challenge • A contract	• A means to an end • Fulfillment
Leadership Style	• Directive • Command-and-control	• Consensual • Collegial	• Everyone is the same • Challenge others • Ask why	• *TBD
Interactive Style	• Individual	• Team player • Loves to have meetings	• Entrepreneur	• Participative
Communications	• Formal • Memo	• In person	• Direct • Immediate	• Email • Voicemail
Feedback and Rewards	• No news is good news • Satisfaction in a job well done	• Don't appreciate it • Money • Title/recognition	• Sorry to interrupt, but how am I doing? • Freedom is the best reward	• Whenever I want it, at the push of a button • Meaningful work

Messages that Motivate	• Your experience is respected	• You are valued • You are needed	• Do it your way • Forget the rules	• You will work with other bright, creative people
Work and Family Life	• Ne'er the twain shall meet	• No balance • Work to live	• Balance	• Balance

*As this group has not spent much time in the workforce, this characteristic has yet to be determined.

Source: Based on Pew Research Center's Internet and American Life Project, 2010.

Figure 23.1
Generational Strengths and Weaknesses

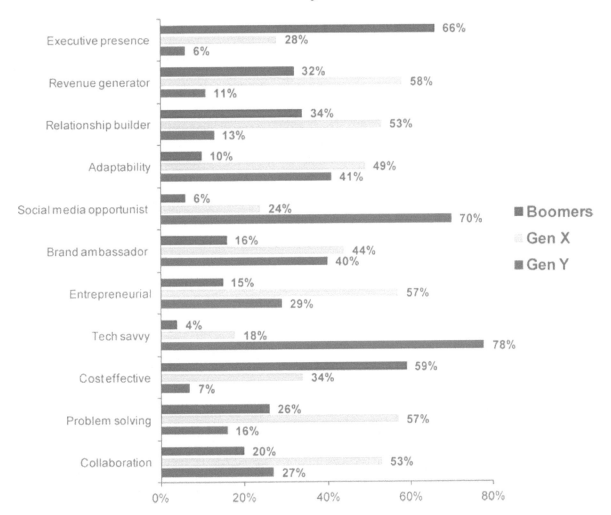

Source: "Here Are the Strengths and Weaknesses of Millennials, Gen X, and Baby Boomers" by Vivian Giang, September 9, 2013, Business Insider. Retrieved from http://www.businessinsider.com/how-millennials-gen-x-and-boomers-shape-the-workplace-2013-9

Generation Y

As the Baby Boomers begin to retire in greater and greater numbers, Generation Y will constitute an increasingly larger proportion of the workforce, eventually becoming the majority. They are viewed as the most highly educated generation and are very skilled in terms of technology. Unlike previous generations, they don't read books or newspapers as frequently as other generations have. When an individual from Generation Y needs or wants to learn something, they go online to the web for easily accessible information. This group also reads more blogs than ever before and continues to embrace new technological advances. [clxix]

In the past, Generation Y has been perceived as the overly demanding generation; however, Randstad USA's 2008 World of Work survey shows that they are beginning to lower their expectations to a more reasonable level. Generation Y "is establishing more realistic views of the workplace, and their once idealistic job expectations are maturing."[3][clxx]

One of the main concerns with Generation Y is the challenge of retaining these young employees and keeping them engaged in their work. Many companies are focusing on college hires as a way to feed future growth and potential within an organization in hopes of narrowing the gap and creating a smooth transition from Baby Boomers to the youngest generation. Employers need to emphasize additional focus on appealing to the younger population. It is vital to create appealing advertising through television and other forms of media. More and more college graduates are searching for jobs on many different websites such as Monster, CareerBuilder, and Facebook. Those employers placing positive focus on these websites will better attract members of Generation Y.

One additional challenge employers will have in attracting and retaining Generation Y is their propensity toward entrepreneurship. Only 7% of Gen Y work for a Fortune 500 company and "owner" is in the top five of most popular Facebook job titles. In addition, the average duration of a first job for a Gen Y worker is two years, as they all expect to job hop throughout their careers. [clxxi]

Devon Scheef's article "Retaining the Four Generations in the Workplace" provides three tips for engaging this generation in the workplace:

- Personalize their work: one size doesn't fit all.

- Make their work interactive, like their technology; and group-oriented, like their social preference.

- Communicate the civic side of your company. [clxxii]

An additional consideration is that social media technology should also be readily available in order attract and retain Gen Y; according to the Cisco world technology report, 56% of all Gen Y indicate they won't work at a company if Facebook is banned. [clxxiii]

Generation X

Generation X individuals follow in the Baby Boomers' shadow, as Time magazine refers to Generation X as the "forgotten" and "under-appreciated." Time indicates that Generation X got lost in the shuffle between the Baby Boomers and their offspring, Generation Y. Originally termed the "spoiled generation," Generation X has proven over time that they are far from spoiled. Due to the fact that Generation X entered the workforce during turbulent economic times, they are very goal-oriented and welcome feedback on their performance. Entrepreneurialism increased significantly as Generation X business involvement created a revival of entrepreneurs. Millions of Generation Xers started their own small businesses, and this generation believed that owning a business and being in control is better than holding an important position in politics or government.[clxxiv] However, as the economy slowed, many small business owners went bankrupt and looked for a way to get out quickly. They became interested in obtaining secure jobs at stable companies, with the goal of making it through tough economic times. Devon Scheef offers the following suggestions for engaging this generation in the workplace:

- Resist micromanaging them.

- Provide flexible work environments (e.g., telecommuting, flex-time).

- Reward their initiative.[clxxv]

Baby Boomers

Baby Boomers grew up in an idealistic society and have impacted the change of the country's social structure. Over time, they created a name for themselves: Rebels. Although Baby Boomers are optimistic in the workplace, they do resist order and conformity. Securing their optimal engagement can be accomplished by:

- Sending the message that long hours at work aren't necessarily a badge of honor

- Redesigning their jobs to provide flexibility

- Spotlighting personal fulfillment, meaningful work, and intangibles[clxxvi]

Veterans

Veterans, also known as the silent generation, built their success on hard work, discipline, and commitment. Veterans want to be publicly recognized for their accomplishments and are interested in the reasoning behind situations. Recommendations for this generation include:

- Provide proactive technology support services if they aren't tech-savvy

- Verbally and publicly acknowledge their experience

- Use due process and explain the reasoning behind decisions[clxxvii]

Workplace Implications

Research continues to indicate that it is important to focus on the interactions between individuals of varying generations to obtain future success within a company. It is evident that many cultural differences exist among these groups. As the age gap within the workplace continues to widen, it is vital that employers proactively manage multiple generations so that they are working together effectively and efficiently.[9][clxxviii]

According to the Society for Human Resource Management's (SHRM) 2004 Generational Differences Survey Report, several positive outcomes result from an intergenerational workforce: 51% of employees from different generations work effectively together, 31% of employees from different generations learn from one another, and 27% of employers report that a better quality of work was performed due to an intergenerational perspective.[10][clxxix] Occasional negative outcomes do exist. The most common example of negative outcomes between generations working together is conflict regarding acceptable working hours between employees of different generations.[11] In addition, 20% of employees feel as though coworkers from different generations do not respect them, and 18% of the communication breakdowns exist between employees of different generations.[clxxx]

In 2009, SHRM revisited this discussion and looked at the differences in attitude toward leadership. Gen X is the product of both parents working, high divorce rates, and job layoffs in the 1980s. As a result, they are skeptical and independent. Gen X prefers to work autonomously, while Baby Boomers have a propensity to feel the need to micromanage to a degree that can create conflict. Gen Y is the product of terrorism and technology; they are team-oriented, patriotic, and social-minded. They were close to their parents and prefer guidance. Baby Boomers also appreciate mentoring, and as a result, Gen Y and Baby Boomers can exist harmoniously in a mentoring environment.[clxxxi]

Growing Age Gap

The aging and retirement of the Baby Boomers is a dramatic demographic transformation for our country. Veterans and Baby Boomers are more frequently expected to work hand in hand with college graduates who support the idea that employers must understand how to adapt to this growing age gap. "According to the U.S. Census Bureau, by 2030, 19.7% of the population, or about 71.5 million Americans, will be 65 or older, compared with just 12.4% in 2000."[clxxxii] The aging of the American people will affect many aspects of our society, from the healthcare system to financial markets, to implications for the labor markets. Employers rely on skills and experience of this older skilled labor pool; therefore, as the population ages and larger numbers of people retire, many industries will face worker and skill shortages.[12][clxxxiii]

The U.S. economy has changed dramatically over the last several years with the downfall of several leading financial companies, a major recession that resulted in a substantial decline in stock prices followed by a significant bull stock market of extended duration, and the deterioration of the housing market, which still hasn't fully recouped lost values completely.

These changes have had a ripple effect on almost every aspect of the economy. The current U.S. economic climate will continue to significantly affect older workers in the workplace. Many Veterans and Baby Boomers who originally anticipated retiring in the near future now find themselves financially unable to do so. Many individuals' 401(k)s and IRAs declined considerably in 2008 and it took a number of years for their values to partially or fully recover. Similarly, this economic crisis forced some of the already retired individuals to return to the workplace due to the sudden decrease in their net worth. In these turbulent times, many employees are suddenly facing a stark situation: they worry that they might have to work five, seven, even 10 years more than planned, perhaps well into their seventies.[clxxxiv]

As retirement age continues to increase, employers will continue to see an increase in the age gap among employees. Baby Boomers have spent at high levels, failed to save, and accumulated unprecedented levels of debt. As the oldest Boomers near retirement, it is estimated that approximately two-thirds of households headed by early Boomers, ages 54 to 63, are financially unprepared for retirement, and many of these Boomers do not realize they are ill-prepared. [clxxxv]

Generational Knowledge Shift

While there is endless debate about the shifting workforce demographics and the reality of a future skilled worker shortage, there is no doubt that in the near future, employers will experience a very real talent shortage. As mentioned earlier, the four generations of workers that comprise the U.S. workforce rarely interact with one another and often do not recognize each other's skills or work ethic. As a result, U.S. businesses risk a shortage of skilled labor due to a limited transfer of knowledge from the Veterans and Baby Boomers to Generation X and Generation Y. According to 2008 U.S. Census Bureau findings, the Generation Y workforce (79.8 million) outnumbered Boomers (78.5 million), "who are perceived as retaining the bulk of working America's institutional brain trust." [16][clxxxvi]

Productivity and Disability Risks

As a result of the combination of slowing economic conditions, Baby Boomers rapidly approaching retirement age, and the fear of a talent shortage, employers are anticipating a number of ways in which they will be affected. About 79 million Baby Boomers are planning on retiring over the next 15 years. [clxxxvii] Companies must assess the risk that is inevitably associated with older workers. The aging process includes loss of muscle strength, tiring easily, and other chronic illnesses such as diabetes and asthma. The odds of employees in the workplace developing any of these ailments increase significantly with age. A study conducted at Michigan State University surveying 153,000 people discovered that most Americans are not doing what they can to lead a healthy lifestyle and that the number of individuals adapting less than healthy habits is only increasing. The characteristics considered vital for a healthy lifestyle are being a nonsmoker; exercising 30 minutes per day, five days a week; and eating five or more servings of fruits and vegetables every day. The study found that only 3% of those surveyed were following all these steps for a healthy lifestyle. [clxxxviii]

The results of the survey, while staggering, are to be expected when you consider that second-hand smoke costs the U.S. economy $10 billion per year; Type II diabetes continues to be the sixth leading cause of death in the United States, affecting 21 million Americans; and 46% of adults consider themselves couch potatoes. The rate of obesity in the United States has increased dramatically during the past 20 years, and research continues to show that obesity is a major contributing factor in workplace incidents. Whether obesity is a directly related cause or prohibits employees from returning to work quickly, the obese file 100% more workers' compensation claims. They exhibit almost seven times higher medical costs and are 13 times more likely to miss work from an occupational injury or illness. [clxxxix]

Economic implications include the decline in the number of working individuals who will contribute to government programs such as Social Security and Medicare, putting more pressure on the younger generations to contribute and carry the burden. Due to the aging of the Baby Boomers, the ratio of seniors to working-age residents will increase by 50% in the in the period between 2010 and 2030. Between 2002 and 2012, the U.S. population over the age of 55 grew 49%, while the portion of the population under age

55 increased 5%. In 1950, there were seven workers for every individual over the age of 65; by 2030, it is expected that there will be three workers for every person over the age of 65.[cxc]

Because many aging individuals are expected to work into their seventies, implications for employers will arise. Employers will most likely see an increase in workers' compensation costs, an increasing number of disability claims, the accommodation of more return-to-work restrictions, and the need to create plans for preventing workplace injuries. Deteriorating health will be seen in such areas as neurological and sensory systems, which demonstrate some of the earliest effects of the aging process, such as a deterioration of hearing, eyesight, and balance. This may result in increased prevalence and severity of workplace injuries. The aging process is inevitable, and we will see the effects of aging on work capacity.

A study in 2008 showed that federal government spending on healthcare is expected to double by 2017 to $4.3 trillion, consuming nearly 20% of the nation's gross domestic product.[cxci] A significant contributor to this increase is mainly due to the Baby Boomer population. Many individuals who are approaching retirement age are enrolling in Medicare, and it is expected that spending for Medicare will account for $884 billion. Similarly, Medicaid is expected to grow by an average of 7.9% per year, reaching $717.3 billion by 2017.[cxcii]

What Employers Can Do

As these numbers continue to rise and more and more individuals are working longer, there are a number of strategies employers can take to more positively manage the impacts of the aging and changing U.S. workforce.

Retention Through Proactive Planning

One of the first effects of the aging population may be labor and skill shortages. Eventually, there will be an inevitable increase in retirement rates, which will cause a potential shortage for employers. Employers will see a drop-off of all levels of employees, ranging from lower-paid positions to presidents and CEOs. This presents potential challenges in recruiting new employees. Some industries that use skilled workers are facing shortages such as mining, welding, construction, and manufacturing. A lot of this was a direct result of the 2008 economic recession as many older skilled workers chose to reenter the workforce in new positions. Construction was hit particularly hard.

Although employers will see a large number of retirees in the future, exactly when is unknown. Due to the struggling economy, older employees may not be ready or able to retire. The reasons vary, often due to lack of planning or current economic conditions, the anticipated loss of Baby Boomers in the workplace may be a few years later than originally anticipated. It is important for companies to be proactive and determine tools for success. Employers must work to create a proactive plan so that they are ready for future career progression. Generation Y must be viewed as the replacements for the Baby Boomers.

Companies have three choices when it comes to understanding the opportunity and reality of Generation Y taking over the workplace. Employers can:

1. Do nothing at all and just wait and see what happens. Most companies are unaware of these changes as they are occurring. Even if they are somewhat aware, they are unsure of the possible impacts.

2. Shut it down; some employers have locked Facebook, YouTube, and other "time-wasters" away from employees, but now with today's pervasive mobile devices, there really is no way to completely restrict access.

3. Make use of the opportunity. Employees, whether they realize it or not, are the front line of the company; they can support, they can manage sales, or they can just be brand promoters.

Now is the time to develop young employees' skills and knowledge in order to feed the future pipeline and create a smooth transition when the time comes for the significant number of Baby Boomers to leave the workforce. It is important to develop strategies and be fully prepared for these shortages. If the gaps fail to be addressed, there will not be a proper and effective transfer of knowledge to Generation X and Generation Y. By proactively retaining skills and exerting leadership to take action prior to the drop off, employers can view this as an opportunity to form mentoring relationships through which the younger workforce may see ways to both learn from and teach the aging population.

Recent research shows that smaller-sized businesses are clearly planning for the drop off of employees better than large companies. A National Association of Professional Employer Organizations press release in March 2008 reported that 28% of small business owners surveyed have planned for the necessary transfer of knowledge across generations. [cxciii] Since smaller businesses generally have fewer employees, all ages have inevitably had no choice but to form working relationships. It is the larger companies that have little to no intergenerational interaction. As Baby Boomers continue to work longer than expected, issues may occur in the workplace that will need to be addressed. The National Resource Center on Aging and Injury acknowledges the fact that older workers tend to be resistant to change. Often older workers tend to be set in their ways, and to create success, employers must encourage them to embrace change because it is often in their best interest.[25]

Interaction Through Understanding and Benefit Design

According to the Randstad's 2008 World of Work survey, when it comes to staying in current jobs, employees from each generation assign varying levels of importance to soft benefits.

Table 23.3

Generational Soft Benefits Preferences

Soft Benefits	Generation Y	Generation X	Baby Boomers	Veterans
Satisfying Work	59%	65%	71%	81%
Pleasant Work Environment	57%	69%	70%	82%
Liking people they work with	57%	65%	62%	70%
Challenging work	42%	52%	59%	71%
Flexible Hours	44%	48%	51%	46%

Source: Limited interactions among generations in the workplace identified as key indicator of coming skilled worker crisis, 2008, May 27, Business Wire.

The survey also showed that the members of each generation have positive views of their current jobs. As shown in Table 23.4, although each generation sees itself as playing a distinct role in the workplace and, for the most part, employees describe the personality of coworkers in their same generation with respect, it is their view of coworkers across different generations that presents a problem. The top-ranked terms vary significantly between Generation Y and Baby Boomers; however, the data reveals that Generation X employees describe coworkers in their own generation as capable of interacting well with all age groups. It is possible that Generation X will serve as the glue, bridging the gap between the oldest and youngest generations in the workplace.

Table 23.4

Top-Ranked Terms Used to Describe Coworkers in Same Generational Cohort			
Generation Y	Generation X	Baby Boomer	Veterans
"Chief friendship officer"	"The Doer"	"Moral authority"	"Moral authority"
Makes personal friends at workplace	Confident	Strong work ethic	Strong work ethic
Sociable	Competent	Competent	Ethical
Thinks outside the box	Willing to take responsibility	Ethical	Committed to the company
Open to new ideas	Ethical	Ability to handle crisis	Competent
Friendly	Willing to work extra time	Willing to take on responsibility	Confident
		Strong communication skills	

Source: Leish, B., Limited interactions among generations in the workplace identified as key indicator of coming skilled worker crisis. Business Wire. 2008, May 27.

To leverage the varying perceptions, employers need to take the time to understand the number and volumes of each cohort that exists within their populations, then work to tailor training programs, team assignments, and even benefit programs to reflect their different needs.

To the extent possible, training about generations should take place in a variety of formats. Mentoring programs can be established to link up the various cohorts so they can establish a stronger connection and understanding among themselves. Continuing education can be geared toward the needs of each generation so that a more level playing field can be established. More specifically, Generation Y was very close to their parents and they tend like receiving guidance, while the Baby Boomers enjoy giving guidance and mentoring. These two generations have an opportunity to function effectively in the workplace under this type of training arrangement.

When it comes to team assignments, efforts can be made to match the workforce to the customer base wherever possible. Further, all generations should be included on boards and councils, and horizontal movement should be promoted as not only good for the work environment but as a means for succession planning as the workforce changes.

Lastly, but very importantly, a wide variety of benefits should be offered with the recognition that a "one size fits all" benefit plan no longer meets people's needs. Employees are looking for flexible access and choices in how they are covered. Most important to them is cost-effective coverage that is portable as they move through their lives. They are interested in various "bundles" of benefits that fit their personal situations.

Overall benefits offerings, whether they be group provided or voluntarily purchased, need to be "life-stage friendly" to include not just the basics of health, dental, life, and disability coverage but go further to include such programs as childcare and eldercare. "Rather than 'flex-time,' employers need to rethink 'flexible work.' These policies include flexible work hours, work from home, part-time work, job sharing, position redesign, and other flexible options that may be necessary to keep valuable employees."[cxciv] Further, employers need to highlight the unique needs that concern each generational group, including such issues as mental health, alcohol and substance abuse, and financial planning that affect the workplace either directly or indirectly.

Productivity Through Tailored Access and Support

When it comes to disability, employees ages 50 to 59 make up approximately 19% of the workforce and have 19% of total short-term and 34% of total long-term disability claims. Conversely, workers ages 30 to 39 make up 22% of the workforce but have 30% of STD claims and only 18% of LTD claims.[31]

Figure 23.2
Unum updated (2013) STD only: Gen Y – 29%, Gen X 33%, Baby Boomers 37%

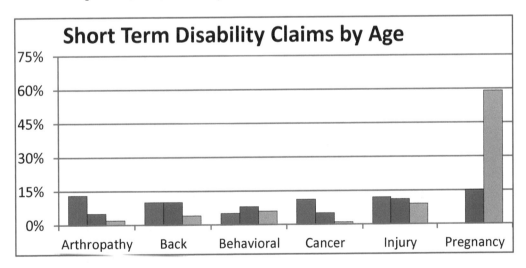

Source: Unum claims database (2013)

Generation Y claims are primarily made up of maternity; as age increases, primary diagnoses become back, arthropathy (joint disease), cancer, and injury.

The breakout for FMLA is similar: Generation Y accounts for 26% of the total, with Generation X at 38%, and Baby Boomers at 35%. Data on intermittent leave for 2012 shows Generation Y primarily out for maternity-related issues, but all generations are most commonly out for their own health. Generations Y and X are out most frequently for child health, and Baby Boomers and the Silent Generation are most commonly out to take care of a spouse. These statistics further demonstrate that each generation can benefit from workplace flexibility.

Figure 6.3

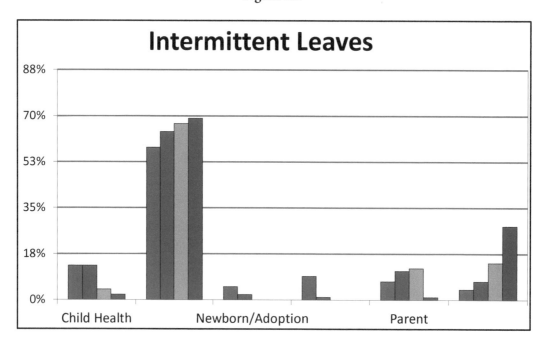

Source: Unum claims database (2012)

Older workers may not go out on STD as frequently or as easily as younger workers; however, older workers' total time out of the office is significantly higher. A Unum study showed that workers over 50 are out of work approximately 11 days longer than those under the age of 50.[cxcv]. As the workforce continues to get older, it is vital that employers anticipate this effect and strategically apply as many tactics as possible to prevent incidences, minimize claims, increase return-to-work efforts, and improve the overall health and productivity of their workforces.

According to the 2005 National Health Interview Survey, 2.9% of respondents between ages 18 and 44 reported themselves as "unable to work" due to a physical, mental, or emotional problem; 8.9% of respondents 45 to 64 and 10.9% of those 65 to 69 reported themselves as unable to work due to one of the three conditions.[cxcvi] The Current Population Survey also reports that 17% of persons ages 55 to 64 have a work-limiting health problem, compared with 9% of persons 40 to 54 and 5% of those 30 to 39.[cxcvii] Further, "UnumProvident Corp.'s long-term disability database indicates that the three most common impairments contributing to long-term work disruption for individuals between the ages of 40 and 60 are:

back disorders and musculoskeletal injuries (accidents), at 25%; cancer, at 17%; and cardiovascular and circulatory disease, at 8%."[cxcviii] This information tells employers that an aging workforce is likely to increase the total cost of their benefits plans, specifically across STD, LTD, health, and overall absence management efforts.

To minimize this effect as much as possible, the physical workplace may need to be redesigned. For example, manufacturers "may find that equipment, vehicles, and related facilities may not meet the usability, size, and safety demands of older [workers]" and "older office staff may require redesigned workstations that provide optimal accessibility and appropriate physical design to manage the fatigue, lower back pain, vision impairment, and other chronic problems that are often associated with mid and later-life."[34][cxcix]

Conclusion

Overall, employers need to think about the breadth and depth of their employee benefit programs and services, and make sure they are structured to respond to all generational needs. Workplace safety, traditionally linked to workers' compensation and other risk management efforts, needs to be expanded to consider the workforce, not just potential claimants. In addition, EAP and behavioral health services can be made part of the disability and workers' compensation management process to manage duration and identify specific resources most applicable to an individual's case. Wellness programs applied broadly to a population can help prevent injuries from even occurring. Work/life programs can mitigate absence by giving people tools that provide alternatives and help them get back to work. Disease management efforts can pinpoint and better manage people's situations so their productivity levels are increased and a support system established.

In these turbulent, uncertain, and rapidly changing times, employers must think creatively and broadly. Employee benefit programs and efforts that were once implemented in silos must be brought together. This must be done not only for the good of the organization but also for the benefit of the multigenerational workforce they will need to employ to ensure future success.

Employer Checklist

Key Questions	Yes/No	Comments
Knowing Your Workforce		
Do you know the population for each generation within your workforce?		
How many of your employees fall within Generation Y?		

How many of your employees fall within Generation X?		
How many of your employees are considered Baby Boomers?		
How many of your employees fall under the category of Veterans?		
Understanding Generational Needs/Motivation		
Do you understand each generation and their needs and motivation?		
How, if at all, are you catering to generational differences?		
Are there training programs you can design to help?		
Are there team assignment changes you can make?		
Are there mentoring relationships you could put in place?		
Considering Benefits Design		
Have you taken proactive steps in anticipation that your organization's benefits costs might increase?		
Are you in a position to expand your wellness and work/life programs to meet varying needs?		

Are there flexible working arrangements you can consider?		
Are there voluntary programs that would complement your overall offering?		
Have you established incentive programs that could be useful?		
Improving Productivity		
Are there physical design changes that could be made?		
How can existing prevention programs be applied more broadly?		
Are there new preventative programs that could be considered?		

Authors/Contributors

Dan Arkins, Regional Director, Group Disability, MetLife

Frank Alverez, Shareholder and National Coordinator of Disability, Leave & Health Management Practice, Jackson Lewis P.C.

Bryon Bass, Director Integrated Disability Management at Pacific Gas and Electric Company

Daniel M. Blaney, III, CEO, ONYX Data Solutions, LLC

Meghan Carrick, Manager, Structured Development Programs at Liberty Mutual Insurance

Michael Clark, Consultant, William Gallagher Associates

Marcia Carruthers, MBA, ARM, CPDM, Chairman, DMEC

Karen English, Partner, CPCU, ARM, Spring Consulting Group, LLC

Emily Ferreira, Consultant, Willis Insurance

Erin Finnemore, Interactive Marketing Manager at Liberty Mutual Insurance

Tracie Foster, Director, Product and Business Development at Anthem

Jay Fundling, Revenue Forecast Analyst at Northeast Utilities

John Garner, CEBS, CLU, CFCI, CMC, Chief Compliance Officer at Bolton & Co.

Diane Gibbins, CEBS, Project Manager, Liberty Mutual

Robert Hall, Ph.D., CRC, CDMS, Hall Associates

Carol A. Harnett, M.S., Executive Director, Counsel for Disability Awareness

Loyd Hudson, Manager, Integrated Disability – HR Recovery Center, American Electric Power

Amor Ibe, Technical Operations Specialist at Maxwell Health

David Kasper, VP of Benefits, Waste Management

Michael Klachefsky, Director, Product Management - Disability & FML/Absence Management at AIG

Alex Korotin, Senior Associate, Global Human Resource Solutions at PwC

Melody Kwok, Business Analyst at Liberty Mutual Insurance

Karin Landry, GBA, Managing Partner, Spring Consulting Group, LLC

Patrick Leary, Principal Benefits Manager, Genentech, Inc.

Daniel Lyons, SVP & Manager-Group Benefits National Accounts, Liberty Mutual

William Molmen, General Counsel, Integrated Benefits Institute

Suzette Moreau, Director, Project Management & HR Policy Development, National Grid

Jeff Nowak, Co-chair of the Labor and Employment practice group at Franczek Radelet P.C.

Carla O'Sullivan, Education Programs Manager, DMEC

Thomas Parry, Ph.D., President, Integrated Benefits Institute

Cheryl Pasa, SPHR, CEBS, CPDM, Owner, CMPasa Associates, LLC

Mark Raderstorf, MA, CRC, CCM, Licensed Psychologist, President, Behavioral Medical Interventions

Terri L. Rhodes, MBA, CPDM, CCMP, CEO, DMEC

Marge Savage, Senior Consultant, MES Consulting

Allison Short, Office Manager, Center for Collaborative Education

Skip Simonds, Managing Principal, Simonds & Associates

Marilyn Taylor, Copy Editor

Kristin Tugman, PhD, Vice President, customer analytics and consultation, Prudential Financial

Nazneen Vimadalal, VP, Group Benefits Marketing, MetLife

Pamela Warren, Ph.D. Licensed Psychologist, Author, Work Loss Data Institute

Teri Weber, Partner, Spring Consulting Group, LLC

NOTES

Chapter 1: WHAT IS INTEGRATED DISABILITY MANAGEMENT (IDM), TOTAL ABSENCE MANAGEMENT (TAM), AND HEALTH AND PRODUCTIVITY MANAGEMENT (HPM)?

[i] English KT. Where does disability insurance fit on the health/productivity continuum. *National Underwriter: Life & Health/Financial Services Edition*. June 23, 2003. Retrieved from http://www.lifehealthpro.com/2003/06/23/where-does-disability-insurance-fit-on-the-healthp

[ii] Towers Watson, (2010/11). *Survey Report on Employee Benefit Policies & Practices*.

[iii] Spring Consulting Group, LLC. (2007/2008). *Integrated Disability/Absence/Health Management Employer Survey*.

[iv] Mercer/Marsh. (2007). *Health, Productivity and Absence Management Programs*.

[v] Spring Consulting Group, LLC. (2007/2008). *Integrated Disability/Absence/Health Management Employer Survey*.

[vi] Mercer/Marsh. (2007). *Health, Productivity and Absence Management Programs*.

[vii] Spring Consulting Group, LLC. (2007/2008). *Integrated Disability/Absence/Health Management Employer Survey*. [I have no more recent source for this data.]

[viii] National Business Group on Health and Watson Wyatt. (2005/2006). *Staying @Work Survey*

[ix] Industry norms and Integrated Benefits Institute Research, 2004.

[x] CIGNA healthcare industry experience, 2006.[The previous comment applies here as well]

[xi] Disability Management Employer Coalition and Liberty Mutual Group. (2007). *Best Practices for Program Integration and Administration*, IDM Leadership Series.

Chapter 2: PROGRAMS THAT CAN BE INTEGRATED

[xii] Spring Consulting Group, LLC. (2007/2008*). Integrated Disability/Absence/Health Management Employer Survey*.

[xiii] Spring Consulting Group, LLC. (2007/2008). *Integrated Disability/Absence/Health Management Employer Survey*.

Chapter 3: STATATORY DISABILITY PLANS

[xiv] http://en.wikipedia.org/wiki/California_State_Disability_Insurance

xv Employment Development Department State of California. (2014). State disability insurance program (DE 8714C Rev. 40) [fact sheet]. Retrieved from http://www.edd.ca.gov/pdf_pub_ctr/de8714c.pdf

xvi State of California Employment Development Department. (2014). Disability Insurance benefits amounts. Retrieved from http://www.edd.ca.gov/Disability/DI_Benefit_Amounts.htm

xvii New York State Worker's Compensation Board. (n.d.). Complying with disability law. Retrieved from http://www.wcb.ny.gov/content/main/DisabilityBenefits/Employer/complyWithLaw.jsp

xviii New York State Worker's Compensation Board. (n.d.). Who is and who is not covered. Retrieved from http://www.wcb.ny.gov/content/main/DisabilityBenefits/Employer/whoCovered.jsp

xix Ibid.

xx New York State Worker's Compensation Board. (n.d.). Cash benefits. Retrieved from http://www.wcb.ny.gov/content/main/DisabilityBenefits/Employer/cashBenefits.jsp

xxi State of New Jersey Department of Labor and Workforce Development. (n.d.). Rates. Retrieved from http://lwd.dol.state.nj.us/labor/ea/rates/rateindex.html

xxii State of New Jersey Department of Labor and Workforce Development. (n.d.). Coverage for temporary disability benefits – state plan employer. Retrieved from http://lwd.dol.state.nj.us/labor/tdi/employer/state/sp_emp_coverage.html

xxiii State of New Jersey Department of Labor and Workforce Development. (n.d.). Wage requirements – state plan. Retrieved from http://lwd.dol.state.nj.us/labor/tdi/content/sp_wage_requirements.html

xxiv State of New Jersey Department of Labor and Workforce Development. (n.d.). How benefits are paid – state plan. Retrieved from http://lwd.dol.state.nj.us/labor/tdi/worker/state/sp_payments.html

xxv State of New Jersey Department of Labor and Workforce Development. (n.d.). Calculating benefit amounts – state plan. Retrieved from http://lwd.dol.state.nj.us/labor/tdi/worker/state/sp_calculating_bene_amounts.html

xxvi RI Department of Labor and Training. (n.d.) TDI quick reference for employers. Retrieved from http://www.dlt.ri.gov/tdi/QuickRef4emp.htm

xxvii Ibid.

xxviii http://www.dlt.ri.gov/tdi/tdifaqs.htm

xxix RI Department of Labor and Training. (n.d.) Frequently asked questions. Retrieved from http://www.dlt.ri.gov/tdi/tdifaqs.htm

xxx Rule 29 Rhode Island Department of Labor and Training -
http://www.dlt.ri.gov/pdf/UITDIRules0614.pdf

xxxi State of Hawaii Disability Compensation Division. (n.d.) Highlights of the Hawaii temporary disability insurance law. Retrieved from http://labor.hawaii.gov/dcd/files/2013/01/TDI-highlights.pdf and see http://labor.hawaii.gov/dcd/files/2013/01/New-Wage-Base.pdf for 2015 statistics.

xxxii State of Hawaii Disability Compensation Division. (n.d.) About temporary disability insurance. Retrieved from http://labor.hawaii.gov/dcd/home/about-tdi/

xxxiii State of Hawaii Disability Compensation Division. (n.d.) 2015 maximum weekly wage base and maximum weekly benefit amount. Retrieved from http://labor.hawaii.gov/dcd/files/2013/01/New-Wage-Base.pdf

xxxiv Secretary of State of Puerto Rico. (2014). Laws of Puerto Rico unannotated. Search http://www.lexisnexis.com/hottopics/lawsofpuertorico/

xxxv Secretary of State of Puerto Rico. (2014). Laws of Puerto Rico unannotated. Search http://www.lexisnexis.com/hottopics/lawsofpuertorico/

xxxvi Secretary of State of Puerto Rico. (2014). Laws of Puerto Rico unannotated. Search http://www.lexisnexis.com/hottopics/lawsofpuertorico/

Chapter 5: OTHER LEAVES OF ABSENCE

xxxvii MetLife. (2008). 6th annual MetLife study of employee benefit trends.

xxxviii Mercer Human Resources Consulting. Survey on the Total Financial Impact of Employee Absences, June 2010

xxxix Bloomberg BNA. (2014, March 17). *Unscheduled absence plunges in the fourth quarter; employee turnover shifts marginally upward, Bloomberg BNA finds.* Retrieved from http://www.bna.com/unscheduled-absence-plunges-pr17179885700/.

xl Milligan, S. (2015, March). The limits of unlimited vacation. *HR Magazine, 60*(2). Retrieved from http://www.shrm.org/publications/hrmagazine/editorialcontent/2015/0315/pages/0315-unlimited-vacation.aspx

xli Society for Human Research Management (SHRM). (2014, November). SHRM survey findings: 2015 holiday schedules [PowerPoint]. Retrieved from http://www.shrm.org/research/surveyfindings/articles/pages/shrm-2015-holiday-schedules.aspx

xlii Mercer Human Resources Consulting. (2003). "2003 Survey Researched at CCH Incorporated." CCH Incorporated. (as cited in SHRM HR Resource Magazine, July, 2007 http://www.shrm.org/publications/hrmagazine/editorialcontent/pages/0707agenda_compben.aspx)

Chapter 6: BEHAVIORAL RISK AND MENTAL HEALTH

[xliii] Kalaydjian, A. P. & Merikangas, K. (2008, September). Physical and mental comorbidity of headache in a nationally representative sample of US adults. *Psychosomatic Medicine, 70*(7)773-780. doi: 10.1097/PSY.0b013e31817f9e80

[xliv] Eaton, W. W. (Ed.). (2006). *Medical and psychiatric Comorbidity over the course of life.* Arlington, VA: American Psychiatric Publishing.

[xlv] O'Connor, C. M. & Joynt, K. E. (2004). Depression: Are we ignoring an important comorbidity in heart failure? *Journal of the American College of Cardiology. (43)*9, 1550-1552. doi: 10.1016/j.jacc.2004.02.003

[xlvi] Waddell, G., Burton, A. K., & Main, C. J. (2003). *Screening to identify people at risk of long-term incapacity for work: A conceptual and scientific review.* London: Royal Society of Medicine Press.

[xlvii] Greco, M. (1998). *Illness as a Work of Thought: Foucauldian Perspective on Psychosomatics* (pp. 1-3, 112-116). New York: Routledge.

[xlviii] Puri, B. K., & Treasaden, I. H. (2011). *Textbook of Psychiatry* (3rd ed.). London: Churchill Livingstone.

[xlix] Milliman, Economic Impact of Integrated Medical-Behavioral Healthcare, August, 2013

[l] National Institute for Mental Health as cited in U.S. Department of Labor, Entering the World of Work: What Youth with Mental Health Needs Should Know About Accommodations, http://www.dol.gov/odep/pubs/fact/transitioning.htm

[li] Ronald C. Kessler, PhD; Patricia Berglund, MBA; Olga Demler, MS; et. al., The Epidemiology of Major Depressive Disorder Journal of the American Medical Association, June 18, 2003, Vol 289, No. 23

[lii] Ibid.

[liii] Hanebuth, D., Meinel, M., & Fischer, J. (2006, January). Health-related quality of life, psychosocial work conditions, and absenteeism in an industrial sample of blue- and white-collar employees: A comparison of potential predictors. *Journal of Occupational and Environmental Medicine. 48*(1), 28-37.

[liv] Langlieb, A.M. & Kahn, J. P. (2005, November). How much does quality mental health care profit employers? *Journal of Occupational and Environmental Medicine. 47*(11), 1099-1109. doi: 10.1097/01.jom.0000177124.60460.25

[lv] American Psychiatric Association. Once again, treatment improves productivity. *MentalHealthWorks.* (2003, Third Quarter).

lvi The Hartford. (2007). *Healthier, more productive employees: A report on the real potential of Employee Assistance Programs (EAP).*

lvii Disability Management Employer Coalition. (2008). *DMEC 2008 employer behavioral risk survey* [white paper]. Retrieved from http://www.workplacementalhealth.org/2008dmec

lviii Jorgensen, D. G. (2005). *The EAP Buyer's Guide.* Arlington, VA: Employee Assistance Professionals Association. Retrieved from http://www.eapnexus.net/Nexus/eap_main/EAPBuyersGuide.pdf

lix Midwest EAP, EAP 101: Why Offer EAP., http://www.midwesteap.com/eap101/why.php

lx See http://www.easna.org/hr-employers/ for a complete list of EASNA corporate winners.

lxi National Institute of Mental Health. (2013). *The numbers count: Mental disorders in America.* Retrieved from http://www.lb7.uscourts.gov/documents/12-cv-1072url2.pdf

lxii Langlieb, A. M., & DePaulo, J. R. (2008, April). *Etiology of depression and implications on work environment. Journal of Occupational and Environmental Medicine,* 50(4), 391-395. doi: 10.1097/JOM.0b013e31816fca08

lxiii Leopold, R. S. (2003). *A Year in the Life of a Million American Workers.* New York: Metlife Group Disability.

lxiv Disability Management Employer Coalition. (2015). *DMEC 2014 Employer Behavioral Risk Survey.* San Diego: DMEC.

Chapter 7: DISEASE MANAGEMENT

lxv Academy of Managed Care Pharmacy, Concept Series Paper on Disease Management, May, 2012 http://www.amcp.org/WorkArea/DownloadAsset.aspx?id=9295

lxvi http://www.cdc.gov/nchs/fastats/leading-causes-of-death.htm

lxvii DeVol, R., & Bedroussian, A. (2007, October). *An unhealthy America: The economic burden of chronic disease—charting a new course to save lives and increase productivity and economic growth.* Santa Monica, CA: Milken Institute. Retrieved from http://www.milkeninstitute.org/publications/view/321

lxviii Academy for Healthcare Management. (n.d.). "Healthcare management: An introduction" [Online course].

lxix DeVol, R., & Bedroussian, A. (2007, October). *An unhealthy America: The economic burden of chronic disease—charting a new course to save lives and increase productivity and economic*

growth. Santa Monica, CA: Milken Institute. Retrieved from
http://www.milkeninstitute.org/publications/view/321

[lxx] CIGNA. (2007, October 15). CIGNA analysis shows integrated medical and disability programs
improve return-to-work rates, productivity [news release]. Retrieved from
http://newsroom.cigna.com/article_display.cfm?article_id=790

Chapter 8: WELLNESS AND WORK/LIFE

[lxxi] *The Kaiser Family Foundation and Health Research and Educational Trust Employer Health
Benefits 2014 Annual Survey*. Retrieved from
https://kaiserfamilyfoundation.files.wordpress.com/2014/09/8625-employer-health-benefits-2014-
annual-survey6.pdf

[lxxii] American Psycological Association Center for Organizational Excellence. (n.d.). Work stress
[web page].Retrieved from http://www.apaexcellence.org/resources/special-topics/work-stress

[lxxiii] The Kaiser Family Foundation, *op. cit.*

[lxxiv] Centers for Disease Control and Prevention. (2014, September 9). Overweight and obesity, adult
obesity facts [web page]. Retrieved from http://www.cdc.gov/obesity/data/adult.html

[lxxv] Centers for Disease Control and Prevention. (2014, April). Fast facts: Cigarette smoking in the
United States. Retrieved from
http://www.cdc.gov/tobacco/data_statistics/fact_sheets/fast_facts/index.htm#use

[lxxvi] Centers for Disease Control and Prevention. (2014, February). Fact sheet: Health effects of
cigarette smoking. Retrieved from
http://www.cdc.gov/tobacco/data_statistics/fact_sheets/health_effects/effects_cig_smoking/
#children

[lxxvii] U.S. Department of the Treasury Internal Revenue Service. (2014, December 10). *Employer's tax
guide to fringe benefits* (IRS Publication 15-B [2015]). Retrieved from
http://www.irs.gov/pub/irs-pdf/p15b.pdf

[lxxviii] U.S. Department of the Treasury Internal Revenue Service. (2006, December 13, p. 75018).
*EBSA final rule: Nondiscrimination and wellness programs in health coverage in the group
market*. Retrieved from http://www.dol.gov/ebsa/regs/fedreg/final/2006009557.htm

[lxxix] http://www.wfcresources.com/articles/cutting-health-care-costs/

Chapter 9: GROUP HEALTHCARE

[lxxx] http://www.epi.org/publication/bp337-employer-sponsored-health-insurance/

[lxxxi] Kaiser Family Foundation. *op. cit.*

[lxxxii] http://kff.org/medicare/state-indicator/medicare-beneficiaries-as-of-total-pop/

[lxxxiii] http://kff.org/health-reform/issue-brief/medicaid-moving-forward/

[lxxxiv] http://www.cdc.gov/nchs/fastats/health-insurance.htm

[lxxxv] Gresham, L. (2008, August 1). Cost cutting goes too deep: Patients in CDHPs forego medications, study finds. *Employee Benefit News*. Retrieved from http://ebn.benefitnews.com/news/cost-cutting-goes-too-deep-patients-629531-1.html

[lxxxvi] http://www.ahrq.gov/professionals/prevention-chronic-care/decision/mcc/mccchartbook.pdf

[lxxxvii] Kaiser Family Foundation/Health Research & Educational Trust. (2005). *Survey of employer-sponsored health benefits*. Menlo Park, CA: Kaiser Family Foundation and HRET.

[lxxxviii] Kaiser Family Foundation (2014), *op. cit.*

[lxxxix] Gurchiek, K. (2008, May 2). Workplace wellness programs on the rise in 2008. *Society of Human Resource Management – HR News*. Retrieved from www.shrm.org/publications/hrnews/pages/wellnessprogramsontherise.aspx

[xc] Kaiser Family Foundation (20140, *op. cit.*

[xci] Dunning, M. (2013, April 7). Employers use penalties to push workers into wellness plans. *Business Insurance*. Retrieved from http://www.businessinsurance.com/article/20130407/NEWS03/304079974

[xcii] Centers for Medicare & Medicaid Services. (n.d.). National health expenditures; aggregate and per capita amounts, annual percent change and percent distribution: Selected calendar years 1960 - 2012. Retrieved from http://www.cms.gov/Research-Statistics-Data-and-Systems/Statistics-Trends-and-Reports/NationalHealthExpendData/Downloads/tables.pdf.

Chapter 10: VOLUNTARY PLANS

[xciii] Society for Human Resource Management. (2012). *2012 Employee benefits: The employee benefits landscape in a recovering economy*. Retrieved from http://www.shrm.org/research/surveyfindings/articles/documents/2012_empbenefits_report.pdf

[xciv] U.S. Department of Labor, Bureau of Labor Statistics. (2015, March 11). *Employer costs for employee compensation —December 2014 (news release USDL-15-0386)*. Retrieved from http://www.bls.gov/news.release/pdf/ecec.pdf

xcv Business Wire. (2015, April 7)). *Voluntary sales were up almost four percent in 2014, according to* Business Wire. (2015, April 7)). *Voluntary sales were up almost four percent in 2014, according to nnual sales study.* Retrieved from http://www.businesswire.com/news/home/20150407005104/en/Voluntary-Sales-Percent-2014-Eastbridge%E2%80%99s-Annual-Sales#.VSQywvnF_II

xcvi MetLife. (2010). *op. cit.*

xcvii U.S. Department of Health and Human Services. (n.d.). *Longtermcare.gov – The basics.* Retrieved from http://longtermcare.gov/the-basics/

xcviii Aetna. (2008, July 18). American Veterinary Medical Association – Group health and life insurance trust, partners with pets best insurance in national pet insurance effort (news release). Retrieved fromhttps://www1.aetna.com/news/newsReleases/2008/0718_AVMA_Aetna.html

xcix Synovate. (2007, November). *Federal Trade Commission – 2006 Identity Theft Survey Report.* Retrieved from https://www.ftc.gov/sites/default/files/documents/reports/federal-trade-commission-2006-identity-theft-survey-report-prepared-commission-synovate/synovatereport.pdf

c Neyer R. *Research Briefings: Analyzing the Size and Potential of Voluntary Worksite Benefits.* LIMRA International, 2007. as cited in A Workforce at Risk, Colonial Life, (2009) https://www.google.com/url?sa=t&rct=j&q=&esrc=s&source=web&cd=1&ved=0CB8QFjAA&url=https%3A%2F%2Fwww.coloniallife.com%2F~%2Fmedia%2FColonial%2FPublic%2520Site%2FWhite%2520Papers%2FSafety%2520Net%2520white%2520paper.pdf&ei=fMB1VaCRFsmusAW9voEY&usg=AFQjCNFPYyY3umXMuMbRlrhNj7kPpoyCHg&sig2=mzXdqjhk4hYPqsiccc2M7Q&bvm=bv.95039771,d.b2w&cad=rjt

Chapter 11: INTAKE AND CALL CENTER MANAGEMENT

ci U.S. Department of Labor, Occupational Safety and Health Administration. (2014). *All About OSHA* (OSHA 3302-09R, p. 17). Retrieved from https://www.osha.gov/Publications/all_about_OSHA.pdf

cii Disability Management Employer Coalition & Liberty Mutual Group. (2005). *2005 call center leadership series: Best practices for managing the cost of absence* (white paper). Retrieved from http://dmec.org/2005/07/02/2005-call-center-leadership-series-best-practices-for-managing-the-cost-of-absence/

Chapter 12: EVENT MANAGEMENT

[ciii] U.S. Department of Labor, Employee Benefits Security Administration. (n.d.). *Filing a Claim for Your Health or Disability Benefits* (web page). Retrieved from http://www.dol.gov/ebsa/publications/filingbenefitsclaim.html

Chapter 13: RETURN-TO-WORK PROGAM DEVELOPMENT AND STAY-AT-WORK PHILOSOPHY

[civ] Kronos. (2010, June 28). *Unplanned absence costs organizations 8.7 percent of payroll, more than half the cost of healthcare, according to new Mercer study sponsored by Kronos* (press release). Retrieved from http://www.kronos.com/pr/unplanned-absence-costs-organizations-over-8-percent-of-payroll.aspx

[cv] Levin-Epstein, J. (2005, February 28*). Presenteeism and paid sick days*. Washington, DC: Center for Law and Social Policy. Retrieved from http://www.clasp.org/resources-and-publications/files/0212.pdf

[cvi] Parry, T. (2008, May). *Filling the black hole of the incidental absence*. San Francisco: Integrated Benefits Institute. Retrieved from http://files.ibiweb.org/uploads/knowledge-bank/content/May_2008_Research_Insights.pdf

Chapter 14: USERRA AND EMPLOYEE REINTEGRATION

[cvii] Uniformed Services Employment and Reemployment Rights Act of 1994, 38 U.S.C. § 4301. Retrieved from http://www.dol.gov/vets/usc/vpl/usc38.htm

[cviii] U.S. Department of Labor. (2014, July).*USERRA fy 2013 annual report to Congress* (p. 1). Retrieved from http://www.dol.gov/vets/programs/userra/USERRA_Annual_FY2013.pdf

[cix] Uniformed Services Employment and Reemployment Rights Act of 1994. Pub. L. no. 4301-4334, (1994). Print.

[cx] U.S. Department of Labor, Office of the Assistant Secretary for Policy. (2009, September). *Employment law guide*. Retrieved from http://www.dol.gov/elaws/elg/userra.htm

[cxi] Ibid..

[cxii] Ibid.

[cxiii] Ibid.

[cxiv] Uniformed Services Employment and Reemployment Rights Act of 1994, As Amended, 38 U.S.C. § 1002.116. Retrieved from http://www.dol.gov/vets/regs/fedreg/final/2005023961.pdf

[cxv] U.S. Department of Labor. (n.d.). *Your rights under USEERA* (web page). Retrieved from http://www.dol.gov/vets/programs/userra/poster.htm

[cxvi] Ibid.

[cxvii] Uniformed Services Employment and Reemployment Rights Act of 1994, 38 U.S.C. § 1002.166. (2005 final rule).

[cxviii] U.S. Department of Labor. (2008, July). *Your rights under USEERA* (poster). Retrieved from http://www.dol.gov/vets/programs/userra/USERRA_Federal.pdf

[cxix] U.S. Department of Labor, Office of the Assistant Secretary for Policy. (2009, September). *Employment law guide.* Retrieved from http://www.dol.gov/elaws/elg/userra.

[cxx] Ibid.

[cxxi] Uniformed Services Employment and Reemployment Rights Act of 1994. 38 U.S.C. § 4316(b)(2)(A)(ii). Retrieved from http://www.dol.gov/vets/usc/vpl/usc38.htm#4316

[cxxii] Uniformed Services Employment and Reemployment Rights Act of 1994. SubSection 1002.123 of the USERRA Regulations. Retrieved from http://www.dol.gov/vets/regs/fedreg/final/2005023961.pdf

[cxxiii] Uniformed Services Employment and Reemployment Rights Act of 1994. SubSection 1002.122 Retrieved from http://www.dol.gov/vets/regs/fedreg/final/2005023961.pdf

[cxxiv] Harty-Golder, B. (2006, September). Supporting troops through USERRA. *Medical Laboratory Observer, 38*(9), 56. Retrieved from http://web.a.ebscohost.com/ehost/pdfviewer/pdfviewer?vid=3&sid=46bc988f-dd4e-42c2-afd1-b20db7405849%40sessionmgr4005&hid=4107

[cxxv] Ibid..

[cxxvi] Doyle, C. (2008, Fall). The effects of reserve component mobilizations on employers. *IDA Research Notes.* Retrieved from https://www.ida.org/~/media/Corporate/Files/Publications/ResearchNotes/RN2008/2008researchnotesfall.pdf

[cxxvii] Ibid.

[cxxviii] Carruthers, M., & Harnett, C. A. (2007). *Workplace Warriors: The Corporate Response to Deployment and Reintegration* [White paper]. San Diego: DMEC.

[cxxix] Bilmes, L. (2007, January). Soldiers returning from Iraq and Afghanistan: The long-term costs of providing veterans medical care and disability benefits (KSG Working Paper No. RWP07-001). doi: org/10.2139/ssrn.939657 .

cxxx Carruthers, M., & Harnett, C. A. (2007). *Workplace Warriors: The Corporate Response to Deployment and Reintegration* [White paper]. San Diego: DMEC.

Chapter 15: AMERICANS WITH DISABILITIES ACT

cxxxi Remarks of President Bush at the signing of the Americans with Disabilities Act, retrieved from http://www.eeoc.gov/eeoc/history/35th/videos/ada_signing_text.html.

cxxxii School Board of Nassau County v. Arline, 480 U.S. 273 (1987).

cxxxiii http://en.wikipedia.org/wiki/ADA_Amendments_Act_of_2008

cxxxiv The ADA is part of section 42 of federal law. References such as "42 U.S.C. Section 12102" refer to specific portions of the actual law. The symbol for "section" is §.

cxxxv Americans with Disabilities Act, 42 U.S.C. § 12102(2) (1990). Retrieved from http://www.gpo.gov/fdsys/pkg/USCODE-2009-title42/pdf/USCODE-2009-title42-chap126-sec12102.pdf

cxxxvi See http://www.eeoc.gov/laws/statutes/adaaa.cfm for full ADAAA text.

cxxxvii See, e.g., Cal. Labor Code § 132a, *Barns v. Workers' Comp. Appeals Bd.*, 216 Cal. App. 3d 524 (1989) (prohibiting termination of employees receiving workers' compensation benefits until they have reached permanent and stationary status, absent a showing of business necessity); Me. Rev. Stat. Ann. Tit. 39-A § 353, *Lindsay v. Great Northern Paper Co.*, 532 A.2d 151 (1987) (holding application of a "no fault" absenteeism to workers' compensation absences as unlawful under the Maine Workers' Compensation Act); Okla. Stat. Tit. 85, § 5, *Keddington v. City of Bartlesville*, 42 P.3d 293 (Okla. Civ. App. 2001) (prohibiting employers from discharging any employee during a period of temporary total disability solely on the basis of absence from work); Cal. Gov't Code § 12945(b) (providing employees with a reasonable period of pregnancy leave not to exceed four months); Conn. Gen. Stat. § 46a-60(a)(7) (providing pregnant employees with a reasonable leave of absence resulting from pregnancy); Conn. Gen. Stat. § 31-51kk et seq. (providing 16 weeks of family and medical leave within a 24-month period for reasons similar to those covered by the FMLA).

cxxxviii The EEOC's guidance on reasonable accommodation and undue hardship can be viewed at http://www.eeoc.gov/policy/docs/accommodation.html.

Chapter 16: WORKPLACE SAFETY AND REGULATORY MANAGEMENT

cxxxix U. S. Dept. of Labor, Occupational Safety and Health Administration. (2005). *Small business handbook*. Washington, DC: GPO.

cxl U. S. Department of Labor, Occupational Safety and Health Administration. (n.d.). *Safety and health program management fact sheet: Creating a safety culture*. Retrieved from https://www.osha.gov/SLTC/etools/safetyhealth/mod4_factsheets_culture.html

cxli Ibid.

cxlii Ibid.

cxliii Hopwood, D. & Thompson, S. (2006.) *Workplace safety: A guide for small and mid-sized companies.* San Diego, CA: Aspen Risk Management Group

cxliv U. S. Department of Labor, Occupational Safety and Health Administration. (2002 revised). *Job hazard analysis* (OSHA 3071). Retrieved from https://www.osha.gov/Publications/osha3071.pdf?utm_source=rss&utm_medium=rss&utm_campaign=job-hazard-analysis-13

cxlv Hopwood, D. & Thompson, S. (2006.) *Workplace safety: A guide for small and midsized companies.* San Diego, CA: Aspen Risk Management Group

No footnotes for chapters 17 & 18.

Chapter 19: RFP AND VENDOR SELECTION

1.   Disability Management Employer Coalition (DMEC). (2004). *Vendor selection and management tools for employers: Vendor scoring tool.* San Diego: DMEC.

2.   Parekh, R. (2006, May 8). Legwork needed to choose a third-party administrator. *Business Insurance*, 40(19), 30.

cxlvi http://www.americanbar.org/publications/blt/2014/02/02_cantley.html

cxlvii Ceniceros, R. (2006, July 24). Data fuels Chevron efforts to reduce disability costs. *Business Insurance.* Retrieved from http://www.businessinsurance.com/article/20060723/ISSUE01/100019355

cxlviii Bridgeford, L. C. (2007, November 1). Falling leaves. *Employee Benefit News.* Retrieved from http://eba.benefitnews.com/news/falling-leaves-301948-1.html

cxlix Mercer/Marsh. (2007). *Survey on Health, Productivity and Absence Management Programs.*

cl Mercer/Marsh. (2007). *Survey on Health, Productivity and Absence Management Programs: 2006 Survey Report.* Retrieved from http://www.protectfamilyleave.org/research/2006_hpam_report_mhb.pdf

cli U.S. Dept. of Labor, Bureau of Labor Statistics. (2005). *Current Population Survey: Circadian Information, Shiftwork Practices.* Washington, DC: GPO.

clii Smith C, C Sippola, R Anfied, K Dunnington. (February 2009). *Predicting Productivity Loss Using Absence and Health Risks.* IBI/NBCH 2009 Health and Productivity Forum.

cliii CIGNA. (2007, November). *Integration value study*. Retrieved from
http://cigna.tekgroup.com/images/56/Study_Summary.pdf

cliv Hudson L. (2009). *CPDM2: IDAM Concepts and Tools*. Santa Ana, CA: Insurance Educational
Association.

clv Mercer. (2008, October). *The total financial impact of employee absences: Survey highlights*.
Retrieved from http://www.fmlainsights.com/wp-
content/uploads/sites/311/2011/09/mercer-survey-highlights1.pdf

clvi Integrated Benefits Institute. (2008). *The business response of employers to absence: Analytic case
studies in three industries: Utilities, finance and retail*. Retrieved from
https://www.ibiweb.org/research-resources/detail/the-business-response-of-employers-to-
absence

clvii Integrated Benefits Institute. (2006, May). *The business value of health: Linking CFOs to health
and productivity*. Retrieved from https://www.ibiweb.org/research-resources/detail/the-
business-value-of-health-linking-cfos-to-health-and-productivity

clviii Editor's Note: The AEP and WM case studies are included without attribution and are based on
work done for them by the Integrated Benefits Institute. Questions on the data cited in these studies
should be directed to IBI.

clix Integrated Benefits Institute. (2008). *The business response of employers to absence: Analytic case
studies in three industries: Utilities, finance and retail*. Retrieved from
https://www.ibiweb.org/research-resources/detail/the-business-response-of-employers-to-
absence

clx Nicholson, S., Pauly, M., Polsky, D., Sharda, C., Szrek, H., & Berger, M. L. (2005, September 30).
Measuring the effects of work loss on productivity with team production. *Health Economics,
15*(2), 111-123. doi: 10.1002/hec.1052

clxi Nicholson, S., Pauly, M. V., Polsky, D., Baase, C. M., Billotti, G. M., Ozminkowski, R. J., Sharda,
C. E. (2005). How to present the business case for healthcare quality to employers. Retrieved
from http://knowledge.wharton.upenn.edu/wp-content/uploads/2013/09/1303.pdf

clxii Loeppke, R., Taitel, M., Haufle, V., Parry, T., Kessler, R. C., & Jinnett, K. (2009, April) Health and
productivity as a business strategy: A multiemployer study. *Journal of Occupational and
Environmental Medicine. 51*(4), 411-428. Retrieved from
https://www.acoem.org/uploadedFiles/Healthy_Workplaces_Now/HPM%20As%20a%20Bu
siness%20Strategy.pdf

clxiii These services include Thomson Reuters (formerly Medstat), Optis,, Ingenix, and Human
Capital Management Services, Inc.

clxiv IBI developed this method of collecting comparison data directly from insurer/TPA claims
administrators and first applied the methodology to its collection of 2005 data. For 2007

data, IBI amassed information on more than 35,000 employer benefits programs comprising 2.32 million claims. IBI adds yearly to this database from vendors and members claims data.

[clxv] Information from the U.S. Census Bureau about the NAICS and SIC systems, including bridges between them, may be found at http://www.census.gov/eos/www/naics/.

[clxvi] Examples of peer-reviewed journals covering these topics include *Health Economics* and the *Journal of Occupational and Environmental Medicine.*

[clxvii] For example: National Business Coalition on Health and American College of Occupational and Environmental Medicine's Blueprint *for Health*; Integrated Benefit Institute's *Health and Productivity Snapshot* developed with Dr. Ron Kessler of Harvard Medical School; National Committee for Quality Assurance's modeling tool, *Quality Dividend Calculator*; Integrated Benefit Institute's free business case DVD, *Winning Ways — How to Gain C-Suite Support for Health & Productivity Improvement.*

[clxviii] Gelston, S. (2008, January 30). Gen Y, Gen X and the Baby Boomers: Workplace generation wars. *CIO.com*. Retrieved from http://www.cio.com/article/2437236/staff-management/gen-y--gen-x-and-the-baby-boomers--workplace-generation-wars.html

[clxix] Corvida. (2008, June 7). Generation Y: Welcome to their world [Online article]. Retrieved from http://readwrite.com/2008/06/07/gen_y_welcome_to_our_world

[clxx] Limited interaction among generations in the workplace identified as key indicator of coming skilled worker crisis: Changes in the workplace reveal new realities for multi-generational workforce. (2008, May 27). *Business Wire*. Retrieved from http://www.businesswire.com/news/home/20080527005042/en/Limited-Interaction-Generations-Workplace-Identified-Key-Indicator#.VUobV_lViko

[clxxi] Walter, E. (2012, January 25). Generation Y: The new kind of workforce. Retrieved from http://thenextweb.com/insider/2012/01/25/generation-y-the-new-kind-of-workforce/

[clxxii] Scheef, D., & Thielfoldt, D. (2004). Retaining four generations in the workplace [Online article]. Retrieved from http://www.spisolutions.com/Articles-Generations0904-Retainthe4Gens.pdf

[clxxiii] Cisco's Connected World Technology Report in 2011 retrieved from: http://www.consejoderectores.cl/boletin_consejo/06_septiembre_2013/Informe_CISCO.pdf

[clxxiv] Stephey, M. J. (2008, April 16). Gen-X: The ignored generation? *Time*. Retrieved from http://content.time.com/time/arts/article/0,8599,1731528,00.html

[clxxv] Scheef, D., & Thielfoldt, D. (2004). Retaining four generations in the workplace [Online article]. Retrieved from http://www.spisolutions.com/Articles-Generations0904-Retainthe4Gens.pdf

[clxxvi] Ibid.

[clxxvii] Ibid.

clxxviii Limited interaction among generations in the workplace identified as key indicator of coming skilled worker crisis: Changes in the workplace reveal new realities for multi-generational workforce. (2008, May 27). *Business Wire*. Retrieved from http://www.businesswire.com/news/home/20080527005042/en/Limited-Interaction-Generations-Workplace-Identified-Key-Indicator#.VUobV_lViko

clxxix Society for Human Resource Management. (2004, August). *2004 Generational Differences Survey Report*. Retrieved from https://www.shrm.org/Research/SurveyFindings/Documents/Generational%20Differences%20Survey%20Report.pdf

clxxx Ibid.

clxxxi Society for Human Resource Management. (2009). Research Quarterly: The multi-generational workforce: Opportunity for competitive success. Retrieved from https://www.shrm.org/Research/Articles/Articles/Documents/09-0027_RQ_March_2009_FINAL_no%20ad.pdf

clxxxii U.S. Department of Labor, Employment and Training Administration. (2008, February). Report of the taskforce on the aging of the American workforce. Retrieved from http://www.doleta.gov/reports/final_taskforce_report_2_27_08.pdf

clxxxiii Ibid.

clxxxiv Martin, K. (2014, October 17). Working into their 70s: The new normal for Boomers [Online article]. Retrieved from http://america.aljazeera.com/watch/shows/real-money-with-alivelshi/2014/10/Workampers-retirement-babyboomers.html

clxxxv Talkin' 'bout my generation: The economic impact of aging US baby boomers, McKinsey, (2008) retrieved from: http://www.mckinsey.com/insights/economic_studies/talkin_bout_my_generation

clxxxvi Limited interaction among generations in the workplace identified as key indicator of coming skilled worker crisis: Changes in the workplace reveal new realities for multi-generational workforce. (2008, May 27). *Business Wire*. Retrieved from http://www.businesswire.com/news/home/20080527005042/en/Limited-Interaction-Generations-Workplace-Identified-Key-Indicator#.VUobV_lViko

clxxxvii McKinsey, *op. cit.*

clxxxviii Reeves, M.J., Rafferty, A.P. (2005) Healthy Lifestyle Characteristics among Adults in the United States. Archives of Internal Medicine, April 2005 retrieved from http://archinte.jamanetwork.com/article.aspx?articleid=486522

clxxxix Østbye, T., Dement, J., Krause, K. (2007) Obesity and Workers' Compensation. Archives of Internal Medicine, April 2007 retrieved from http://archinte.jamanetwork.com/article.aspx?articleid=412250

cxc Ortman, J., Victoria, A. (2014) An Aging Nation: The Older Population in the United States. U.S. Dept of Commerce, retrieved from http://www.census.gov/prod/2014pubs/p25-1140.pdf

cxci Casale, J. (2008, February 26). U.S. health care spending could double by 2017: CMS. *Business Insurance.* Retrieved from http://www.businessinsurance.com/article/20080226/NEWS/200012368/u-s-health-care-spending-could-double-by-2017-cms

cxcii Ibid.

cxciii National Association of Professional Employer Organizations (NAPEO). (2008, March 5). Small businesses outpace larger ones in planning for impact of aging workforce, NAPEO survey shows [Press release]. Retrieved from https://www.napeo.org/media/pressreleases/pr_030508.cfm

cxciv Coughlin, J. F. (2007). Are you ready for the new older workplace? Aging baby boomers and the evolving role of employers (AgeLab 2008-01). Retrieved from http://web.mit.edu/coughlin/Public/Publications/AgeLab%20I2%202008-1%20Coughlin%20Wide%20Version.pdf

cxcv Tugman, K. (2013, June). Return to work: Aging workforce update. *Professional Case Management, 18*(3), 155-157. doi: 10.1097/NCM.0b013e31828ad597

cxcvi Adams, P. F., Dey, A. N., & Vickerie, J. L. (2007). Summary health statistics for the U.S. population: National health interview survey, 2005. *Vital and Health Statistics. Series 10, Data from the National Health Survey,* (233), 1-104.

cxcvii Bureau of Labor Statistics, United States Department of Labor. (2007). *Current population survey 1990-2007.* Retrieved November 1, 2007, from http://data.bls. gov/PDQ/outside.jsp?survey=ln

cxcviii Mitchell, K. (2006, March 26). Productivity does not end with age. *Business Insurance.* Retrieved from http://www.businessinsurance.com/article/20060326/ISSUE0401/100018573

cxcix Coughlin, J. F. (2007). Are you ready for the new older workplace? Aging baby boomers and the evolving role of employers (AgeLab 2008-01). Retrieved from http://web.mit.edu/coughlin/Public/Publications/AgeLab%20I2%202008-1%20Coughlin%20Wide%20Version.pdf